T0205761

Communications in Computer and Information Science 2115

Rationale

The CCIS series is devoted to the publication of proceedings of computer science conferences. Its aim is to efficiently disseminate original research results in informatics in printed and electronic form. While the focus is on publication of peer-reviewed full papers presenting mature work, inclusion of reviewed short papers reporting on work in progress is welcome, too. Besides globally relevant meetings with internationally representative program committees guaranteeing a strict peer-reviewing and paper selection process, conferences run by societies or of high regional or national relevance are also considered for publication.

Topics

The topical scope of CCIS spans the entire spectrum of informatics ranging from foundational topics in the theory of computing to information and communications science and technology and a broad variety of interdisciplinary application fields.

Information for Volume Editors and Authors

Publication in CCIS is free of charge. No royalties are paid, however, we offer registered conference participants temporary free access to the online version of the conference proceedings on SpringerLink (http://link.springer.com) by means of an http referrer from the conference website and/or a number of complimentary printed copies, as specified in the official acceptance email of the event.

CCIS proceedings can be published in time for distribution at conferences or as postproceedings, and delivered in the form of printed books and/or electronically as USBs and/or e-content licenses for accessing proceedings at SpringerLink. Furthermore, CCIS proceedings are included in the CCIS electronic book series hosted in the SpringerLink digital library at http://link.springer.com/bookseries/7899. Conferences publishing in CCIS are allowed to use Online Conference Service (OCS) for managing the whole proceedings lifecycle (from submission and reviewing to preparing for publication) free of charge.

Publication process

The language of publication is exclusively English. Authors publishing in CCIS have to sign the Springer CCIS copyright transfer form, however, they are free to use their material published in CCIS for substantially changed, more elaborate subsequent publications elsewhere. For the preparation of the camera-ready papers/files, authors have to strictly adhere to the Springer CCIS Authors' Instructions and are strongly encouraged to use the CCIS LaTeX style files or templates.

Abstracting/Indexing

CCIS is abstracted/indexed in DBLP, Google Scholar, EI-Compendex, Mathematical Reviews, SCImago, Scopus. CCIS volumes are also submitted for the inclusion in ISI Proceedings.

How to start

To start the evaluation of your proposal for inclusion in the CCIS series, please send an e-mail to ccis@springer.com.

Constantine Stephanidis · Margherita Antona ·
Stavroula Ntoa · Gavriel Salvendy
Editors

HCI International 2024 Posters

26th International Conference
on Human-Computer Interaction, HCII 2024
Washington, DC, USA, June 29 – July 4, 2024
Proceedings, Part II

 Springer

Editors
Constantine Stephanidis
University of Crete and Foundation for
Research and Technology - Hellas (FORTH)
Heraklion, Crete, Greece

Margherita Antona
Foundation for Research and Technology -
Hellas (FORTH)
Heraklion, Crete, Greece

Stavroula Ntoa
Foundation for Research
and Technology - Hellas (FORTH)
Heraklion, Crete, Greece

Gavriel Salvendy
University of Central Florida
Orlando, FL, USA

ISSN 1865-0929   ISSN 1865-0937 (electronic)
Communications in Computer and Information Science
ISBN 978-3-031-61946-5   ISBN 978-3-031-61947-2 (eBook)
https://doi.org/10.1007/978-3-031-61947-2

This Springer imprint is published by the registered company Springer Nature Switzerland AG
The registered company address is: Gewerbestrasse 11, 6330 Cham, Switzerland

If disposing of this product, please recycle the paper.

Foreword

This year we celebrate 40 years since the establishment of the HCI International (HCII) Conference, which has been a hub for presenting groundbreaking research and novel ideas and collaboration for people from all over the world.

The HCII conference was founded in 1984 by Prof. Gavriel Salvendy (Purdue University, USA, Tsinghua University, P.R. China, and University of Central Florida, USA) and the first event of the series, "1st USA-Japan Conference on Human-Computer Interaction", was held in Honolulu, Hawaii, USA, 18–20 August. Since then, HCI International is held jointly with several Thematic Areas and Affiliated Conferences, with each one under the auspices of a distinguished international Program Board and under one management and one registration. Twenty-six HCI International Conferences have been organized so far (every two years until 2013, and annually thereafter).

Over the years, this conference has served as a platform for scholars, researchers, industry experts and students to exchange ideas, connect, and address challenges in the ever-evolving HCI field. Throughout these 40 years, the conference has evolved itself, adapting to new technologies and emerging trends, while staying committed to its core mission of advancing knowledge and driving change.

As we celebrate this milestone anniversary, we reflect on the contributions of its founding members and appreciate the commitment of its current and past Affiliated Conference Program Board Chairs and members. We are also thankful to all past conference attendees who have shaped this community into what it is today.

The 26th International Conference on Human-Computer Interaction, HCI International 2024 (HCII 2024), was held as a 'hybrid' event at the Washington Hilton Hotel, Washington, DC, USA, during 29 June – 4 July 2024. It incorporated the 21 thematic areas and affiliated conferences listed below.

A total of 5108 individuals from academia, research institutes, industry, and government agencies from 85 countries submitted contributions, and 1271 papers and 309 posters were included in the volumes of the proceedings that were published just before the start of the conference, these are listed below. The contributions thoroughly cover the entire field of human-computer interaction, addressing major advances in knowledge and effective use of computers in a variety of application areas. These papers provide academics, researchers, engineers, scientists, practitioners and students with state-of-the-art information on the most recent advances in HCI.

The HCI International (HCII) conference also offers the option of presenting 'Late Breaking Work', and this applies both for papers and posters, with corresponding volumes of proceedings that will be published after the conference. Full papers will be included in the 'HCII 2024 - Late Breaking Papers' volumes of the proceedings to be published in the Springer LNCS series, while 'Poster Extended Abstracts' will be included as short research papers in the 'HCII 2024 - Late Breaking Posters' volumes to be published in the Springer CCIS series.

I would like to thank the Program Board Chairs and the members of the Program Boards of all thematic areas and affiliated conferences for their contribution towards the high scientific quality and overall success of the HCI International 2024 conference. Their manifold support in terms of paper reviewing (single-blind review process, with a minimum of two reviews per submission), session organization and their willingness to act as goodwill ambassadors for the conference is most highly appreciated.

This conference would not have been possible without the continuous and unwavering support and advice of Gavriel Salvendy, founder, General Chair Emeritus, and Scientific Advisor. For his outstanding efforts, I would like to express my sincere appreciation to Abbas Moallem, Communications Chair and Editor of HCI International News.

July 2024   Constantine Stephanidis

HCI International 2024 Thematic Areas
and Affiliated Conferences

- HCI: Human-Computer Interaction Thematic Area
- HIMI: Human Interface and the Management of Information Thematic Area
- EPCE: 21st International Conference on Engineering Psychology and Cognitive Ergonomics
- AC: 18th International Conference on Augmented Cognition
- UAHCI: 18th International Conference on Universal Access in Human-Computer Interaction
- CCD: 16th International Conference on Cross-Cultural Design
- SCSM: 16th International Conference on Social Computing and Social Media
- VAMR: 16th International Conference on Virtual, Augmented and Mixed Reality
- DHM: 15th International Conference on Digital Human Modeling & Applications in Health, Safety, Ergonomics & Risk Management
- DUXU: 13th International Conference on Design, User Experience and Usability
- C&C: 12th International Conference on Culture and Computing
- DAPI: 12th International Conference on Distributed, Ambient and Pervasive Interactions
- HCIBGO: 11th International Conference on HCI in Business, Government and Organizations
- LCT: 11th International Conference on Learning and Collaboration Technologies
- ITAP: 10th International Conference on Human Aspects of IT for the Aged Population
- AIS: 6th International Conference on Adaptive Instructional Systems
- HCI-CPT: 6th International Conference on HCI for Cybersecurity, Privacy and Trust
- HCI-Games: 6th International Conference on HCI in Games
- MobiTAS: 6th International Conference on HCI in Mobility, Transport and Automotive Systems
- AI-HCI: 5th International Conference on Artificial Intelligence in HCI
- MOBILE: 5th International Conference on Human-Centered Design, Operation and Evaluation of Mobile Communications

List of Conference Proceedings Volumes Appearing
Before the Conference

1. LNCS 14684, Human-Computer Interaction: Part I, edited by Masaaki Kurosu and Ayako Hashizume
2. LNCS 14685, Human-Computer Interaction: Part II, edited by Masaaki Kurosu and Ayako Hashizume
3. LNCS 14686, Human-Computer Interaction: Part III, edited by Masaaki Kurosu and Ayako Hashizume
4. LNCS 14687, Human-Computer Interaction: Part IV, edited by Masaaki Kurosu and Ayako Hashizume
5. LNCS 14688, Human-Computer Interaction: Part V, edited by Masaaki Kurosu and Ayako Hashizume
6. LNCS 14689, Human Interface and the Management of Information: Part I, edited by Hirohiko Mori and Yumi Asahi
7. LNCS 14690, Human Interface and the Management of Information: Part II, edited by Hirohiko Mori and Yumi Asahi
8. LNCS 14691, Human Interface and the Management of Information: Part III, edited by Hirohiko Mori and Yumi Asahi
9. LNAI 14692, Engineering Psychology and Cognitive Ergonomics: Part I, edited by Don Harris and Wen-Chin Li
10. LNAI 14693, Engineering Psychology and Cognitive Ergonomics: Part II, edited by Don Harris and Wen-Chin Li
11. LNAI 14694, Augmented Cognition, Part I, edited by Dylan D. Schmorrow and Cali M. Fidopiastis
12. LNAI 14695, Augmented Cognition, Part II, edited by Dylan D. Schmorrow and Cali M. Fidopiastis
13. LNCS 14696, Universal Access in Human-Computer Interaction: Part I, edited by Margherita Antona and Constantine Stephanidis
14. LNCS 14697, Universal Access in Human-Computer Interaction: Part II, edited by Margherita Antona and Constantine Stephanidis
15. LNCS 14698, Universal Access in Human-Computer Interaction: Part III, edited by Margherita Antona and Constantine Stephanidis
16. LNCS 14699, Cross-Cultural Design: Part I, edited by Pei-Luen Patrick Rau
17. LNCS 14700, Cross-Cultural Design: Part II, edited by Pei-Luen Patrick Rau
18. LNCS 14701, Cross-Cultural Design: Part III, edited by Pei-Luen Patrick Rau
19. LNCS 14702, Cross-Cultural Design: Part IV, edited by Pei-Luen Patrick Rau
20. LNCS 14703, Social Computing and Social Media: Part I, edited by Adela Coman and Simona Vasilache
21. LNCS 14704, Social Computing and Social Media: Part II, edited by Adela Coman and Simona Vasilache
22. LNCS 14705, Social Computing and Social Media: Part III, edited by Adela Coman and Simona Vasilache

https://2024.hci.international/proceedings

Preface

Preliminary scientific results, professional news, or work in progress, described in the form of short research papers (4–11 pages long), constitute a popular submission type among the International Conference on Human-Computer Interaction (HCII) participants. Extended abstracts are particularly suited for reporting ongoing work, which can benefit from a visual presentation, and are presented during the conference in the form of posters. The latter allow a focus on novel ideas and are appropriate for presenting project results in a simple, concise, and visually appealing manner. At the same time, they are also suitable for attracting feedback from an international community of HCI academics, researchers, and practitioners. Poster submissions span the wide range of topics of all HCII thematic areas and affiliated conferences.

Seven volumes of the HCII 2024 proceedings are dedicated to this year's poster extended abstracts, in the form of short research papers, focusing on the following topics:

- Volume I: HCI Design Theories, Methods, Tools and Case Studies; User Experience Evaluation Methods and Case Studies; Emotions in HCI; Human Robot Interaction
- Volume II: Inclusive Designs and Applications; Aging and Technology
- Volume III: eXtended Reality and the Metaverse; Interacting with Cultural Heritage, Art and Creativity
- Volume IV: HCI in Learning and Education; HCI in Games
- Volume V: HCI in Business and Marketing; HCI in Mobility and Automated Driving; HCI in Psychotherapy and Mental Health
- Volume VI: Interacting with the Web, Social Media and Digital Services; Interaction in the Museum; HCI in Healthcare
- Volume VII: AI Algorithms and Tools in HCI; Interacting with Large Language Models and Generative AI; Interacting in Intelligent Environments; HCI in Complex Industrial Environments

Poster extended abstracts were accepted for publication in these volumes following a minimum of two single-blind reviews from the members of the HCII 2024 international Program Boards, i.e., the program committees of the constituent events. We would like to thank all of them for their invaluable contribution, support, and efforts.

July 2024

Constantine Stephanidis
Margherita Antona
Stavroula Ntoa
Gavriel Salvendy

26th International Conference on Human-Computer Interaction (HCII 2024)

The full list with the Program Board Chairs and the members of the Program Boards of all thematic areas and affiliated conferences of HCII 2024 is available online at:

http://www.hci.international/board-members-2024.php

HCI International 2025 Conference

The 27th International Conference on Human-Computer Interaction, HCI International 2025, will be held jointly with the affiliated conferences at the Swedish Exhibition & Congress Centre and Gothia Towers Hotel, Gothenburg, Sweden, June 22–27, 2025. It will cover a broad spectrum of themes related to Human-Computer Interaction, including theoretical issues, methods, tools, processes, and case studies in HCI design, as well as novel interaction techniques, interfaces, and applications. The proceedings will be published by Springer. More information will become available on the conference website: https://2025.hci.international/.

General Chair
Prof. Constantine Stephanidis
University of Crete and ICS-FORTH
Heraklion, Crete, Greece
Email: general_chair@2025.hci.international

https://2025.hci.international/

Contents – Part II

Aging and Technology

Inclusive Designs and Applications

Smart Signage with Augmented Reality: Inclusive Coworking

Hugo Arias-Flores[1] , Carlos Borja-Galeas[1](✉) , and Mario Piedra[2]

[1] Centro de Investigación en Mecatrónica y Sistemas Interactivos – MIST, Universidad Indoamérica, Av. Machala y Sabanilla, Quito, Ecuador
{hugoarias,carlosborja}@uti.edu.ec
[2] Independent Investigator, Av. Machala y Sabanilla, Quito, Ecuador

Abstract. This project focuses on the implementation of augmented reality signage designed to enhance user experience in a coworking space. The signage integrates 2D animations and virtual tours to provide an intuitive and immersive experience, from entry to the desired destination within the establishment. At the main entrance, a totem with a coworking directory features a QR code that visitors can scan to access an interactive directory. The 2D animations, thoughtfully designed with an inclusive approach, utilize validated corporate colors to ensure accessibility, especially for individuals with color vision deficiencies. Each business in the coworking space is identified by a unique corporate color, and internal business floor plans use analogous colors, adjusted to maintain aesthetic coherence and accessibility. In addition to being an effective navigation tool, these animations reinforce the visual identity of the coworking space. Each business within the establishment has an interactive virtual tour that guides visitors from entry to their final destination, providing real-time visual information for effective orientation. The signage system is based on WordPress to offer a seamless and efficient experience without the need to download a specific application. Upon scanning the QR code, users are redirected to a mobile-optimized web page. This page not only provides access to the 2D animations and virtual tours but also offers useful information such as business hours, links to the businesses' and coworking space's social media, and other relevant details for the visit. This augmented reality signage approach not only enhances the functionality of the space but also ensures that all visitors, regardless of their needs, enjoy an inclusive and efficient experience in the coworking space.

Keywords: QR codes · Coworking spaces · User experience · Mobile navigation · Digital signage

1 Introduction

The present research focuses on the implementation of a new augmented reality signage system in a coworking environment, with the primary purpose of enhancing user experience. This signage integrates 2D animations and virtual tours to provide an intuitive and accessible experience from the moment visitors enter until they reach their desired

C. Stephanidis et al. (Eds.): HCII 2024, CCIS 2115, pp. 3–11, 2024.
https://doi.org/10.1007/978-3-031-61947-2_1

destination within the establishment. Emphasis is placed on inclusive design, particularly considering the needs of individuals with color vision deficiencies, a condition that affects a significant number of people worldwide. Recent statistics indicate that approximately 350 million people worldwide have color vision deficiencies, underscoring the importance of addressing this concern in signage design.

In line with the pursuit of inclusion, specific assistive technologies have been applied, such as image modification through algebraic operations and saturation adjustments, to ensure the accessibility of visual elements for individuals with different color perceptions. This approach extends not only to physical signage in the coworking environment but also to web interface design, where interface adaptation techniques are evaluated to enhance accessibility through recoloring algorithms.

The consideration of user diversity, their needs, and individual preferences is fundamental in the development of adaptive systems. Recognizing the variety of user profiles that may interact with signage, it is essential to design solutions that cater to a wide spectrum of characteristics and requirements, from specific visual abilities to navigation preferences. This approach involves not only technical adjustments in signage and interfaces but also a deep understanding of user experiences and perspectives, including their potential sensory limitations.

Through the implementation of this intelligent augmented reality signage, the aim is not only to improve the functionality of the coworking space but also to ensure an inclusive and satisfactory experience for all visitors, regardless of their visual capabilities or specific needs. This user-centered and inclusive design approach constitutes an important step towards creating more accessible and welcoming environments in both work and commercial settings.

Color vision deficiency, a condition affecting millions worldwide, presents significant challenges both in social integration and in digital interface interaction [1]. An assistive technology designed for individuals with deuteranopia has been successfully developed and validated, highlighting its potential to enhance the visual experience of users with color vision deficiency [2]. Accessibility in web interfaces is compromised by the emphasis on color usage, driving the search for adaptation techniques that enable a more inclusive experience for users with different visual abilities [2]. The consideration of user diversity and their individual needs becomes crucial in the design of digital products, emphasizing the importance of developing solutions that encompass a wide range of profiles, abilities, and skills [3]. To address the specific challenges faced by individuals with color vision deficiency in interpreting images, an innovative algorithm based on prominence has been proposed, aimed at improving chromatic perception and visual comprehension [4].

Furthermore, recent studies have employed virtual reality technology and data analysis to investigate how the layout and positioning of signage affect its effectiveness in communicating important information [5]. On the other hand, digital simulation of visual impairments has emerged as a valuable tool for enhancing techniques for detecting and understanding color vision deficiencies, surpassing the limitations of traditional detection methods [6].

In the context of digital signage, in the study by Nahyeong Kim et al. [7] They explore the usability and accessibility of symbols in automotive environments, specifically targeting individuals with color vision deficiency (CVD). Their research highlights the importance of designing more accessible symbols to improve the understanding of visual information in digital environments. This perspective offers valuable lessons applicable to the design of signage in coworking spaces, where accessibility is crucial to ensuring an inclusive experience for all users.

On the other hand, augmented reality (AR) presents particular challenges for individuals with color vision deficiency, as highlighted by Sundus Fatima & Jannicke Baalsrud Hauge [8]. Their research emphasizes the need to adapt educational technologies to address the specific needs of this population. By integrating these findings into the implementation of smart AR signage in coworking environments, the navigation experience can be enhanced, facilitating information comprehension for users with varying visual abilities.

The focus on empathy and understanding the experiences of people with visual disabilities, as addressed in Jialiang Bai's study [9], It is essential for inclusive design. The introduction of tools such as mixed reality-based ocular disease simulators can assist designers in better understanding the needs and challenges of this user group. By considering these empathetic perspectives, signage solutions can be developed to be more intuitive and accessible for all users, regardless of their visual abilities.

The research by Michael J Fliotsos [10] The research highlights the importance of assessing color vision using mobile applications. By comparing a mobile app for color vision assessment with standard tests, their approach underscores the feasibility of digital tools for diagnosing visual impairments. This methodology provides an accessible and convenient way for individuals to assess their color vision, potentially leading to early detection of visual deficiencies and thus appropriate intervention.

On the other hand, the study by Naomi Woods & Johanna Silvennoinen [11] proposes innovative digital authentication methods focused on the memorability and security of passwords. Their approach to using color signals as memory underscores the importance of enhancing user experience and online security. This proposal paves the way for more secure and easily remembered passwords, potentially increasing the adoption and effectiveness of security measures in digital environments.

2 Methods and Materials

Design of Augmented Reality Signage. The implementation of augmented reality signage was based on a multidisciplinary approach, combining expertise in graphic design, augmented reality technologies, and accessibility considerations. An interdisciplinary team was formed, consisting of graphic designers, software developers, and usability experts, with the aim of ensuring an effective and accessible implementation of the signage (Fig. 1).

Development of 2D Animations and Virtual Tours. The 2D animations and virtual tours were designed with special attention to inclusion and accessibility. Advanced graphic design tools were used to create intuitive and user-friendly animations, employing validated corporate colors to ensure accessibility, particularly for individuals with color

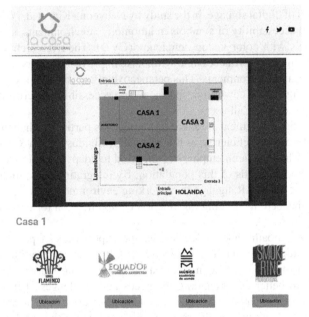

Fig. 1. The image depicts the homepage of the site, displaying the directory of all establishments within the coworking space, providing an overview of the layout and organization of the spaces for users.

vision deficiency. The development of virtual tours was carried out using specialized augmented reality software, aiming to provide an immersive and effective experience for users (Fig. 2).

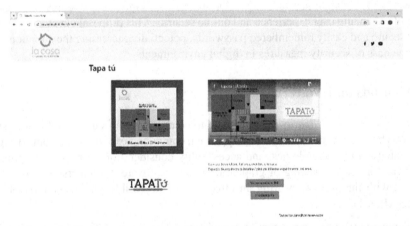

Fig. 2. The image illustrates how each establishment is equipped with a map and a 2D animation guiding individuals on how to reach the venture from the main totem, facilitating navigation and location within the coworking space

Integration of Assistive Technologies. Specific assistive technologies were evaluated and applied to enhance the accessibility of the signage for individuals with color vision deficiency. This included the use of recoloring algorithms to adapt web interfaces to the needs of colorblind users, as well as the development of a prominence-based image correction algorithm to improve the visualization of highlighted areas in images.

Testing and Validation. The augmented reality signage underwent comprehensive testing to ensure its effectiveness and accessibility. Usability tests were conducted with representative users, including individuals with different visual abilities, to assess the ease of use and effectiveness of the signage. Additionally, formal validation of the assistive technologies used, including user testing with colorblind individuals, was carried out to ensure their functionality and effectiveness in real-world environments.

Technology Used. The development of the augmented reality signage relied on advanced technologies, including graphic design software, augmented reality development platforms, and accessibility tools. Software such as WordPress was utilized for the implementation of the signage, enabling an agile and efficient experience for users without the need to download a specific application.

3 Proposed Model

The proposed model represents an innovative and meticulously designed approach to implementing smart signage with augmented reality in coworking environments. It is grounded in the fundamental premise of enhancing the user experience and ensuring accessibility for all individuals, regardless of their visual capabilities.

First and foremost, the model distinguishes itself through its comprehensive focus on accessibility. It acknowledges that traditional signage can pose significant barriers for individuals with color vision deficiency and other visual impairments. Therefore, inclusion has been prioritized at every stage of design and implementation. Validated corporate colors and specific recoloring algorithms are utilized to ensure that the signage is legible and understandable for all users (Figs. 3 and 4).

Furthermore, the model leverages advanced assistive technologies to further enhance the accessibility of the signage. Image correction algorithms based on prominence are implemented, specifically designed to assist users with color vision deficiency in distinguishing colors and highlighting important areas in the images. This integration of assistive technologies not only improves accessibility but also demonstrates a commitment to innovation and technical excellence.

In terms of technological platform, the model relies on WordPress, a robust and widely used platform that offers flexibility and scalability. This strategic choice enables the implementation of signage in an agile and efficient manner, without the need to develop a specific application. Additionally, it provides a consistent and seamless experience for users, regardless of the device they use to access the signage.

The model also includes a rigorous process of testing and validation to ensure the effectiveness and quality of the signage. Exhaustive usability tests are conducted with representative users, as well as specific accessibility tests with individuals with color vision deficiency. This empirical validation allows for the identification and addressing

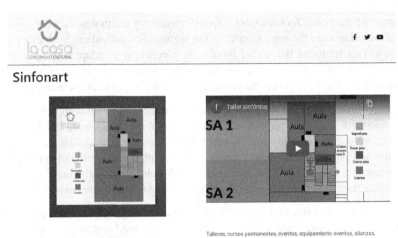

Sinfonart

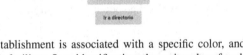

Fig. 3. The image illustrates how each establishment is associated with a specific color, and some of them are located on upper floors. To facilitate floor identification, the main color of each establishment was used, along with its respective variant validated for individuals with color vision deficiency, thus ensuring an inclusive and accessible experience for all users.

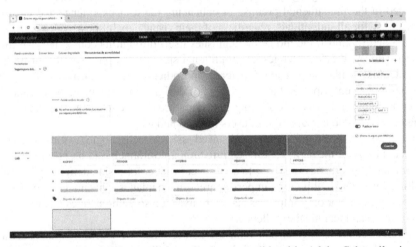

Fig. 4. As observed in the image, the use of color was validated in Adobe Color, allowing for the creation of a harmonious color scheme that is especially functional for individuals with color vision deficiency.

of any issues or limitations in the signage, ensuring a satisfactory experience for all users.

Ultimately, the model is committed to continuous improvement. Feedback and input from users are actively collected to iterate and constantly improve the signage. This user-centered approach allows for adaptation to the changing needs of the user community and ensures that the signage remains relevant and effective over time.

4 Discussion

The present study has explored the implementation of smart signage with augmented reality in a coworking environment, with a particular focus on improving user experience and ensuring accessibility for individuals with different visual abilities. Through the integration of innovative technologies and inclusive design practices, a model has been developed that offers significant benefits for both users and coworking space owners.

One of the highlights of this study is the careful attention paid to accessibility. It is recognized that traditional signage can present significant challenges for people with color vision deficiency and other visual impairments, and therefore, inclusion has been prioritized at every stage of the design and development process. The integration of specific assistive technologies, such as recoloring algorithms and image correction, has proven effective in enhancing the readability and comprehension of signage for this user group.

Furthermore, the choice of a robust and scalable technological platform, such as WordPress, has facilitated the agile and efficient implementation of the signage, without compromising the user experience. This platform provides a solid foundation for future improvements and updates, ensuring that the signage remains relevant and effective over time.

The process of testing and validation has been crucial to ensuring the effectiveness and quality of the signage. Exhaustive usability and accessibility tests have identified and addressed potential issues and limitations, ensuring a satisfactory experience for all users. Additionally, continuous user feedback has been essential for iterating and constantly improving the signage, demonstrating a commitment to excellence and continuous improvement.

In summary, this study demonstrates the potential of smart signage with augmented reality to enhance user experience and ensure accessibility in coworking environments. The integration of innovative technologies and inclusive design practices offers significant benefits for both users and coworking space owners, laying the groundwork for future research and developments in this promising field.

5 Conclusions

The implementation of smart signage with augmented reality in coworking environments presents a unique opportunity to enhance user experience and ensure accessibility for individuals with diverse visual abilities. Through this study, several important conclusions have been identified, highlighting the effectiveness and potential of this innovative approach.

Firstly, it has been demonstrated that the integration of augmented reality technologies and inclusive design can significantly improve the readability and comprehension of signage for people with color vision deficiency and other visual impairments. Careful attention to the selection of validated corporate colors and specific recoloring algorithms has been crucial in ensuring an inclusive experience for all users.

Furthermore, it has been confirmed that the choice of a robust and scalable technological platform, such as WordPress, facilitates the efficient implementation of signage without compromising the user experience. This platform provides a solid foundation for future enhancements and updates, ensuring that the signage remains relevant and effective over time.

The process of testing and validation has been essential in identifying and addressing potential issues and limitations in the signage. Exhaustive usability and accessibility testing have ensured a satisfactory experience for all users, while continuous user feedback has been crucial for iterating and constantly improving the signage.

In summary, this study highlights the potential of smart signage with augmented reality to transform the user experience in coworking environments. The integration of innovative technologies and inclusive design practices offers significant benefits for both users and coworking space owners, laying the groundwork for future research and developments in this promising field.

6 Gratitude

We would like to express our sincere gratitude to Casa Coworking in Quito, Ecuador, for their invaluable collaboration in conducting this study. We want to especially acknowledge Mr. Gonzalo Proaño, the site administrator, for his generous willingness to grant us access to the facilities and efficiently coordinate communications with all the businesses housed in the coworking space during the research process. His support and cooperation have been essential to the success of this project, and we are sincerely grateful for his contribution.

References

1. Delgado-Cedeño, D., Chacón-Rivas, M.: Image adaptation based on color saturation and linear matrices for people with deuteranopia-type color blindness. In: Antona, M., Stephanidis, C. (eds.) UAHCI 2021, pp. 349–368. Springer, Cham (2021). https://doi.org/10.1007/978-3-030-78092-0_23

2. Guilei, S.: Research on location of emergency sign based on virtual reality and eye tracking technology. In: Ahram, T. (ed.) AHFE 2019. AISC, vol. 973, pp. 401–408. Springer, Cham (2020). https://doi.org/10.1007/978-3-030-20476-1_40

3. Narayanan, A., Venkadesan, M., Krishnamurthy, S.S., Hussaindeen, J.R., Ramani, K.K.: Dalton's pseudo-isochromatic plates and congenital colour vision deficiency. Clin. Exp. Optom. **103**(6), 853–857 (2020). https://doi.org/10.1111/cxo.13034

4. de Araújo, R.J., Dos Reis, J.C., Bonacin, R.: Understanding interface recoloring aspects by colorblind people: a user study. Univers. Access Inf. Soc. **19**(1), 81–98 (2020). https://doi.org/10.1007/s10209-018-0631-7

5. Georgakas, D.: Tell me what to do: designing for people with disabilities. In: A11Y Unraveled, pp. 37–65. Apress, Berkeley, CA (2023). https://doi.org/10.1007/978-1-4842-9085-9_5

6. Li, J., Feng, X., Fan, H.: Saliency-based image correction for colorblind patients. Comput. Vis. Media **6**(2), 169–189 (2020). https://doi.org/10.1007/s41095-020-0172-x

7. Kim, N., et al.: Usability evaluation of symbols in digital cluster for drivers with color vision deficiency. Univers. Access Inf. Soc. **22**(3), 903–917 (2023). https://doi.org/10.1007/s10209-022-00898-4

8. Fatima, S., Hauge, J.B.: Challenges in designing Augmented Reality (AR) in serious games and gamification for students with colorblindness. In: Haahr, M., Rojas-Salazar, A., Göbel, S. (eds.) JCSG 2023, pp. 447–454. Springer, Cham (2023). https://doi.org/10.1007/978-3-031-44751-8_41

9. Bai, J., Yu, Z., Zhang, F., Cheng, Y.: Empathy tool design-eye disease simulator based on mixed-reality technology. In: Stephanidis, C. (ed.) HCII 2019. CCIS, vol. 1032, pp. 235–242. Springer, Cham (2019). https://doi.org/10.1007/978-3-030-23522-2_30

10. Fliotsos, M.J., Zhao, J., Pradeep, T., Ighani, M., Eghrari, A.O.: Testing a popular smartphone application for colour vision assessment in healthy volunteer subjects. Neuro-Ophthalmology **45**(2), 99–104 (2021). https://doi.org/10.1080/01658107.2020.1817947

11. Woods, N., Silvennoinen, J.: Enhancing the user authentication process with colour memory cues. Behav. Inf. Technol. **42**(10), 1548–1567 (2023). https://doi.org/10.1080/0144929X.2022.2091474

Use of Technologies to Improve Quality of Life and Well-Being in People with Autism (ASD) and Chronic Anxiety and/or Depression from a Gender Perspective

Gema Benedicto Rodriguez[1]([✉]), Vanessa Zorrilla-Muñoz[2,3,8],
María Silveria Agulló-Tomás[3,4], Carmen Lillo-Navarro[5], Eduardo Fernandez[2,7],
and Jose Manuel Ferrandez-Vicente[1,6]

[1] Polytechnic University of Cartagena, Murcia, Spain
gema.benedicto@edu.upct.es, jm.ferrandez@uptc.es
[2] Bioengineering Institute, Miguel Hernández University of Elche, Elche, Spain
{vzorrilla,nicolas.garcia,e.fernandez}@umh.es
[3] Institute of Gender Studies, University Carlos III of Madrid, Gatafe, Spain
msat@polsoc.uc3m.es
[4] Department of Social Analysis, University Carlos III of Madrid, Gatafe, Spain
[5] Center for Translational Research in Physiotherapy (CEIT), Department of Pathology and Surgery, Miguel Hernández University, Alicante, Spain
mclillo@umh.es
[6] National Network on Artificial Intelligence for Neuroscience and Mental Health, Madrid, Spain
[7] CIBER BBN, Elche, Spain
[8] University Miguel Hernandez, Getafe, Spain

Abstract. Individuals with Autism Spectrum Disorder (ASD) often experience anxiety and/or depression, complicating their diagnosis due to sensory hypersensitivity and social difficulties, with negative impacts on well-being and quality of life. Social stigma worsens mental health issues, particularly affecting women and older individuals. New technologies may be a key for enhancing well-being by addressing communication gaps and reducing anxiety and depression levels. The main objective of this chapter is to explore the current use of technologies and the perception of their impact on people diagnosed with ASD, chronic anxiety, and/or depression. This goal will be obtain answer of human computer interaction in social robots and other technologies used in ASD to reduce anxiety and depression levels. For this purpose, we used secondary data from the "Survey on Disability, Personal Autonomy and Dependency Situations (EDAD)" of the National Institute of Statistics (INE, 2020, Spain) regarding people with chronic anxiety (n = 2070), chronic depression (n = 2179) and ASD (n = 241). The results show a correlation between the improvement in quality of life and the use of technologies in these three groups of people from a gender and intergenerational perspective. Devices such as the Empatica E4 show alterations in autistic children undergoing robotic therapy, so this may be useful for personalized and autonomous interventions. All of these technologies and different forms of AI could currently provide benefits for other more vulnerable groups, such as minors, women, and older people.

C. Stephanidis et al. (Eds.): HCII 2024, CCIS 2115, pp. 12–20, 2024.
https://doi.org/10.1007/978-3-031-61947-2_2

Keywords: Happiness · quality of life · well-being · technologies · autism · chronic anxiety · chronic depression · gender · intergenerational · social robots

1 Introduction

Persons affected by Autism Spectrum Disorder (ASD) often experience anxiety and/or depression, complicating their diagnosis due to sensory hypersensitivity and social difficulties. Moreover, multiple diagnosis produced negative impacts on their quality of life (QoL). New technologies may be a key for enhancing well-being and improving QoL by addressing communication gaps and reducing anxiety and depression levels. However, the global technologies use has generated a widespread stigma towards certain devices perceived as unduly dangerous or simply. Despite a high market demand, still seems to be inappropriate for therapeutic use, as happens with social robots [4]. Some research suggests there is a high scientific interest in technological evaluation based on its therapeutic benefits, in various population groups, such as patients with ASD [5], where the results suggest social robots and other types of Internet of Things (IoT) technologies such as portable and mobile devices can be used in patients with ASD, Chronic Anxiety (CA) and Chronic Depression (CD) [2]. Moreover, ASD is on the rise and is more prevalent in men than in women, with a rate of 23.6 per thousand inhabitants in men and 5.3 per thousand inhabitants in women in the United States [2].ASD has historically been identified with a strong male bias in prevalence, which has affected scientific knowledge of autism in women. However, in recent years, there has been growing interest in understanding sex and gender differences (s/g) in ASD, which has led to an increased number of investigations on this topic [11].

Additionally, sex and gender differences in the core symptoms of ASD have shown inconsistent results, but it has been observed that women tend to have fewer restrictive and repetitive behaviors, although they may face greater difficulties in social-communicative skills and adaptive functioning than men. In addition, girls with ASD tend to use camouflage strategies to hide their social difficulties, which can make diagnosis more difficult [12]. In this context, research have also revealed differences in the detection and diagnosis of ASD between men and women, suggesting that the case verification methodology influences the prevalence ratio between the sexes. It has been proposed that s/g differences in ASD prevalence are influenced by genetic, environmental, and hormonal factors [13].

Regarding the neuroanatomy of ASD, although some differences have been identified between boys and girls, more research is needed to fully understand its role in the etiopathogenesis of the disorder. In addition, a co-occurrence of ASD and gender dysphoria has been suggested, highlighting the importance of understanding the interactions between these conditions and their implications for diagnosis and treatment [1].

Symptoms of ASD begin in childhood and persist throughout life, with variations in evolution and functioning depending on factors such as language, intellectual development, age, and the presence of comorbidities. Early detection of ASD is crucial, but there are currently no biological tests for its diagnosis; therefore, it is based on assessment through validated scales, which influences the clinical evolution and quality of life of those who suffer from it [2].

Quality of life (QoL) refers to how people perceive their lives in relation to their goals, expectations, and standards within their cultural and value environments. This perception is linked to happiness and can influence physical and mental health [6]. Individuals with Autism Spectrum Disorder (ASD) may experience comorbidities with other mental disorders such as anxiety. Anxiety can manifest in individuals with ASD as autistic traits are evident in people with anxiety. The coexistence of ASD and anxiety affects a significant percentage (39.6%) of people under 18 years of age. A higher percentage of anxiety is observed in young people with ASD, where some have traditional anxiety disorders and others show atypical symptoms related to ASD. The simultaneous prevalence of ASD and anxiety remains controversial in the scientific community [5]. In addition, adolescents with Anxiety Disorders who present with autistic traits experience higher levels of social anxiety and depressive symptoms, which makes it difficult to manage uncertainty and daily activities, impacting their quality of life [3, 4].

Depression can negatively impact the quality of life of individuals with Autism Spectrum Disorder (ASD). It is estimated that approximately 5% of adults experience depression, affecting children and young people as well, with rates of 2.8% in children under 13 years of age and 5.6% in adolescents. Studies have shown that the combined rates of depression and ASD vary between 23–37% over the lifespan, suggesting an increased risk of depressive disorders in people with ASD compared with those without ASD [8].

The exact cause of depression in ASD is not clearly defined, with different researchers pointing to external factors, such as socioeconomic conditions, genetic predisposition, stressful events, loss, or disappointment, as possible triggers. Depression in childhood can be related to social, family, personal, and educational aspects, manifesting over time as an emotional response (van Heijst, 2020). It is important to note that children with ASD may struggle to manage stress and react disproportionately to environmental stimuli, which may influence their emotional development. Learning emotion regulation strategies in people with ASD could play a crucial role in reducing the risk of anxiety and depression in stressful situations [7].

Recently, the beneficial use of disruptive technologies with a social base has been shown to improve emotional regulation in individuals with Autism Spectrum Disorder (ASD), as well as in patients with anxiety and depression. These technologies could be key to improving quality of life by reducing the communication gap and aiding in the management of stressful situations [9]. Some people with severe disabilities have reported a high quality of life, including perceived health, despite their conditions, which is known as the "disability paradox" [10]. A person's perception of technology, in relation to their daily challenges, is critical. Therefore, the importance of understanding the technological perception of individuals with ASD, anxiety, and depression is highlighted to improve the design, development, and innovation of accessible and effective technologies in therapies [9].

2   Methods

The main objective is to explore the current use of technologies and the perception of their impact on people diagnosed with ASD, chronic anxiety, and/or depression. This goal will be obtain answer of human computer interaction in social robots and other technologies used in ASD to reduce anxiety and depression levels. For this purpose, we used secondary data from the "Survey on Disability, Personal Autonomy and Dependency Situations (EDAD)" of the National Institute of Statistics (INE) [14] regarding people with chronic anxiety (n = 2070), chronic depression (n = 2179) and ASD (n = 241). The questionnaire used applies aspects related to QoL based on the WHO dimensions of the WHOQOL-100 scale, which focuses on describing "the person's physical health, their physiological state, the independence level, their social relationships and with their environment" [9]. Specifically, this questionnaire included facets from the domains of "Social relationships" (interpersonal relationships were added) and "Psychological" (communication and learning). It is based on data from two different types of questionnaires. Table 1 shows the main domains, aspects and variables considers in the analysis.

Table 1. Domains, items and variables of the EDAD questionnaire.

Domains	Items	Variables
Social relationships and	Interpersonal relationships	3
Psychological item	Communication	6
	Learning	6

To carry out the statistical analysis, the question that relates the perception of technology with the improvement of quality of life is used as a dependent variable: "Do you think that the use of new technologies has improved aspects of your daily life?", using a score of 1 to 4 points, where the minimum value is 1 being "Yes, has improved a lot" and the value of 4 the maximum difficulty with "It has made my daily life worse".

A second part of the analysis was carried out based on the data available from the ENCAGE Program, ENCAGEn-CM (https://encage-cm.csic.es/) and the ENVACES project. It is based on a total of 118 documents and 124 labeled codes. The search for discursive extracts was carried out with the following subcodes: 'Technology', 'anxiety', 'depression' and 'gender'. The software used was Atlas.ti. Finally, the codes and speeches were taken to the Artificial Intelligence APP (OpenArt) to create images that summarized the aspects analysed.

3   Results

The results show a correlation between the improvement in QoL and the use of technologies in these three groups of people from a gender and intergenerational perspective. An example is a $p < 0.001$ for ASD and CD in the variable "Understand the meaning of what others say to you when you receive help" into the item *Communication*. Moreover, ASD persons manifest to have more difficulties in technologies based on mobiles and touch-screen and there are not data available to consider social robots interactions (Table 2).

Table 2. Difficulties levels variables related to communication, learning and interpersonal relationships items. Pearson analysis for ASD, CA and CD.

	Difficulty levels variables to…	Pearson ASD	Pearson CA	Pearson CD
COMMUNICATION	…speak in a manner understandable or say meaningful phrases when you use the assistive device	−0.0949	0.4391*	0.2547
	…understand the meaning of what others say when get help	−0.2196*	−0.1392	−0.0893
	…understand and express yourself through written language	−0.2029*	0.0233	−0.0290
	…understand and express yourself through gestures, symbols, drawings or sounds	−0.3054*	−0.0187	−0.0681
	…use systems written communication to distance	−0.0948	−0.0633	−0.1385*
	…use systems written communication to distance when receiving aid	−0.2925*	−0.0932	−0.1478
LEARNING	…pay attention with the gaze or hold the attention with ear	−0.3149*	−0.1465	−0.1085
	…to learn to do simple things	−0.2614*	−0.1231	−0.1596*
	…to learn to do simple things when receive help or personal assistance	−0.2317*	0.0897	−0.0372
	…carry out tasks simple	−0.3621*	−0.0633	−0.1294
	…carry out tasks complex	−0.2165*	−0.1470*	−0.0975

(*continued*)

Table 2. (*continued*)

	Difficulty levels variables to...	Pearson ASD	Pearson CA	Pearson CD
	...carry out tasks complex when receive help or personal assistance	−0.2100*	0.0720	0.0711
INTERPERSONAL RELATIONSHIPS	...relate to Unknown people	−0.1751*	−0.0649	−0.1219*
	...create and maintain relationships with friends, neighbors, acquaintances, subordinate people, higher positions or companions	−0.1662	−0.1611*	−0.1366*
	...create and maintain relations sentimental, couple or sexual	−0.0840	−0.2059*	−0.2430*

* p < 0.001

Regarding the discourse results, there is fear about how the technology could affect further and new generations and how the codes and caregivers and speeches were the new technological world, especially, when person has a disability as autism.

"*...There is enormous social anxiety with automation and robotization and everyone finds themselves, themselves or their children, in the gutter.*"(*Business Man*).

In this sense, there is also concern about the multiple comorbidities that autistic people, like other people affected by disabilities, can develop in adulthood and around ageing. In the spotlight is the anxiety of not having nearby resources available, the loss of friendships, unconditional support.

"*... I get anxiety attacks, and if I stay at home it's worse, so I start thinking about a place and how and with whom I should go... Because I'm at home all day and at five in the afternoon, as a rule, I go out and return home at nine at night.*" (*Older woman*).

Last but not least, it should not be ignored that certain states or situations such as unwanted loneliness and social isolation can influence the appearance of mental illnesses, such as anxiety and depression. Here any type of person, as well as autistic people, must face a paradigm shift in their life, through social integration in order to improve the QoL and well-being.

"*...In the end what made him change is the paradigm shift regarding diseases. That is, achieving greater health through integration, regardless of their illnesses that were the root of unwanted loneliness, depression and decay. This type of thing has more to do with social issues.*" (*Man, program expert of institutional services*).

Beyond this, there is a problem in adulthood related to isolation and unwanted loneliness and programs, whether technological or not, can encourage the person to participate. Technology itself can be a factor in attracting the attention of the affected person. From a gender perspective, the great handicap is attracting the attention of men, since they are less participatory than women in any program or action.

"We have to try to redirect them, so that they are not left alone in their houses, treat depression, social isolation... we have a great role in promoting this type of activities and for them to intervene... But really, the problem is to capture the person." (Man, program expert of institutional services).

"The woman is active when she is an adult and close to old age, the man may feel displaced... With retirement will come depression." (Older woman).

Under the base of the discourses, several AI image model was created with the subcodes "autism", "older man and woman", "depression", "anxiety".

4   Conclusion

It is known that most emerging technologies are being used to address the limitations and challenges of children with Autism Spectrum Disorder (ASD), anxiety, and/or chronic depression in areas such as communication and social skills, improving quality of life. Despite this, stigmas continue to exist in technologies, such as social robots.

With the aim that this does not affect its acceptance and use in the treatment of conditions such as autism and its comorbidities, it would be of great relevance to carry out an evaluation of the technologies according to the different population groups, always from a therapeutic perspective, that is, how autistic people perceive and respond to these technologies. Likewise, it is suggested to explore the perception of technologies from a gender and intergenerational perspective, determining how it influences men and women differently, and how they could be adapted to the specific needs of each group.

However, it is true that technology is increasingly growing in research, especially in autism, detecting needs and establishing clear objectives, as is the case in studies that focus on emotional areas and learning, which are the most studied fields. For technology to systematically enrich any activity, there are two blocks of applications: personal support and learning.

In the case of learning, there are technological resources that can be used in mathematics and digital whiteboards, and in personal support, there are devices and applications that help in communication and understanding of the environment.

The importance of technology in the quality of life of individuals with ASD must be highlighted. When the use of technology is appropriate, there are many advantages to its use, such as individualization and personalization for each person, also considering the methodological principles of intervention, assuming the inclusion of vulnerable groups, an improvement in emotional regulation, and sensory balance. In addition, it can mean improvements in orientation and autonomy, therapeutic treatment of phobias, and situations that cause stress, along with home automation, which provides well-being in the domestic environment.

This is where the intervention of social robots takes precedence, which not only provides a therapeutic benefit for people with autism, but also provides the intention to play and have fun through different activities and games, currently also beneficial for other groups. The most vulnerable, such as minors, women, and the elderly.

5 Fundings and Grants

This work is part of the grant PID2020-115220RB-C22 funded by MCIN/AEI/ https://doi.org/10.13039/501100011033 and, as appropriate, by "ERDF A way of making Europe", by the "European Union" or by the "European Union NextGenerationEU/PRTR of the Polytechnic University of Cartagena (PR: Jose Manuel Ferrandez-Vicente); ENCAGEn-CM R&D Activities Program (Ref. H2019/HUM-5698) (Community of Madrid-FSE. PR: G. Fernandez-Mayoralas, C Rodriguez-Blazquez, M.S. Agullo-Tomas, M.D. Zamarron, and M.A. Molina) and; Proyecto INNTA1/2022/23 "Innovation Agent for the Bioengineering Institute of the Miguel Hernandez University o Elche", co-financed by the UE in the Program FEDER, Valencian Community 2021–2027.

This project has received funding by and was funded in part by grants DTS19/00175 and PDC2022–133952-100 from the Spanish "Ministerio de Ciencia, Innovación y Universidades" and by the European Union's Horizon 2020 Research and Innovation Programme under Grant Agreement No. 899287 (NeuraViPeR), as well as the "Premio Tecnologías Accesibles de Indra y Universia Fundación".

References

1. Calderoni, S.: Sex/gender differences in children with autism spectrum disorder: a brief overview on epidemiology, symptom profile, and neuroanatomy. J. Neurosci. Res. **101**(5), 739–750 (2023)
2. McCarty, P., Frye, R.E.: Early detection and diagnosis of autism spectrum disorder: why is it so difficult? Seminars in Pediatric Neurology **35**, 100831. WB Saunders (2020)
3. Moss, P., Mandy, W., Howlin, P.: Child and adult factors related to quality of life in adults with autism. J. Autism Dev. Disord. **47**, 1830–1837 (2017)
4. Williams, Z.J., Gotham, K.O.: Assessing general and autism-relevant quality of life in autistic adults: a psychometric investigation using item response theory. Autism Res. **14**(8), 1633–1644 (2021)
5. Zaboski, B.A., Storch, E.A.: Comorbid autism spectrum disorder and anxiety disorders: a brief review. Future Neurol. **13**(1), 31–37 (2018)
6. WHO. WHOQOL - Measuring Quality of Life. (6 de diciembre de 2023). Obtenido de The World Health Organization. https://www.who.int/tools/whoqol
7. Khanna, R., Jariwala-Parikh, K., West-Strum, D., Mahabaleshwarkar, R.: Health-related quality of life and its determinants among adults with autism. Res. Autism Spectrum Disorders **8**(3), 157–167 (2014)
8. Hollocks, M.J., Lerh, J.W., Magiati, I., Meiser-Stedman, R., Brugha, T.S.: Anxiety and depression in adults with autism spectrum disorder: a systematic review and meta-analysis. Psychol. Med. **49**(4), 559–572 (2019)

9. Lara, M.H., Caro, K., Martínez-García, A.I.: Technology for supporting emotion regulation of individuals with developmental disabilities: a scoping review. Res. Dev. Disabil. **136**, 104467 (2023)

10. Henao Lema, C.P., Gil Obando, L.M.: Calidad de vida y situación de discapacidad. Hacia la Promoción de la Salud **14**(2), 114–127 (2009)

11. de Haro, E.O.: Las diferencias de género en el TEA. Intervención psicoeducativa en una niña de 3 años

12. Montagut Asunción, M., Mas Romero, R.M., Fernández Andrés, M.I., Pastor Cerezuela, G.: Influencia del sesgo de género en el diagnóstico de trastorno de espectro autista: una revisión. Escritos de Psicología (Internet) **11**(1), 42–54 (2018)

13. Beacher, F.D.C.C., et al.: Sex differences and autism: brain function during verbal fluency and mental rotation. PLoS One **7**(6). https://doi.org/10.1371/JOURNAL.PONE.0038355.

14. INEbase/Sociedad/Salud/Encuestas de discapacidades/Resultados. 2020. INE. Recuperado 9 de enero de 2024, de https://www.ine.es/dyngs/INEbase/es/operacion.htm?c=Estadistica_C&cid=1254736176782&menu=resultados&idp=1254735573175

Reliability of the Metric to Evaluate the Ergonomic Principles of Assistive Systems, Based on ISO 92419

Azadeh Braun[1], Karsten Nebe[1(✉)], and Rüdiger Heimgärtner[2]

[1] Rhine-Waal University of Applied Sciences, Friedrich-Heinrich-Allee 25,
47475 Kamp-Lintfort, Germany
azadehrf@gmail.com, karsten.nebe@hochschule-rhein-waal.de
[2] IUIC, Lindenstrasse 9, 93152 Undorf, Germany
ruediger.heimgaertner@iuic.de

Abstract. To develop Assistive Systems that are well-adjusted to users' needs, one approach is the usage of international standards, for example, DIN or ISO norms. In this paper, we consider a questionnaire by Azevedo, Heimgaertner, and Nebe [17] designed to evaluate the ergonomics principles of Assistive Systems according to DIN EN 92419 [8]. As an example of an available Assistive System, Amazon Echo was chosen. We ran the survey with 18 participants. To evaluate the reliability of the questionnaire, Cronbach's alpha is calculated. Moreover, we investigate the questions in more detail and give recommendations for improving the questionnaire.

Keywords: Assistive Systems · Reliability Assessment · Cronbach's alpha · Usability Survey · Ergonomics

1 Introduction

The World Health Organization (WHO) highlights in its reports [15, 16] the limited access to Assistive Systems in low to middle-income countries, ranging from 5% to 15%, often due to the lack of accessibility standards [9]. Studies indicate users may abandon Assistive Systems if adaptation is required [12], leading to a mismatch between user needs and system offerings [10]. International standards like DIN or ISO norms are crucial for aligning Assistive Systems with user needs. The WHO categorizes diverse groups as needing these systems, while DIN 92419 includes even those without specific health conditions [8, 17]. This broadens the scope of Assistive Systems, potentially impacting broader societal goals like the SDGs [13, 14]. Azevedo et al. developed a metric based on DIN 92419 to evaluate Assistive Systems' ergonomics, though empirical validation is needed [17]. This paper validates the reliability of Azevedo et al.'s survey using Amazon Echo as a case study and offers improvements for efficiency and applicability.

C. Stephanidis et al. (Eds.): HCII 2024, CCIS 2115, pp. 21–32, 2024.
https://doi.org/10.1007/978-3-031-61947-2_3

1.1 Research Questions

The main focus of this paper is to assess the reliability of the questionnaire. In addition, there are more questions to consider:

- What are the strengths and weaknesses of this questionnaire?
- To what extent is this questionnaire usable?
- Is the number of questions regarding each principle appropriate?
- Can the questionnaire be adapted for various contexts or different systems?

By considering these questions, we are aiming to understand the capabilities, usability, and limitations of this questionnaire.

1.2 Methodology

This study distributed an online questionnaire in English and German to evaluate its reliability. We calculated Cronbach's alpha for the overall questionnaire and for each principle. Adhering to Bonett's formula [4], a minimum of 18 participants was determined as the necessary sample size. The alpha values were derived from the data using Excel.

1.3 Goals and Innovative Aspects

This study's main aim is to assess the reliability of the newly developed questionnaire, previously untested in practical scenarios. It critically reviews the questionnaire, highlighting its merits and limitations, and suggests ways to improve it for subsequent studies. Another key goal is to fine-tune the questions for better usability. The research provides insights for enhancing the questionnaire's application in evaluating and advancing Assistive Systems, focusing on their assessment, development, and standardization.

2 Concepts

2.1 Assistive Systems

In contemporary societies, assisting individuals such as the elderly, those with cognitive impairments like dementia, and people with functional disabilities is increasingly vital. Assistive Technologies, designed to aid these groups, are essential given the growing global population and longer life expectancies. These technologies range from hearing aids and cognitive aids to AI-enhanced devices [5]. This paper expands the definition of "Assistive System" to include technologies used by the general population, like navigation systems, storage solutions, smartwatches, and automatic emergency braking systems.

2.2 Ergonomics

Defined by ISO 26800:2011 [11], ergonomics is the study of human interactions within systems, aiming to optimize well-being and system performance. It involves designing hardware, software, and work environments to prevent negative outcomes like inefficiency and injuries [6]. Ergonomic applications, guided by scientific knowledge and situational methods [3], are versatile, addressing existing system issues, shaping new system designs, and aligning with organizational goals.

2.3 DIN Ergonomic Principles of Assistive Systems

DIN 92419 [8] outlines six principles for the ergonomic design of Assistive Systems to enhance human-machine interaction quality:

- Acceptance: Defined as the user's affirmative choice to use a system, based on its added value and positive user experience. Recommendations include making the system enjoyable, providing extra value, ensuring trust, and being unobtrusive.
- Safety, Security, and Privacy: Focuses on minimizing risks and unauthorized activities, ensuring user privacy, and transparent handling of personal data.
- Optimization of Resultant Internal Load: Aims to improve overall external load for users, by managing the internal load and using it for encouragement.
- Controllability: Ensures the system is predictable and influenceable by users, with transparency in its support extent.
- Adaptability: Allows users to tailor the system's functionality to their context, including modifying privacy settings and the level of support.
- Perceptibility and Identifiability: Ensures all components and information of the system are understandable and identifiable by users, catering to multiple senses.

3 Information Gathering

3.1 Survey

We evaluated Amazon Echo with a questionnaire completed by 18 individuals, a sample size justified in the Cronbach's alpha section. Table 1 provides the participants patterns of Alexa usage.

Among the survey respondents, 13 resided in Germany, 1 in Italy, 1 in Canada, and 2 in the US, with one participant's location unspecified. The gender distribution was 8 women, 8 men, and 2 undisclosed, ranging in age from 26 to 72 years, averaging at 39 years.

Results. In [1], we provide 36 charts, illustrating the user ratings for Alexa in different categories. The charts show the breakdown of each principle into different subcategories, aligning with the division outlined in the research by Azevedo et al. [17].

The results in the charts are shown in Likert-scales. They are all aligned on the answer "neutral", to make it easily perceivable if the answers tend more to the positive or negative sides of the scale. An indicator shows the average score of the answers in the sense of how positive the answers are; a high score means that the answers were more positive. The answers "Not applicable" are illustrated separately, next to the scale.

Table 1. Usages of the participants from Alexa.

Usage	Participants
Playing music (including controlling the music in different areas at home)	16
Getting information	10
Adjusting the lights in the house	9
Setting an alarm	8
Turning on/off the TV	6
Setting routines	5
Finding your other devices at home	4
Shopping or making a shopping list or ordering items	4
Checking your calendar	3
Assisting in the kitchen (recipes, grocery lists, etc.)	3
Adjusting the temperature in the house	2
Making calls (including emergency calls)	2
Listening to news or putting notifications for news channels	2
Playing games	1
Play dog bark when an outdoor camera sees a human on the property at night	1*
Switching lights and devices in the garden	1*
Alexa Prize Social Bots were fun until ChatGPT nuked them into irrelevance	1*
Answering the door	0
Locking the door(s)	0
Scheduling a meeting	0
Alexa together	0
Assisting with kids (homework, routines, playing games, etc.)	0
Photos (taking a selfie, showing them, making albums, sharing them, etc.)	0

*: Three of the items were not on our list; the participants wrote them as "other" usages

User ratings for Amazon Echo, evaluated across 36 charts, revealed varied responses in different categories based on the principles from Azevedo et al. [17]:

- Acceptance: High ratings for usefulness and ease of use, agreeable attitudes, and positive effects on self-efficacy without affecting self-esteem negatively. The system was seen as compatible but average in creating trust. Social influence and presence received lower ratings.
- Safety, Security, and Privacy: Generally, below average. Privacy design and legal compliance were average, with mixed feelings about transparency. Users expressed concerns about privacy for others and potential system errors, yet felt generally safe.
- Optimization of Resultant Internal Load: Above average ratings, with questions only partly applicable, suggesting low physical or mental demand.

- Controllability: Generally found controllable, but some questions deemed irrelevant.
- Adaptability: High ratings for adaptability to user preferences.
- Perceptibility and Identifiability: Positive feedback on system outputs and information clarity, minimal distractions, and high identifiability of visual outputs.

Based on these results, we conduct an analysis of the questionnaire in Sect. 4.1 and suggest a revision of it in Sect. 4.2.

3.2 Cronbach's Alpha

The Cronbach's alpha index assesses a questionnaire's reliability by gauging its internal consistency. Higher values of this index denote increased reliability among the questions [7]. A typical formula for the calculation of Cronbach's alpha is:

$$\alpha = \frac{k}{k-1}\left(1 - \frac{\sum_{i=1}^{k}\sigma_i^2}{\sigma_t^2}\right)$$

where k is the number of items in a scale, σ_i^2 is the variance of the i-th item, and σ_t^2 is the variance of the total scores. In our methodology, we modified the use of Cronbach's alpha to include the "Not applicable" response. Following the procedure in [2], we first calculated a raw scale score with relevant responses, then scaled it to the entire questionnaire by the ratio of applicable items to total items:

$$adjusted\ scale\ score = \frac{raw\ scale\ score}{number\ of\ applicable\ items} \times number\ of\ items\ in\ the\ scale$$

In our case, we have $k = 108$, $\sum_{i=1}^{k}\sigma_i^2 = 234.61$, and $\sigma_t^2 = 3149.1..$ This yields a (raw) Cronbach's alpha of $\alpha_{raw} = 0.9341$, that is, around 93.41%.

Conducting Arifin's method of also regarding the N/A answers, we obtain 3184.02 as the variation of the scaled sums. This yields a scaled Cronbach's alpha of $\alpha_{sc} = 0.935$, that is, around 93.5%. So, the difference of the two values for alpha is less than 0.09%. The fact that these two values are so close to each other shows that the N/A answers do not have a big influence on the reliability of the questionnaire.

Results. Also, we calculated the adjusted Cronbach's alpha (with N/A option) for each principle separately. The results can be seen in Table 2. All calculations were made in Google Sheets.

Table 2. Cronbach's alpha for each principle separately.

Acceptance	Safety, Security, and Privacy	Optimization of Resultant Internal Load	Controllability	Adaptability	Perceptibility and Identifiability
0.87	0.91	0.80	0.77	0.80	0.76

Cronbach's alpha for the questionnaire was a robust 0.93, affirming its reliability. Each principle individually surpassed the 0.7 reliability threshold, with Safety, Security, and Privacy highest at 0.91 and Perceptibility and Identifiability lowest at 0.76. The other principles are between these two values. Item-level analysis for outliers showed minimal deviation from the overall alpha, with the most notable differences observed in questions regarding privacy settings and system intimidation, yielding alphas of 93.21% and 93.75%.

4   Discussion

4.1   Analysis of the Questionnaire

Analyzing the questionnaire's questions revealed several areas for improvement:
   Similar Questions

- **Issue**: Repetitive questions in different forms, e.g., "I find the system scary" vs. "I find the system intimidating", leading to potential confusion, especially for non-native English or German speakers.
- **Impact**: Non-native speakers may struggle to distinguish subtly different questions, affecting response accuracy.

   Survey Fatigue

- **Issue**: Lengthy questionnaire (110 questions) causing participant fatigue.
- **Feedback**: Participants expressed exhaustion, affecting the quality of responses.

   Imbalance in Question Numbers

- **Issue**: Disproportionate number of questions among principles, e.g., 49 in "Acceptance" but only 4 in "Controllability".
- **Implication**: Comparisons between principles are unreliable due to this imbalance.

   Negative Question Framing

- **Issue**: Inconsistent use of negatively framed questions, with only four marked for reverse scoring.
- **Suggestion**: Revise the questionnaire to balance positive and negative questions and ensure accurate scoring.

The importance of "Context of Use" in evaluating assistive systems like Amazon Echo is paramount. Researchers should consider creating multiple questionnaire versions for different contexts or weighting questions according to their relevance in each specific context [8]. The functionality assessment of a system can significantly vary based on its application. For example, the ease of use for complex operations like integrating with home systems could differ from basic functions like alarm setting. Also, the usefulness perception can change based on the tasks considered, like comparing information retrieval to list-making. Furthermore, user experiences, such as feedback loudness, can be subjective and vary across different environments and times. This necessitates a context-driven approach to accurately gauge a system's performance in various real-life scenarios.

Our study's objective was to evaluate the questionnaire's effectiveness, yet we encountered several limitations. The primary challenge was engaging Amazon Echo users; hence, we conducted an online survey instead of personal interviews. Interviews might have provided deeper insights, including clarifications and participants' comprehension of questions. Budget limitations also impacted our study, restricting our ability to incentivize participation. Despite extensive outreach efforts to over 35 Alexa users, the final participant count was limited to 18.

4.2 Proposed Revision of the Questionnaire

From some participants we received the feedback that they found some questions repeating. This motivated us to investigate in more detail which questions could be eliminated or merged. Further, after collecting the data, when it came to analyzing the findings about Amazon Echo, for some questions it was not fully clear on how to interpret them.

In addition to this paper, under [1] we share the full list of questions together with our suggested improvements. The revised questionnaire is as follows:

Acceptance – Perceived Usefulness	1. I think the system is useful to me and can help me with many things 2. The system was able to provide the support I needed
Acceptance – Perceived Ease of Use	1. I find the system easy to use 2. I think I can use the system without any help (from a person, a technical person, or a manual)
Acceptance – Attitude Toward Technology	1. The system would make life more interesting 2. It's good to make use of the system
Acceptance – Perceived Enjoyment	1. I enjoy the system interacting with me 2. I find the system enjoyable
Acceptance – Anxiety	1. If I should use the system, I would be afraid to make mistakes with it. (inverted) 2. I find the system intimidating. (inverted)
Acceptance – Self Efficacy	1. I felt confident using the system 2. I could do easy adjustments on the system by myself
Acceptance – Social Influence	1. I think the people around me would like it if I would use the system 2. The product is also usable for the people who interact with me
Acceptance – Perceived Sociability	1. I consider the system a pleasant conversational partner 2. I find the system pleasant because it interacts with me 3. I feel the system understands me

(continued)

(continued)

Acceptance – Perceived Usefulness	1. I think the system is useful to me and can help me with many things 2. The system was able to provide the support I needed
Acceptance – Social Presence	1. When interacting with the system I felt like I'm talking to a real person 2. I can imagine the system to be a living creature 3. Sometimes the system seems to have real feelings
Acceptance – Trust	1. I would trust the system if it gave me advice 2. I would follow the advice the system gives me 3. This system is trustworthy
Acceptance – Impact on Self Esteem	1. The system does not draw unwanted attention to me 2. The system does not make me look dependent or weak
Acceptance – Facilitating Conditions	1. I have the resources necessary to use the technology 2. I have the knowledge necessary to use the technology 3. The technology is not compatible with other technologies I use. (inverted) 4. A specific person (or group) is available for assistance with difficulties related to the technology I use
Acceptance – Intention to Use	1. I'm certain to use the system 2. Whenever I think I would need it, I use the system
Safety, Security, and Privacy – Privacy by Design (PbD)	1. I could adapt the privacy settings to fit my preferences
Safety, Security, and Privacy – Transparency	1. I can clearly understand what data of mine is processed
Safety, Security, and Privacy – Legal Compliance	1. I think my rights and freedom are protected by the system
Safety, Security, and Privacy – Feeling of Safety	1. The system does not impose a biological hazard on me. (e.g. contact with viruses, bacterias etc.) 2. The system does not impose a chemical hazard on me 3. The system does not impose a physical hazard to me (e.g., getting physically hurt) 4. The system does not impose a psychosocial hazard on me (e.g., mental stress, social isolation etc.)

(continued)

(*continued*)

Acceptance – Perceived Usefulness	1. I think the system is useful to me and can help me with many things 2. The system was able to provide the support I needed
Safety, Security, and Privacy – Reliability	1. The system works reliably 2. A system malfunction is likely. (inverted) 3. The system might make sporadic errors. (inverted) 4. I don't fear that the information the system provides me can be false
Safety, Security, and Privacy – Intimacy preservation	1. The system could invade my privacy. (inverted) 2. I am not worried about my confidential information being exchanged by the system 3. I do not feel under constant surveillance while using the system 4. I feel free to be myself using the system 5. I am afraid the system could record me without notifying me (by audio or video). (inverted)
Safety, Security, and Privacy – Confide	1. I can decide on which information I want to share with whom 2. I am asked for consent if I allow my data to be shared to other companies or institutes
Optimization of resultant internal load – Physical Demand	1. Completing the task with the system was Physically demanding. (inverted)
Optimization of resultant internal load – Mental Demand	1. Completing the task with the system was mentally demanding. (inverted)
Optimization of resultant internal load – Temporal Demand	1. Completing the task with the system was hurried or its pace was rushed. (inverted)
Optimization of resultant internal load – Performance	1. I was successful in accomplishing what I was asked to do
Optimization of resultant internal load – Effort	1. I did not have to work hard to accomplish my level of performance
Optimization of resultant internal load – Frustration	1. I was insecure, discouraged, irritated, stressed, or annoyed. (inverted)
Controllability – Autonomy & Control Balance	1. I did not feel the system was controlling me 2. I have the impression I had full control of the system 3. If the system is doing something wrong, I could find a way to change its behavior
Adaptability – Adaptability to Context	1. The system can be adapted according to the environment I am in
Adaptability – Adaptability to User Models	1. The system is adaptable to my preferences 2. The system is adaptable to my health conditions

(*continued*)

(continued)

Acceptance – Perceived Usefulness	1. I think the system is useful to me and can help me with many things 2. The system was able to provide the support I needed
Adaptability – Temporal Adaptability	1. I think the system will only do what I need at that particular moment 2. I think the system will help me when I consider it to be necessary 3. The system did not need much time to adapt itself
Perceptibility and Identifiability – Communicate Meaning	1. I understand what the system's outputs mean 2. The system's actions made sense to me
Perceptibility and Identifiability – Perceptibility	1. I could clearly recognize the system's outputs independent of my perspective 2. I could clearly recognize the system's outputs independent of light conditions 3. I could clearly recognize the system's outputs independent of the external noise 4. I could clearly recognize the system's outputs independent of the external physical disturbance (e.g. vibration from a bumpy road) 5. I could clearly read the visual information the system displayed
Perceptibility and Identifiability – Distraction Avoidance	1. The system does not distract me from my task 2. The system helps me to stay engaged in the task
Perceptibility and Identifiability – Feedback Intensity	1. The system displays so many outputs that I started to ignore them. (inverted) 2. The duration of the feedback seems too long. (inverted) 3. The feedback is too loud to me. (inverted) 4. The feedback was annoying to me. (inverted)
Perceptibility and Identifiability – Visual Attention	1. It was easy for me to identify the system's visual feedback 2. The system displayed outputs in the places where I expected them to be 3. It was easy for me to identify the different components of the controls and displays

We also like to share some recommendation on the application of the questionnaire: *a) User Test or Evaluation.* It is important to know how we are going to use the metric. If it is for doing user tests, in the process of the HCI cycle of a system, then it makes sense to ask questions more accurately or in detail and avoid the merged questions. For example, consider the question: "I was insecure, discouraged, irritated, stressed, or annoyed." If we just want to know whether the system can cause frustration in the user, then it is okay to ask the question as it is. But if we want to know exactly what the user is experiencing, e.g., being annoyed or stressed, then we need to put them in separate questions. b) *Survey or Interview.* We can consider whether it will be a survey to fill out or if we are going to use the metric in an interview, in which case we might need to adjust the questions again. If it will be an interview, an additional set of questions as follow-up questions could also be prepared. As some questions are not clear enough, it will be recommended to have the presence of the researcher during the test or while the participant is filling out the survey. c) *Comparing Assistive Systems.* We can consider the metric as a usable set of questions to test an assistive system, but it is necessary to know that each system has its own context of use and specific group of users. Therefore, it might not be sensible to conclude that these systems are eligible under ISO principles and compare two systems with each other. d) *Assistive System for Users with Disabilities.* There should be a consideration before conducting the test whether, for users who have disabilities, some questions might not be applicable based on their usage.

5   Conclusion

The DIN document [8] shows a way to design a system in an ergonomic way. While striving to achieve this goal during the design process (for example, for a questionnaire), on the other hand it is also necessary to measure whether the final system is fulfilling the aspects that are mentioned in the DIN document. The metric [17] used in this research is newly composed and was not used before. This research was an analysis on testing the metric regarding its usability. Besides gathering data about an assistive system and gaining an experience with the metric, the reliability of the questionnaire was calculated by using Cronbach's alpha. It was shown that the set of questions are sufficiently reliable to be used in the future. Based on this experience, we gathered some noticeable points regarding this metric that can be considered in the further uses. Some aspects can help to develop an improved version of the metric that might work more accurately and make the questions more purposeful (they are listed in Chapter 4). In this research, the metric was used with the minimum number of participants to calculate Cronbach's alpha. This research can be repeated with more participants to confirm the accuracy of the data and the results. Still, this is a new metric, and having more research and studies using it and sharing the experience will give us a better insight into the usability of the metric itself. On the other hand, it is good to have data gathered by using the metric on other assistive systems with different levels of complexity [15].

Disclosure of Interests.   The authors have no competing interests to declare that are relevant to the content of this article. Author B & C are member of the DIN committee NA 023-00-04-09 AK Ergonomic aspects of AAL (ambient assisted living) and assistive systems.

References

1. Additional Files: https://www.hochschule-rhein-waal.de/de/fakultaeten/kommunikation-und-umwelt/organisation/professorinnen/prof-dr-karsten-nebe/publikationen-1
2. Arifin, W.N.: Calculating the Cronbach's alpha coefficients for measurement scales with "not applicable" option (2018). https://doi.org/10.13140/RG.2.2.16955.87843

3. Baber, C., Young, M.S.: Making ergonomics accountable: reliability, validity and utility in ergonomics methods. Appl. Ergon. **98**, 103583 (2022). https://doi.org/10.1016/j.apergo.2021. 103583

4. Bonett, D.G.: Sample Size Requirements for Testing and Estimating Coe. (2002)

5. Bourbakis, N.G., Esposito, A., Tsihrintzis, G.A., Virvou, M., Jain, L.C.: Introduction to advances in assistive technologies. In: Tsihrintzis, G.A., Virvou, M., Esposito, A., Jain, L.C. (eds.) Advances in Assistive Technologies. LAIS, vol. 28, pp. 1–7. Springer, Cham (2022). https://doi.org/10.1007/978-3-030-87132-1_1

6. Bridger, R.S.: Introduction to Human Factors and Ergonomics. Routledge & CRC Press. (2017)

7. Bujang, M.A., Omar, E.D., Baharum, N.B.: a review on sample size determination for Cronbach's alpha test: a simple guide for researchers. Malays J. Med. Sci, **25**(6), 85–99 (2018). https://doi.org/10.21315/mjms2018.25.6.9

8. DIN 92419:2020-01. Principles of the ergonomic design of assistive systems (Standard). International Organization for Standardization (2020). https://doi.org/10.31030/3106725

9. Holloway, C. Disability interaction (DIX). Interactions **26**(2), 44–49 (2019). https://doi.org/ 10.1145/3310322

10. Holloway, C., Dawes, H.: Disrupting the world of disability: the next generation of assistive technologies and rehabilitation practices. Healthcare Technol. Lett. **3**(4), 254–256 (2016). https://doi.org/10.1049/htl.2016.0087

11. ISO 26800:2011. Ergonomics – General approach, principles and concepts. International Organization for Standardization (2011). https://www.iso.org/obp/ui/#iso:std:iso:26800:ed-1:v1:en

12. Mavrou, K., Hoogerwerf, E.-J.: Towards full digital inclusion: The ENTELIS manifesto against the digital divide. J. Assist. Technol. **10**(3), 171–174 (2016). https://doi.org/10.1108/ jat-03-2016-0010

13. Tebbutt, E., Brodmann, R., Borg, J., MacLachlan, M., Khasnabis, C., Horvath, R.: Assistive products and the sustainable development goals (SDGs). Globalization and Health, **12**(1) (2016). https://doi.org/10.1186/s12992-016-0220-6

14. United Nations General Assembly. The 2030 agenda and the sustainable development goals (2015). https://sustainabledevelopment.un.org/content/documents/212 52030%20Agenda%20for%20Sustainable%20Development%20web.pdf

15. World Health Organization. World report on disability (2011). https://www.who.int/disabi% 20lities/world_report/2011/report.pdf. Accessed 14 Mar 2022

16. World Health Organization. Global priority research agenda for improving access to high- quality affordable assistive technology (2017). https://apps.who.int/iris/handle/10665/ 254660. Accessed 14 March 2022

17. Xavier Macedo de Azevedo, F., Heimgaertner, R., Nebe, K.: Development of a Metric to Evaluate the Ergonomic Principles of Assistive Systems, based on the DIN 92419. Rhine-Waal University of Applied Science, Germany (2022)

Educational Recreational Family Garden Project for People with Autism

Rubén Galicia Mejía[1]($\boxtimes$), Erika Hernández Rubio[2], and Berenice Galicia Moreno[3]

[1] Instituto Politécnico Nacional México, Mexico City, Mexico
rgaliciam@ipn.mx
[2] Escuela Superior de Cómputo, Av Othon de Mendizabal s/n, Ciudad de México, Mexico
ehernandezru@ipn.mx
[3] El Jito de Mati, Mexico City, Mexico

Abstract. Nowadays there is a large quantity of people diagnosed with autism spectrum disorder (ASD). Due to lack of daily life activities, playful opportunities at early ages and unemployment resources and labor training in young adults and adults some autistic people can show high levels of stress and anxiety. There are methods that has proven that visual instructions, including photos, drawings or physical objects are highly motivational and can engage people with ASD to follow instructions and perform guided activities. This paper proposes horticultural activity by a sensory instrumented hort as the way to improve cognitive, social, physical and psychological skills in autistic people. This is translated to reduce stress and anxiety levels as a result of an outdoor activity. The system is designed with visual supports, like pictures or animations, that can show children or adults the activity to be performed, and the current health of plants in the hort. The system will show graphically if plants need attention and attend the scheduled activities, anticipating the action that they have to do. The name of the project has been called " El Jito de Mati", one of the plants grown in the experience are the Tomatoes due to the color, height and natural growing process of the plant is very visual. The system captures humidity, temperature and sunlight from different digital electronic sensors placed in the hort, this information is sent to a cloud-based app by internet in a Wi-Fi protocol, the system works anywhere there is internet access.

Keywords: Autism · System · Project · Garden

1 Introduction

The benefits of outdoor activities as horticultural therapy have been widely reported [1], in last decades children who live in cities have a nature deficit [2, 3], it is important to bring children closer to nature for all the benefits that come with it, physical, psych emotional, behavioral, and cognitive. There are reduced recreational opportunities for Autistic children so the horticultural represent a beneficial way to enhance the mentioned skills, whether is a child, adolescent, or adult. By means horticultural therapy autistic person have the place to structure their thinking and integrate into a unique and playful

© The Author(s), under exclusive license to Springer Nature Switzerland AG 2024
C. Stephanidis et al. (Eds.): HCII 2024, CCIS 2115, pp. 33–36, 2024.
https://doi.org/10.1007/978-3-031-61947-2_4

family environment for each of the members see Fig. 1. On the other hand, autistic people have important challenges in areas such as communication, sensory, social, thought process; Horticultural therapy comprehensively manages these challenges in a respectful way. For an autistic person the world is full of surprises and prediction errors [4, 5] People with autism can show high levels of stress as they do not perceive changing situations like most people [6, 7]. This is one of the arguments why it is suggesting the use of visual supports like drawings, diagrams, photos [8, 9]. Autistic people need structure in their daily lives. Because they cannot perceive those changes, when they are taken to a natural setting, their stress levels lower.

Fig. 1. Set of benefits of the proyect.

2   Methods

The electronic part of *Jito de Mati* project consist of 2 main modules; hardware and software, which are implemented in sub modules, hardware module consists of 3 processes, the analog sensors are read by an open-hardware based acquisition system, then converted to digital data and finally send to a database in the cloud, while software is composed of 2 processes; download the information from the cloud database and display of data in a user-friendly way [10, 11]. The hardware module is configured to connect

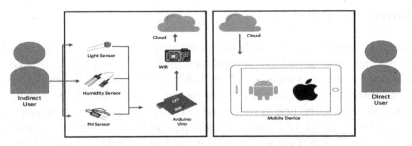

Fig. 2. System diagram

directly to the home network and powered by either batteries or a 5V DC power supply. The autonomy of the device will depend on the power supply selected. All the tests were performed under the supervision of an adult or a school guide see Fig. 2.

3 Results and Discussion

The *Jito de Mati* project was implemented in a family environment and in a semi-scholar manner at Atzan Institute [12], during the 2023–2024 school year in Guadalajara Mexico. The system was used by six autistic children, aged between 7 and 10 years old, who had contact with the garden [13], once a week at the Atzan institute and once at home. During the test period, it was observed the interest of the children in this activity, upon having stimuli with the garden. Figures 3 and 4 show some activities performed during school hours.

Fig. 3. Sowing activities   **Fig. 4.** Activities contact with the sowingland

Figures 5 and 6 show the activities performed at home during test periods and the prototypes developed for this project.

Fig. 5. Garden care   **Fig. 6.** Electronic monitoring system

4 Conclusions

The educational recreational family garden, was applied with some autistic children, who through the system developed with humidity, ph, and sunlight sensors, and the objectives set out in this work were met throughout its development, the system's sensors were calibrated to obtain the most accurate values possible and thus have greater precision when informing the status of the garden to autistic children. In addition, a server was enabled with the application so that any user can view the application regardless of the device they connect to.

Acknowledgments. The garden therapy system will be applied ATZAN Psycho Pedagogical and Psychotherapeutic Center to support needs of children with several neurodevelopmental conditions.

References

1. Fan, M.S.N.: Nature-based interventions for autistic children a systematic review and meta-analysis. JAMA Netw Open. **6**(12), e2346715 (2023). https://doi.org/10.1001/jamanetworko pen.2023.46715
2. Louv, R.: Last Child in the Woods: Saving Our Children from Nature-Deficit Disorder. Algonquin Press, Chapel Hill (2008)
3. https://link.springer.com/article/10.1007/s10571-017-0564-3
4. Apoyos Visuales World Health Organization. Autism spectrum disorders. https://www.who. int/es/news-room/fact-sheets/detail/autism-spectrum-disorders. Accessed October 2020
5. National Institute of Neurological Disorders and Stroke, "Rett Syndrome," (2010). https://espanol.ninds.nih.gov/trastornos/el_sin-drome_de_rett.htm. Accessed Aug-Sept 2020
6. Stress and Parents of Children with Autism: Susan Bonis A Review of Literature: available https://www.tandfonline.com/doi/abs/10.3109/01612840.2015.1116030
7. Autism and the predictive brain. Peter Vermeulen 2021, Perlego
8. la Garriga, P.A.: Autism: Definition, Symptoms and Indications (2016). https://www.autismo.com.es/autismo/que-es-el-autismo.html. Accessed Feb-Mar 2020
9. https://journals.sagepub.com/doi/abs/10.1177/004005991104300603
10. Rezayi, S., Tehrani-Doost, M., Shahmoradi, L.: Features and effects of computer-based games on cognitive impairments in children with autism spectrum disorder: an evidence-based systematic literature review https://www.scopus.com/record/. Accessed Dec 2022
11. Galicia, R., Hernández, E., Escareño, J.: therapy oriented garden monitoring system gardening for autistic children. In: Stephanidis, C., Antona, M., Ntoa, S., Salvendy, G. (eds.) HCII 2023. LNCS, vol. 1833, Springer, Cham (2023). https://doi.org/10.1007/978-3-031-35992-7_40. Accessed November 2023
12. Psychopedagogical and Psychotherapeutic Center, "ATZAN Psychopedagogical and Psychotherapeutic Center". https://www.atzan.com.mx. Accessed Jan 2021
13. International University of Valencia. The different types of the autism spectrum (ASD): characteristics and forms of intervention in the classroom (2018). https://www.universidadviu.com/los-distintos-tipos-de-tras-torno-del-espectro-autista-tea-caracteristicas-y-formas-de-intervencion-en-el-aula/. Accessed Aug-Sept 2020

Design of Oral Muscle Training Device for Infants and Toddlers in Early Language Development Period

Zilin Hu[✉], Jiajun Tan, Yue Qiu, and Lixuan Zhao

School of Design, South China University of Technology, Guangzhou 510006, People's
Republic of China
1397348897@qq.com

Abstract. Currently, language development disorders in children have attracted
much attention. For infants and toddlers in the early language development period,
oral muscle training has become an important intervention. During this critical
period of growth, parental-led training is crucial for promoting the coordination
of children's oral muscles, accurate pronunciation, and improvement of language
expression. Therefore, this study aims to explore the behavior of infants and toddlers and their parents in language training, and propose a solution for oral muscle training combining interest-based learning - motivating children's breathing
training through music and painting creation. This study explores the challenges
and needs faced by children's families in language development through methods such as user observation and interviews, analyzes the pain points of users in
the training process, and ultimately designs an oral muscle training device based
on interest-based learning. Finally, the researchers developed a prototype of the
device and recruited 5 groups of children and parents to test the training, evaluating
the accuracy of children's vocalization before and after training, as well as their
emotional changes during the process. The results indicate that the oral muscle
training device, as a fun tool, can provide children with easy and effective family oral muscle training. This research not only provides new ideas and methods
for solving children's language development issues, but also provides important
reference for the future development and optimization of oral muscle training.

Keywords: Oral muscle training · Interest-based learning ·
Language development · Music and painting creation · Design · Breathing
training

1 Introduction

1.1 Problem of Developmental Language Disorder in Children

Developmental language disorder in children refers to the phenomenon of language
delay caused by normal growth in a normal environment, normal intelligence development, excluding reasons such as hearing impairments or other pathological factors

C. Stephanidis et al. (Eds.): HCII 2024, CCIS 2115, pp. 37–48, 2024.
https://doi.org/10.1007/978-3-031-61947-2_5

[1]. Studies have shown that the prevalence of developmental language disorders in Mandarin-speaking children is about 8.5%. This means that in a class of 40 people, there are 3 children suffering from this disease. This prevalence rate is comparable to that of English-speaking children (7%–9%) [2]. On a social level, problems with developmental language disorders in children are often caused by family and kindergarten factors, but because of the high rate of illness and difficulty in detection, sickest children lack education and guidance from close groups such as parents and teachers [3]. On the pathological level, the emergence of this problem is largely due to the slow development and lack of exercise of children's oral muscles, and parents find it difficult to master the correct methods of assistance in training [4].

1.2 Current Status of the Language Training Market

More and more domestic and foreign medical industries are beginning to invest in the language training market, providing correctional assistance for patients with various language disorders. According to data, there are 186,000 speech therapists in the United States, 25,000 in the UK, and only about 10,000 in mainland China, which is far from the increasing number of children with developmental language disorders in China [5]. At the same time, therapists spend limited time with children, the treatment cost is high, and not widely applicable to all families. Studies have shown that family-centered early behavioral language development intervention treatments can improve developmental language disorders in children [6]. But the existing market's home training competitors are highly homogenized and lack scientific training methods.

1.3 Interest-Based Learning

Interest-based learning methods refer to using a person's curiosity and desire to explore a certain thing, or purely interest, to arouse enthusiasm for learning, thereby cultivating long-term effective learning habits [7]. Studies have shown that the right use of children's interests to build learning methods is effective in exercising children's daily language ability and treating autism [8, 9]. During development, children's language ability develops along with multiple senses such as vision, hearing, and smell. Children are easily interested in external stimuli such as colors and sounds, which further stimulates their own development [10]. Hence, the derived music therapy and painting therapy that mobilize children's emotions and stimulate children's creativity, as well as the mimicry therapy in families led by parents to read interesting fairy tales.

2 Evaluation

2.1 Competitive Product Analysis

As Fig. 1 shows, due to the limited type and outdated forms of children's language training products on the market, to understand the products in this field from more angles, we selected some concept products (from competitions, literature research) and landed products for comparative analysis. A horizontal comparison is made from the perspectives of target users, user age, usage methods, functional points, and innovation points.

Name of competitor	Introduction	Target User	User age	Source	Application method	Function Points	Innovation points
Oral muscle training flute	The product is equipped with some oral/speech training videos and manuals to help children with pronunciation correction	Inarticulate children	Under 5 years old	Products already on shelves	Use the product for blowing exercises, pumping training, tongue contraction and slow connection, lip closing exercises, etc	- Physiologically address language delays by training the mouth	/
Portable language training learning machine	A portable language training learning machine as the core, with the teacher side APP and parents side APP together to form a service system, the main function is to photograph recognition pronunciation teaching.	Preschool children with hearing impairment	3-6 years old	Documentary research	The basic process of use includes: photo identification, learning video, feeling vibration, imitating reading after reading, viewing ratings, and practicing related vocabulary.	- Multi-end design of supporting app to improve intervention behavior of parents and teachers - Based on the characteristics of children's curiosity design, stimulate children's learning motivation	1. Cooperate with APP to form education system 2. Scene learning - "photo recognition" inspires children's behavioral motivation 3. Real oral English teaching design
Card follower reader	The product is equipped with a set of cartoon object cards, which can be inserted into the learning machine to play Chinese and English pronunciation, combined with objects in life, to guide children's cognition	Normal children	0-6 years old	Products already on shelves	Children insert pictures of different cartoon objects into the learning machine and automatically play the Chinese and English pronunciation of the cards	- Help children grow and enlighten - Combine objects in your life to enhance your cognition - Simple interaction	1. Card interaction is simple and easy to use
Fun train	A parent-child interactive product, by the parent-child interaction loading, arranging train to achieve the effect of children's language training. By allowing parents and children to interact, cards with different meanings are loaded on the carriage of the small train, children are guided to complete sentence arrangement and language telling, and the starting device of the small train is controlled, so as to carry out language expression and logic training.	Language impaired children	0-6 years old	Documentary research	In the process of parent-child interaction, parents lead children to understand the language of the card, and parents will insert the corresponding card into the car in a disorderly order, so that children will install the car in the order of the sentence on the train, and correct pronunciation, through voice recognition control, the small train starts, and repeat the correct pronunciation, to encourage children.	- Enhance parent-child interaction and help strengthen the training effect - Fun, stimulate children's interest	1. Emphasize parents' participation and interaction effects 2. Inspire interest in the form of a train game
Smartstones Touch	Smartstones Touch is a palm-sized, pebblestone shaped smart device, and different movements can trigger Smartstone preset patterns such as light, sound or vibration, so that autistic patients can get tactile feedback during the communication process.	Autistic children	/	Conceptual design	Children can ask the App to 'say' pre-programmed words aloud by tapping and swiping. Different actions can trigger the Smartstone's preset patterns of light, sound or vibration.	- Easier communication, suitable for autistic children - Interactive approach combined with consideration of the child's stereotypical behavior	1. Design sentences according to your needs and activities 2. Provide consistent speech demonstrations and associations between words and actions

Fig. 1. Competitive product analysis.

Through the design analysis of competitive products, the following key points are summarized:

- Products often guide children's vocal training by playing recordings.
- Enhancing parent-child interaction is beneficial to improving participation pleasure and reinforcing the training effect.
- Multisensory stimulation and interest help to stimulate children's learning behavior motivation.
- Combining the cognitive basis of daily objects is key to the development of children's language ability.
- For the language disorder group, it is necessary to provide a communication training method with stronger assistance.
- Intelligent technologies are conducive to innovating training scenarios and forms.

2.2 User Research

User Observation. As shown in Fig. 2, through searching for the living status of children with developmental language disorders on short video platforms and related educational institution's intervention treatment processes, we understand their daily learning, living, and training details.

Fig. 2. User observation.

The following key points are summarized:

- Institutional teachers use professional equipment to help improve physiological pronunciation problems such as oral and lingual muscles, which can easily cause children to resist stereotyped training.
- However, the cultivation of cognitive foundations relies more on family intervention, and combining scene teaching is effective.
- When conducting cognitive training, the child's eye gaze is very important.
- In the initial stage of training, children are segmented by age for articulation training (such as "ji" sound, "ke" sound).

User Interviews. Targeting three parents of age-appropriate children, we conducted user interviews. Their children are between 1 and 5 years old and are receiving family-based language skills training in their daily lives. The goal of user interviews is to investigate the guiding methods used by parents in daily training, the problems they

Table 1. Interview Outline.

Areas of focus	Question
Basic information	The child's age, gender, personality and other basic information
About vocalization and speaking	Q1: How old do children start vocalizing? Did you intentionally lead before?
	Q2: When you grow up, do you pay attention to your child's voice and language ability? Do you find that your child has some difficulties in the process of vocalizing? -- if yes: How do specific difficulties manifest themselves?
	Q3: Is there anything you do to help train your child's voice and language skills? What are the specific methods? -- if yes: Why this approach? How does it work?
	Q4: Have you also adopted some auxiliary cultivation methods for children's phrasing ability in the post-vocal stage? -- if yes: Why this approach? How does it work?
Information about buying toys	Q1: Do you usually buy toys for your children? What is the frequency of purchase?
	Q2: What kind of toys do you buy for your children? What kind of toys are your children interested in?
	Q3: In the process of purchasing toys, do you consider the cultivation of children's abilities in all aspects of the product, and purchase toys for them with a purpose? -- if yes: What are the types of toys purchased and their functional forms? What's the feedback from the child?
	Q4: Do you use toys to develop children's voice and language organization (words and sentences)? -if yes: What approach to take? How does it feel? -if no: Do you think that the use of toys to develop children's vocal ability is a reasonable way, is it attractive to you?
	Q5: Does the child play with toys independently or with others? What kind of play do children prefer? - if you play by yourself: What is the state and time of play? - if playing with others: With whom does the child get more excited?

encounter, and their expectations for relevant products. The interview outline is shown in Table 1 below.

The main points concluded from the interviews are:

- In training, parents rely on their own understanding and the internet for guidance, with great uncertainty in the methods.
- Parents are often confused about how to evaluate and choose products for language training, and they feel that the products are not personalized.
- Children often lose interest in repetitive training, making it difficult to maintain long-term training.
- Parents express a strong desire for intelligent, entertaining, and effective language training products that can attract children's attention and are easy to operate.

2.3   User Persona

Based on field research and user studies, we have constructed the user personas of our target users, which include two groups: children and parents. We listed the pain points and goals of children with language disorders and their parents during the home-based language learning process. The user personas for the two groups are shown in Fig. 3.

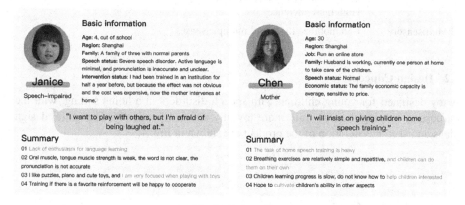

Fig. 3. Personas.

3   Solution

3.1   Product Elements/Features

Based on the results of the preliminary research and the pain points reflected by the two types of user personas, we propose a solution with lower operational and financial costs. This solution combines interest-based learning therapy with the commonly used blow-type oral muscle training in one toy device, hence it can be called the Oral Muscle Training Device for Infants and Toddlers. The product elements of this trainer are shown in Table 2.

Table 2. Product elements of this trainer.

Element	Details
1.Interest	· Engage children in repeated play · Suitable for low neck children (4–14 years old) · Strong sense of game
2.Emotion	· Give children the confidence to learn · Can promote children's relationships with others
3.Shape	· Cute and round appearance · In line with children's cognition
4.Interaction	· Can enhance children's communication with others · High playability of toys
5.Innovation	· Conform to the general perception of known things · Different from competitive products, giving people a refreshing feeling
6.Safety	· Material safety · Not easy to swallow · It is not easy to cause other harm to children
7.Ease of Use	· Able to get timely feedback · Enable children to get started quickly · High fault tolerance
8.Multisensory	· Can mobilize the use of multiple senses

3.2 Design Concept

A toy designed for young children with speech disorders in a home setting, with the purpose of helping them to train more joyfully and independently. The initial design plans and sketches iteration of the product are shown in Fig. 4.

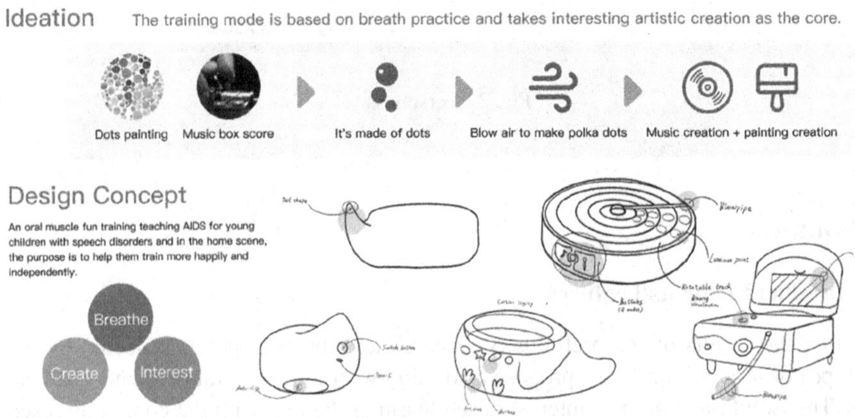

Fig. 4. Design concept.

3.3 Usage Process Schematic

As shown in Fig. 5, the process of using the Oral Muscle Training Device by users is displayed. Parents connect the tablet to the Oral Muscle Training Device and guide the child to blow air into the round hole of the trainer using a blowpipe. The app on the tablet will simultaneously display the annular dot matrix graphics data activated by blowing, allowing the child to create music or paintings through blowing, thus forming an interest-based oral muscle training method.

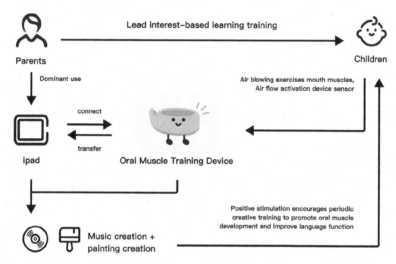

Fig. 5. Usage process schematic.

4 Prototype Design

4.1 Product Design

In terms of product appearance, it follows the human-centered design principles, adopting bionic design methods for young children, with animal tails as the core inspiration to design a shape that can place an iPad and has three common operation buttons. The size of the product is 300 mm*260 mm*200 mm, and the basic shape is a short cylinder, with gentle curves to meet user's expectations for the image of children's toy products.

As shown in Figs. 6 and 7, the product uses translucent silicone material, HDPE transparent plastic, and PC plastic, ensuring the safety of food-grade inlets, and also cares for children's vision and skin with warm-toned skin-friendly materials.

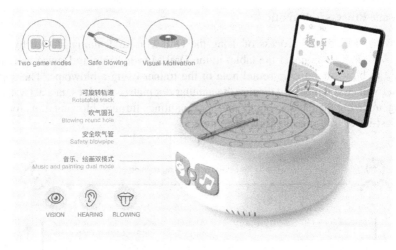

Fig. 6. Product appearance (1).

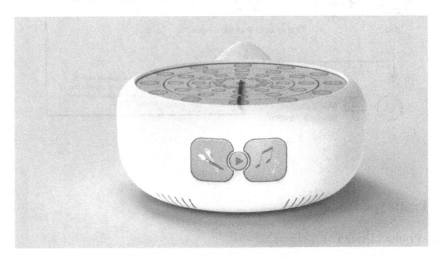

Fig. 7. Product appearance (2).

4.2 APP and IP Design

An APP design for use on tablet devices has been completed to accompany the product (see Fig. 8). It introduces game scenarios through graphic animations, interactively guiding children in their blowing exercises and providing visual and auditory feedback to engage their senses and encourage their participation. At the same time, the animal IP image designed based on the product's physical shape is friendly and attractive, helping to establish an interactive creative storytelling scenario.

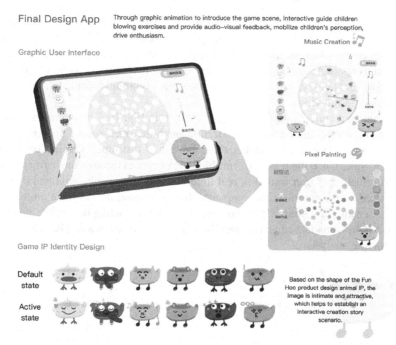

Fig. 8. APP and IP design.

4.3 Complete Process

The complete usage process of the product is shown in Fig. 9.

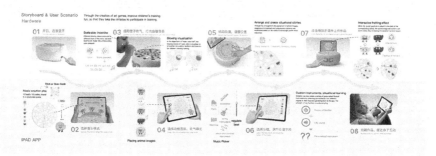

Fig. 9. Complete process.

4.4 Technical Development

The system development is specifically divided into two parts: the mobile application and the hardware device. As it is a basic technology prototype, to ensure usability and lower implementation costs, the two modules communicate data via a wired connection. Firstly, the mobile application is implemented using JavaScript through the Vue.js framework and is displayed on the mobile iPad via a web page. The development is completed in the Visual Studio Code editor. The program runs on the child's tablet device, providing functions for music and painting creation. Secondly, the interactive hardware is developed using an Arduino microcontroller, along with a series of technologies such as 3D printing technology, air pressure sensors, serial communication, etc., to achieve the corresponding functions.

The technical architecture of the system is shown in Fig. 10. The interactive music function of the mobile application is realized through the open-source Tone.js, which endows it with the ability to personalize the definition of instruments, adjust pitch, and range. Meanwhile, when the user performs blowing exercises through the hardware, the blowing information is transmitted in real time to the mobile application and dynamically rendered to the interface, accompanied by corresponding interface animations (implemented using Bootstrap, CSS, and echarts.js), thus attracting the child's attention and focus. All blowing data can subsequently be sent and stored in a database for future user information analysis.

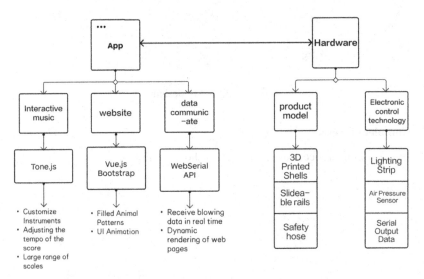

Fig. 10. Technical development.

5 Testing and Experimentation

Finally, with the system prototype developed by our team, we conducted research tests on 5 groups of users (children + parents). In the research tests, users were required to use the device to complete training tasks as per the given instructions and afterwards provide feedback on the usage process.

In user testing, we focused on several important indicators such as children's vocal accuracy, emotional changes, and task completion efficiency. Therefore, we recorded their vocal frequencies, facial expressions, and task completion data.

- Children's vocal accuracy: Users were asked to train with the device for a week. After a week of training, we led the children to read the vowels /a/, /o/, /e/, /i/, /u/ under the four tones. Our team analyzed the children's vocal accuracy by extracting the formant peaks (F1, F2) and duration using the Praat speech analysis software on the voice recordings. The results showed a reduction in the error rate of the vowel four tones, especially the accuracy of F2 for /i/ and /u/ showed significant differences before and after training. Therefore, it indicates that the design of this study has improved children's vocal accuracy and can provide a reference for oral muscle training.
- Emotional changes: Through single training observations, we found that children's emotional state transitioned from calm to excited during the training process, especially during the interest creation process, this was more pronounced. Also, children were often eager to actively share their creations with their parents, and most would attempt to create repeatedly, indicating that interest-based therapy effectively stimulated children's emotions and enhanced their enthusiasm.
- Task completion efficiency: Each user had tasks set to be completed, such as a single blow, creating a musical score after blowing, and reviewing created works. Usability tests showed a task completion rate of 70%; additionally, the average time taken to complete each task was close to 6 s, indicating good integration of each function within the device and high user efficiency. Additionally, their feedback included the following aspects through recording and observation:
- Overall use was relatively smooth with a low learning curve
- Suggestions for making the device appearance more affable
- Interface animal images sparked children's associations and questions
- Rich game sound feedback

Significant enhancement in interaction between child and parent This test helped us understand the usability and effectiveness of the system prototype based on the actual use by children and parents and was also helpful in understanding the satisfaction with each part of the software and hardware. More importantly, it evaluated the effectiveness of interest-based therapy as a method for home language training for children.

6 Conclusion

The results show that the oral muscle training device, as an effective intervention tool, has the potential to become an important aid in the treatment and training of children's language development disorders. Compared with traditional children's toys, our device and application are more attractive, interactive with children, and promote cognitive training and creativity. Therefore, using our device, children can effectively perform oral muscle training at home and track their progress.

The results of this study not only provide new ideas and methods for solving children's language development problems but also offer important references for the future development and optimization of oral muscle training.

References

1. Zhou, Y.: Clinical diagnosis of developmental language disorder in children: research approach and injury characteristics (2023)
2. Nan, Z., Mei, W.: The prevalence rate of developmental language disorder in children is 8.5%, Who will fill the shortage of therapists (2023)
3. Wu, S., et al.: Prevalence, co-occurring difficulties, and risk factors of developmental language disorder: first evidence for mandarin-speaking children in a population-based study. Lancet Regional Health–Western Pacific. 100713 (2023)
4. Liu, L., Huang, L.: A review of the intervention effect of oral muscle training on children with speech disorder in China (2023)
5. Shi, D., Yang, Y.: Language disorders and speech therapy in China: Current situation analysis and development ideas (2020)
6. Meng, Q., Huang, Z.-H., Shao, P., et al.: Effect evaluation of family-centered intervention model for early childhood language and behavior development (2023)
7. Guo, J.: Dewey's Theory of Educational Purpose and Interest: A review and reflection (2023)
8. Dunst, C.J., Raab, M., Hamby, D.W.: Interest-based everyday child language learning. Revista de Logopedia, Foniatria y Audiologia **36**(4), 153–161 (2016)
9. Dunst, C.J., Trivette, C.M., Masiello, T.: Exploratory investigation of the effects of interest-based learning on the development of young children with Autism. Autism **15**(3), 295–305 (2011)
10. Xu, F., Zhou, R., Zhou, J., et al.: Intervention effect of speech function training combined with multi-sensory stimulation on intellectual and language rehabilitation of children with total developmental delay (2022)

Developing a Mobile Application Linking the Microsystems of Young Children with Delays or Disabilities: A Case Study and Guidelines

Young Eun Jeon[✉] ⓘ, Hye Jun Park ⓘ, Hye Min Suh ⓘ, Soo Jung Kim ⓘ, and Eun Ji Jeon ⓘ

Seoul National University, Seoul, Republic of Korea
youngeunjeon@snu.ac.kr

Abstract. Early intervention for young children with delays or disabilities is universally recognized as essential for helping children develop to their fullest potential. Despite worldwide efforts to implement various forms of Early Intervention, it remains a challenge for families to navigate the services without support. This study presents the collaborative program development of *LinkI*, a mobile application that can support families by enhancing integrated communication among the child's microsystems (e.g., parents, therapists, and teachers). The stakeholders took a participatory role in sharing their experiences with early intervention and providing feedback regarding the preliminary design of *LinkI*. A qualitative analysis of the interviews highlighted the importance of incorporating a family-centered approach and the need for an efficient method of collaboration. Informed by the findings, we made revisions to create our final prototype of *LinkI*. This study anticipates facilitating mobile application development for comprehensive early intervention support through our suggested program design recommendations.

Keywords: early intervention · family-centered approach · interdisciplinary practice · mobile application · *LinkI*

1 Introduction

Approximately 240 million children worldwide are estimated to have disabilities (UNICEF 2021). Children with disabilities are at higher risk of compromised well-being outcomes (e.g., health, education, and protection) than children without disabilities. Receiving the proper support during early developmental stages is essential because it strongly impacts their ability to counter disadvantages and provides opportunity to develop to their fullest potential. Early intervention was created to support families of young children with delays or disabilities. The program usually provides services such as detecting and evaluating developmental delays or disabilities as well as providing support through necessary therapies (Brown & Guralnick 2012). In recognition of the universal significance of early intervention, many nations have adopted various early intervention programs to support families of children with delays or disabilities.

C. Stephanidis et al. (Eds.): HCII 2024, CCIS 2115, pp. 49–56, 2024.
https://doi.org/10.1007/978-3-031-61947-2_6

Often fully or partially funded by the government, early intervention programs are increasingly offered to families of children with delays or disabilities worldwide. Yet, countries are evidently at varying stages of development due to the existence of considerable barriers (e.g., cultural stigma, political system, and societal commitment) in implementing a suitable program (Guralnick 2008). In South Korea, a voucher program was established, offering qualified families to receive a designated amount to use towards their child's therapy sessions. However, these vouchers are administered on a local district level with various requirements (e.g., income level and designated clinic centers), and a comprehensive program guide to early intervention is unavailable. Without a systemic early intervention program, services are not integrated, leaving families to navigate the complex microsystems alone.

With the intention of providing immediate and easily accessible early intervention support to families of children with disabilities or delays in South Korea, we designed a mobile app program called *LinkI*. This app helps families navigate the child's complex microsystems (e.g., family, teachers, and therapists) by providing a communication platform tailored to the family's schedule. This study aimed to illustrate the program development process, emphasizing the importance of the stakeholders' experiences and input. Taking a participatory approach, we made conscious efforts to include the stakeholders through interviews to gain a deeper insight into how our initial prototype can support them and incorporated their feedback to craft our revised prototype design.

1.1 Ecological Systems Theory

Early intervention was formulated with many foundational concepts rooted in Bronfenbrenner's ecological systems theory (Bronfenbrenner, 1979). This theory identified five complex layers (microsystem, mesosystem, exosystem, macrosystem, and chronosystem) of environment systems that affect the child's short- and long-term development. The interactions between the systems experienced by the child are the processes that impact the child's trajectory throughout life. The microsystem is the layer closest to the child and consists of the relationships in the immediate surroundings, such as with family, therapists, and caregivers. The mesosystem consists of the interactions linking the microsystems that directly influence the child and family outcomes. Therefore, a proficient early intervention program considers the ecosystem of the child, primarily focusing on strengthening the mesosystem through interactions among the microsystems, which often includes the family, therapist(s), and other caregivers (e.g., daycare teacher). In order for a strong mesosystem, interactions should be meaningful, forming collaboration through teamwork.

1.2 Service Coordination

Similar to many other countries with developing early intervention programs, South Korea does not yet have a systematic early intervention that provides service coordination. Service coordinators have an important role as the single point of contact to help families receive the services they need and manage the collaborative relationship between the family and therapists. Since early intervention consists of various services, the service coordinator helps integrate the services to facilitate the multifaceted process for families. Without service coordination, many families are burdened with juggling their busy schedules while being accountable for being the communicator between the service providers. While policy establishment or reformation would be the ideal solution in the long run, parents who currently have children with delays or disabilities need immediate remediate that can be easily accessible.

2 Methods

We strategically adapted the first five steps of the Collaborative Family Program Development (CFPD) Model (Fraenkel, 2006) to our program development. The CFPD model emphasizes treating the stakeholders as experts to address community-based issues, in our case, early intervention. By incorporating the CFPD approach, we created a meaningfully conceptualized program development with the collaboration of the stakeholders.

2.1 Initiating the Project

In forming a professional team, we strived to involve members having experience working with the targeted community. Our final team consisted of graduate students and the supervising professor from the SPECTRUM (Special Education & Translational Research for Universal Design and Inclusive Minds) lab in Seoul National University. In addition, one member had basic tech knowledge for application development. The different expertise of our team members (i.e., early intervention therapists, early childhood center director and teacher) helped identify various issues that needed to be addressed in South Korea's early intervention.

2.2 Interviewing

Focus group interviews (FGI) of the families and professionals were conducted separately, consisting of two main parts. Part one comprised of semi-structured questions that were mostly open-ended questions that focused on how communication was happening between the microsystem, what types of collaboration were available, and the communication experiences between the microsystems. In the second part of the interview, we introduced our preliminary protocol version of *LinkI* through a short PowerPoint presentation and a video explaining its different features (see Fig. 1). We then asked the participants for feedback and any questions they might have.

2.3 Qualitative Coding

The focus group interviews were recorded, transcribed and analyzed thematically (Braun & Clark, 2006). Four researcher members coded the interview responses independently. Afterwards, they came together to cross-check the codes and were able to find three main themes.

Fig. 1. The main program features translated into English are as the following: a) child information, b) shared access code, c) daily log, d) treatment notes, e) assessment records, and f) developmental checklist.

2.4 Creating Program Format (Revised Prototype)

The app program content and features were revised based on the feedback and the themes discovered through the interviews. Some features were eliminated, and new features were added to address the needs expressed by the stakeholders.

3 Results

3.1 Themes

Three main themes found through qualitatively analyzing the interviews were the following: "Need for Family-Centered Approach", "Desire for More Opportunities of Involvement", and "Challenges Without a Systemic Early Intervention".

Feedback on Initial Prototype. While considering these themes, we gained further insight to the stakeholders' needs through their feedback about the presented initial prototype (see Table 1).

3.2 Revisions

We used the main findings from our interviews and feedback to make the key revisions to create our final prototype. Some features were eliminated, and new features were added to address the needs expressed by the stakeholders (see Fig. 2). The developmental milestones checklist was deleted entirely because the mothers shared that various resources regarding it was already available in hospital settings. Treatment notes were also eliminated to prevent an overwhelming workload for the therapists.

To address the parents' desire for involvement with the child's therapy, we created the individualized functional outcomes" feature (see Fig. 3). In this feature, the family

Table 1. Summary of Feedback for *Linkl*.

Domains	Feedback
Beneficial	• A holistic view of the child • Including the microsystems of the child (i.e., father and teachers) • Less burden on main caregiver as the messenger between microsystems • Accountability of all microsystems • Keeping a record of the child's progress through the assessment feature
Concerns	• Increased workload • Too time-consuming • Sustainability • Interpretation of the notes • Discrepancies in the treatment notes
Additional features	• Treatment notes should focus on practical skills rather than sessions • Minimize the content that needs to be uploaded by the professionals • Collaboration on shared target goals • Resources on information regarding centers/clinics

inputs what they would like their child to work on tailored to their daily routine. These goals are functional outcomes that are meaningful to the family's routine. For example, a child might have difficulty with "handwashing." The family could input, "Riley will wash her hands after using the bathroom." We also incorporated the feedback from the therapists regarding how workload would be decreased if there were unified goals that all therapists could target as a team. The "individual functional outcome" target goals that are not domain specific, and require the therapists to utilize their expertise to come up with ways to achieve the goal. For example, in continuation with the "handwashing" example, the speech therapist might write in the "progress notes" section, "*The child responds best with a verbal and visual prompt before heading to the bathroom. The verbal prompt used is "Let's go to the bathroom (do not use question form). Please refer to the uploaded picture for the visual prompt.*" Then the occupational therapist might input, "*Child prefers to wash hands in cold water,*" while the child's teacher might add, "*Singing the ABCs encourages the child tow wash their hands thoroughly.*" Expectedly, therapists will have overlapping as well as different approaches that can be collaborated to better support the family and child. The tips from other disciplines allows all members to have more holistic view of the child. This helps not only achieve the unified target goals more efficiently but also provides a wider lens on how to approach different goals. For example, after the teacher reads the tip on using a visual prompt to transition to the bathroom for "handwashing," the teacher might try using visuals for the child's other challenging transitions at school. Such collaboration helps achieve family-centered goals efficiently and enhances interdisciplinary practice across all team members.

3.3 Design Recommendations

When designing a support program for families of children with disabilities or delays, we found the following recommendations to be helpful.

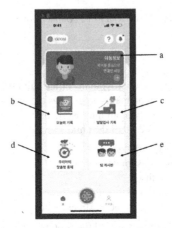

Fig. 2. The revised version of the main menu shows the following features: a) child information, b) daily notes, c) assessment records, d) individualized functional outcomes, and e) collaboration board.

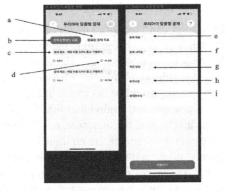

Fig. 3. The newly added individualized functional outcome has the following features: a) completed goals list, b) current goals list, c) individualized outcome(s), d) progress notes, e) target goal, f) goal start date, g) intervention tips, h) things to note/avoid, and i) target goal met to date.

Form a Team w/Diverse Expertise. When initiating a project for making an app for families of children with disabilities or delays, having a collaborative team with diverse expertise is advantageous for identifying problems and solutions from different perspectives.

Include Stakeholders Meaningfully. Utilizing a participatory approach by including the stakeholders kept the checks in balance, reiterating important features and detecting components needing revision. Through the interviews of the stakeholders, we discovered the critical need to expand the family-centered approach communication to include routine-based functional outcomes to support the child and family.

Utilize a Family-Centered Approach. A family-centered approach was used by focusing on individualized family outcomes embedded within daily routines. The most significant advantage of incorporating individualized outcomes is that the feature becomes malleable in any context. Individualized family outcomes are universally applicable since the family is responsible for crafting outcomes based on how they perceive the child and what they have been informed by other microsystems in how the child is perceived in particular settings. Moreover, we were able to mindfully avoid discipline-specific jargon and use simple language throughout the app to facilitate implementation and smoother translation process.

Collaboration Shouldn't Increase in Workload. The reoccurring hesitance in our interviews for administering the app for the child's early intervention was rooted in the concern of increased workload. Therapists expressed that they are already overworked in their line of work. To address this concern we eliminated the treatment notes feature. In contrast to the therapists' concern, prior studies established that interdisciplinary practice reduces the problem-solving workload and enhances the tools for targeting outcomes (Kilgo & Bruder, 1997; Stayton & Bruder, 1999). Instead, we incorporated the "progress notes" feature to the "individualized family outcomes" to encourage efficiently targeting a unified goal.

4 Conclusion

Our final prototype highlighted the importance of the family-centered approach and integrated collaboration amongst the microsystems by adding the "individualized outcome" and "progress feature." The concept of routine-based family outcomes and how they should be administered may be unfamiliar to the stakeholders. Therefore, for the next steps of our app development, a short video or informative document routine-based functional outcomes will be helpful. Furthermore, a follow-up study with representative sampling will be conducted regarding the app's usage and effectiveness through pilot testing. Although we anticipate facilitated implementation in other similar contexts (e.g., countries without a systemic early intervention system), validating this expectation through future studies would be worthwhile.

In this study, we reported the meaningfully construed development process of an app, *LinkI*, designed to support families of young children with disabilities or delays. The design focused on linking the microsystems to enhance integrated communication to facilitate the families and children's early intervention process. The process highlights a collaborative, participatory approach to meaningfully co-designing the app with the stakeholders. The case study emphasizes the importance of a family-centered approach and the focus group interviews demonstrated the need for the transition to inter/transdisciplinary methods in early intervention. Through the findings from this study, we were able to revise the key features of the final prototype. Overall, the participants voiced enthusiasm about using the app when launched in the near future. We hope that our findings will provide design guidelines and recommendations for developing accessible support for families of children with delays and disabilities, conceivably expanding implementations to other countries with similar implications with early intervention.

Disclosure of Interests. The authors have no competing interests to declare that are relevant to the content of this article.

References

Braun, V., Clarke, V.: Using thematic analysis in psychology. Qualitative Res. Psychol. **3**(2), 77–101 (2006). https://doi.org/10.1191/1478088706qp063oa

Bronfenbrenner, U. (1979). The ecology of human development: Experiments by nature and design. Harvard university press

Brown, S.E., Guralnick, M.J.: International human rights to early intervention for infants and young children with disabilities: tools for global advocacy. Infants Young Child. **25**(4), 270–285 (2012). https://doi.org/10.1097/IYC.0b013e318268fa49

Fraenkel, P.: Engaging families as experts: collaborative family program development. Fam. Process. **45**(2), 23–257 (2006). https://doi.org/10.1111/j.1545-5300.2006.00093.x

Guralnick, M.J.: International perspectives on early intervention: a search for common ground. J. Early Interv. **30**(2), 90–101 (2008)

Kilgo, J., Bruder, M.B.: Creating new visions in institutions of higher education: Interdisciplinary approaches to personnel preparation in early intervention. Reforming personnel preparation in early intervention: Issues, models, and practical strategies, pp. 81–101. Paul H. Brookes (1997)

Stayton, V., Bruder, M.B.: Early intervention personnel preparation for the new millennium: early childhood special education. Infants Young Child. **12**(1), 59–69 (1999)

Design of the Challenging Behavior Monitoring System for Children with Developmental Disabilities that Combines ConvLSTM and Skeleton Keypoint

Jonguk Jung and Yoosoo Oh[✉]

Daegu University, Gyeonsan-Si, Republic of Korea
yoosoo.oh@daegu.ac.kr

Abstract. This paper proposes a system to monitor the challenging behaviors of children with developmental disabilities by utilizing the method combining ConvLSTM and Skeleton Keypoint information. The system consists of a behavior classification module, a data storage and analysis module, and an intervention module. By utilizing ConvLSTM and MoveNet, the proposed system accurately classifies challenging behaviors into various types, helping early detection and intervention. Experimental results demonstrate the effectiveness of the proposed system. By learning ConvLSTM on a challenging behavior dataset, the system achieves high accuracy even when classified into segmented types. In addition, it can be confirmed that LSTM is superior at processing keypoint information compared to other machine learning algorithms such as SVM and KNN. The proposed system has important implications for the field of developmental disability and behavioral analysis. It reduces the burden on caregivers by enabling continuous monitoring and early intervention. And Second, through intervention through Positive Behavior Support, a positive environment for children with developmental disabilities can be established.

Keywords: ConvLSTM · Human Pose Estimation · Skeleton Keypoint · Challengeing Behavior

1 Introduction

Challenging behavior refers to behavior that threatens or harms oneself and others. In particular, challenging behavior of people with developmental disabilities who do not develop mentally and physically as their peers is characterized by a very high frequency. The challenging behavior of people with developmental disabilities in childhood appears as self-harming behavior targeting themselves and aggressive behavior targeting others. The burden on caregivers is considerable because a lot of time and money are required to mediate the challenging behavior of people with developmental disabilities [1]. Also, it is commonly mentioned that caregivers need services that can be used continuously for a long time [1, 2]. Challenging behavior is a behavior that attacks using part of the

© The Author(s), under exclusive license to Springer Nature Switzerland AG 2024
C. Stephanidis et al. (Eds.): HCII 2024, CCIS 2115, pp. 57–65, 2024.
https://doi.org/10.1007/978-3-031-61947-2_7

body, and aggressive behavior, self-harm behavior, destructive behavior, and obstructive behavior are included in the challenge behavior [2]. For the treatment of children with developmental disabilities, it is necessary to detect challenging behavior and analyze challenging behavior that can help in the treatment process. In addition, it is necessary to prepare a system that can help the treatment process by detecting challenging behavior in the early stages of the development of challenging behavior. In addition, an intervention system through PBS is needed because intervention with praise and compensation through Positive Behavior Support (PBS), which consists of individual interventions, is effective in the treatment of people with developmental disabilities. PBS is used in schools, workplaces, and homes, but rather than simply punishing problematic behaviors of people with developmental disabilities, it is an approach to identify the cause and induce positive changes. PBS builds a positive environment, analyzes the cause, and consists of continuous support and monitoring [3–5]. However, continuous support and monitoring is one of the reasons that make caregivers feel a time and economic burden. To solve this problem, a monitoring system that can analyze the frequency of challenging behaviors and frequently occurring challenging behaviors is needed. Therefore, this paper proposes a system for monitoring challenge behaviors of children with developmental disabilities that combines ConvLSTM and Skeleton Keypoint.

2 Related Works

2.1 Human Activity Recognition Using ConvLSTM and Keypoint

Human focuses on detecting what a person is doing in images or videos. Yadav Santosh Kumar, Tiwari Kamlesh, and Pandey Hari Mohan Akbar Shaik Ali used Kinect v2 to extract human joint information through a total of seven behaviors: Standing, Walking Slow, Walking Fast, Sitting, Bending, Fall, and Lying Down. Yadav Santosh Kumar, Tiwari Kamlesh, and Pandey Hari Mohan Akbar Shaik Ali constructed the dataset by collecting a total of 130,000 data. Keypoint was learned using LSTM, CNN, and ConvLSTM to classify human behavior. As a result of learning, ConvLSTM, CNN, and LSTM have accuracy of 98.89%, 93.89%, and 92.75%, respectively, and ConvLSTM performed the best [6]. However, there is a limitation in that a dedicated sensor (Kinect v2) should be used, human behavior was classified into only seven behaviors, and the video itself was not used for learning. Therefore, this paper photographs a person's behavior with a general camera, extracts keypoint information of a person appearing in an image using MoveNet [7], and classifies the behavior of children with developmental disabilities into 19 challenging behaviors (kick, no action, pinch, push, throw, hit, pull, extort, tear, swing, bit, blocking, smash, self-bending, self-bending, self-bumping, and one no action). In addition, the goal is to apply image data by frame of image data to learning to proceed with the coarse classification, and to classify the behavior of children with developmental disabilities using the extracted keypoint information for learning.

2.2 Challenging Behavior Detect System with Wearable Sensors

Challenging behaviors of children suffering from the spectrum, one of the types of developmental disabilities, show more frequent aggressive behaviors. Such challenging behaviors can lead to injuries. Alban Ahmad Qadeib, et al. designed a wristband-shaped wearable device to collect heart rate (IBI, HR), acceleration, skin conductivity, temperature, and Blood Volume Pulse (BVP) of children with developmental disabilities. Ahmad Qadeib, et al. divided the challenging behaviors of children with developmental disabilities into six behaviors (head banging, hand flapping, kicking others, hand beating, and scoring) in the sensor data collected, and compared and analyzed the performance of three algorithms: machine learning algorithms Support Vector Machine (SVM), Multilayer Perception (MLP), and Decision Tree (DT). As a result of the analysis, applying all features to the learning of the Multilayer Perception (MLP) algorithm was the best, showing performance of 0.90, 0.97, and 0.90 respectively, Recall, and F1 scores [8]. However, there is a limitation in that children with developmental disabilities can only recognize the challenging behavior of children with developmental disabilities by wearing wearable devices, and machine learning time-series information cannot be used. Therefore, this paper focuses on recognizing the challenging behavior of people with developmental disabilities using Keypoint information extracted through cameras without the need for wearable devices (Fig. 1).

3   Proposed Methodology

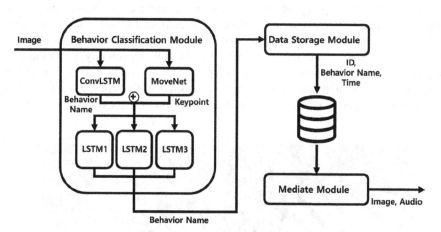

Fig. 1. System Configuration Diagram

The proposed system consists of a behavior classification module, a data storage analysis module, and an intervention module. The behavior classification module consists of the ConvLSTM layer, the MoveNet [7], the LSTM1 layer, the LSTM2 layer, and the LSTM3 layer, and is trained through the challenging behavior image dataset. In this paper, image data is inputted into ConvLSTM and MoveNet [7] to learn the challenging behavior of children with developmental disabilities and to extract Skeleton Keypoint data. The proposed system predicts the challenging behavior of children with developmental disabilities through multiple classification layers by extracting spatial feature multiplication and temporal feature map. The proposed system converts the image data into a 5D sensor. By inputting the image data converted into the 5D sensor into the ConvLSTM layer, the input data is classified into (attacking others with hands, attacking others with their torso, and self-harming behavior). In addition, through the MoveNet [7], the 17 joints of a person (nose, left eye, right eye, left early, right shoulder, right shoulder, right elbow, right elbow, left wrist, right hip, right hip, left knife, right knife, left knee, left ankle, right angle) are entered into the MoveNet [7] to extract the x coordinates and y coordinates of each of the 17 joints of the person (nose, left eye, right eye, right eye, right eye). When the result value of ConvLSTM is an action of attacking another person with a hand, the Skeleton Keypoin extracted with the MoveNet [7] is inputted into the LSTM1 layer and classified into 9 actions (scratch, pinch, push, throw, hit, pull, extort, tear, swing). When the result of ConvLSTM is an action of attacking another person with a body, it is inputted into the LSTM2 layer and classified into 5 actions (bite, choking, kick, strike, smash). When the result of ConvLSTM is self-harming behavior, it is classified into 6 behaviors (self-bending, self-biting, self-chewing, self-bumping, no action) through the LSTM3 layer.

The behavior text extracted from the behavior classification module is stored in a database and inputted into the data storage analysis module to analyze the challenge behavior occurring with the highest frequency. It is stored in a database composed of a table composed of names, behavior names, and times of children with developmental disabilities in the database.

When a new challenging behavior is stored in the database, the intervention module outputs a warning voice made of TTS(Text-to-Speech), including the name of a child with a developmental disability and the challenging behavior in action, and a voice that induces meditation through the intervention module. On the contrary, when the most frequent behavior did not occur during the specified time, a praise voice is output to create a positive environment and lead to positive behavior through praise. In addition, if you enter the name of a child with a developmental disability, the data storage analysis

Fig. 2. A figure caption is always placed below the illustration. Short captions are centered, while long ones are justified. The macro button chooses the correct format automatically.

module can check the behavior name of the child with a disability and the number of times by date along with the graph. Figure 2 shows a scene that provides positive behavior support. The left is the screen that comes out when the challenge action has not been performed for a certain period of time, and the right is the screen that induces meditation when the challenge action occurs.

3.1 Dataset Building

This paper constructs a challenging behavior dataset to train ConvLSTM, LSTM1, LSTM2, and LSTM3 models used in the behavior classification module. The dataset was built by recording 10 s videos of 20 behaviors (scratch, pinch, push, throw, hit, pull, extort, tear, swing, bite, kick, chocking, strike, smash, self-banging, self-bitting, self-chewing, self-hitting, self-bumping, no action) from 80 university students at Daegu University. The constructed dataset consists of a total of 16,620 videos, with 800 videos for each of the 19 behaviors (kick, no action, pinch, push, throw, hit, pull, extort, tear, swing, bite, chocking, strike, smash, self-banging, self-bitting, self-chewing, self-hitting, self-bumping), and 820 videos for "no action". Table. 1 illustrates the composition of the challenging behavior dataset.

Figure 3 presents exemplar images extracted from the challenge behavior dataset, illustrating distinct behaviors. The left side is one of kick data, and the right side is one of pull data.

Table 1. The composition of the challenging behavior dataset

Name of Challenging Behavior	Number of Video	Name of Challenging Behavior	Number of Video
pinch	800	chocking	800
push	800	strike	800
throw	800	smash	800
hit	800	scratch	800
pull	800	self bitting	800
extort	800	self chewing	800
tear	800	self hitting	800
swing	800	self bumping	800
bite	800	self banging	800
kick	800	no action	820
all	16,620		

Fig. 3. Presents exemplar images extracted from the challenge behavior dataset.

4   Experiment and Evaluation

4.1   Human Activity Recognition Using ConvLSTM with Video

ConvLSTM [6] is used to extract spatial features through CNN and use temporal prediction through LSTM [6, 9]. This paper conducted learning by dividing the challenging behavior dataset into two methods of learning it in ConvLSTM.

1. ConvLSTM classifies into 20 classes
2. ConvLSTM classifies into three classes

The first method is to classify all 20 actions (scratch, pinch, push, throw, hit, pull, extort, tear, swing, bit, kick, chucking, strike, smash, self-banging, self-bending, self-chewing, self- heating, self-bumping, and no action). The second method is to learn by rearranging the 20 actions into three major categories (attacking another person with body, attacking other person with arm, self-arm). Figure 4 is the result of ConvLSTM, which is classified into 20 classes.

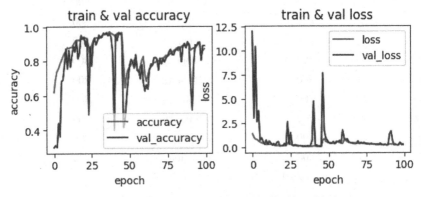

Fig. 4. Result of ConvLSTM, which is classified into 20 classes.

ConvLSTM classified into 20 classes shows the performance of the maximum value of training account 0.97 and the maximum value of validation account of 0.95. However, there are many sections in which the value of the graph is unstable. This is the same for training loss and validation loss. Figure 5 is the learning result of ConvLSTM classified into three classes.

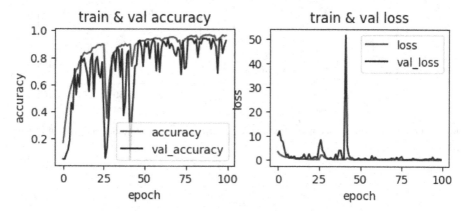

Fig. 5. Result of ConvLSTM, which is classified into 20 classes.

The three major categories are divided into "attacking other person with body" (bite, kick, kick, and smash), "attacking other person with arm" (scratch, pinch, push, throw, hit, pull, extort, tear, swing), and "self-bending," "self-bending," "self-beating," "self-chewing," "self-bumping," and "no action." When learning with data divided into three major categories, the maximum value of training accuracy is 0.96 and the maximum value of validation accuracy is 0.94. ConvLSTM, which is classified into 20 categories, shows higher accuracy, but the three major categories of data are upward-sloping in most parts of the graph. In addition, there are significantly fewer parts where the loss value changes rapidly than ConvLSTM, which is classified into 20 categories.

4.2 Training LSTM, SVM, KNN

This paper learns and compares human Keypoint information using LSTM that can learn information for a unit time, SVM that is lighter and shows compliance performance compared to deep learning models, and KNN, which is the lightest. Figure 6 is a graph of LSTM [9]'s Training Accuracy, Trainnig Loss, Validation Accuracy, and Validation Loss.

Both Training Accuracy, Validation Accuracy increase steadily and both Training Losss, Validation Loss are steadily decreasing. The highest training accuracy of LSTM is 0.92 and validation accuracy is 0.93. The lowest training loss is 0.47 and validation loss is 0.48. In order to analyze the performance of LSTM, the machine learning classification algorithms Support Vector Machine (SVM) and K-Nearest-Neighbor (KNN) learned keypoint information (x, y-coordinates) of people appearing in images and compared the accuracy. Figure 7 is a graph for accuracy analysis of SVM, KNN, and LSTM.

The accuracy of LSTM, SVM, and KNN was found to be 0.72, 0.86, and respectively. Therefore, the proposed system employs the LSTM algorithm for learning Key point information.

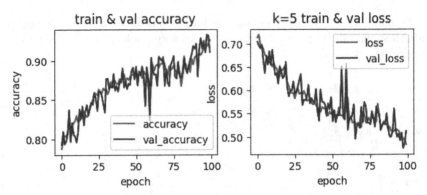

Fig. 6. Graphs of training accuracy, training loss, verification accuracy, and verification loss of LSTM.

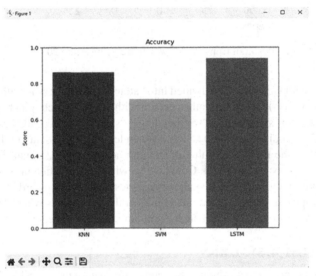

Fig. 7. A graph for accuracy analysis of SVM, KNN, and LSTM

5   Conclusion and Future Work

This paper proposed a system for monitoring challenging behaviors of children with developmental disabilities by combining ConvLSTM and Skeleton Keypoint information. The system consists of a behavior classification module, a data storage analysis module, and an intervention module. By leveraging ConvLSTM and MoveNet, the proposed system accurately classifies challenging behaviors into various categories, aiding in early detection and intervention. The experimental results demonstrated the effectiveness of the proposed system. By training ConvLSTM on challenging behavior datasets, the system achieved high accuracy in classifying behaviors, even when categorized into finer subgroups. Furthermore, comparison with other machine learning algorithms such as SVM and KNN highlighted the superiority of LSTM in handling Keypoint information for behavior recognition.

The proposed system has several implications for the field of developmental disabilities and behavior analysis. Firstly, it provides caregivers with a tool for continuous monitoring and analysis of challenging behaviors, reducing the burden of manual observation. Secondly, early detection facilitated by the system allows for timely interventions, potentially preventing escalation of challenging behaviors. Future work could focus on enhancing the system's scalability and real-time performance. Additionally, integrating feedback mechanisms based on intervention outcomes could further optimize the effectiveness of the system in supporting individuals with developmental disabilities and their caregivers. Moreover, expanding the dataset to encompass a broader range of challenging behaviors and demographic diversity would improve the system's generalizability and applicability in real-world settings.

Acknowledgements. This work was supported by the Ministry of Education of the Republic of Korea and the National Research Foundation of Korea(NRF-2022S1A5C2A07091326).

References

1. Hyuksang, K., Chul, K.S.: The implications of parents' experiences on lifelong education for adults with autism spectrum disorder. J. Emot. Behav. Disord. **34**(4), 477–500 (2018)
2. Mi, Y.S., Chung, Y., Jun, Y.: Mothers' perception and experiences of the challenging behavior of their children with developmental disabilities in transition to adulthood. J. Emot. Behav. Disord. **38**(3), 411–440 (2022)
3. Lorena, B., et al.: Positive behavioural support for children and young people with developmental disabilities in special education settings. J. Appl. Res. Intellectual Disab. 719–735 (2022)
4. Morris Kelsey, R., Horner, R.H.: Positive behavior support. In: Handbook of Evidence-Based Practices in Intellectual and Developmental Disabilities, pp. 415–441 (2016)
5. Singh Nirbhay, N., et al.: Caregiver training in mindfulness-based positive behavior supports (MBPBS): effects on caregivers and adults with intellectual and developmental disabilities. Front. Psychol. **7** (2016)
6. Kumar, Y.S., Kamlesh, T., Mohan, P.H., Ali, A.S.: Skeleton-based human activity recognition using ConvLSTM and guided feature learning. Soft Comput. 877–890 (2022)
7. Rishabh, B., Joshi, D.: Movenet: a deep neural network for joint profile prediction across variable walking speeds and slopes. IEEE Trans. Instrum. Meas. **70**, 1–11 (2021)
8. Qadeib, A.A., et al.: Detection of challenging behaviours of children with autism using wearable sensors during interactions with social robots. In: 2021 30th IEEE international conference on robot & human interactive communication (RO-MAN). IEEE (2021)
9. Jian, C., Li, J., Zhang, M.: LSTM-based dynamic probability continuous hand gesture trajectory recognition. IET Image Process. 2314–2320 (2019)
10. Lee, S., et al.: SVM-based pose estimation algorithm for gesture recognitions. J. Inst. Control Robot. Syst. **2014**(11), 65–68 (2014)
11. Zhang, M.-L., Zhou, Z.-H.: ML-KNN: a lazy learning approach to multi-label learning. Pattern Recogn. 2038–2048 (2007)

Sensitize and Qualify University Teachers for Digital Accessibility

Judith Kuhlmann[1]([email]) [ORCID], Kim Helen Althoff[2], Anna-Maria Kamin[1] [ORCID],
and Michael Johannfunke[2]

[1] Faculty of Educational Science, Bielefeld University, Universitätsstraße 25,
33615 Bielefeld, Germany
jkuhlmann3@uni-bielefeld.de
[2] Bielefeld University, ZAB - Accessibility Services, Universitätsstraße 25,
33615 Bielefeld, Germany

Abstract. University teachers face new challenges, particularly in the context of digital teaching and learning. However, teachers often encounter obstacles in implementing digital accessibility in their teaching. One of the challenges is disproportionate additional time effort as well as technical and didactic compatibility issues. The SHUFFLE project aims to support teachers with their needs in designing accessible digital teaching concepts through a material package based on the concept of Universal Design for Learning. The package includes checklists, guides, and a knowledge database, which covers various aspects related to digital teaching – accessible to everyone. The checklists offer advice and assistance on technical and didactic requirements, and the guidelines provide detailed instructions for implementation The knowledge database provides additional information on other aspects of making digital teaching accessible. The material is available in German and English under the Creative Commons license CCBY.

Keywords: digital accessibility · material packages · higher education · inclusion · universal design for learning

1 Introduction: Digital Accessibility in Higher Education

University teachers are particularly challenged in the context of digitally supported teaching and learning [3]. Digitization processes open up both new potential and challenges. In view of the increasing heterogeneity of students at German universities, the risks with regard to comprehensive technical and didactic accessibility of teaching must be addressed [1, 8]. In order to guarantee the right to equal participation, increasingly digitalized university teaching must be accessible to all students.

Although accessibility is enshrined in policy and/or law worldwide, the requirements are still insufficiently implemented in everyday university life [10]. Despite the obligation arising from the UN Convention on the Rights of Persons with Disabilities to make universities a place of non-discriminatory participation for all students through accessibility and reasonable accommodation, students with disabilities continue to encounter barriers. These relate to structural, communicative, organizational and didactic factors and prevent equal opportunities for students [4]. This applies not only to individual students, but to an increasingly large group. In summer 2021, around 16% of students in Germany reported an impairment that made studying difficult, compared to 8% and 11% in 2011 and 2016 respectively [4]. Similar figures can also be seen in other countries such as Canada and the United Kingdom (11%), while in the USA the figure is as high as 21.9% [10].

The increasing number of students with disabilities or more difficult study conditions point to the urgency of anchoring digital accessibility in university teaching. Education policy in Germany has responded by launching a series of initiatives and funding projects for digital accessibility at universities. This is because expertise in the areas of equality, diversity and accessibility can counteract the risk of reproducing and reinforcing disadvantage and discrimination through digitalization in the university context [7].

Current projects are mostly aimed at students and teachers. For example, the Kompetenzzentrum digitale Barrierefreiheit.NRW[1] was founded for the federal state of North Rhine-Westphalia. The Uni digital & inklusiv[2] project at the European University Viadrina Frankfurt Oder also provides various services to promote digital accessibility at German universities. All projects offer support for students in reducing barriers in teaching, address individual needs and work together to find access and solutions. Among other things, training and advisory services are developed and provided for teachers in the implementation of inclusive teaching. The creation of accessible teaching and learning material (PDF, PPT, videos) is also part of the support developed in the projects. However, it should be noted that the offers are usually not made available in a bundled form, meaning that teachers have to obtain information from various platforms.

This is where the package of accessible teaching materials developed in the SHUFFLE joint project comes in. Central assistance and materials for teachers are bundled in a learning management system and thus offer a low-threshold solution for increasing digital accessibility in university teaching. In addition, the material package not only provides concrete implementation aids for digital accessibility, but also content that is intended to help raise awareness. They therefore take into account the specific needs of teachers. The basis is the Universal Design before Learning (UDL) model (see chapter 3).

2 Needs Analysis: Results of a Teacher Survey

In order to gain more detailed insights into accessible, digital teaching, an empirical needs analysis was carried out as part of the SHUFFLE joint project in spring 2022. To this end, a standardized online questionnaire survey (N = 179) was conducted at the four universities[3] participating in the project at the beginning of 2022. Among other things, the questionnaire asked about the level of knowledge, personal attitudes and experiences regarding digital accessibility.

---

[1] Further information: Kompetenzzentrum digitale Barrierefreiheit.NRW: https://barrierefreiheit. dh.nrw/.

[2] Further information: Uni digital & inklusiv: https://www.europa-uni.de/de/struktur/zll/ueber-uns/auszuege-aus-unserer-arbeit/abgeschlossene-projekte/digitalinklusiv/index.html.

[3] Bielefeld University, Stuttgart Media University, Freiburg University of Education and Heidelberg University of Education.

In addition, 30- to 60-min guided interviews were conducted with six teachers from the four universities. The sample was interdisciplinary and covered as wide a range of experiences as possible in terms of teaching formats and experiences. The interviews focused on the key question of how teachers deal with digital barriers in their teaching. In addition to the individual understanding of digital accessibility, the researchers were particularly interested in the assessment of possibilities, opportunities and risks in the implementation of digital accessibility as well as wishes and challenges for the future. The qualitative data was evaluated using content analysis [6], while frequency counts were carried out for the quantitative data. The overall results paint a comprehensive and detailed picture of the importance of digital accessibility for the respondents as well as their motivation, wishes and concerns regarding implementation [5].

Teachers' knowledge proved to be a key factor influencing the implementation of digitally accessible teaching. The question about the subjective assessment of the level of knowledge about digital accessibility shows that just under 6% of teachers ascribe extensive knowledge to themselves. The majority of respondents (58%) ranked their own knowledge in the middle range and more than a third (36%) ascribed very little knowledge to themselves. In the free text responses, some of the teachers also stated that they did not feel that they knew enough to identify all possible barriers. The subjectively perceived low level of knowledge is also reflected in the qualitative data. Overall, although teachers are fundamentally aware of many aspects of digital accessibility, in-depth knowledge is only available in isolated cases.

When explicitly asked about difficulties in designing accessible teaching materials, a lack of knowledge about implementation was also mentioned in addition to time-related difficulties. One interviewee summarized: "The main problem, however, is that many others, like me, probably don't know exactly what I have to do to ensure accessibility".

The attitude of teachers towards digital, accessible teaching can be identified as another influencing factor. Both the quantitative data and the analysis of the qualitative interviews confirm the sometimes-contradictory attitudes of teachers. On the one hand, teachers fear the disproportionate additional work involved in implementing digital accessibility. Teachers express concerns and doubts about the implementation of digital accessibility, particularly with regard to the additional time (67%), technical (54%) and didactic (34%) effort involved. Various statements in the interviews with teachers support this information. In addition, some teachers express considerable doubts about the relevance of the topic. For example, teachers ask in the survey: "Accessible, for whom?" and thus highlight concerns about actual occasions.

Despite the extensive concerns and doubts, on the other hand, there appears to be an awareness of and interest in digital accessibility as well as a willingness to engage with and provide further training on these topics. The majority of the teachers interviewed were in favor of integrating this topic into university didactics: "I do believe that we should get involved and agree on a minimum level of accessibility that can be implemented." The quantitative survey also illustrates a fundamental interest in further education courses on digital accessibility. For example, 64.25% of respondents stated that they would be interested in a corresponding offer.

The question of what teachers would like to see in terms of digital accessibility in teaching opens up clear starting points for the implementation of the materials package.

In addition to more time or personnel resources, teachers would primarily like to see "measures that are easy to implement", "tools that are easy and time-saving to use" and "guidelines with brief explanations" with "examples and descriptions of use". Teachers' limited knowledge can be assumed to be one reason for doubts about the balance between (additional) effort and (added) value. However, the willingness of teachers to expand their knowledge through further or advanced training can be seen as an opportunity not only to expand the skills of teachers and thus minimize the additional workload, but above all to sensitize them to the needs of students and thus emphasize the importance of digital accessibility.

The results of the survey in the context of the discussion about a (digital) university for all make it clear that teachers need to be qualified for the cross-cutting issues of digitalization and heterogeneity in the context of university teaching and the associated challenges. It is also clear that teachers need more intensive support at various levels in this regard. As outlined above, they primarily need technical and didactic skills to design digitally accessible teaching. The findings of the needs analysis were used to develop support measures for digital teaching that is as accessible as possible and were incorporated into the development of the materials package.

3 Material Package: Implementing Digital Accessible Teaching

The aim of the material package developed in Shuffle is to open up low-threshold access to the complex topic of digital accessibility and to provide concrete assistance in designing digitally accessible university teaching. In addition to specific wishes and needs expressed by teachers in the surveys, the material package also takes into account findings with regard to the state of research on digital accessibility. It is therefore primarily aimed at teaching staff at universities and is intended to support them in designing accessible digital teaching. However, it can also serve as an aid for other university stakeholders in the design of accessible digital content.

The accessibility of this support is ensured by making all materials available in a learning management system (Open Moodle). This central collection enables uncomplicated and bundled availability of support aids: Materials for creating accessible documents (1) and materials for designing accessible teaching (2) as well as a topic-specific knowledge database (3).

The core of the material package consists of clear checklists on various aspects of accessible digital teaching. These provide tips and assistance for creating documents and teaching situations that are as accessible as possible. They contain simply formulated checkpoints to tick off as well as a supplementary implementation aid with detailed descriptions of the aspect. The material package is completed by the knowledge database.

Checklists for Word, PowerPoint, Excel and PDF are available for creating accessible documents. These checklists are primarily based on the European standard (EN 301 549) for digital accessibility, which specifies requirements for the accessibility of information and communication technology. However, in order to create legally compliant accessible documents, many technical criteria must be taken into account, some of which are less relevant in practice. For example, the requirements for video embedding were excluded from the Word checklist. In order to ensure the low-threshold nature of the checklists, some of these criteria, which are rarely used in practice, were not included in the lists. By reducing the checklists to the central criteria used in practice and adding didactically relevant checkpoints, checklists were created that are specifically adapted to everyday university teaching and the needs of teachers. In order to ensure clear orientation in the checklists, the checkpoints are also divided into different areas depending on the document format. For example, the checkpoints relate to general document settings, text, links, headings, graphics and tables (see Fig. 1).

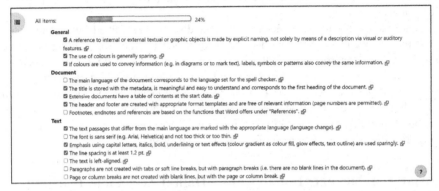

Fig. 1. Accessible Word checklist with links

If help is needed with the implementation of individual aspects, users can use a link at each checkpoint to go directly to the implementation aids, which provide them with further information. This implementation aid contains a detailed description of the aspect to be checked off under the heading "What does this mean?". The section "Why is it important?" describes which barriers are removed with the respective aspect and for which groups of people this is essential. Finally, under the heading "How can I implement/check this?" you will find detailed instructions on how to implement or check the respective aspect (see Fig. 2). The implementation guide therefore not only provides concrete support for the implementation of accessible document creation, but also raises awareness. Mentioning the groups of people who benefit from the various aspects can raise awareness of the fact that many more people benefit from accessibility than is apparent at first glance.

Several checklists have also been compiled in the material package for the design of accessible courses. On the one hand, information has been compiled to help design courses in the Moodle learning management system to be as accessible as possible. This includes both structural aspects (e.g. course format, table of contents, activities) and content-related aspects (e.g. materials used). As video productions such as instructional videos, screencasts or explanatory videos have also become a central component of digital university teaching, information is also compiled in a checklist to help make these video productions accessible. Further checklists are intended to support the planning of inclusive digital teaching. The various design aspects are structured according to the chronological course of the semester and the seminar and supplemented by measures and precautions for the atmosphere of an inclusive classroom (e.g. group size, diversity-sensitive communication). The points to be ticked off consist of instructions that can be implemented quickly and easily.

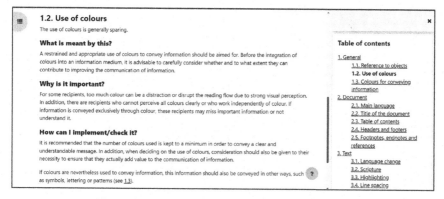

Fig. 2. Accessible Word implementation guide

These checkpoints are also supplemented with information about which student groups find it particularly helpful to take these aspects into account. This is intended to raise awareness of different needs. At the same time, it shows that in terms of UDL, a large target group can benefit from small changes. UDL refers to the creation of teaching materials and learning environments that are designed from the outset to meet the needs of as many learners as possible, including students with disabilities [2]. In this respect, the integration of UDL concepts into higher education can help to create a more inclusive and accessible learning environment that meets the individual learning needs of all students. In this context, the importance of digital accessibility is particularly emphasized, as learning processes today are increasingly supported by digital technologies. In addition to illustrating the content, the presentation of good practice offers guidance. At the same time, examples of successful implementations serve as models of good practice and can therefore be motivating.

The knowledge database is a collection of further information on relevant topics of accessible, digital teaching. In addition to recommendations on the use of methods and social forms, information is also provided on accessible (specialist) literature, accessible language and compensating for disadvantages. The information is selected in such a way that it is relevant for teachers. Particularly in the case of complex topics, such as compensation for disadvantages, this means that some information is merely referenced. In many places, the knowledge database is also supported with examples of good practice, so that the transfer to your own teaching can be successful.

To enable flexible use, the content is available in various formats. All checklists are created as progress lists in the Moodle course. These progress lists make it easy to check them off digitally and also show the growth in accessibility (see Fig. 1). The detailed implementation aids and the knowledge database are laid out in book format. The division into chapters with links makes it easy to navigate and find the desired information quickly (see Fig. 2). The checklists and implementation aids are also available as accessible Word documents for download. In addition, the document checklists were implemented in an Office add-in (Word, PowerPoint, Excel Accessibility Checker - WEPAC), which can be integrated directly into the Office tools and thus into the workflows of the teachers (see Fig. 3).

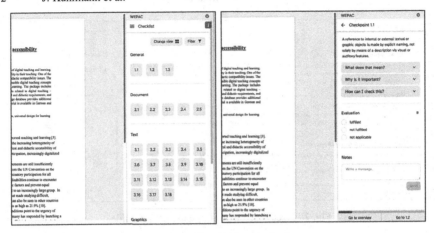

Fig. 3. Office add-in: WEPAC

The entire material package is available in German and English under the Creative Commons License CCBY and is freely accessible as a Moodle course in German under the name "Materialpaket barrierefreie Lehre"[4] and in English under the name "Material package accessible teaching"[5].

In summary, the material package presented offers teachers a starting point on the topic of accessibility in digital university teaching. In particular, it addresses the obstacles that teachers perceive when designing accessible digital lessons. It offers low-threshold materials that teachers can use, even with limited time resources, to make their teaching as accessible as possible. The additional information helps to increase awareness and knowledge about accessibility. Based on the concept of Universal Design for Learning (UDL), the needs of as many people as possible are already taken into account during the development of the materials, so that major adaptations afterwards or (necessary) individual solutions are avoided. This ensures accessibility on a technical and didactic level from the outset. The materials also enable teachers to independently check their teaching materials for a certain degree of accessibility.

4   Conclusion and Outlook

With the material package, a solution approach was created to expand the skills of teachers at a low threshold to entry, to support them in the challenges of implementing accessible teaching and to sensitize them to the needs of students with individual impairments. At the same time, the use of the checklists and tips enables a large number of students to benefit from accessible content. This makes it possible to stimulate a change in values and culture. According to Rabbel and Porsche (2021), this can help to ensure that digital accessibility is actively and naturally considered and integrated into everyday

---

[4] Click here for the German course: Materialpaket barrierefreie Lehre: https://openmoodle.uni-bielefeld.de/course/view.php?id=46.

[5] Click here for the English course: Material package accessible teaching: https://openmoodle.uni-bielefeld.de/course/view.php?id=79.

university life in all status groups in the future. Awareness-raising and education are two important pillars for enabling all students to participate fully in everyday university life.

The material package was presented at Bielefeld University and in the context of several university didactic conferences and made available for testing. Encouragingly, a total of 94 people have registered to use the course so far, and 13 people have taken part in the evaluative feedback survey. The survey shows that despite a fundamental interest on the part of teachers to consider digital accessibility in teaching, given the low response rate, presumably only a few teachers have extensively tested the materials. Therefore, a central aspect in the integration of digital accessibility at the university is the accompanying guidance for teachers. This ensures that digital accessibility not only exists as a concept, but is firmly anchored in the structures of the universities. According to Rabbel and Porsche (2021), it is worth taking a look at the US higher education system, as it plays an exemplary role in terms of framework conditions and support structures. The authors refer to a study[6] that shows that internal university organizational structures have a major influence on the number, structure and target groups of support services. In order to fully and comprehensively integrate digital accessibility into university teaching, it is therefore necessary to define clear responsibilities within the university organization and ensure the broad participation of IT services, centers for didactics and digital teaching as well as the university administration [9]. Accordingly, an inclusive educational environment for a heterogeneous student body can be pursued, which also takes pedagogical-didactic aspects into account in an appropriate manner. It is not only permanent contact points at universities that could promote the implementation of digital accessibility. The integration of digital accessibility training into existing processes such as onboarding, further education and training is also crucial. One suggestion would be to introduce training on digital accessibility as a mandatory program, similar to safety training in the workplace.

In order to realize a university for all, it is essential to provide teachers with comprehensive support and further training opportunities such as the materials package. This equips them for the new challenges they face when implementing digital, accessible teaching. Only the additional consolidation of digital accessibility in university structures, clear regulations and the provision of specific materials can ensure that educational opportunities are opened up equally for all students and an inclusive learning environment is created. After all, digital accessibility is not just an obligation, but a benefit for everyone.

Acknowledgments. The SHUFFLE project is funded by the Stiftung Innovation in der Hochschullehre, Treuhandstiftung in Trägerschaft der Toepfer Stiftung gGmbH.

Disclosure of Interests. The authors have no competing interests to declare that are relevant to the content of this article.

---

[6] Further information: Informationsportale für eine barrierefreie digitale Lehre. Was können deutsche Hochschulen von den USA lernen?

References

1. Berghoff, S., Horstmann, N., Hüsch, M., Müller, K.: Studium und Lehre in Zeiten der Corona-Pandemie - Die Sicht von Studierenden und Lehrenden. CHE Impulse 3, (2021). https://www.che.de/download/studium-lehre-corona/
2. Burgstahler, S.: Designing inclusive formal and informal online learning. what do instructors need to know? In: Digital Accessibility. Policies, Practices and Professional Development, pp. 113–128. Routledge, New York (2023)
3. Chan, R.Y.: The future of accessibility in higher education: making college skills and degrees more accessible. In: Disability and Equity in Higher Education Accessibility, pp. 1–45. IGI Global, USA (2017)
4. Deutsches Zentrum für Hochschul- und Wissenschaftsforschung GmbH (DZHW): Die Studierendenbefragung in Deutschland: best3. Studieren mit einer gesundheitlichen Beeinträchtigung. DZHW, Hannover (2023)
5. Kuhlmann, J., Günter, J., Kamin, A.-M.: Digitale Hochschullehre für Alle gestalten. Ergebnisse einer Lehrendenbefragung an vier Hochschulen. Jahrbuch MedienPädagogik 20: Zeitschrift für Theorie und Praxis der Medienbildung, pp. 169–182 (2023). https://doi.org/10.21240/mpaed/jb20.X
6. Mayring, P.: Qualitative Inhaltsanalyse: Grundlagen und Techniken. 13th edn. Beltz, Weinheim Basel (2022)
7. Orwat, C.: Risks of Discrimination through the Use of Algorithms. Federal Anti-Discrimination Agency, Berlin (2020). https://www.antidiskriminierungsstelle.de/EN/homepage/_documents/download_diskr_risiken_verwendung_von_algorithmen.pdf?__blob=publicationFile&v=1
8. Podszus, M.: Diversität im universitären Kontext!? Lehre zugänglicher gestalten – Perspektivwechsel für ein reicheres Bild der Lernenden!. In: Jahn, D., Kenner, A., Kergel, D., Heidkamp-Kergel, B. (eds.) Kritische Hochschullehre. Diversität und Bildung im digitalen Zeitalter, pp. 113–131. Springer, Wiesbaden (2019). https://doi.org/10.1007/978-3-658-25740-8_6
9. Rabbel, I., Porsche, C.: Barrierefreiheit in der digitalen Lehre: Die USA als Vorbild für deutsche Hochschulen? Hochschulforum Digitalisierung (2021). https://hochschulforumdigitalisierung.de/blog/barrierefreiheit-in-der-digitalen-lehre-die-usa-als-vorbild-fuer-deutsche-hochschulen/
10. Seale, J. (ed.): Improving Accessible Digital Practices in Higher Education. Springer, Cham (2020). https://doi.org/10.1007/978-3-030-37125-8

Towards Inclusive Voice User Interfaces: A Systematic Review of Voice Technology Usability for Users with Communication Disabilities

Kimberly R. Lin[✉] [iD]

Google, New York, NY, USA
linkimberly@google.com

Abstract. Voice technology has the potential to empower users with disabilities to be independent, communicate, and access information. However, voice technology is not always accessible or usable for people with speech and language disabilities. A systematic literature review was conducted to identify the needs, pain points, and attitudes of users with speech and language disabilities towards consumer voice user interface products, such as virtual assistants and voice assistive technologies. Thematic analysis was used to highlight key opportunities to improve the voice user interface experience for users with speech and language disabilities. Common pain points include poor speech recognition accuracy, difficult to pronounce wake words, premature end point detection, rigid query language, poor error handling, lack of voice output customization, and lack of cross-product integration. These pain points decrease the usability of voice technology for users with communication disabilities and reinforce negative user sentiment. For voice user interface products to be truly accessible, the responsibility of accessibility must shift from the user to the product team. Considerations for inclusive voice user interface research and design are proposed.

Keywords: Accessibility · Voice user interface · Speech and language disability · Inclusive design

1 Introduction

From mobile and automotive assistants to smart home controls and more, the increased prevalence of voice technology over the years has allowed people to access information and technology with increased ease and efficiency. In the United States alone, 135 million adults own a smart home device (52% of the US adult population), and nearly 60% of smart device owners use voice activation to interact with their smart home technology [16]. Globally, 37% of the online population uses voice search on smart devices [21]. The use of voice technology is expected to increase as automatic speech recognition (ASR) models improve and voice input/output become further integrated into everyday devices, services, and routines.

C. Stephanidis et al. (Eds.): HCII 2024, CCIS 2115, pp. 75–85, 2024.
https://doi.org/10.1007/978-3-031-61947-2_9

Voice input and multimodal or hands-free experiences are especially useful to people who may have difficulty accessing technology due to a mismatch between the environment and their needs. For example, someone who has their hands busy while cooking may use a voice assistant to set a timer. Similarly, someone with an upper motor disability who experiences pain or fatigue in their arm/hand when typing on a keyboard may use voice dictation to more easily compose a message.

However, voice user interface (VUI) products are not always accessible or usable for people with speech and language disabilities. Communication disabilities that might prevent voice technology from correctly understanding someone's speech (e.g., disfluency, word finding difficulty, inconsistent volume or quality of speech, etc.) affect approximately 10% of the US population [1]. Furthermore, improving voice technology has curb cut effects for users with no disabilities, including young children, those with accents or dialectal language differences, and those with situational constraints (e.g., loud environments, etc.). Given the rapid growth of voice technology, understanding the needs of users with speech and language disabilities and improving the accessibility of voice technology is key to upholding equity and inclusion across products.

This research aims to explore the state of voice technology accessibility and identify pain points and opportunities to improve voice user interface experiences for users with communication disabilities. The study was guided by the following research questions:

1. What are the needs and expectations of users with speech/language disabilities when interacting with voice user interface (VUI) technology?
2. What are the attitudes of users with speech/language disabilities towards VUI?
3. What are opportunities to improve the accessibility and usability of VUI for users with speech/language disabilities? How does current VUI technology address or not address their needs?

2   Method

A systematic literature review was conducted to understand the accessibility and usability of voice technology for users with speech and language disabilities.

2.1 Search Strategy

The Association for Computing Machinery (ACM) Digital Library and Google Scholar were searched and filtered to identify relevant literature. Database search methodology utilized AND/OR Boolean operators across technology and disability concepts, including ("speech recognition" OR "ASR" OR "voice assistant" OR "intelligent personal assistant" OR "smart assistant" OR "voice user interface" OR "conversational user interface") AND ("speech disability" OR "speech disorder" OR "speech impair*" OR "language disability" OR "language disorder" OR "language impair*" OR disfluen* OR "unconventional speech"), published from the year 2017 onwards. Articles were first manually reviewed for broader relevance to the literature review research goals. Remaining articles were then reviewed against a set of inclusion criteria. Articles that: 1) included end users with speech or language disabilities (or co-occurring cognitive or motor disabilities), 2) focused on consumer voice assistants or voice assistive technology, and 3) primary or secondary sources were included in the review. The initial search surfaced 307 results (193 from ACM Digital Library, 114 from Google Scholar). After manual review and application of the inclusion criteria, 14 articles were ultimately included for analysis.

2.2 Analysis

Data was extracted from the 14 included articles, including study metadata (author, year, source type), study content (method, sample size, user group, product, research questions, objectives), and study outcomes (results, recommendations, next steps). Inductive coding was used to identify themes across articles, and each theme was mapped to the literature review research questions. Frequency counts of each theme were aggregated to identify highly prevalent user pain points, needs, attitudes, and opportunities for VUI improvement.

3 Results

3.1 User Needs and Characteristics

Users included in the reviewed articles had various communication disabilities, spanning across speech production, language expression, language comprehension, and pragmatic language disabilities. These were often co-occurring with motor disabilities (e.g., brain injury, Parkinson's, multiple sclerosis, amyotrophic lateral sclerosis, etc.) or cognitive learning disabilities (e.g., dementia, brain injury, dyslexia, etc.). As such, users with motor-speech and cognitive-language disabilities have notable, intersectional needs that impact their access to technology. Despite the wide range of speech and language disabilities included, three common themes emerged in the literature, regarding user needs for communication, independence, and flexibility.

Communication: expression, comprehension, and repair. Communication is a basic human right that affects one's autonomy, social well-being, and access to information [4]. Clear and efficient communication with others and with technology is a primary need of people with speech and language disabilities, as they may face difficulty with expressing their thoughts, understanding what's communicated to them, and/or repairing conversational breakdowns. People who have difficulty with word finding, forming sounds for words, or understanding complex sentences and social cues often benefit from extra time to communicate, multimodal options, and communication partners who adapt to their communication styles [1].

Independence and Environmental Control. Controlling the environment (e.g., temperature, lights, sounds, positioning, etc.) is essential to one's independence and well-being. Alternative access to items in the environment is particularly useful for people with motor-speech disabilities, who may have difficulty completing daily tasks when physical interaction is not an option [10]. Similarly, people with co-occurring cognitive-language disabilities have challenges with memory, organization, attention, and/or formulating thoughts into words. They often benefit from supports such as reminders, suggestions, repetition, and multimodal guidance (e.g., auditory + visual options) to maintain independence in daily tasks [19].

Flexibility. People with speech and language disabilities may have changing needs that impact their ability to complete their goals at any given time, depending on the context. For example, some people who stutter report experiencing more disfluencies in the presence of unfamiliar communication partners. People who stutter also report experiencing different frequencies of disfluencies depending on whether they're communicating in-person or on a phone/video call [3]. Additionally, progressive conditions such as ALS or dementia, cause an individual's motor or cognitive needs to increase over time and across contexts as well. Choice of when and how to interact with the environment allows people with speech and language disabilities to maintain their personhood and autonomy in the midst of changing circumstances.

3.2 Voice User Interface Usability and Accessibility

Voice technology takes on several different roles in addressing the needs of people with speech and language disabilities. This section summarizes VUI accessibility progress and pain points across digital assistants and voice assistive technologies. Pain points are categorized across voice input, voice output, and system-level barriers.

Input Pain Points

Automatic speech recognition models are not accurate for all varieties of speech. Users expect voice activated digital assistants to understand their voice. However, users with speech and language disabilities report several pain points related to speech recognition accuracy and adaptation. In studies comparing the word error rates of Deaf/hard of hearing speech to hearing speech, commercial voice user interfaces performed significantly worse for users with speech disabilities [11].

Many efforts to improve automatic speech recognition for people with speech disabilities have been documented [22]. Notably, cross-industry collaborations such as the Speech Accessibility Project aim to improve automatic speech recognition models by collecting more diverse speech data [28]. Other initiatives, such as VoiceItt and Google's Project Relate, offer users personalized speech models after inputting a number of speech recordings. Such efforts seem promising, evidenced by improved word error rates for read sentences using personalized models compared to out of the box models [29].

However, these data largely focus on dysarthric speech, which is only one type of speech disability caused by difficulties with speech-motor control. Other qualities of speech in addition to dysarthria, such as stuttering disfluencies or apraxia, should garner equal attention [8]. Preliminary research on speech disfluencies has shown that collecting and publishing large, annotated datasets of disfluent speech (e.g., Sep-28k) can be used to develop models that detect stuttering events and improve the voice input experience for people who stutter [18]. With larger, more inclusive datasets comes a greater variance of speech and more opportunity to improve automatic speech recognition models for a wider range of users.

The context of speech also impacts ASR performance and must be accounted for. Research on stuttering shows that spontaneous conversational speech often contains more disfluencies than read speech [26]. Similarly, users who speak quietly may experience more barriers using voice technology in environments with loud background noise compared to others. Creating models that adapt to users' changing speech over time (e.g., degenerating speech, fatigue, etc.) and across contexts (e.g., background noise) requires product teams to innovate and push the bounds of voice technology.

In addition to collecting more diverse speech data, while metrics like word error rate are often used to evaluate the performance of speech recognition models, usability research involving end users with speech and language disabilities remains very limited [6]. Including users with communication disabilities in product research is critical to identifying and improving VUI usability issues.

Poor end point detection interrupts users who need time to express their thoughts. Users across speech and language disabilities have expressed frustration when voice technology times out or interrupts them before they complete their thought [2]. While natural conversational turns are determined by a combination of verbal cues (e.g., syntactic completion), prosody (e.g., pitch, intonation), breath, and nonverbal cues (e.g., eye gaze, gestures, etc.), current VUI technology determines conversational turns by using explicit direct cues (e.g., wake word indicates the user has something to say) or silence detection (e.g., preset time threshold). However, silence detection thresholds have limitations. If time-out thresholds are too short, users are interrupted when pausing to think. If time-out thresholds are too long, users may think the system is unresponsive [27]. Researchers have been reimagining how voice assistants determine when a user has finished their utterance, including the use of continuous models that combine prosodic and verbal cues to predict turns [20]. Nonetheless, more work is needed to develop improved models that detect end points and conversational turns in naturalistic ways.

Wake words are difficult to pronounce for some. For users who have difficulty remembering specific words or pronouncing specific speech sounds, wake words pose a major blocker to independently utilizing voice assistants [3]. While push to talk features exist as alternative methods to invoke voice assistants, hands-free interactions for users with communication disabilities remain inaccessible. Additionally, the issue persists for users with co-occurring motor disabilities. Hands-free alternatives to wake words, including customizable phrases or removing wake words altogether, are worth exploring. Current features, such as Google's Look and Talk, Quick Phrases, or Amazon's Conversation Mode have the potential to improve the accessibility of voice assistants for people with speech and language disabilities by removing the barrier of hard to pronounce wake words; however, these features are currently limited to certain devices and use cases. Further testing with users with disabilities is warranted to better understand the usability and accessibility of such solutions.

Query language is rigid and difficult to discover. Rigid query language is one barrier that prevents people with language disabilities from accessing voice assistants. For example, similar Google Assistant queries such as "Show me my sleep results" and "How did I sleep last night?" yield different responses. When one query works as intended while similar alternatives yield errors, inflexible query language causes increased frustration and cognitive load for voice assistant users with language disabilities, who have difficulty verbally expressing grammar and vocabulary [9]. In fact, in a study on voice assistant users with cognitive-linguistic disabilities, the usability of a voice assistant was more affected by a user's communication skill rather than their cognitive ability [19]. Supportive features such as word prediction, suggestions, auto-correct, and auto-complete help users with language disabilities formulate search queries with increased ease and efficiency [17]. Increasing the discoverability of possible query phrases, improving language models, and exploring language supports such as multimodal suggestions and word prediction are prime opportunities to improve the VUI experience for users with language disabilities.

Output Pain Points

Speech output is not fully customizable. In natural conversations, factors such as a speaker's voice (e.g., pitch, intensity, intonation, etc.), rate of speech, and vocabulary all affect how well one is understood. When utilizing voice assistants, some users with communication disabilities experience difficulty understanding the output when voice assistant responses are too lengthy or when the speaking rate is too quick. While some products have settings to change the output voice and verbosity, these settings remain limited [22]. Further customization of speech output, including speaking rate and pitch, may particularly improve the accessibility of voice assistants for users with language disabilities who have difficulty comprehending spoken language, or those with speech and hearing disabilities who have difficulty processing certain sound frequencies.

Customizable voice output is especially critical for products that utilize text-to-speech (TTS) or speech-to-speech technology to provide voice output for the purpose of real time user communication. Augmentative and alternative communication (AAC) systems provide people with speech and language disabilities a means of communication other than oral speech [12]. AAC systems are often highly personalized, following a systematic feature-matching process to match a user's strengths and needs to available communication tools and features (e.g., input method, size and positioning of device, vocabulary, etc.) [25]. In fact, users often refer to their AAC devices as part of their identity, as opposed to a separate tool [31]. While advancements in voice technology have largely focused on the clarity of TTS voices, developing voices that are authentic and representative of the user for the purposes of communication are only starting to garner attention. Making authentic voices more widely available to AAC users has great potential impacts on one's social identity and increases user adoption of voice technology [7, 23].

Poor error handling leaves users uncertain when errors occur. During communication breakdowns, VUIs do not always give users enough feedback for error recovery [3, 5]. Poor error handling especially causes frustration for users with speech and language disabilities because without clear redirection, the onus is on the user to determine whether the error was due to their query language, speech pronunciation, technical limitations, or otherwise. For users with speech disabilities, repeating speech to be louder or clearer may be effortful. As fatigue increases, one's speech may be further negatively impacted. Thus, poor error handling creates a cycle of frustration.

System Integration Pain Points

Lack of support for assistive technology prevents equal access to voice technology. Assistive technology (AT) is any tool or system that is used to increase, maintain, or improve the functional capabilities of people with disabilities [30]. Voice activated assistive technologies, such as Voice Control or Dictation, help users with motor disabilities access technology and maintain environmental control. Given the high co-occurrence of speech and motor disabilities, it is crucial to evaluate the usability of voice-activated assistive technology with the perspective of users with multiple disabilities.

When assistive technologies are not compatible with other products, platforms, or systems, users with disabilities lose access to control and independence within their technology ecosystem. This issue is commonly evidenced when using multiple voice input/output products (e.g., Voice Control + voice search, voice assistant + video conferencing platform, etc.) [24]. When faced with incompatible assistive technology, users must seek assistance from others at the sake of privacy and independence, avoid products, and/or fail to meet their goals altogether.

Lack of cross-product integration emphasizes the need for alternative access and multimodal options in VUI products. People with disabilities often use one or a combination of assistive technologies, depending on their needs [15]. Likewise, people with speech and language disabilities may use multiple means of interaction depending on their level of fatigue, including verbal speech, text, images, or gestures, etc. Providing users with multiple means of access allows them to choose what works best for them at any given time.

3.3 User Attitudes and Perceptions

As consumer voice technology becomes more integrated into everyday devices and improves in speech recognition and natural language processing, there is growing expectation for the technology to listen well, communicate clearly, and adapt to user needs and contexts. As such, how well voice technology listens and speaks to the user inevitably influences their perceptions of the device.

Users with speech and language disabilities have expressed overall positive sentiment regarding the usefulness of products like voice assistants [10, 13, 24]. When voice technology works, it has the potential to increase user independence, control, and efficiency with everyday tasks and information seeking.

Despite this, outstanding pain points related to being misunderstood increase frustration and abandonment of voice assistants. When voice input or output technology fails to meet the needs of users with speech and language disabilities, users report feeling invisible. Internalized pain points cause users to put pressure on themselves to perform better - they try to speak faster, louder, more clearly, more fluently - and attempt to fill the gaps of an ultimately inaccessible product design. The prior or anticipated negative experiences thus lead to users avoiding voice technology altogether [3, 9, 14].

4 Discussion

Given the state of limited voice user interface usability and accessibility, the burden currently lies on users to change their speech and language to access a product that was not built for them. For voice user interface products to be truly accessible, the responsibility of accessibility must shift from the user to the product team. When products are designed for accessibility from the start, all users – both with and without disabilities – benefit from a more inclusive, usable product.

4.1 Design Considerations

Communication Disabilities are Wide-Ranging. Whether building automatic speech recognition models, designing voice user interface features, or conducting user experience research, consider the needs of users not only with speech production disabilities, but those with language expression, comprehension, fluency, and co-occurring disabilities as well.

Voice User Interface Usability Extends Beyond Automatic Speech Recognition Accuracy. Metrics such as word error rate do not represent the holistic voice user interface experience. Include end users with speech and language disabilities in foundational and evaluative research to better understand their perspectives on voice user interface accessibility. Consider prioritizing usability testing in naturalistic environments, co-design, or participatory design methods to ensure users with disabilities are directly included in the product design process.

Users Expect Representation in Voice Output. As voice is tied to identity, consider the social implications of text-to-speech voices across products. When designing voice output, consider how users may have different expectations of voices depending on their goal. User expectations for the voice output of a voice assistant may be different from expectations for a reading tool or a communication application.

Speech and Language Needs Changes Over Time and Across Contexts. Users with speech and language disabilities may have difficulties that change in severity in certain times, environments, or social situations. Provide choices for customization that allow users to choose the settings or modalities that work best for them at any given time, preserving user independence and control.

Appropriate Error Handling Minimizes Fatigue for Users with Disabilities. For many users with speech and language disabilities, talking is tiring. Clearly identify issues and provide instructions for repair to prevent users from exerting extra effort repeating themselves through trial and error. Surface alternatives to voice input when appropriate.

Assistive Technology is Often not Used in Isolation. Users with disabilities utilize assistive technology to access the world. It is critical that voice assistive technologies are compatible with other voice technologies so that users with disabilities maintain independence and control. Consider users' technology ecosystem and how assistive technologies are integrated with voice input/output products.

4.2 Limitations and Future Work

While this study explored the experiences of users with speech and language disabilities using voice user interfaces, disability is just one dimension of the user experience. Future work should consider the intersectionality of additional user factors such as language,

age, or technology affinity, in addition to disability, to more holistically understand and design equitable, inclusive voice input and output technologies.

Additionally, more research is needed to ensure that voice technology realistically addresses the complex needs of users with multiple or changing disabilities – across severity, time, and contexts. Current literature including users with communication disabilities is limited, and the available literature does not clearly describe the severity or communication characteristics of the user groups included. Future product research should reflect this variance in communication disabilities to ensure that voice technology is usable for those who may have nuanced interaction needs depending on temporal, environmental, or social constraints. Including representative samples of end users with disabilities in VUI research is critical to centering users with disabilities in product research, design, and innovating alongside the disability community.

5 Conclusion

This systematic literature review identified themes describing the needs, pain points, and attitudes of users with speech and language disabilities using voice technology. While significant efforts have been made to improve the diversity of data included in automatic speech recognition models, usability issues around voice input, output, and system-level integration remain. These usability issues cause a cycle of frustration for users with communication disabilities, who often carry the burden of altering their own speech or language to interact with inaccessible voice input and output systems. As product teams continue to invest in voice user interfaces, it is critical that users with a wide range of communication disabilities are included in research and design so that all users can access communication, independence, and flexibility with voice technology.

Disclosure of Interests.   The authors have no competing interests to declare that are relevant to the content of this article.

References

1. ASHA Quick Facts. https://www.asha.org/about/press-room/quick-facts/. Accessed 06 Jan 2023
2. Ballati, F., et al.: Assessing virtual assistant capabilities with Italian dysarthric speech. In: Proceedings of the 20th International ACM SIGACCESS Conference on Computers and Accessibility (ASSETS 2018), pp. 93–101. Association for Computing Machinery, New York, NY, USA (2018)
3. Bleakley, A., et al.: Exploring smart speaker user experience for people who stammer. In: Proceedings of the 24th International ACM SIGACCESS Conference on Computers and Accessibility (ASSETS '22), pp. 1–10. Association for Computing Machinery, New York, NY, USA (2022)
4. Brady, N.C., et al.: Communication services and supports for individuals with severe disabilities: guidance for assessment and intervention. Am. J. Intellect. Dev. Disabil. **121**(2), 121–138 (2016)

5. Brewer, R., et al.: An empirical study of older adult's voice assistant use for health information seeking. ACM Trans. Interact. Intell. Syst. **12**(2), 1–32 (2022)

6. Cave, R., Bloch, S.: The use of speech recognition technology by people living with amyotrophic lateral sclerosis: a scoping review. Disabil. Rehabil. Assist. Technol. **18**(7), 1043–1055 (2021)

7. Cave, R., Bloch, S.: Voice banking for people living with motor neurone disease: views and expectations. Int. J. Lang. Commun. Disord. **56**(1), 116–129 (2020)

8. Clark, L., et al.: Speech diversity and speech interfaces: considering an inclusive future through stammering. In: Proceedings of the 2nd Conference on Conversational User Interfaces (CUI 2020), pp. 1–3. Association for Computing Machinery, New York, NY, USA (2020)

9. Duffy, O., et al.: Attitudes toward the use of voice-assisted technologies among people with Parkinson disease: findings from a web-based survey. JMIR Rehab. Assist. Technol. **8**(1), e23006 (2021)

10. Friedman, N., et al.: Voice assistant strategies and opportunities for people with tetraplegia. In: Proceedings of the 21st International ACM SIGACCESS Conference on Computers and Accessibility (ASSETS 2019), pp. 575–577. Association for Computing Machinery, New York, NY, USA (2019)

11. Glasser, A.T., et al.: Feasibility of using automatic speech recognition with voices of deaf and hard-of-hearing individuals. In: Proceedings of the 19th International ACM SIGACCESS Conference on Computers and Accessibility (ASSETS 2017), pp. 373–374. Association for Computing Machinery, New York, NY, USA (2017)

12. Hartmann, A.: What is AAC?. https://www.assistiveware.com/learn-aac/what-is-aac. Accessed 06 Jan 2023

13. Jefferson, M.: Usability of automatic speech recognition systems for individuals with speech disorders: past, present, future, and a proposed model. University of Minnesota Digital Conservancy (2019)

14. Kane, S.K., et al.: Sense and accessibility: Understanding people with physical disabilities' experiences with sensing systems. In: Proceedings of the 22nd International ACM SIGAC-CESS Conference on Computers and Accessibility (ASSETS 2020), pp. 1–14. Association for Computing Machinery, New York, NY, USA (2020)

15. Kbar, G., et al.: Assistive technologies for hearing and speaking impaired people: a survey. Disabil. Rehabil. Assist. Technol. **12**(1), 3–20 (2017)

16. Kinsella, B., Herndon, A.: Smart home consumer adoption report. Voicebot.ai (2022)

17. Kvikne, B., Berget, G.: "My words were completely gone" a qualitative study of the information seeking behaviour of people with aphasia. Inform. Res. **27**(1), 916 (2022)

18. Lea, C., et al.: Sep-28k: a dataset for stuttering event detection from podcasts with people who stutter. In: ICASSP 2021, IEEE International Conference on Acoustics, Speech, and Signal Processing, pp. 6798–6802. IEEE (2021)

19. Lewis, L., Vellino, A.: Helping persons with cognitive disabilities using voice-activated personal assistants. In: 8th International Conference on ICT & Accessibility (ICTA), pp. 1–3, Tunis, Tunisia (2021)

20. Li, S., et al.: When can I speak? Predicting initiation points for spoken dialogue agents. In: Proceedings of the 23rd Annual Meeting of the Special Interest Group on Discourse and Dialogue, pp 217–224. Association for Computational Linguistics, Edinburgh, UK (2022)

21. Mander, J., Buckle, C.: Voice search: a deep-dive into the consumer uptake of voice assistant technology. Global Web Index (2018)

22. Ngueajio, M.K., Washington, G.: Hey ASR system! What aren't you more inclusive? In: Chen, J.Y.C., Fragomeni, G., Degen, H., Ntoa, S. (eds.) HCI International 2022 - Late Breaking Papers: Interacting with extended Reality and Artificial Intelligence, HCII 2022, LNCS, vol. 13518, pp. 421–440. Springer, Cham (2022). https://doi.org/10.1007/978-3-031-21707-4_30

23. Patel, R., Threats, T.T.: One's voice: a central component of personal factors in augmentative and alternative communication. Perspect. ASHA Special Interest Groups 1(12), 94–98 (2016)
24. Pradhan, A., et al.: "Accessibility came by accident": use of voice-controlled intelligent personal assistants by people with disabilities. In: Proceedings of the 2018 CHI Conference on Human Factors in Computing Systems (CHI 2018), pp 1–13. Association for Computing Machinery, New York, NY, USA (2018)
25. Shane, H., Costello, J.: Augmentative communication assessment and the feature matching process. In: Mini-seminar presented at the Annual Convention of the American Speech Language Hearing Association, ASHA, New Orleans, LA (1994)
26. Sheikh, S.A., et al.: Machine learning for stuttering identification: review, challenges, and future directions. Neurocomputing 514(1), 385–402 (2022)
27. Skantze, G.: Turn-taking in conversational systems and human-robot interaction: a review. Comput. Speech Lang. 67, 1–26 (2021)
28. Speech accessibility project: coming together to expand voice recognition. https://speechaccessibilityproject.beckman.illinois.edu/. Accessed 06 Jan 2023
29. Tomanek, K., et al.: On-device personalization of automatic speech recognition models for disordered speech. arXiv preprint arXiv:2106.10259 (2021)
30. What is AT?. https://www.atia.org/home/at-resources/what-is-at/. Accessed 06 Jan 2023
31. Zack, A.H., Konyn, L.: How to talk about AAC and AAC users (according to them). https://www.assistiveware.com/blog/how-to-talk-about-aac. Accessed 06 Jan 2023

Visualizing the Road Ahead: Human-Centered Dashboard Design for an Individualized Driving Simulator

Isaiah Osborne[1]([⊠]), Abigale Plunk[2], Nathan Bolick[4], Siddhardha Chedella[4], Revanth Kommu[4], Drew Lickman[4], Warren Russell[4], Usman Saeed[4], Nilanjan Sarkar[1,2,3], and Medha Sarkar[4]

[1] Department of Computer Science, Vanderbilt University, Nashville, TN 37212, USA
isaiah.osborne@vanderbilt.edu
[2] Department of Electrical and Computer Engineering, Vanderbilt University, Nashville, TN 37212, USA
[3] Department of Mechanical Engineering, Vanderbilt University, Nashville, TN 37212, USA
[4] Department of Computer Science, Middle Tennessee State University, Murfreesboro, TN 37132, USA

Abstract. Obtaining a driver's license is pivotal for independence among teenagers and young adults, yet autistic individuals acquire their license less often and later than their non-autistic peers. This leads to decreased employment opportunities necessitating intervention. While existing studies have examined the complexities of driving challenges for autistic individuals, solutions are scarce. To address this gap, we developed a Simulator for Individualized and Adaptive Driving (SIAD). SIAD captures multimodal data that encapsulate driving performance and attention. In this work, we present a companion data visualization dashboard to provide driving therapists and autistic individuals insights into their attentional patterns and driving performance. We conducted a brief series of case studies involving autistic individuals driving in the simulator and a driving therapist. Feedback from these case studies informs ongoing refinement of the dashboard, demonstrating its potential to support driving education for autistic individuals.

Keywords: Driving Simulator · Autism · Dashboard

1 Introduction

Earning a driver's license is critical in gaining independence and autonomy for teenagers and young adults [2]. Deficits in motor skills and the ability to infer the thoughts and intentions of others make learning to drive more difficult for individuals with autism spectrum disorder (ASD) [1,9]. Due to these deficits, autistic [1] adolescents and young adults are less likely to obtain their driver's license

---

[1] We have chosen to use identity-first language (e.g., autistic individual) as opposed to person-first (e.g., individual with autism) because recent surveys of autistic self-advocates suggest a preference for identity-first language [10].

C. Stephanidis et al. (Eds.): HCII 2024, CCIS 2115, pp. 86–93, 2024.
https://doi.org/10.1007/978-3-031-61947-2_10

compared to their non-autistic peers. Fewer than 30% of driving-age autistic individuals are licensed to drive [2]. This, in turn, leads to fewer opportunities for employment making intervention critical [6,8,12]. Studies have investigated the complexities that lead to challenges the autistic population may face while driving, however, studies to overcome these barriers are limited. Current driving programs are not designed with neurodiversity in mind.

Advancements in virtual reality have enabled us to develop a diverse range of simulated driving scenarios, resulting in the ability to practice driving in a safe and controlled environment. In doing so, we have designed and developed an adaptable driving simulator that considers anxiety and different attention patterns of autistic individuals called the Simulator for Individualized and Adaptive Driving (SIAD) [11]. This driving simulator, which was developed in Unity, captures multimodal signals regarding both driver performance and attention. The multimodal data captured is summarized in Table 1. In the current work, our objective is to create a companion application that visualizes data collected from this driving simulator for the following purposes: (1) to provide driving therapists with quantitative insights into attention patterns and driving performance so they can be more informed as to why a person is driving the way they are and (2) to provide autistic individuals with their own attentional and performance data, allowing them the opportunity to potentially gain insights through review, either independently or with the assistance of a driving therapist.

Table 1. Mulitmodal data Collected by the driving simulator.

Modality	Units
Eye Gaze	x,y screen coordinates
Speed	Miles per Hour (MPH)
Wheel Rotation	Degrees (°)
Gas Pedal Force	Normalized value between 0 and 1
Brake Pedal Force	Normalized value between 0 and 1
Heart Rate	Beats per Minute (BPM)
Electrodermal Activity (EDA)	microSiemens

We designed a dashboard to allow autistic individuals and their driving therapists to review data collected with the driving simulator including gaze patterns and driving performance metrics. Our approach includes the systematic development process integrating technology tailored to the unique needs of autistic individuals learning to drive. We began by conducting a needs assessment involving consultations with experts in autism and driving education. This phase aimed to identify specific challenges faced by autistic individuals during driving and inform the design requirements for the dashboard. This dashboard facilitates comprehensive visualization and analysis of driving behaviors.

To test the value of this information, we carried out a short series of case studies wherein autistic individuals drove an introductory level in the simulator. After completing the level, the participants reviewed their performance in the dashboard and engaged in a qualitative interview with a researcher to discuss their experience. Evaluation metrics include the ease of use of the dashboard, its effectiveness in conveying driving-related insights, and feedback from both autistic individuals and a driving therapist.

2   Data Visualization Dashboard

To build the dashboard, we utilized Plotly, a Python data visualization library, and Plotly Dash, a Python-based web application development tool, to build our dashboard for the driving simulator study [5]. Plotly allowed us to create clear and interactive visual representations of the quantitative data from the simulator. Backend analysis and file manipulation are handled by Pandas, NumPy, and other standard Python libraries. Iterative design sessions ensured the incorporation of features sensitive to diverse attentional patterns and driving behaviors. The dashboard captures and interprets multimodal data streams generated during simulated driving sessions. Figure 1 shows example data visualizations. With its capabilities, we can present essential metrics effectively, making the data more accessible and user-friendly.

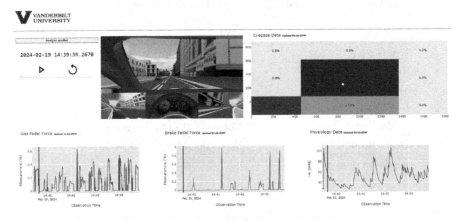

Fig. 1. Full view of the driving simulator dashboard including a screen recorded video, eye gaze plot, gas and brake plots, and physiology plot.

2.1   Eye Gaze Data

We collect eye gaze data with a Tobii Pro X3, which samples data at up to 120 Hz. The eye gaze visualization shows the percentage of time spent looking at each area of the screen, while also showing the live location of the participant's eye gaze as a scatter dot on top of the heatmap. This graph has higher latency and updates less frequently but also offers more information about the participant's eye gaze data. Figure 2 shows an example of the eye gaze plot in the dashboard.

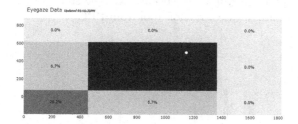

Fig. 2. Eyegaze Data Chart. The white dot shows the current X, Y coordinates the participant is looking at, while the heatmap shows the distribution of the participant's gaze.

2.2   Pedal Data

Pedal data is collected through a Logitech G920 wheel and pedals using their Unity SDK. The pedal data are normalized. A pedal value of 1 corresponds to pressing the pedal all the way down, and 0 corresponds to not touching the pedal. Therefore, spikes in either the gas or brake pedal typically correspond to unsmooth driving which can be dangerous and leads to increase wear on the vehicle. The pedal data is presented as a line graph in order to visualize the transitions between speeding up and slowing down as shown in Fig. 3.

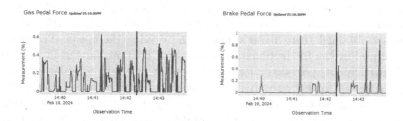

Fig. 3. Gas and Brake Pedal Force Chart. The two graphs are synced together, and the black line corresponds to the current time being analyzed.

2.3   Physiology

We collect physiology data using an EmotiBit, which is an open-source wearable physiological sensing platform [7]. The EmotiBit measures electrodermal activity (EDA), multi-wavelength photoplesmography (PPG) which can be used to derive heart rate (HR), skin temperature, and motion with a 9-axis IMU. Physiology can be used to predict affective states such as stress which is a cited adversity to driving for autistic individuals [3,4]. Therefore, incorporating physiology into the dashboard is critical. When loading the dashboard, one physiology modality is chosen to plot along with the gaze data, video, and pedal data. Figure 4 shows an example of a physiology graph, the specific example shows HR which is derived using EmotiBit's standard conversion tool from PPG.

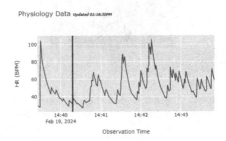

Fig. 4. Heart Rate Chart. The black line corresponds to the current time being analyzed.

3   Case Studies

We hypothesized that (a) driving data including pedal information, eye gaze, and physiology would be feasible and suitable for visualization within the dashboard; (b) autistic individuals and driving therapists would find initial value in the components of the dashboard; and (c) qualitative feedback from autistic individuals and driving therapists would reveal new insights into more effective ways to present information in the dashboard. To test these hypotheses, we conducted a small series of case studies with autistic individuals who have previously obtained their driver's license and driving therapists. The research was approved by the Institutional Review Board (IRB) at Vanderbilt University and all participants provided informed consent or assent in accordance with the requirements set forth by the IRB. Personnel conducting the sessions had several years of experience performing human subjects research involving autistic individuals and were well-equipped to address accommodations that might have arisen during the sessions.

3.1   Feedback from Autistic Individuals

Four autistic adults, all licensed drivers, participated in the study. After consent, the participants began driving in the driving simulator. All participants drove two onboarding levels to familiarize themselves with the gas and brake pedals before driving in a 5-minute guided drive through a city. Throughout the guided drive, they were required to turn left and right at stoplights, yield to pedestrians, slow down for a school zone with a school bus loading students, and carefully pass a broken-down vehicle. Afterward, researchers loaded the data collected during the guided drive into the dashboard data visualization. Then, the researcher and participant engaged in a qualitative interview to discuss the dashboard visualization. All participants completed the study without any adverse events or loss of data.

The four participants had varied levels of driving experience. All four received their license between the ages of 16 and 18, but one soon quit driving and hasn't driven in years since. None of the four had an official driver's training course and thought the simulator with the accompanying data visualization dashboard would have been a helpful tool when learning. Despite varying driving experiences, common themes emerged regarding the dashboard's strengths and areas for growth. Participants appreciated the clarity and comprehensiveness of the visualizations, particularly the ability to track eye gaze patterns and physiological responses. None of the participants found the visualizations to be overwhelming. However, one participant did note that adding an information/help screen about each of the visualizations could help with initial understanding. All participants found that the dashboard was well organized, presented information clearly, and could potentially help guide new drivers.

There were a few notable suggestions for improving the dashboard. One person suggested placing the gaze heatmap on top of the video so it was more clear what each area mapped to. Additionally, it was suggested to show anxiety/stress levels based on physiology rather than the raw physiology signal as not everyone would know what it means. One participant suggested having scrolling plots rather than showing the entire level with a line indicating the time. The participants also recommended other metrics that would be beneficial for neurodivergent drivers, including respiration rate, grip strength, and the positioning of their hands on the steering wheel. These insights highlighted the value of the visualizations in supporting diverse driving needs.

3.2 Feedback from Driving Therapist

We conducted an in-depth qualitative discussion about the dashboard with a certified driver rehabilitation therapist who has extensive experience in supporting autistic individuals in learning to drive. The driving therapist found the dashboard's visualizations and metrics to be easy to comprehend and visually appealing. They particularly liked that the graphics were large, and there were not too many of them which would risk making it overwhelming. Additionally, they found the drag feature to be a nice addition. They emphasized the potential usefulness of the eye gaze features which could be used to identify errors during coaching sessions. One point for improvement was to make the y-axis of the pedal plots fixed between 0 and 1 as it is currently confusing since it can be inconsistent between drivers as the axes dynamically adjust based on the minimum and maximum value. Additionally, they suggested integrating error detection into the simulator and dashboard so they can isolate the data around these errors to identify mistakes and highlight areas for improvement. The coach acknowledged the dashboard's potential for guiding new drivers but underscored the need for future development. They recommended adding a plot selection tool to allow focus on one plot at a time to prevent overwhelming new drivers. The therapist provided critical insights into the visualization's strengths while isolating areas that still need to be refined.

4   Discussion and Conclusion

Feedback from autistic drivers and driving therapists supported our hypotheses that (a) driving data including pedal information, eye gaze, and physiology would be feasible and suitable for visualization within the dashboard; (b) autistic individuals and driving therapists would find initial value in the components of the dashboard; and (c) qualitative feedback from autistic individuals and driving therapists would reveal new insights into more effective ways to present information in the dashboard.

First, we demonstrated that driving data is suitable for visualization by developing a dashboard in Python using Plotly. Next, in a small feasibility study, we found that all of our participants found value in the dashboard and thought it would have helped them when learning to drive. Finally, valuable insights were made into how we can improve the dashboard. For example, it was suggested that we make the y-axis of the plots consistent and that we embed an error detection system so we can see what is happening when errors are made.

While the current study validates the usefulness of a personalized dashboard within the SIAD framework, future research is needed to further refine individualization strategies. Based off of the feedback and suggestions from our autistic individuals and driving coaches, we want to explore methods to tailor intervention strategies based on the diverse cognitive profiles and behavioral characteristics of autistic individuals, focusing on providing easily interpreted measures of stress. This could involve developing algorithms or decision support systems within the dashboard framework to recommend personalized coaching strategies based on real-time analysis of physiology data, grip data, or eye-gaze data. Using this real-time analysis, we would like to establish a mechanism for direct user feedback within the dashboard interface, extending the dashboard to provide more directly actionable feedback for autistic individuals and driving instructors. This feedback loop would empower autistic individuals and driving therapists to provide input on the efficacy and relevance of the dashboard's personalized features, contributing to continuous improvement of the SIAD framework.

References

1. Cox, S.M., et al.: Driving simulator performance in novice drivers with autism spectrum disorder: the role of executive functions and basic motor skills. J. Autism Dev. Disord. **46**(4), 1379–1391 (2016). https://doi.org/10.1007/s10803-015-2677-1

2. Curry, A.E., Yerys, B.E., Huang, P., Metzger, K.B.: Longitudinal study of driver licensing rates among adolescents and young adults with autism spectrum disorder. Autism: Int. J. Res. Pract. **22**(4), 479–488 (May 2018). https://doi.org/10.1177/1362361317699586

3. Fok, M., Owens, J.M., Ollendick, T.H., Scarpa, A.: Perceived driving difficulty, negative affect, and emotion dysregulation in self-identified autistic emerging drivers. Front. Psychol. **13** (2022). https://www.frontiersin.org/journals/psychology/articles/10.3389/fpsyg.2022.754776

4. Healey, J., Picard, R.: Detecting stress during real-world driving tasks using physiological sensors. IEEE Trans. Intell. Transport. Syst. **6**(2), 156–166 (Jun 2005). https://doi.org/10.1109/TITS.2005.848368, http://ieeexplore.ieee.org/document/1438384/

5. Inc., P.T.: Collaborative data science (2015). https://plot.ly

6. Kersten, M., Coxon, K., Lee, H., Wilson, N.J.: Independent community mobility and driving experiences of adults on the autism spectrum: a scoping review. Am. J. Occup. Therapy: Off. Public. Am. Occup. Therapy Assoc. **74**(5), 7405205140p1–7405205140p17 (2020). https://doi.org/10.5014/ajot.2020.040311

7. Montgomery, S.M., Nair, N., Chen, P., Dikker, S.: Introducing EmotiBit, an open-source multi-modal sensor for measuring research-grade physiological signals. Sci. Talks **6**, 100181 (May 2023). https://doi.org/10.1016/j.sctalk.2023.100181, https://www.sciencedirect.com/science/article/pii/S2772569323000567

8. Myers, E., Davis, B.E., Stobbe, G., Bjornson, K.: Community and social participation among individuals with autism spectrum disorder transitioning to adulthood. J. Autism Dev. Disord. **45**(8), 2373–2381 (2015). https://doi.org/10.1007/s10803-015-2403-z

9. Sheppard, E., van Loon, E., Ropar, D.: Dimensions of self-reported driving difficulty in autistic and non-autistic adults and their relationship with autistic traits. J. Autism Dev. Disord. **53**(1), 285–295 (2023). https://doi.org/10.1007/s10803-021-05420-y

10. Taboas, A., Doepke, K., Zimmerman, C.: Preferences for identity-first versus person-first language in a US sample of autism stakeholders. Autism: Int. J. Res. Pract. **27**(2), 565–570 (Feb 2023). https://doi.org/10.1177/13623613221130845

11. Wade, J., et al.: A pilot study assessing performance and visual attention of teenagers with ASD in a novel adaptive driving simulator. J. Autism Develop. Disorders **47**(11), 3405–3417 (Nov 2017). https://doi.org/10.1007/s10803-017-3261-7, https://www.ncbi.nlm.nih.gov/pmc/articles/PMC5693648/

12. Zalewska, A., Migliore, A., Butterworth, J.: Self-determination, social skills, job search, and transportation: Is there a relationship with employment of young adults with autism? J. Vocational Rehab. **45**(3), 225–239 (Nov 2016). https://doi.org/10.3233/JVR-160825, https://www.medra.org/servlet/aliasResolver?alias=iospress&doi=10.3233/JVR-160825

Serious Games Created for Cognitive Rehabilitation: A Systematic Review

Carlos Ramos-Galarza[1]([envelope]) [iD], Patricia García-Cruz[2] [iD],
and Mónica Bolaños-Pasquel[1] [iD]

[1] Centro de Investigación en Mecatrónica y Sistemas Interactivos - MIST, Facultad de Psicología, Universidad Tecnológica Indoamérica, Quito, Ecuador
carlosramos@uti.edu.ec

[2] Facultad de Psicología, Pontificia Universidad Católica del Ecuador, Quito, Ecuador

Abstract. Cognitive rehabilitation is a process by which people who have suffered some type of brain impairment recover their mental abilities. This type of treatment has classically been carried out with concrete materials of pencil and paper, however, currently the use of technology has provided a significant contribution to improve the motivation and interest of patients involved in this process. In this research, a systematic review of the main studies that have generated some type of technology for the cognitive stimulation and rehabilitation process was carried out. In the collection of studies, 24 published articles were found that allowed understanding aspects such as sample size, age, gender, countries, continents, type of interventions and the main technological developments that have been developed in recent years in favor of cognitive stimulation and rehabilitation. The results are discussed in relation to the importance of conducting this type of studies in favor of the treatment processes and the need to improve the quality of the treatment process.

Keywords: Cognitive rehabilitation · technological innovation · systematic review · virtual reality · neuropsychology

1 Introduction

The process of cognitive rehabilitation involves activities aimed at helping a human being who has suffered brain damage [1]. They include strategies such as restoration, compensation or substitution of mental abilities in order for the subject to recover the brain functions affected by the deficit suffered [2]. Restoration consists in the stimulation and re-building of the affected function, in compensation a preserved brain function takes over the role of a damaged one and substitution is based on external resources used to take over the damaged brain function [3]. There is a wide variety of pencil-and-paper tools that the clinician can use in all three of these strategies; however, recently there has been significant interest in including technological devices to aid in the neuropsychological therapy process [4].

Cognitive rehabilitation is part of the development of neuropsychology, because, thanks to advances and discoveries about the conditions of psychological processes, areas

C. Stephanidis et al. (Eds.): HCII 2024, CCIS 2115, pp. 94–103, 2024.
https://doi.org/10.1007/978-3-031-61947-2_11

of the brain and their functions, techniques were generated to rehabilitate these areas [5]. Since the Second World War, it was possible to learn more about cognitive rehabilitation; the most prominent authors in its beginnings were Kurt Goldstein, Alexander Luria, Richie Russell, Henry Head, Henri Hecaen, because they incorporated the importance of taking several factors and approaches when rehabilitating people, beyond physical rehabilitation [6].

Throughout the world a significant percentage of people suffer brain damage. According to the Spanish Federation of Brain Injury, there are more than 435,400 people with Acquired Brain Injury [7]. On the other hand, approximately 1.7 million people in the United States have a diagnosis of brain damage [8]. The consequences that people with a brain injury have to experience are physical, mental and sensory, which can trigger other problems that both patients and their families must face, which is why the cost of living of these people and their families is significant.

The population that benefits from cognitive rehabilitation has to do with acquired brain damage produced by various causes such as traumatic brain injury, brain tumors, nervous system infections, cerebrovascular disease, nervous system immaturity, among other causes of clinical interest [9]. This type of affectation produces a series of neuropsychological disorders known as: agnosia, apraxia, amnesia, aphasia, frontal syndrome, attentional disturbances, mood difficulties, learning problems, behavioral and cognitive disorders [10].

In the cognitive rehabilitation process there are classically developed elements to be used with pencil, paper and the use of concrete materials. For example, puzzles, cubes, worksheets to locate elements, incomplete drawings, copying text or graphics, reproduction of towers, use of tools, among other elements, are used. In recent years, technological development has become important in neuropsychological rehabilitation and nowadays web pages, applications for smartphones, electronic devices and others have been developed, which make the treatment process more attractive [11].

The use of technology in the context of neuropsychological rehabilitation generates several positive aspects, for example, (a) it increases patient motivation, (b) it generates greater interest in performing cognitive exercises, (c) it is possible to configure the exercises to the patient's level of functioning, (d) there is a wide variety of proposals, (e) it is possible to use characters that are to the patient's liking, among other benefits of technology for the treatment of human beings with some type of brain alteration [12].

Many people around the world have a diagnosis of Brain Injury that has affected their cognitive functions and quality of life. In the same way, due to the increase in this and other diagnoses that deteriorate the development and cognitive functions of people, it is important to discover accessible and innovative ways that can favor both the evaluation and the forms of intervention of cognitive rehabilitation. We hope that this research provides more information and sources that help the treatment of more people.

2 Method

2.1 Research Design

In this research we worked on a systematic review of games that have been applied for psychological treatments with humans. The present research was carried out by means of a systematic review methodology of the collection of 24 academic articles [13–36]. Figure 1 describes the method and process followed in this research.

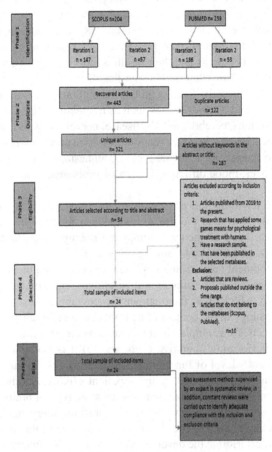

Fig. 1. Flow Chart of Methodology

3 Results

In the present systematic review, 24 scientific articles were obtained from different prestigious health journals. In each of the articles, information was obtained about different games that are used to cognitively rehabilitate different types of populations, being some instruments used for the evaluation of the effects of rehabilitation and other games used for intervention.

4 Sample Size

In the 24 investigations, a minimum of 7 participants were found in the effectiveness testing of the different game models and a maximum participation of 1139 people. From these values, a mean of 111.33 and a standard deviation of 227.03 were obtained. These values can be seen in Fig. 2.

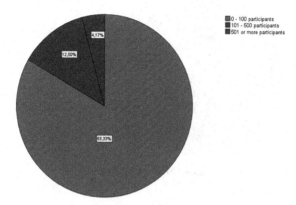

Fig. 2. Sample Size

4.1 Age of Participants

The participants who took part in the different investigations belonged to different age ranges, with the youngest persons being 9 years old and the oldest persons 89 years old. The mean age of the participants was 43.79 and the standard deviation was 23.01 (Fig. 3).

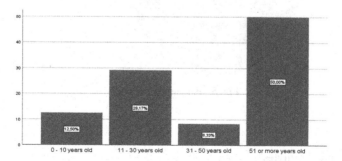

Fig. 3. Age of participants

4.2 Gender of Participants

In the research, 2 genders were found to participate, who were mostly male with a minimum of 3 males and a maximum of 831 participants, whose mean is 56.25 and standard deviation is 165.49. The following information can be seen in Fig. 4.

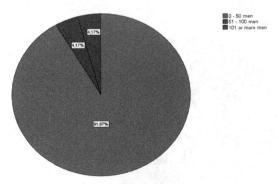

Fig. 4. Male Participants

On the other hand, the investigations found a minimum of 3 women who participated and a maximum of 308 women, with a mean of 49.83 and a standard deviation of 61.50. The following information can be seen in Fig. 5.

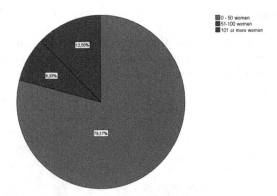

Fig. 5. Female Participants

4.3 Research Countries

When analyzing all the research, it was observed that there is a great deal of interest in this topic around the world, with the United States being the country with the most games and studies that favor cognitive rehabilitation, followed by Canada, Brazil and Mexico. This information can be seen in Fig. 6.

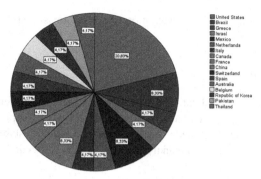

Fig. 6. Research Countries

According to these data, the continent with the most research on games that favor cognitive rehabilitation was America with 45.82%, followed by Europe with 29.16% and Asia with 20.85%. This information can be seen in Fig. 7.

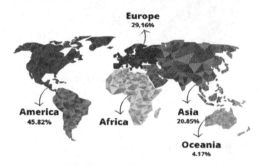

Fig. 7. Research Continents

4.4 Types of Applications

According to the data obtained in the different investigations, two main forms of application of these games in cognitive rehabilitation are recognized. Most of them are applied

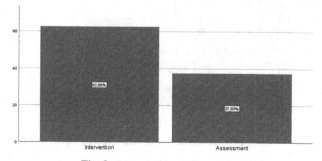

Fig. 8. Intervention & Assessment

for intervention and others for the evaluation of the progress or state of rehabilitation. Figure 8 shows these data.

4.5 Time Intervention

In relation to the time of application of the different games, a difference of weeks is evident. Most of the studies established a time of up to 1 week of application, however, there are other researches that made more longitudinal studies establishing more than 6 weeks for the application and the analysis of the effects. This can be seen in Fig. 9.

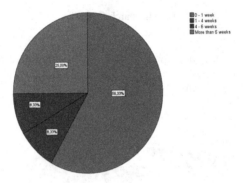

Fig. 9. Time Intervention

4.6 Technological Devices Developed

When analyzing the proposed technological developments, it was found that 7 studies developed virtual reality, 5 proposed computerized evaluations, 6 proposed neuropsychological stimulation platforms, 5 proposed serious video games and 1 study proposed mobile applications. Figure 10 shows the percentages of this result.

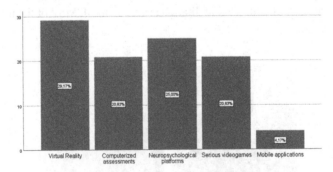

Fig. 10. Technological Devices Developed

5   Conclusions

In this research, a systematic review of the main studies that have generated some type of technology for the cognitive stimulation and rehabilitation process was carried out. In the collection of studies, 24 published articles were found that allowed understanding aspects such as sample sizes, age, gender, countries, continents, type of interventions and the main technological developments that have been developed in recent years in favor of cognitive stimulation and rehabilitation.

Among the main results found in the systematic review, the following can be highlighted: (a) the age group that most receives technological research in favor of cognitive stimulation is the elderly (51 years of age or older), (b) men are the ones who most receive technological innovations, (c) in terms of countries, the United States is the place where most research is conducted in this type of studies and (d) the main technological development has to do with the use of virtual reality and technological platforms for neuropsychological stimulation.

For mental health professionals in the clinical area, this study provides relevant information to innovate the way of evaluating and rehabilitating patients with cognitive disorders. In addition, being interactive games, they can be used with different age groups, from children to older adults. On the other hand, since most of the games have a short application time, the cognitive rehabilitation processes can be more agile and efficient, and since they are games that can be used for more than one occasion, it helps accessibility both for the psychologists who apply them and for the patients.

The main limitation of this work that should be highlighted is the fact that we do not have access to all the articles published in this line of research, especially the papers that must be paid for in order to download them; however, with the authors' university affiliation accounts we were able to access the studies included in this work.

As future research, we plan to carry out new studies in which we will perform meta-analysis of the results found in the different investigations and thus determine a statistical index of improvement of the technological innovation developed. In addition, we are interested in making a technological proposal to be applied in Latin American population that suffers some kind of alteration in their cognitive functioning.

References

1. Ramos-Galarza, C., et al.: Fundamental concepts in the neuropsychological theory. Revista Ecuatoriana de Neurología, **26** (1), 53–60, (2017). https://revecuatneurol.com/magazine_issue_article/conceptos-fundamentales-en-la-teoria-neuropsicologica-fundamental-concepts-neuropsychological-theory/
2. Ramos-Galarza, C., Benavides-Endara, P., Bolaños-Pasquel, M., Fonseca-Bautista, S., Ramos, D.: Scale of clinical observation to evaluate the third functional unit of the Luria theory: EOCL-1. Revista Ecuatoriana de Neurología. **28** (2), 83–91 (2019). https://revecuatneurol.com/wp-content/uploads/2019/10/2631-2581-rneuro-28-02-00083.pdf
3. Chantsoulis, M., Mirski, A., Kropotov, J., Pachalska, M.: Neuropsychological rehabilitation for traumatic brain injury patients. Ann. Agric. Environ. Med. **22**(2), 373–384 (2015)
4. Ramos-Galarza, C., Acosta-Rodas, M., Sánchez-Gordón, S., Calle-Jiménez, T.: Mobile technological apps to improve frontal lobe functioning. Adv. Intell. Syst. Comput. **1201**, 89–93 (2021). https://doi.org/10.1007/978-3-030-51041-1_13

5. Rufo-Campos, M.: La neuropsicología: historia, Revista de neurología, vol. 43, no. 1, pp. 57–58 (2006)
6. Mateer, C.A.: Introducción a la Rehabilitación Cognitiva, Avances en Psicología Clínica Latinoamericana, vol. 21, pp. 11–20 (2003)
7. FEDACE: Federación Española de Daño Cerebral. 2022. https://fedace.org/cifras_dano_cerebral
8. Georges, J.M.D.: National library of medicine. 2 January 2023. https://www.ncbi.nlm.nih.gov/books/NBK459300/
9. Wilson, B.: Neuropsychological rehabilitation: state of the science. S. Afr. J. Psychol. **43**(3), 267–277 (2013). https://doi.org/10.1177/0081246313494156
10. Silva-Barragán, M., Ramos-Galarza, C.: Brain organization models: a neuropsychological journey. Revista Ecuatoriana de Neurología **29**(3), 74–83 (2020). https://doi.org/10.46997/revecuatneurol29300074
11. Ramos-Galarza, C., Arias-Flores, H., Cóndor-Herrera, O., Jadán-Guerrero, J.: Literacy toy for enhancement phonological awareness: a longitudinal study. In: Miesenberger, K., Manduchi, R., Covarrubias Rodriguez, M., Peňáz, P. (eds.) ICCHP 2020. LNCS, vol. 12377, pp. 371–377. Springer, Cham (2020). https://doi.org/10.1007/978-3-030-58805-2_44
12. Gaibor-Estévez, J., Ramos-Galarza, C.: Neuropsychological analysis of a case with anosognosia. Rev. Chil. Neuropsiquiatr. **58**(3), 294–299 (2020). https://doi.org/10.4067/S0717-92272020000300294
13. Kozora, E., Zell, J.L., Baraghoshi, D., Smith, R.M., Strand, M.: Improved executive function in patients with systemic lupus erythematosus following interactive digital training. Lupus **31**(8), 910–920 (2022)
14. Goulart, A.A., et al.: Comparison of digital games as a cognitive function assessment tool for current standardized neuropsychological tests. Braz. J. Anesthesiol. (English Ed.) **72**(1), 13–20 (2022)
15. Lucatelli, A., et al.: Assessment of a digital game as a neuropsychological test for postoperative cognitive dysfunction. Braz. J. Anesthesiol. (English Ed.) **72**(1), 7–12 (2022)
16. Iliadou, P., Paliokas, I., Zygouris, S., Lazarou, E., Votis, K., Tzovaras, D., et al.: A comparison of traditional and serious game-based digital markers of cognition in older adults with mild cognitive impairment and healthy controls. J. Alzheimer's Dis. **79**(4), 1747–1759 (2021)
17. Menascu, S., Aloni, R., Dolev, M., Magalashvili, D., Gutman, K., Dreyer-Alster, S., et al.: Targeted cognitive game training enhances cognitive performance in multiple sclerosis patients treated with interferon beta 1-a. J. NeuroEng. Rehabil. **18**(1), 1–8 (2021)
18. Gómez-Tello, M.F., Rosetti, M.F., Galicia-Alvarado, M., Maya, C., Apiquian, R.: Neuropsychological screening with TOWI: performance in 6- to 12-year-old children. Appl. Neuropsychol. Child **11**(2), 1–10 (2022)
19. Rosetti, M.F., Gómez-Tello, M.F., Maya, C., Apiquian, R.: Feasibility of TOWI as a cognitive training video game for children. Int. J. Child-Comput. Interact. **25**, 100172 (2020)
20. Van De Weijer, S.C.F., Duits, A.A., Bloem, B.R., De Vries, N.M., Kessels, R.P.C., Köhler, S., et al.: Feasibility of a cognitive training game in Parkinson's disease: the randomized Parkin'play study. Eur. Neurol. **83**(4), 426–432 (2020)
21. Pitteri, M., Dapor, C., Ziccardi, S., Guandalini, M., Meggiato, R., Calabrese, M.: Visual-attentional load unveils slowed processing speed in multiple sclerosis patients: a pilot study with a tablet-based videogame. Brain Sci. **10**(11), 871 (2020)
22. Tong, T., Chignell, M., DeGuzman, C.A.: Using a serious game to measure executive functioning: response inhibition ability. Appl. Neuropsychol. Adult **28**(6), 673–684 (2021)
23. Benoit, J.J., Roudaia, E., Johnson, T., Love, T., Faubert, J.: The neuropsychological profile of professional action video game players. PeerJ **8**, e10211 (2020)

24. Burdea, G.C., Grampurohit, N., Kim, N., Polistico, K., Kadaru, A., Pollack, S., et al.: Feasibility of integrative games and novel therapeutic game controller for telerehabilitation of individuals chronic post-stroke living in the community. Topics Stroke Rehab. **27**(5), 321–336 (2020)
25. Perrot, A., Maillot, P., Hartley, A.: Cognitive training game versus action videogame: effects on cognitive functions in older adults. Games Health J. **8**(1), 35–40 (2019)
26. Pin, T.W., Butler, P.B.: The effect of interactive computer play on balance and functional abilities in children with moderate cerebral palsy: a pilot randomized study. Clin. Rehab. **33**(4), 704–710 (2019)
27. Bove, R.M., Rush, G., Zhao, C., Rowles, W., Garcha, P., Morrissey, J., et al.: A videogame-based digital therapeutic to improve processing speed in people with multiple sclerosis: a feasibility study. Neurol. Ther. **8**(1), 135–145 (2019)
28. Boivin, M.J., Sikorskii, A., Nakasujja, N., Ruiseñor-Escudero, H., Familiar-Lopez, I., Opoka, R.O., et al.: Evaluating immunopathogenic biomarkers during severe malaria illness as modifiers of the neuropsychologic benefits of computer cognitive games rehabilitation in Ugandan children. Pediatr. Infect. Dis. J. **38**(8), 840–848 (2019)
29. Nef, T., Chesham, A., Schütz, N., Botros, A.A., Vanbellingen, T., Burgunder, J.M., et al.: Development and evaluation of maze-like puzzle games to assess cognitive and motor function in aging and neurodegenerative diseases. Front. Aging Neurosci. **12**, 87 (2020)
30. Faust, M.E., Multhaup, K.S., Ong, M.S., Demakis, G.J., Balz, K.G.: Exploring the specificity, synergy, and durability of auditory and visual computer gameplay transfer effects in healthy older adults. J. Gerontol. Psychol. Sci. Soc. Sci. **75**(6), 1170–1180 (2020)
31. Palaus, M., Viejo-Sobera, R., Redolar-Ripoll, D., Marrón, E.M.: Cognitive enhancement via neuromodulation and video games: synergistic effects? Front. Hum. Neuroscie. **14**(235), 539373 (2020)
32. McCord, A., Cocks, B., Barreiros, A.R., Bizo, L.A.: Short video game play improves executive function in the oldest old living in residential care. Comput. Hum. Behav. **108**, 106337 (2020)
33. Bellens, A., Roelant, E., Sabbe, B., Peeters, M., van Dam, P.: A video-game based cognitive training for breast cancer survivors with cognitive impairment: a prospective randomized pilot trial. Breast **53**, 23–32 (2020)
34. Song, H., Yi, D.J., Park, H.J.: Validation of a mobile game-based assessment of cognitive control among children and adolescents. PloS One **15**, e0230498 (2020)
35. Amjad, I., Toor, H., Niazi, I.K., Pervaiz, S., Jochumsen, M., Shafique, M., et al.: Xbox 360 Kinect cognitive games improve slowness, complexity of EEG, and cognitive functions in subjects with mild cognitive impairment: a randomized control trial. Games Health J. **8**(2), 144–152 (2019)
36. Jirayucharoensak, S., Israsena, P., Pan-Ngum, S., Hemrungrojn, S., Maes, M.: A game-based neurofeedback training system to enhance cognitive performance in healthy elderly subjects and in patients with amnestic mild cognitive impairment. Clin. Interv. Aging. **14**, 347–360 (2019)

Enhancing Affordance Through the Use of Sign Language in Virtual Reality

Gapyuel Seo[✉]

Hongik University, Sejong 30016, South Korea
gapseo@hongik.ac.kr

Abstract. In this paper, we introduce the usage of sign language in a virtual reality game that can strengthen affordance by making important information, cues, or instructions perceptible to general players as well as those who rely on sign language as a primary means of communication. The use of sign language gestures in a game can be considered a way of strengthening affordance, particularly in the context of accessibility. Affordance refers to the perceived and potential actions that players can take with an entity or within an environment. Strengthening affordance involves making these potential actions more apparent and easily understood by players. In this study, we suggested various sign language gesture hints through the agent that can provide potential actions that are more apparent and easily understood by players to induce natural progression. We implemented sign language gestures that represent the nine actions and six emotional expressions that players need to solve puzzles and explore to progress through the game. These sign language gestures help players identify puzzle elements. Players can decide on a specific puzzle or task and understand and put into action the essential elements or steps needed to solve a puzzle. We suggest the broader concept of enhancing affordance through the use of sign language gestures, where games are designed to be playable by all people, to the greatest extent possible, without the need for adaptation or specialized design.

Keywords: Virtual Reality Game · Affordance · Sign Language

1 Introduction

The development of virtual reality technology is evolving into a way in which information is delivered through more active participation and intuitive interaction of users. Virtual reality is a new medium of technological advancement, and much research is being done to find a more popular and effective method of communication. It is recognized for its expansion potential as a new communication method that combines rapidly developing digital technology, artificial intelligence, and video technology. In virtual reality, users wear a head-mounted display (HMD) to focus on what the virtual environment provides and become immersed by excluding external stimuli from the physical environment. In other words, the player can only see the virtual world by completely blocking the real world by covering the field of view with the HMD and can maximize immersion by

C. Stephanidis et al. (Eds.): HCII 2024, CCIS 2115, pp. 104–110, 2024.
https://doi.org/10.1007/978-3-031-61947-2_12

interacting with the provided sensory information and feeling as if the virtual world is real. Unlike the passive attitude of unilaterally accepting information, users of virtual reality have the characteristic of being able to actively participate and interact with situations and events as in reality. The user's active participation leads to the stage of immersion in virtual reality, and immersion can lead to a sense of presence that gives the player the experience of actually existing in the virtual world [1, 2]. This sense of presence leads to the complete immersion stage through perceptual and psychological immersion through the experiencer's natural interaction [3]. Immersion through natural interaction in virtual reality means forgetting oneself and forming realistic beliefs in the virtual world by performing a role with a new identity acquired through empathy with others [4]. In order to realize the highly immersive environment pursued by virtual reality, behavioral induction for natural interaction is essential to achieve the fusion of the user's various senses and perceptions. In particular, virtual reality games require a design that induces user action for efficient and smooth progress based on real-time interaction. Virtual reality games allow users to experience the intended story through user interaction. To achieve this, they must be able to satisfy the need for information while remaining faithful to the sensory experience elements of immersion and experience. In addition, there is an essential goal in planning to solve manipulation and control problems through natural user interaction. However, there is a lack of research on users' flexibility with physical difficulties in virtual reality games. In game production, there is a need for a design that can accommodate a wide range of personal preferences, disabilities, and abilities so that even users with physical limitations can induce natural behavior by providing smooth information.

This study aims to explore the use of sign language gestures in a virtual reality game to enhance affordance. These gestures can strengthen affordance by making important information, cues, or instructions perceptible to general players as well as those who rely on sign language as a primary means of communication.

2 Affordance

Virtual reality maximizes immersion by making users feel as if they are experiencing it themselves based on sensory information processing such as seeing, hearing, and feeling through the user's active participation. In particular, in immersive virtual reality games to enhance such experiences, the affordances of interaction design that mediate between the user and the virtual space are more important than anything else. Affordance is the delivery of information using text, images, graphic symbols, and metaphors to convey meaning or purpose in a way that users can easily understand without being controlled by restrictive language [5, 6]. Norman studied the interaction between humans and the environment by focusing on the concept of 'user-centered design' through affordance theory. The importance of affordances is also growing in immersive virtual reality environments where users' natural interactions must be encouraged, and actions required to progress the story must be predicted. He classified affordances into physical and cognitive affordances according to the characteristics of helping users decide and perform actions. Physical affordances are characteristics that help and encourage the user to perform specific physical actions. Cognitive affordances help users recognize what is happening and predict the results of their actions [7]. Hartson classified the affordances that appear in interaction design into four types. These are physical affordances that help users perform physical actions with an interface, cognitive affordances that help them know something, sensory affordances that help them perceive things with their senses and functional affordances that help them accomplish specific tasks [8]. Even in virtual reality, users must be designed to perceive information provided by cognitive affordances, naturally understand physical affordances, and achieve their goals by supporting sensory and functional affordances [9]. These affordances can form a complementary relationship, leading to effective exploration and interaction with the virtual environment. Virtual reality games are real-time-based digital media that are played by interacting with the environment through the user's direct actions. In games where users interact with virtual objects in real-time, creating a virtual environment with realistic affordances is necessary to induce actions similar to those in the real world. Affordance-based interaction design is essential in shaping the user's interaction with virtual objects and environments, thereby designing virtual reality games that provide a more intuitive and attractive experience, increasing user immersion and satisfaction.

3   Agency Affordance

Characters serve as agencies that help the story flow in the virtual environment. Agencies are classified into agents and avatars depending on the controlling entity. An agent is an entity controlled by a computer. An avatar is an entity that a player can control in real time [10, 11]. In a virtual environment, an avatar is a character that a player can control. Players must sympathize with the virtual character that drives the story's progress and create the illusion of becoming a character in the story. An avatar in a virtual reality space establishes an individual's presence and can construct self-consciousness by expressing various facial expressions, movements, and physical abilities in real-time. In particular, players can embodied interact realistically through avatars in virtual reality. It allows you to express and perform yourself through a wide range of communication modalities, including verbal and nonverbal interactions such as voice, gestures, gaze, facial expressions, and movement in a 3D virtual space. Agent refers to a character or object controlled by a computer algorithm and refers to an animal or human that exists in a virtual environment. In addition to language, gestures, and facial expressions, these agents include autonomous movement and environmental interaction [12]. Autonomous agents, also a research field in artificial intelligence, are becoming active research activities as the number of research groups increases [13]. In particular, agents with human anatomy can now communicate naturally with players through conversation or nonverbal communication. Agents suitable for virtual reality situations must be created and deployed to help players progress through the story more smoothly and increase their understanding of the situation. In particular, nonverbal communication theory can be used to communicate smoothly with agents. Nonverbal communication is communication using methods other than language. It is a theory that various nonverbal communication elements can increase engagement and create effective communication [14]. The player can mediate the inner and outer world while performing nonverbal communication through agency and can be visualized as a virtual object and become an object of control. Players have perspectives on themselves and others regarding technologically mediated objects, and as subjects of virtual reality, they experience and acquire knowledge and form their own identities [15]. Through agency in the virtual world, we not only play a role in self-performance but can also feel a sense of social presence and guide our actions.

4 Nonverbal Communication

We rely more on nonverbal means, such as body language and facial expressions than verbal messages In communication [16]. Many studies have also shown that the proportion of nonverbal communication in actual communication situations is much more significant than that of verbal communication [17, 18]. Nonverbal communication is communication in a way other than language, which is the theory that various non-verbal communication elements can increase immersion and create effective communication. The character's physical appearance and kinesics are important elements of nonverbal communication. The physical appearance of a character can be thought of as face, body shape, height, hairstyle, costume and ornaments of a character, and kinesics of a character are gestures, facial expression, and voice. In particular, nonverbal communication theory can be used for smooth communication with the agent. The physical appearance and kinesics of virtual reality characters can be crucial factors for enhancing user's immersion and reliability [19].

5 Design Process

The use of sign language gestures in a game can be considered a way of strengthening affordance, particularly in the context of accessibility. Players are often frustrated because they don't know what to do when entering a new environment and having to solve a puzzle. The problem can be severe for players who cannot receive help from sound. Affordance refers to the perceived and potential actions that players can take with an entity or within an environment. Strengthening affordance involves making these potential actions more apparent and easily understood by players. In this study, we suggested various sign language gesture hints through the agent that can provide potential actions that are more apparent and easily understood by players to induce natural progression. We implemented sign language gestures representing the nine actions and six emotional expressions of American Sign Language (ASL) that players need to solve puzzles and explore to progress through the game as shown in Fig. 1.

We tested the enhancement of affordances due to the sign language gesture of the push action. We created a puzzle situation in which the player had to move the position of the statue to pass through a passage blocked by a thorny vine obstacle. We experimented by creating versions of two situations. One version presented only visual effect clues for where the statue should be moved, and the other presented both push sign language gestures and visual effect clues. To investigate the relationship between strengthening interaction through sign language clues, we conducted an experiment with 14 college students who had experience playing virtual reality games. After teaching students about sign language gestures related to eight actions, we experimented. Although there was no significant difference in the experimental results between the two versions, we found it

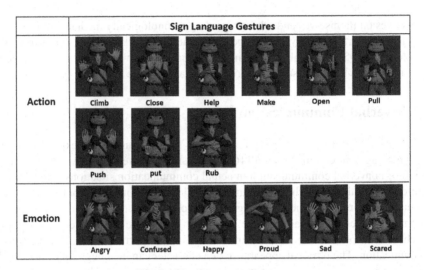

Fig. 1. Sign Language Gestures

easier to solve the puzzle when there were visual effects and sign language clues were presented together (Fig. 2).

Fig. 2. Affordances for Gameplay

These sign language gestures help players identify puzzle elements. Players can decide on a specific puzzle or task and understand and put into action the essential elements or steps needed to solve a puzzle.

6   Conclusion and Future Work

The purpose of strengthening affordances is to provide clues that can be easily recognized and acted upon in terms of player interaction, allowing users to immerse themselves and play naturally. In this way, interaction design with improved usability is essential in providing players with an intuitive and attractive experience to enjoy content. As a result, strengthening affordances allows the player to perceive the state according to the user's expectations and abilities and predict the function, helping the user achieve the desired purpose without additional explanation or display. This concept of affordance has essential implications for interaction design strategies that can induce user-driven immersion in virtual reality. Players can control and explore based on interaction design through active voluntary participation in the virtual world. However, in order for the player to be proactively immersed, we need to provide sufficient information and sensory clues to enable natural interaction with virtual objects and environments. Additionally, we can ensure that players can effectively navigate and interact with virtual environments, regardless of their previous experience or physical abilities. Based on this, players can naturally immerse themselves by exploring the information provided in the virtual space and perceiving manipulation and functional affordances to proceed to the next step through successive affordances. We suggest the broader concept of enhancing affordance through the use of sign language gestures, where games are designed to be playable by all people, to the greatest extent possible, without the need for adaptation or specialized design. In this study, we discovered the possibility of using nonverbal communication as a clue to convey information through the medium of sign language in the area of affordances. In future research, we will supplement facial expressions and sign language and conduct research targeting not only general players but also players who use sign language as their primary means of communication.

References

1. Heeter, C.: Being there: the subjective experience of presence. Presence: Teleoperators Virtual Environ. **1**, 262–271 (1992)
2. Minsky, M.: Telepresence. Omni **2**, 44–52 (1980)
3. McMahan, A.: Immersion, engagement and presence. In: Wolf, M.J., Perron, B. (eds). The video game theory reader, Psychology Press, pp. 67–86 (2003)
4. Murray, J.H.: Hamlet on the Holodeck: The Future of Narrative in Cyberspace (1997)
5. Gaver, W.W.: Technology affordances. In: Proceedings of the SIGCHI Conference on Human Factors in Computing Systems, pp. 79–84 (1991)
6. Norman, D.A.: Affordance, conventions, and design. Interactions **6**(3), 38–43 (1999)
7. Norman, D.: The Design of Everyday Things: Revised and Expanded Edition. Constellation (2013)
8. Hartson, R.: Cognitive, physical, sensory, and functional affordances in interaction design. Behav. Inform. Technol. **22**(5), 315–338 (2003)
9. Seo, G.: Exploring an immersive user interface in virtual reality storytelling. In: Stephanidis, C., Antona, M., Ntoa, S. (eds.) HCI International 2021 - Late Breaking Posters: 23rd HCI International Conference, HCII 2021, Virtual Event, July 24–29, 2021, Proceedings, Part I, pp. 385–389. Springer International Publishing, Cham (2021). https://doi.org/10.1007/978-3-030-90176-9_50

10. Nowak, K.L., Biocca, F.: The effect of the agency and anthropomorphism on users' sense of telepresence, copresence, and social presence in virtual environments. Presence: Teleoperators Virtual Environ. **12**(5), 481–494 (2003)

11. Fox, J., Ahn, S.J., Janssen, J.H., Yeykelis, L., Segovia, K.Y., Bailenson, J.N.: Avatars versus agents: a meta-analysis quantifying the effect of agency on social influence. Hum.-Comput. Interact. **30**(5), 401–432 (2015)

12. Luck, M., Aylett, R.: Applying artificial intelligence to virtual reality: intelligent virtual environments. Appl. Artif. Intell. **14**(1), 3–32 (2000)

13. Aylett, R., Brazier, F., Jennings, N., Luck, M., Nwana, H., Preist, C.: Agent systems and applications. Knowl. Eng. Rev. **13**(3), 303–308 (1998)

14. Seo, G.: Study on the diegetic user interface meditated as illusion factor for virtual reality interactive storytelling, Doctor of Fine Art Dissertation, Sejong University (2019)

15. Bricken, M.: Virtual worlds: no interface to design. In: Benedikt, M.L. (ed.) Cyberspace: first steps, pp. 363–382. MIT Press, Cambridge (1991)

16. MacLachlan, J.: What people really think of fast talkers. Psychol. Today, 113–117 (1979)

17. Birdwhistell, R.L.: Introduction to kinesics: (An annotation system for analysis of body motion and gesture). Department of State, Foreign Service Institute (1952)

18. Jolly, S.: Understanding body language: Birdwhistell's theory of kinesics. Corporate Commun. Int. J. **5**(3), 133–139 (2000)

19. Knapp, M.L., Hall, J.A., Horgan, T.G.: Nonverbal communication in human interaction. Holt, Rinehart and Winston, New York, vol.1, pp. 978 (1978)

Analyzing How Social Service Organizations Utilize Video-Sharing and Video-Meeting Platforms for People with Disabilities in Mitigating Social Isolation Post-Covid

Abigail Wilson, Isaac Tomeho, Lev Roland-Kalb, Vachaspathi Tirukkoveluru, Shuo Niu, and John Magee$^{(\boxtimes)}$

Computer Science Department, Clark University, Worcester, USA
abwilson@clarku.edu , jmagee@clarku.edu

Abstract. The Covid-19 pandemic reshaped human interaction, necessitating a pivot to digital platforms for social engagement. This shift presented unique challenges for individuals with disabilities, who already faced significant barriers to participation in social activities. The enhanced isolation during the pandemic had a serious and detrimental impact on their mental health. Our study explores how social service organizations utilized video-sharing and video-meeting platforms to mitigate social isolation and enable interaction for people with disabilities during and after the pandemic. To this end, we conducted interviews with two assistive technology professionals at two different social service organizations to evaluate the impacts of their various programs implemented during this time.

Keywords: Social service organizations · Video-sharing platforms · Video-meeting platforms · Inclusive digital strategies · Mitigating social isolation · Post-Covid adaptation

1 Introduction

Social service organizations discovered that platforms like Zoom were instrumental in decreasing social isolation among people with disabilities. These platforms provided accessible and comfortable alternatives to in-person meetings, which often pose challenges for this group [3]. Activities such as collaborative gaming and martial arts lessons facilitated through Zoom were not only interactive but also significantly enjoyed by participants.

The primary contributions of this work are: (1) an analysis of themes conducted in interviews with two assistive technology professionals, (2) a comparison of different video-meeting and video-sharing platforms to assess the ones with best effectiveness for socialization, and (3) a way to integrate digital mediums and traditional in-person meeting in a way that helps mitigate social isolation in the most effective way in this changed environment post-Covid.

C. Stephanidis et al. (Eds.): HCII 2024, CCIS 2115, pp. 111–115, 2024.
https://doi.org/10.1007/978-3-031-61947-2_13

2   Use of Video-Meeting Platforms

Collaborative gaming and martial arts lessons, as mentioned above, by a professional instructor via Zoom were notably interactive and enjoyed by participants (as stated by one of the Programming Specialist we interviewed). One of Zoom's strengths throughout these activities was allowing participants to focus automatically on the active speaker. This helped to simulate a conversational environment in which attention would be naturally directed. While this feature was beneficial to facilitating discussions, it did not allow participants to reach the same levels of dialogue they experienced during in-person meetings. Organizers we spoke to indicated finding no true replacement for authentic social interactions in addressing feelings of isolation.

3   Impact of Covid-19 on Video-Meeting Utilization

With the onset of the Covid-19 pandemic, social service organizations found themselves heavily reliant on video-meeting platforms like Zoom to facilitate social activities for their clients, particularly those with disabilities. As the pandemic disrupted traditional in-person gatherings, these digital platforms became a vital means of mitigating social isolation and fostering a sense of community among their patrons.

Post-pandemic efforts to resume in-person sessions were met with limited success due to ongoing barriers faced by individuals with disabilities. Challenges such as physical limitations, social barriers, and transportation difficulties persisted, hindering their ability to attend on-site events. Recognizing these challenges, the social service organizations adopted a hybrid approach, integrating virtual and in-person components.

The hybrid model ensured continued access and inclusivity for those confronting various obstacles, enabling them to participate in social activities from the comfort and safety of their preferred environments. Video-meeting platforms like Zoom proved instrumental in this endeavor, offering a range of accessibility features that catered to the diverse needs of participants. Features like closed captioning, screen sharing, and automatic speaker focus facilitated an enriching and inclusive experience, fostering a sense of community and belonging.

As one of the organizations highlighted, their clients expressed a strong preference for continuing virtual martial arts sessions via Zoom, even after the pandemic subsided. The convenience and accessibility of these digital platforms outweighed the barriers associated with attending in-person classes, such as transportation constraints and personal care requirements. This feedback underscored the significance of video-meeting platforms in addressing the unique challenges faced by individuals with disabilities.

Moreover, the organizations actively gathered feedback from their patrons, particularly those with disabilities, to assess the effectiveness and user-friendliness of the digital platforms employed. Surveys and direct feedback during virtual meetings provided valuable insights, enabling the organizations to make necessary adjustments and ensure a better experience for their clients.

The inclusive nature of these digital platforms, coupled with their accessibility features and the flexibility of the hybrid model, proved pivotal in fostering a sense of community and belonging among individuals with disabilities during the challenging times of the Covid-19 pandemic. As the organizations navigate the post-pandemic landscape, they remain committed to integrating these digital strategies with traditional in-person interactions, optimizing the social experience for their clients while addressing their unique needs and preferences.

4   The Role of Video-Sharing Platforms

Beyond video-meeting platforms like Zoom, video-sharing sites like YouTube have emerged as vital tools for the accessible dissemination of information and content tailored to individuals with disabilities during and after the Covid-19 pandemic [4]. These platforms allowed social service organizations to sidestep common pitfalls of traditional in-person event planning, such as scheduling conflicts, space limitations, and accommodation challenges. By regularly uploading new content, organizations fostered para-social relationships with clients, providing a virtual sense of community and kinship.

Importantly, video-sharing platforms complemented the use of video-meeting services by serving as accessible repositories for previously recorded sessions. Clients could revisit activities like martial arts lessons or virtual tours at their convenience, catering to diverse schedules and learning preferences. This function of video-sharing platforms as an online library highlights a key strength of the digital approach which will likely lead to lasting changes in how organizations engage their community's post-pandemic [5].

However, the social service organizations expressed concerns over limited user engagement on these one-way video platforms compared to live, interactive digital events or in-person gatherings. While invaluable for content dissemination, passive video consumption did not foster the same levels of dialogue and connection as more immersive virtual experiences. This underscored the continued need for innovative, highly interactive digital solutions to effectively mitigate social isolation among people with disabilities.

As society emerged from strict pandemic conditions, forward-thinking organizations carefully integrated video-sharing platforms alongside video-meetings and the gradual return of select in-person events. This hybrid model leveraged the unique strengths of each medium to provide an enriching, inclusive experience tailored to the diverse abilities and preferences of clients with disabilities. Ongoing feedback and assessment further optimized this comprehensive digital-physical approach to combat social isolation in our new reality following Covid-19.

5   Changes to Specific Programs Due to the Pandemic

A notable shift occurred as organizations transitioned from pre-recorded YouTube sessions to live Zoom sessions for activities like martial arts, leading to increased participation. This change underscored the significance of interactive and real-time digital experiences in fostering engagement and mitigating social isolation during the pandemic.

Participants reported heightened involvement and enjoyment during the live Zoom martial arts sessions, which allowed for real-time interactions, immediate feedback, and a more dynamic experience akin to in-person classes. The ability to receive instant guidance from instructors and the camaraderie fostered through shared virtual spaces contributed to an immersive and rewarding experience.

Complementing this transition, the organizations explored integrating interactive technologies like iPads into their programming, presenting both opportunities and challenges. These devices opened new avenues for accessible engagement, enabling participants to leverage apps and functionalities tailored to their needs. The portability and user-friendly interface made iPads valuable tools for individuals with diverse abilities.

However, effective implementation required substantial staff training, not only in technical aspects but also in facilitating engaging sessions through these platforms. Organizations had to allocate resources for comprehensive training programs and manage device maintenance, software updates, and IT support, presenting ongoing challenges.

Despite these hurdles, the organizations remained committed to leveraging interactive technologies to enhance programming and better serve individuals with disabilities. Through continuous adaptation, staff development, and technological improvements, they aimed to create an environment fostering meaningful social connections, learning opportunities, and overall well-being for their clients.

6   Conclusion

Our study underscores the pivotal role of digital platforms in addressing the socialization needs of individuals with disabilities during the COVID-19 pandemic. It highlights the innovative strategies employed by social service organizations to adapt to this new reality, revealing the potential of these platforms to enhance accessibility and interaction. As we transition away from strict social distancing measures, the insights gained from this study offer valuable guidance on integrating digital strategies with traditional in-person interactions to optimize the social experience for individuals with disabilities. This research contributes to the existing body of knowledge by providing practical insights into the use of digital platforms for social engagement during prolonged crises, aligning with and extending the findings of earlier studies. Past research has shown that there are both positive and negative experiences for people trying to socialize on digital platforms [2], so our research focuses on how these digital strategies can be best integrated with traditional in-person interactions post-Covid to create the most positive experience for the users. Building on the findings of Pellicano et al. [1] and McCausland et al. [2], our study addresses a crucial gap in understanding the digital engagement of individuals with disabilities and their caregivers.

It underscores the need for inclusive, accessible digital solutions that cater to diverse needs and preferences.

Acknowledgements. We thank the representatives of the social services organizations who discussed their experiences with video meeting and video sharing platforms.

References

1. Pellicano, E., et al.: COVID-19, social isolation and the mental health of autistic people and their families: a qualitative study. Autism: Int. J. Res. Pract. **26**(4), 914–927 (2022). https://doi.org/10.1177/13623613211035936
2. McCausland, D., McCarron, M., McCallion, P.: Use of technology by older adults with an intellectual disability in Ireland to support health, well-being and social inclusion during the COVID-19 pandemic. Br. J. Learn. Disab. **51**(2), 175–190 (2023). https://doi.org/10.1111/bld.12514
3. Birnbaum, M.L., Rizvi, A.F., Confino, J., Correll, C.U., Kane, J.M.: Role of social media and the Internet in pathways to care for adolescents and young adults with psychotic disorders and non-psychotic mood disorders. Early Interv Psychiatry **11**(4), 290–295 (2017). https://doi.org/10.1111/eip.12237
4. Morris, A., Goodman-Deane, J., Brading, H.: Internet use and non-use: views of older users. Universal Access Inf. Soc. **6**, 43–57 (2007). https://doi.org/10.1007/s10209-006-0057-5
5. Niu, S., Manon, H., Bartolome, A. Ha, N.B., Veazey, K.: Close-up and whispering: an understanding of multimodal and parasocial interactions in YouTube ASMR videos. In: ACM CHI Conference on Human Factors in Computing Systems, 30 April–6 May 2022 (CHI 2022), New Orleans. ACM, New York (2022). https://mathcs.clarku.edu/~shniu/pdf/Niu%20-%20CHI22%20-%20ASMR.pdf

Achieving an Inclusive and Accessible DSpace: University of Oregon's Approach and Outcomes

Le Yang(✉) ⓘ and Zhongda Zhang ⓘ

University of Oregon, Eugene, OR 97405, USA
yanglegd@gmail.com

Abstract. DSpace is a widely used open-source repository system that offers various functionalities for disseminating and preserving digital assets. However, it also suffers from a poor user interface and low digital accessibility. To remedy this, DSpace 7 has incorporated significant improvements in digital accessibility. Nevertheless, DSpace 7.6 still falls short of meeting the minimum accessibility requirement of WCAG 2.2 AA standard. This poses a major barrier for users who need to access digital objects, as well as for institutions who want to adopt DSpace as their institutional repository. To address the accessibility issues of DSpace repository for the benefit of the organization and the community, the University of Oregon DSpace project team conducted a thorough analysis of the WCAG 2.2 AA standard document and identified 56 accessibility items that are essential for the repository to comply with the standard. The team classified the items into six key categories: Keyboard Accessibility, Screen Reader Compatibility, ARIA Support, Color Contrast, Captioning, and Navigation Skip. After resolving each accessibility issue on the list and verifying them by WAVE and Axe testing tools, the project team developed a comprehensive solution package that can enable UO Libraries to create an inclusive and accessible digital environment on the institutional repository, ensuring that the published digital assets are accessible and usable by all users, regardless of their abilities.

Keywords: Digital Repository · Digital Interface · DSpace · Digital Accessibility

1 Introduction

1.1 DSpace

DSpace is recognized as the preeminent software solution for digital repositories and archives worldwide, a status supported by quantitative metrics collected from OpenDOAR, ROAR, and DuraSpace registry, suggesting that DSpace commands a dominant share of the global institutional repository market [1]. Scholarly literature underscores DSpace's pivotal role as a frontrunner in open-source software for digital repositories, significantly advancing open science endeavors and facilitating the dissemination of knowledge within the scholarly community and the public domain [2].

DSpace 7, as evaluated by the extensive developer community, introduces significant alterations and integrates novel features compared to its predecessors. These enhancements not only elevate the system's overall functionality but also address critical functionalities and known issues [3–5]. A noteworthy advancement lies in the decoupling of back-end and front-end interfaces [6], which facilitates the adoption of Angular technology on the user interface. This transition results in improved user experiences, including faster loading times, native responsiveness, efficient web harvesting, customizable interfaces, and enhanced accessibility features [6, 7].

Due to substantial disparities between the earlier iterations of DSpace and the current DSpace 7, a direct migration route from the previously employed XMLUI or JSPUI to the novel user interface is unavailable. In essence, developers are required to construct and adopt an entirely new web-based user interface within the DSpace 7 framework.

1.2 Digital Accessibility

The expanding diversity of student populations and the growing digitization of the education sector underscore the need to deliberate on inclusive access to digitally available information, lectures, and learning materials within various educational contexts. Additionally, it is crucial to examine the information and communication technology (ICT) systems employed by students within educational institutions to ensure equitable participation and engagement [8].

In a 2018 survey of students, it was found that approximately 18% of higher education students self-reported having a disability or chronic illness [9]. More recently, in 2023, The University of Oregon reported that 46.5% of incoming UO undergraduates identified as having a disability or being neurodivergent; additionally, 2.1% of incoming UO undergraduates encountered challenges related to computer and mobile device usage due to their reported disabilities, impairments, or neurodivergence [10].

Research indicates that accessibility barriers within learning platforms and educational materials hinder students' full participation in higher education, ultimately impacting their academic success [11–13]. As libraries and higher education institutions increasingly prioritize accessibility initiatives, various groups will need to revisit and reevaluate their services to enhance digital accessibility. Importantly, these efforts must be undertaken with minimal additional resource allocation, as the majority of institutions operating repositories face limitations in available resources, preventing them from extending beyond the pre-existing accessibility features inherent in widely adopted repository platforms [14].

In the context of institutional repositories (IRs), the emphasis on availability should not be perceived as entirely detrimental. However, it is essential to recognize that web accessibility remains a challenge for many IR managers; and these difficulties arise when integrating accessibility principles into both the software architecture and content of IRs [14]. A significant proportion of institutions operating IRs lack the necessary resources to extend beyond the pre-existing accessibility features inherent in widely adopted repository platforms. Consequently, the majority of IR software implementations do not incorporate stringent accessibility measures. This situation underscores the need for continued efforts to enhance accessibility within IRs, ensuring equitable access for all users [15].

2 Identified Problems

2.1 WCAG

The World Wide Web Consortium (W3C), with the objective of establishing a unified standard for ensuring accessible web content, introduced the Web Content Accessibility Guidelines (WCAG). These guidelines delineate a comprehensive set of testable criteria that must be met to guarantee equitable access to web-based information for individuals with disabilities. WCAG is structured around four fundamental principles, Perceivable, Operable, Understandable, and Robust, succinctly summarized by the acronym POUR. Each principle has specific guidelines and success criteria that outline how to achieve accessibility. For example, providing alternative text for images makes web content perceptible, allowing users to navigate with a keyboard ensures the platform is operable, using clear and consistent navigation guarantees web content is understandable, and using semantic HTML markup contributes to robustness.

Table 1. Differences in WCAG 2.0, 2.1, & 2.2.

WCAG	Release Date	Content	Purpose	Scope
2.0	Dec. 2008	The original version of WCAG, consisting of 12 guidelines organized under four principles: Perceivable, Operable, Understandable, and Robust (POUR)	Provides guidelines and success criteria for making web content accessible to people with disabilities	Focuses on basic accessibility requirements and is widely used as a reference for accessibility standards
2.1	Jun. 2018	An extension of WCAG 2.0, introducing 17 new success criteria to address additional accessibility needs and emerging technologies	Includes enhancements for mobile accessibility, low vision, and cognitive and learning disabilities	Adds support for new technologies such as touch interfaces, mobile devices, and responsive design
2.2	Jun. 2021	Another extension of WCAG 2.0, introducing 9 new success criteria to further improve accessibility standards	Focuses on addressing issues related to mobile accessibility, users with cognitive or learning disabilities, and users with low vision or color vision deficiencies	Provides guidance on making websites and web applications more accessible and user-friendly for a wider range of users

The rapid evolution of technology necessitates continuous updates to accessibility guidelines, ensuring their relevance across novel platforms and devices. Specifically, WCAG 2.1 and 2.2 were developed to address emerging trends, including mobile devices, touch interfaces, and responsive design. These iterations aim to enhance inclusivity, making digital content accessible to a broader spectrum of users with diverse abilities and varying assistive technology requirements.

The iterative development of WCAG involves the continual enrichment of its framework by introducing novel success criteria, guidelines, and recommendations (see Table 1). These enhancements are essential to remain aligned with technological progress and to enhance accessibility for all users. Notably, WCAG 2.1 and 2.2 extend the purview of accessibility requirements, addressing emerging technologies and accommodating diverse user needs beyond the scope of WCAG 2.0. To assess an application's accessibility, WCAG employs a three-tiered conformance model, namely A, AA, and AAA [16].

2.2 DSpace 7 Accessibility Status

The DSpace community, comprising both users and developers, diligently endeavors to create an accessible and user-friendly interface aligned with the Web Content Accessibility Guidelines (WCAG). Specifically, DSpace aims to meet the WCAG level AA standards, recognizing that achieving full compliance is an ongoing process. In order to do so, The DSpace community places a strong emphasis on accessibility during active development. Guided by design principles and coding standards that prioritize accessibility considerations, they conduct automated accessibility scans as part of rigorous testing procedures. Furthermore, institutions are required to share their accessibility testing outcomes with DSpace, which informs subsequent releases. Notably, in 2021, DSpace underwent an accessibility audit conducted by Deque, informing refinements to design and coding standards [17].

Accessibility issues are meticulously tracked within the DSpace GitHub issue tracker, using the "accessibility" label. Given the reliance on volunteer contributions for DSpace development, some accessibility tickets may await assignment to available volunteers. Urgent matters receive prompt attention, while non-urgent ones are addressed as resources permit. DSpace actively encourages contributions aimed at enhancing accessibility. Institutions with developers engaged in accessibility work are invited to contribute fixes back to the DSpace ecosystem.

3 Proposed Solutions

3.1 Accessibility Testing

The evaluation and testing of web accessibility lack a standardized, formalized approach. While existing steps for web accessibility audits are presented, they do not constitute a cohesive, controlled process. Furthermore, there is a dearth of information regarding the systematic grouping of applied methods and tools, aligned with their specific stages of application [18]. Consequently, we advocate for an organized audit process that adheres to the following stages, analysis and planning, field work, creating a report, and follow-up activities [19].

Numerous instruments exist for the assessment of WCAG guidelines. These include automated testing tools such as the W3C Validation Service, WebAIM's WAVE, Google Chrome's Lighthouse, Siteimprove Accessibility, Deque's Axe, and the Paciello Group's WAVE Accessibility Checker. Additionally, manual tools such as Screen Reader Simulation Tools like NVDA and VoiceOver, Keyboard Navigation Testing, and Color Contrast Checkers are also utilized.

DSpace employs an automated accessibility scanning tool, Axe by Deque, to conduct end-to-end testing across the user interface. This testing is executed via Cypress. Each GitHub pull request submitted to the UI code repository is subject to these automated tests. In our specific instance, we employ the browser extension WAVE to test the DSpace 7 front end (see Fig. 1). This ensures that our digital resources are accessible and adhere to the highest standards of web accessibility [14, 19].

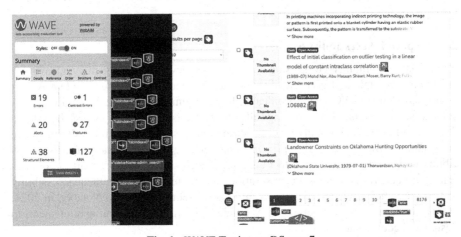

Fig. 1. WAVE Testing on DSpace 7.

In the context of DSpace 7, a comprehensive evaluation of each design element is crucial, with a specific focus on accessibility during practical testing. While automated tools like WAVE can swiftly identify common accessibility issues and expedite their resolution, manual testing remains an indispensable component of the accessibility review process. Human-led testing adds a personalized dimension to the evaluation process, facilitating a thorough and detailed analysis. This involves rigorous testing using keyboard navigation, screen readers, and other assistive technologies commonly employed by individuals with disabilities. Manual testing emphasizes critical aspects such as efficient focus management, keyboard input functionality, and compatibility with screen readers. By conducting automatic scanning and manual assessments, we can uncover both subtle and obvious issues, and then identify and categorize the 56 identified issues into six primary categories, including Keyboard Accessibility, Screen Reader Compatibility, ARIA Support, Color Contrast, Captioning, and Navigation Skip.

3.2 Solutions in DSpace 7

Based on the findings from the accessibility testing, we aim to propose a solution package that can function as an initial toolkit and a set of best practices for developers and digital library practitioners to reference when they are tasked with addressing DSpace accessibility issues. The solution package commences with the utilization of the most current versions of web browsers, such as Chrome, Firefox, Edge, Safari, etc., which are furnished with a variety of inherent features to ensure that web content is accessible to all users. Additionally, we have implemented some coding enhancements on the DSpace interfaces predicated on the six categories we identified.

"Keyboard Accessibility" is a critical aspect of web accessibility, enabling users to navigate and interact with a website solely through the use of a keyboard, eliminating the need for a mouse. Essential elements encompass keyboard focus, logical tab order, keyboard shortcuts, the absence of keyboard traps, managing focus for dynamic content, and accessible forms. In this discourse, we advocate for the utilization of the most recent browser versions to guarantee that web content is accessible to all users, thereby diminishing the requirement for extensive JavaScript development by programmers. Furthermore, we have undertaken testing and implemented enhancements, with a particular emphasis on customized keyboard focus, logical tab order, and accessible forms.

"Screen Reader Compatibility" pertains to the assurance that websites and web applications are capable of effectively interfacing with screen readers. Websites that are not accessible can present substantial obstacles for screen reader users, including complications such as absent alternative text (alt text) for images, incorrect usage of headings, and a lack of keyboard accessibility. To enhance accessibility, we employ appropriate HTML elements like heading tags, lists, and tables (such as < header >, < nav >, < main >, < article >, < section >, < footer >, < h1 > - < h6 >, < button >, < input >) to communicate the structure and significance of the content to screen readers. Providing alt text descriptions for all images ensures that screen readers can accurately interpret the visual content.

"Accessible Rich Internet Applications" (ARIA) functions as an instrumental resource for web developers, facilitating the bridging of the divide between complex web functionalities and assistive technologies. The support provided by ARIA encompasses the definition of roles and properties, the addressing of dynamic content, and the enhancement of user experience. We have invested significant effort into labeling. Labeling provides mechanisms to furnish both visible and invisible labels for elements, thereby augmenting the context or supplying additional information that assistive technologies can relay to users. This includes the attributes aria-label, aria-labelledby, and aria-describedby. The deficiencies we have identified in DSpace 7, utilizing WAVE and other tools, primarily consist of empty headings, missing or empty form labels, empty buttons, missing or empty table headers, empty links, broken ARIA references, and issues with dynamic content such as those discovered in the ui-switch. Our primary method of improving ARIA support has been through the addition of ARIA attributes.

"Color Contrast" denotes the disparity in luminosity between two colors, specifically between text and its corresponding background. The WCAG AA stipulates a contrast ratio of at least 4.5:1 for small text and 3:1 for large text. Color contrast is not solely confined to text. It is integral for various user interface (UI) components such as buttons, icons, and form elements. Upholding sufficient contrast between these elements and the background ensures they are distinctly discernible for all users. We employed contrast checkers to scrutinize nearly all pages, with a particular emphasis on augmenting the color contrast for breadcrumbs, which possess a contrast ratio of less than 4.5:1, and the graphical objects and user interface components. We modified some ratios to align with the guidelines.

"Captioning" constitutes the textual depiction of audio content in videos or audio tracks, thereby rendering content accessible to all, inclusive of individuals who are deaf or hard of hearing, possess auditory processing disorders, or are situated in noisy environments. Captions articulate spoken dialogue and delineate non-speech information, such as sound effects and speaker identification, which are vital for comprehending the context and content of media. DSpace allows for the submission of files, inclusive of video and audio files. However, this may precipitate issues with captioning. To rectify this, we necessitate the inclusion of video and audio descriptions or the submission of a vtt file (Web Video Text Tracks File) to ensure compliance with accessibility standards.

"Navigation Skip" or "Skip to Content" links constitute a web accessibility feature that permits users to circumvent repetitive navigation links and directly access the primary content of a page. We conducted a comprehensive review and customization of the features in our DSpace 7 project, strategically positioning the navigation skip link at the apex of the page to guarantee it is the initial focusable element for users of screen readers and keyboard navigation. We also undertook a review of as many pages as feasible, with a particular emphasis on the customization sections, to ensure the skip link is visually conspicuous with unambiguous labeling.

4   Conclusion

Several considerations have emerged in the post-project phase. Notably, accessibility is an integral facet of web development, and it should be ingrained from the project's inception rather than treated as an afterthought. This underscores the need for seamless integration of accessibility principles into development tools and frameworks, ensuring that accessibility becomes a foundational element of the entire development process.

Our DSpace-based project places a strong emphasis on digital accessibility and usability for individuals with disabilities, not only on the interfaces but also on the digital content. To achieve this, we will incorporate a diverse array of features and tools, aiming to make digital content accessible and usable for all users, regardless of their abilities. By steadfastly adhering to these principles and accounting for various dimensions of accessibility, our goal is to create a web environment that is truly inclusive and accessible to a wide spectrum of users.

Disclosure of Interests. The authors have no competing interests to declare that are relevant to the content of this article.

References

1. Formanek, M.: DSpace 7 benefits: is it worth upgrading? Inform. Technol. Libraries **42**(3) (2023). https://doi.org/10.5860/ital.v42i3.16209

2. Research: Technologies and services to ensure sustained access. https://www.lyrasis.org/membership/Pages/Research.aspx. Accessed 12 Mar 2024

3. The DSpace 7 Project – A Simple Summary. https://dspace.lyrasis.org/the-dspace-7-project-a-simple-summary. Accessed 12 Mar 2024

4. Available Now: DSpace 7 preview release. http://www.atmire.com/articles/detail/available-now-DSpace-7-preview-release. Accessed 12 Mar 2024

5. DSpace 7 Press Release. https://dspace.lyrasis.org/dspace-7-press-release. Accessed 12 Mar 2024

6. Release notes. https://wiki.lyrasis.org/display/DSDOC7x/Release+Notes. Accessed 12 Mar 2024

7. DSpace 7 UI project plain language summary. https://wiki.lyrasis.org/display/DSPACE/DSpace+7+UI+Project+Plain+Language+Summary. Accessed 12 Mar 2024

8. Sanderson, N., Kessel, S., Chen, W.: What do faculty members know about universal design and digital accessibility? A qualitative study in computer science and engineering disciplines. Univ. Access Inf. Soc. **21**(2), 351–365 (2022). https://doi.org/10.1007/s10209-022-00875-x

9. Hauschildt, K., Vögtle, E.M., Gwosć, C.: Social and economic conditions of student life in Europe. EUROSTUDENT VI 2016–2018 | Synopsis of Indicators. German Centre for Higher Education Research and Science Studies (DZHW) (ed.) (2018)

10. Disabilities Data. https://digitalaccessibility.uoregon.edu/about/data. Accessed 12 Mar 2024

11. Kent, M.: Disability and eLearning: opportunities and barriers. Disabil. Stud. Q. 35(1) (2015). https://doi.org/10.18061/dsq.v35i1.3815

12. Sachs, D., Schreuer, N.: Inclusion of Students with disabilities in higher education: performance and participation in student's experiences. Disabil. Stud. Q. **31**(2) (2011). https://doi.org/10.18061/dsq.v31i2.1593

13. Seale, J.: When digital capital is not enough: reconsidering the digital lives of disabled university students. Learn. Media Technol. **38**(3), 256–269 (2013). https://doi.org/10.1080/17439884.2012.670644

14. McLaughlin, M., Hoops, J.: Web accessibility in the institutional repository: crafting user-centered submission policies. Serials Librarian **80** (1–4), 41–46 (2021). https://doi.org/10.1080/0361526X.2021.1868217

15. Bankier, J., Gleason, K.: Institutional Repository Software Comparison. UNESCO, Paris (2014)

16. Web Content Accessibility Guidelines (WCAG) 2.2. https://www.w3.org/TR/WCAG22. Accessed 12 Mar 2024

17. Accessibility. https://wiki.lyrasis.org/display/DSDOC7x/Accessibility. Accessed 12 Mar 2024

18. Gay, G.: Professional Web Accessibility Auditing Made Easy: Essential Skills for Web Developers, Content Creators, and Designers. Toronto Metropolitan University, Toronto (2019)

19. Nacheva, R.: Digital inclusion through sustainable web accessibility. Commun. Comput. Inform. Sci. **1503**, 83–96 (2022). https://doi.org/10.1007/978-3-030-93715-7_6

Aging and Technology

Do Old People in Rural Areas Go Online, and Should They Do that?

Mariia Bochkova[1]([⊠]) [iD] and Triin Liin[2] [iD]

[1] Department of Geography, University of Tartu, Vanemuise 46, 51003 Tartu, Estonia
mariia.bochkova@ut.ee
[2] Department of Psychology, University of Tartu, Näituse 2, 50409 Tartu, Estonia
triin.liin@ut.ee

Abstract. Despite Estonia's reputation as an e-country and a pioneer in e-governance solutions, a digital divide persists, leading to a double exclusion of rural elderly. This paper aims to address this challenge by examining digital learning among elderly as a means to overcome this exclusion. The analysis of focus groups and expert interviews revealed that due to the lack of digital skills, the elderly in rural Estonia experience difficulties with using basic digital services (e-governance, e-banking, e-health, e-commerce) as well as accessing social networks. Furthermore, the elderly usually leave a very small digital footprint, which makes this community irrelevant for the service developers and further increases the digital divide. Four groups of needs were identified: access to the digital world, alleviation of fears and knowledge of secure conduct in the digital world, basic skills in accessing and navigating the digital world, and ability to communicate through e-services. We developed an intervention to overcome these deficiencies. The intervention is planned for the second half of 2024 and will be held in randomized controlled trials (RCT). While the experimental group is learning to use digital devices in small groups led by a local community researcher, the control group initially receives materials for self-study and participates in the intervention after the experimental group has completed their lessons. After the intervention, we can find out how the development of digital skills affects elderly well-being and inclusion in digital society. This research is supported by the Estonian Research Council grant PRG1919.

Keywords: digital skills · rural elderly · learning · digital divide · e-governance

1 Introduction

It has been said that one of the main principles of democracy is that all people should be treated equally, they should not be discriminated against, and they should have equal access to the free enjoyment of their rights [1]. In The Universal Declaration of Human Rights [2] it is stated that everyone has the right of equal access to public service in his country and the right freely to participate in the cultural life of the community, to enjoy the arts and to share in scientific advancement and its benefits. Despite this there still exist many different inequalities based on physical, socio-economic, and other factors.

One of these is digital one [3], which was underlined by forced isolation during COVID-19. In the beginning, the definition of digital divide was based on access possibility [4]. Even in developed countries, rural areas still experience it [5] due to the low population density which makes it not profitable for providers to create and/or develop better access [5, 6]. Today, in addition to access, skills, and outcomes of using the internet are also considered part of the divide [7, 8]. There are many studies demonstrating that education, age, gender, income, and space are factors that define the digital divide [9–11].

The COVID-19 crisis highlighted that in the absence of conventional face-to face interaction, certain members of the community face a lack of access to everyday services [12–14]. More specifically, the combination of high health risks, which made it particularly important for the elderly to comply with isolation rules, and their lower access to digital services, led to an increased risk of exclusion [15–17].

Bridging the digital divide in this age group is particularly relevant as the uptake of ICT among older people reduces social isolation, increases social inclusion, improves cognitive abilities and overall well-being [18–20]. Furthermore, the divide tends to expand with technological progress [21], thereby affecting the inclusion of the elderly in the network society, especially in rural areas, where a double exclusion is prevalent as a combination of lower skills and lower access possibilities.

Old people themselves are interested in learning these skills for individual, social and technical reasons - some older adults learn digital skills to form and/or improve relationships while others wish to reduce dependence on others or just to improve themselves [20, 22, 23].

However, even when elderly agree that learning ICT skills might benefit them, they still often fail to act due to numerous fears and barriers. For example, older adults might find it difficult to use the touch screen or they might become impatient when programs do not work properly or internet access is irregular [24, 25]. There are also concerns of privacy and safety, e.g., that unauthorized people might gain access to their medical information or bank account [25, 26]. Therefore, when preparing the learning environment for elderly, special attention should be paid to these topics. For example, elderly should receive support during the educational sessions, and as the possibility of social contact with peers might be an additional motivating and encouraging factor for the elderly, community-based programs should be considered [23, 24, 27, 28]. The instruction should consider that elderly prefer non-technical wording in explanations and user manuals [29]. To further support the adoption of digital devices, the intervention should also create positive emotions with respect to digital technology by being fun and familiar [24].

The following topics have previously been suggested for skills development: mastering a device, social contact (e-mail, skype, social media), surfing the web (google search etc.), entertainment (puzzles, games, movies, radio, podcasts, music), taking pictures and managing files, online shopping and banking, planning (calendar, trip-planners, reminders) [18, 20, 25].

As meeting the participants' expectations has been shown to be an integral part of learning motivation and thus an important aspect of planning an educational intervention for the elderly [22], our first aim was to find out the needs of the elderly that might be met by learning new digital skills. For that aim we conducted expert interviews with specialists who work with elderly every day and have first-hand experience with their skills and needs. We provide an overview of the results.

The second aim of the study was to develop a curriculum that would support the acquisition of digitals skills related to the identified needs in a manner that is suitable for the elderly. We introduce the preliminary study-plan for digital skills.

2   The Identification of the Fields of Smart in Need of Improvement

2.1   Participants, Method, and Procedure

To understand the needs and motivations of the elderly, semi-structured expert interviews (32 interviews, 36 participants) and focus-group interviews (4 interviews, 25 participants) were conducted. The interviewees were divided into four groups of stakeholders based on their every position or role in the local community. When one person had several roles, classification was based on the role they identified themselves with. The following groups of stakeholders were identified: officials from local municipalities, providing the perspective of politicians; point persons from volunteer organizations, offering insights from elderly associations; specialists whose everyday work involves interacting with the elderly or elderly communities; and representatives from development and innovation centers, contributing perspectives on innovation, projects, and social developments.

Two types of topics were covered in the interviews: the first focused on the digital life experiences of the elderly and the second on the digital needs and visions of the municipality. This strategy allowed us to consider the broader picture of the entire municipality as well as the local level perspective (e.g., one village or community). Participant sampling for the first round was based on desk research and included representatives from various levels of municipalities and communities. For the second round, the snowball method was applied. The interviews were done by project work group members and completed during the fieldwork from October 2023 till February 2024. For each interview we obtained an informed consent from the participants, a short form ((i.e. a protocol filled in by interviewers to provide a brief background of the experts, record notes about the interview, and collect metadata), and a voice recording. Access to this material was strictly limited with project workgroups members. After the end of fieldwork, transcriptions were created by Taltech webtrans [30] and overviewed by team members. We employed a deductive approach to identify areas of elderly exclusion and their digital needs. Additionally, we explored widespread attitudes and users' experiences in the digital realm, which should be considered when designing the intervention.

2.2   Results

Based on the interviews, four groups of needs were identified. The number of stakeholders mentioning a topic is in Table 1.

First, *access to the digital world* can be restricted due to the lack of devices and/or internet access. For example, the following comments were made: "Internet access can be poor in remote areas, elderly people often have cordless phones and cannot access the internet, and even some public internet points are closed." However, it seems that

Table 1. The needs of the elderly identified by different stakeholders.

Identified needs	Number of stakeholder interviews mentioning a topic[a]				
	Officials from the local municipalities (6)	Point persons of volunteer organizations (14)	Specialist working directly with the elderly (16)	Representatives of development & innovation centers (5)	Summary number of interviews (37)
Access to the digital world	6	9	7	4	26
Alleviation of fears and safe conduct in the digital world	2	13	6	1	22
Basics skills to navigate the digital world	3	7	9	4	23
Communication via e-services	6	14	6	4	30

[a] Double mentions are possible

it is beyond the capacity/agency of the municipality to solve access problems: "The municipality lacks the funds for smart homes for the elderly." or "Education programs need to be financed, but municipalities lack those funds." The problem of access can be caused by skills related to login information as elderly "...sometimes lose their access codes and passwords." These results confirm rural elderly's double exclusion caused by lower internet access in rural areas and lack of skills. We found an opinion that providing equipment could motivate and encourage the use of digital services "...if they (the elderly) have a smart device, they become more interested in the digital world." Moreover, English language, the specific technical terms of digital solutions and the unfamiliar architecture of most programs are also defined as a blocking factor in program use.

Second, the introduction of new and/or unfamiliar procedures tends to create anxiety; therefore, addressing *fears* and providing guidance *on safe conduct in the digital world* are necessary topics. The stakeholders' comments illustrate this topic: "On the one hand, elderly people are afraid of becoming victims of online scams, but on the other hand, they share their access codes with relative strangers because they need help to use services." Because of lack of knowledge about how computer security works "...they tend to trust officials they know with private information." They also look for additional guidance and support when using digital services, because "...they (elderly) want somebody help them; they don't trust themselves."

Third, the elderly *need basic skills to access and navigate the digital world.* When they have somebody who helps them, the elderly tend to rely on them and become less independent. Some examples from interviews: "They have become dependent on others because they lack the skills;" "Some of them lack all skills, others have some knowledge, but often children do most of the elderly's' digital transactions;" "Elderly need help setting up emails, user accounts and finding services..." For the elderly, this solution often seems easier than skill acquisition, but learning might help them regain at least some independence. For example, when driving a car is no longer manageable and the public transport system is not comfortable for the transportation of goods, digital commerce and supply chain management could solve the issues. It was said that e-commerce services "...are important issues in rural areas..." but they find the necessary technology challenging. Continuous and quick development of digital world also undermines the motivation for gaining new knowledge: "Their skills get old; it is like rowing upstream." It was mentioned several times that systems which are supposed to make everyday life easier (for example public transport schedules) are often too complex and confusing for the elderly. This indicates that services are often not user friendly and the needs of older users have not been taken into account during the design stage [31].

Fourth, only if the elderly have the necessary skills can they *communicate via e-services*, where two levels of communication were mentioned. On one hand communication with the government and vital services (banks, medicine) was deemed necessary. Though Estonia is famous for their e-government system, older adults cannot always use it. Several interviews mentioned that access to banking services is the most needed, but they also need to use e-government and medical services. However, personal communication theme also appeared. It was said, that "They wish to share pictures and use Facebook" and "...make video calls...". They want to communicate and maintain relationships with children who live somewhere else, sometimes even in a foreign country and they also wish to communicate with people from the same age group and form the same community.

3 Discussion and Conclusions

In designing the intervention plan, we drew on the themes raised in the interviews and the literature [see also 17, 24]. Accounting for the digital divide in terms of digital infrastructure, we make sure to provide them with a tablet with internet access that they get to keep after the intervention.

In choosing the websites and applications that are covered by the curriculum the conditions affordability, usability, and accessibility had to be met [see also 19]. This means that we will mainly use applications and websites that are free of charge, that are available in the official language (interviews suggested, that elderly often struggle with foreign languages) and have been available to the public for at least a year (learning to navigate a website takes time for the elderly and thus we choose those with a higher probability of being maintained). We will mostly focus on guided action which improves performance on specific training materials, but we also implement guided attention training by presenting examples of similar services with different designs in the hopes of improving the participants' general digital skills [see also 32].

We will begin the intervention by assessing the digital skills, wellbeing, and personality traits of all volunteers. The chosen participants (individuals are eligible for participation if they are at least 65 years old, have low digital skills, and no mental illness) in each municipality are first randomly divided into the first and second wave of the intervention. After the introductory lesson about security and safe conduct all participants will be given a tablet with an identification code that contains all the materials used in instruction and a booklet explaining the video.

Participants in the first wave are then divided into small groups, each containing up to 5 people from the same municipality [see also 25]. Group based is also in accordance with a topic that emerged in several interviews, namely that though elderly need digital skills, they wish to interact face to face as well. Groups meet twice a week in a quiet place accessible for the group members (e.g., library, community center etc.). Each group has a supervisor who has been trained to conduct the intervention. Each lesson (except the first one, where no homework is discussed) follows the same structure:

1. A short written reflection of the previously covered topic.
2. Discussion of the homework.
3. A short video on that week's topic (15 min). All videos are pre-recorded specifically for the intervention to minimize the influence of different instructors on the learning of the material.
4. Participants try the activities described in the video. If necessary, help can be sought from the supervisor.
5. After the group practice, participants will be given a homework assignment to revisit what they have learned and to try out the new skills at least 2 times during the following days.

The following topics will be covered:

- Topic 0. Introductory lecture. A general overview of security issues and safe conduct on the web for all participants. The procedures in place to protect the privacy of the participants. An overview of the participation procedures.
- Topic 1. Introduction. Getting to know your group. Tablet basics, including physical components and system navigation (e.g., turning the tablet on/off, unlocking with a passcode, keyboard, settings, organization of app icons (pre-designed gates for different services that will be covered in later lessons), volume buttons, navigating between different pages. How to take screenshots. Calendar reminders. Homework - Watch the tutorial video. Follow the steps described in the video by yourself at least twice before the next meeting. Charge the tablet to make sure it is usable at the second meeting. Take a screenshot. Set a reminder for the week.
- Topic 2. Basic skills to navigate the web. Creating and using e-mail. Searching the web (e.e., google search). Taking pictures and sharing them via e-mail. Homework - Watch the tutorial video. Follow the steps described in the video by yourself at least twice during the week. NB! You do not have to re-create an e-mail account! Send an e-mail. Search for information on the web.
- Topic 3. Social networks and communication. New ways to connect with others – videocalls, chatting, voice messages, shorts (e.g., Facebook, Skype, Instagram, Tik-tok). Creating a shared document (Google Docs). How to set up your FB page, to create a group chat, and a group page in FB. Sharing pictures and stories on the web. Homework - Watch the tutorial video. Follow the steps described in the video by

yourself at least twice before the next meeting. Visit your FB page and your groups' FB page. Read and/or send a message on the group chat.

- Topic 4. Accessing the services of e-government (Riigiportaal, webpage and/or FB page of local municipality). How to set up a digital signature and how to give a digital signature. How to connect with local government services. Homework - Watch the tutorial video. Follow the steps described in the video by yourself at least twice before the next meeting. Access the e-government webpage. Use that information to connect with a local government representative (e.g., social worker, ordering demand-based transport).
- Topic 5. E-banking. Digital health services (e.g., Terviseportaal). Online booking for doctors' appointments. Homework - Watch the tutorial video. Follow the steps described in the video by yourself at least twice before the next meeting. Access your bank account. Check your prescriptions online. Check for available doctors' appointments.
- Topic 6. Online shopping. Overview of grocery stores that deliver goods to your home (e.g., Selver, Coop, Rimi). Shopping for non-edible products online (e.g., Kaup24). Overseas shopping (e.g. Amazon, eBay). Homework - Watch the tutorial video. Follow the steps described in the video by yourself at least twice before the next meeting. Make a shopping list in an e-shop. Find out the price of a product.
- Topic 7. Travel and entertainment. How to plan a trip (bus schedules, train schedules, ride sharing, peatus.ee). E-library. Free games and puzzles (e.g., Nutiristsõnad, chess.com, sudokuonline). Free online television and videos (ERR, Youtube). Homework - Watch the tutorial video. Follow the steps described in the video by yourself at least twice before the next meeting. Plan a trip to a destination of your choosing. Do at least one of the following: order a book from the library, play a game/puzzle online, watch a video online.

Participants in the second wave receive only study-materials without any further instructions during the first 4 weeks. After the first wave has completed the lessons, the digital skills and wellbeing of all participants are assessed. After the second assessment has been completed, activities for the second-wave participants will follow the same procedure as the first wave, followed by another digital skills and wellbeing assessment. Finally, 3 months after the intervention follow-up interviews are conducted to investigate changes in social inclusion. We hope to demonstrate that crossing the digital divide leads to greater inclusion.

Acknowledgments. This research is supported by the Estonian Research Council grant PRG1919.

Disclosure of Interests. The authors have no competing interests to declare that are relevant to the content of this article.

References

1. Day, J.: 14 Principles of democracy. https://www.liberties.eu/en/stories/principles-of-democracy/44151. Accessed 20 Feb 2024
2. United Nations General Assembly: The Universal Declaration of Human Rights (UDHR). https://www.un.org/en/about-us/universal-declaration-of-human-rights. Accessed 20 Feb 2024
3. Robinson, L., et al.: Digital inequalities and why they matter. Inf. Commun. Soc. **18**, 569–582 (2015). https://doi.org/10.1080/1369118X.2015.1012532
4. van Dijk, J., Hacker, K.: The digital divide as a complex and dynamic phenomenon. Inf. Soc. **19**, 315–326 (2003). https://doi.org/10.1080/01972240309487
5. Salemink, K., Strijker, D., Bosworth, G.: Rural development in the digital age: a systematic literature review on unequal ICT availability, adoption, and use in rural areas. J. Rural. Stud. **54**, 360–371 (2017). https://doi.org/10.1016/j.jrurstud.2015.09.001
6. Bosworth, G., Price, L., Collison, M., Fox, C.: Unequal futures of rural mobility: challenges for a "smart countryside." Local Econ. **35**, 586–608 (2020). https://doi.org/10.1177/0269094220968231
7. van Deursen, A.J.A.M., van Dijk, J.A.G.M., Peters, O.: Rethinking Internet skills: the contribution of gender, age, education, Internet experience, and hours online to medium- and content-related Internet skills. Poetics **39**, 125–144 (2011). https://doi.org/10.1016/j.poetic.2011.02.001
8. van Dijk, J.: The Digital Divide. Wiley (2020)
9. Bauer, J.M.: The Internet and income inequality: Socio-economic challenges in a hyper-connected society. Telecommun. Policy. **42**, 333–343 (2018). https://doi.org/10.1016/j.telpol.2017.05.009
10. Cruz-Jesus, F., Vicente, M.R., Bacao, F., Oliveira, T.: The education-related digital divide: an analysis for the EU-28. Comput. Hum. Behav. **56**, 72–82 (2016). https://doi.org/10.1016/j.chb.2015.11.027
11. Elena-Bucea, A., Cruz-Jesus, F., Oliveira, T., Coelho, P.S.: Assessing the role of age, education, gender and income on the digital divide: evidence for the European union. Inf. Syst. Front. **23**, 1007–1021 (2021). https://doi.org/10.1007/s10796-020-10012-9
12. Lai, J., Widmar, N.O.: Revisiting the digital divide in the COVID-19 era. Appl. Econ. Perspect. Policy **43**, 458–464 (2021). https://doi.org/10.1002/aepp.13104
13. Seifert, A., Cotten, S.R., Xie, B.: A double burden of exclusion? Digital and social exclusion of older adults in times of COVID-19. J. Gerontol. Soc. Sci. **76**, 99–103 (2021)
14. Zapletal, A., Wells, T., Russell, E., Skinner, M.W.: On the triple exclusion of older adults during COVID-19: technology, digital literacy and social isolation. Soc. Sci. Humanit. Open. **8**, 100511 (2023). https://doi.org/10.1016/j.ssaho.2023.100511
15. Litchfield, I., Shukla, D., Greenfield, S.: Impact of COVID-19 on the digital divide: a rapid review. BMJ Open **11**, e053440 (2021). https://doi.org/10.1136/bmjopen-2021-053440
16. van Jaarsveld, G.M.: The effects of COVID-19 among the elderly population: a case for closing the digital divide. Front. Psychiatry. **11** (2020). https://doi.org/10.3389/fpsyt.2020.577427
17. Konstabel, K., et al.: Eesti rahvastiku vaimse tervise uuring. Lõpparuanne. Tervise Aren-gu Instituut ja Tartu Ülikool (2022)
18. Chan, M.Y., Haber, S., Drew, L.M., Park, D.C.: Training older adults to use tablet computers: does it enhance cognitive function? Gerontologist **56**, 475–484 (2016). https://doi.org/10.1093/geront/gnu057
19. Choi, H.K., Lee, S.H.: Trends and effectiveness of ICT Interventions for the elderly to reduce loneliness: a systematic review. Healthcare. **9**, 293 (2021). https://doi.org/10.3390/healthcare9030293

20. Hasan, H., Linger, H.: Enhancing the wellbeing of the elderly: social use of digital technologies in aged care. Educ. Gerontol. **42**, 749–757 (2016). https://doi.org/10.1080/03601277.2016.1205425

21. Hilbert, M.: The bad news is that the digital access divide is here to stay: domestically installed bandwidths among 172 countries for 1986–2014. Telecommun. Policy. **40**, 567–581 (2016). https://doi.org/10.1016/j.telpol.2016.01.006

22. Ackermann, T.P., Seifert, A.: Older adults' engagement in senior university lectures and the effect of individual motivations. Front. Educ. **6** (2021)

23. Pihlainen, K., et al.: Older adults' reasons to participate in digital skills learning: an interdisciplinary, multiple case study from Austria, Finland, and Germany. Stud. Educ. Adults. **55**, 101–119 (2023). https://doi.org/10.1080/02660830.2022.2133268

24. Blažič, B.J., Blažič, A.J.: Overcoming the digital divide with a modern approach to learning digital skills for the elderly adults. Educ. Inf. Technol. **25**, 259–279 (2020). https://doi.org/10.1007/s10639-019-09961-9

25. Chaudhry, B., Dasgupta, D., Mohamed, M., Chawla, N.: Teaching tablet technology to older adults. In: Stephanidis, C., Harris, D., Li, W.-C., Schmorrow, D.D., Fidopiastis, C.M., Antona, M., Gao, Q., Zhou, J., Zaphiris, P., Ioannou, A., Sottilare, R.A., Schwarz, J., Rauterberg, M. (eds.) HCII 2021. LNCS, vol. 13096, pp. 168–182. Springer, Cham (2021). https://doi.org/10.1007/978-3-030-90328-2_11

26. Vassli, L.T., Farshchian, B.A.: Acceptance of health-related ICT among elderly people living in the community: a systematic review of qualitative evidence. Int. J. Hum.-Comput. Interact. **34**, 99–116 (2018). https://doi.org/10.1080/10447318.2017.1328024

27. Fields, J., et al.: In-home technology training among socially isolated older adults: findings from the tech allies program. J. Appl. Gerontol. **40**, 489–499 (2021). https://doi.org/10.1177/0733464820910028

28. Trenorden, K.I., Hull, M.J., Lampit, A., Greaves, D., Keage, H.A.D.: Older adults' experiences of a computerised cognitive training intervention: a mixed methods study. Aust. J. Psychol. **74**, 2036581 (2022). https://doi.org/10.1080/00049530.2022.2036581

29. Pajalic, Z., et al.: Welfare technology interventions among older people living at home—a systematic review of RCT studies. PLOS Digit. Health. **2**, e0000184 (2023). https://doi.org/10.1371/journal.pdig.0000184

30. Olev, A., Alumäe, T.: Estonian Speech Recognition and Transcription Editing Service. Balt. J. Mod. Comput. **10**, (2022). https://doi.org/10.22364/bjmc.2022.10.3.14

31. Leppiman, A., Riivits-Arkonsuo, I., Pohjola, A.: Old-Age digital exclusion as a policy challenge in estonia and finland. In: Walsh, K., Scharf, T., Van Regenmortel, S., Wanka, A. (eds.) Social Exclusion in Later Life. IPA, vol. 28, pp. 409–419. Springer, Cham (2021). https://doi.org/10.1007/978-3-030-51406-8_32

32. Hickman, J.M., Rogers, W.A., Fisk, A.D.: Training older adults to use new technology. J. Gerontol. Ser. B. **62**, 77–84 (2007). https://doi.org/10.1093/geronb/62.special_issue_1.77

Analysis of Spatial Interaction Model of Quanzhou Aged Community Based on Evidence-Based Design Theory

Geng Kun Cheng and Yu Zhai[✉]

Xiamen Academy of Arts and Design, FuZhou University, Xiamen 361021, Fujian, China
miazhai@fzu.edu.cn

Abstract. With the acceleration of population aging, China faces significant challenges in meeting the complex needs of its elderly population within urban communities. This study focuses on the aging population in Quanzhou, Fujian Province, aiming to enhance their sense of belonging and security within their communities and transform traditional neighborhoods into elderly-friendly environments. Drawing on evidence-based design theory and the Kano model, this research identifies key attributes driving elderly satisfaction with community environments. Using the evidence-based design framework, the study examines elderly groups, social organizations, and service facilities as subjects, with the elderly and related groups serving as receptors. The Kano model categorizes elderly needs into basic and expected categories, with factors such as pressure alleviation, empowerment, and positive experiences shaping the evidence-based elements like activity spaces, facilities, and green spaces. Satisfaction evaluation, informed by Kano model insights, aims to enhance the quality of elderly community life. Data collection through questionnaires and interviews provides insights into the demographic, health, and economic profiles of the aging community. This data, categorized through evidence-based design and Kano model analysis, informs tailored interventions at various levels of community needs. By leveraging evidence-based analysis, this study offers scientifically informed design standards and strategies for aging communities, contributing to their objective development and transformation. Ultimately, this research aims to chart a path for the future development of aging communities, offering a data-driven direction for their evolution and improvement.

Keywords: aging community · gender composition · evidence-based subject · spatial interaction model · sense of control

1 Introduction

China is in the predicament of accelerating population aging, and coping with the aging problem has become the core link of the national population development strategy. In order to properly meet this challenge, the government has implemented a series of policies to promote the all-round development of diversified pension models, including home-based pension, community-based pension and institutional pension. In view of the diverse needs of the elderly and the complex and changeable community environment, how to use data for accurate guidance and analysis to build a positive and sustainable community environment has become an important issue. Based on evidence-based design theory, combined with space interaction model, this paper discusses the innovative development direction of community pension space design in depth, and puts forward corresponding design strategies for reference by relevant stakeholders.

The author will take Dongmen Community in Quanzhou Old Town-Licheng District as the investigation area, explore the current situation of public space, the needs of the elderly, the management and service mode, etc., and collect data from various parties such as site information, environmental factors, cultural connotation, etc., so as to find new solutions and strategies for the contradictions arising from the sustainable development of the old-age community, and provide certain reference value for related research (Fig. 1).

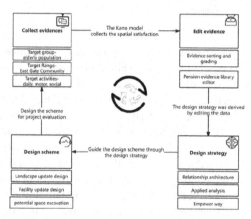

Fig. 1. Evidence-based design process (Photo source: author self-painting)

2 The Research Background

2.1 Community Ageing and Elderly Groups

Community aging refers to the phenomenon that the proportion of the elderly population in the community continues to rise compared with other age groups. This phenomenon is manifested in the gradual expansion of the proportion of the elderly population, the aging of the population structure, the increasing demand for social services and the adjustment of community facilities, etc. The core of which lies in the change of community spatial elements. In view of the aging community, its connotation can be summarized into the following two levels: First, the aging community means that the proportion of the elderly population in the community continues to rise and occupies a dominant position. This phenomenon is particularly prominent in first-tier and second-tier cities, which is mainly due to the overall aging of permanent residents. Secondly, the community itself is also experiencing an "aging" process. Community aging is an inevitable stage in the life cycle of the community. How to revive the vitality of the community and achieve sustainable development has become an urgent problem to be solved (Fig. 2).

Fig. 2. Daily life scene of Dongmen Community, Licheng District, Quanzhou City, Fujian Province, China (Source: Self-made by the author)

According to the classification of the World Health Organization, people aged 60 to 74 are regarded as young and old people, while those over 75 are called old people. In addition, people over 90 years old are known as long-lived old people. In China, Article 2 of the Law on the Protection of the Rights and Interests of the Elderly clearly stipulates that the starting point of the age of the elderly is 60 years old, which means that all Chinese citizens who have reached the age of 60 are regarded as elderly people. Many researchers often regard the elderly as a kind of "burden", and the measures designed for them are more for the purpose of protection. However, these designs do not bring long-term well-being to the elderly, on the contrary, they are only a series of protection measures that restrict group activities. In fact, the elderly are a group with unlimited potential. Their existence can not only enrich community life, improve community culture level, but also stimulate young people's upward spirit. Researchers should face up to their needs, fully tap their potential, and make them active participants and leaders in community activities (Fig. 3).

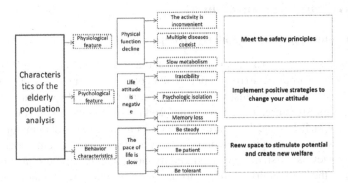

Fig. 3. Analysis of the elder population characteristics (Photo source: self-made by the author)

2.2 Evidence-Based Design and Kano Model

This study focuses on the elderly in the community, which is in the stage of physical function decline, and its disease incidence is similar to that of the elderly patients studied by evidence-based medicine. In view of the fact that the source of evidence-based design is evidence-based medicine, the relevant research and data analysis provided by it are abundant and reliable.

By actively solving the aging problem in the community, tapping the potential of the community, empowering the elderly, optimizing the community environment, and improving the happiness and satisfaction of the elderly (Fig. 4).

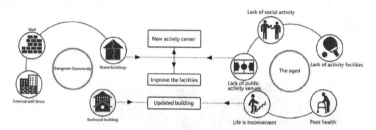

Fig. 4. Community vitality stimulation path (Photo source: homemade by the author)

Under the advocacy of active aging, applying evidence-based design theory to the design process of old-age community will help empower the community and ensure its sustainable development. Kano model, invented by Tokyo Institute of Technology professor Noriaki Kano, is a tool for classifying and prioritizing user needs. The model analyzes user requirements and user satisfaction, reflects the non-linear relationship between functional requirements satisfaction and user satisfaction, and is an effective method to accurately judge the key factors affecting user satisfaction. In practical application, users' evaluation of each influencing factor is collected through questionnaires, and the statistical results of questionnaires are classified according to Kano model evaluation table, and then Better-Worse satisfaction coefficient is used for analysis, and the needs are prioritized (Fig. 5).

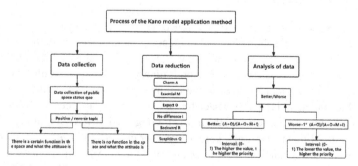

Fig. 5. Spatial interaction model process from the perspective of event-based design (Photo source: author homemade)

3 Research Methods and Demonstration Construction

3.1 Research Methodology

At the initial stage of the study, it is necessary to collect relevant site information on the spot, including target population and target range, and analyze the activities of target population through spatial interaction model, such as daily life, leisure and entertainment, physical exercise and social activities. We will collate and analyze the collected evidence, which is mainly divided into sorting and grading of community pension evidence and editing of community pension evidence database. By editing the data, the design strategy is put forward, and the evidence is critically understood and collected. The strategy covers the elderly groups with different needs, and strives for innovative attempts to obtain valuable feedback (Fig. 6).

Fig. 6. Real picture of the current situation of Dongmen Community (photo source: made by the author)

3.2 Research Process

According to the activity nature and preferences of the elderly in Dongmen Community of Licheng District, Quanzhou City, the influencing factors, namely demand indicators, are divided into three categories, including safety and comfort needs, mental health needs and social dependence needs. The preliminary investigation results show that the public space in the residential area in the community is spacious, but the planning is unreasonable, and there is a public space for development; The streets in the cultural and entertainment areas are narrow and the traffic is congested. In the community, there is an open park with Minnan traditional garden style for citizens to have a rest. Community service stations are located in the center and provide convenient services. The dense population in the community brings a stable community atmosphere and makes the community life rich and colorful. At the same time, the existence of office population indicates that the community includes commercial or office areas. There are commercial centers, office buildings or enterprises and institutions in the community, which provide employment and commercial services for residents and constitute a relatively perfect community system.

Generally speaking, the community population composition shows a balanced community structure: both the resident population forms a relatively stable community life, and the office population injects commercial and employment elements into the community, thus constructing a relatively comprehensive community (Fig. 7).

Type of activity	Activity time	Concentrated location	Activity content	Concentrated point diagram	Field photos	Demand index content	
Daily life	Long time	Park, community	Take care of your baby and buy food			Safe and comfortable	A1.Elderly-friendly rehabilitation facility
							A2.Real-time security detection
							A3.Barrier-free structures
Leisure and entertainment	Time is moderate	Street, park	Play cards, pick up children				A4.Medical security
						Mental health	B1.Respect and love the elderly propaganda
Physical fitness	Short time	Community, street	Fitness exercise				B2.Psychological service
							B3.Love activities
						Social dependency	C1.Group space
Social dependency	Time is moderate	Green space, community mouth	Chat, read newspapers				C2.Help the elderly activities
							C3.Make friends organization

Fig. 7. Analysis of the elements of Dongmen Community life Scene (Photo source: homemade by the author)

Through KANO model, the community space is deeply studied. The model divides the key elements and influencing factors into five categories: Attractive Quality, One-dimensional Quality, Must-be Quality, Reverse Quality and Indifferent Quality. In the practical application process, through the questionnaire survey to collect the user's evaluation opinions on each influencing factor, according to the KANO evaluation table to classify the questionnaire statistical results, and further use Better-Worse satisfaction coefficient analysis, and to prioritize the needs. Better-Worse satisfaction coefficient is an evaluation index for calculating demand index items and user satisfaction, and analyzes the importance between this satisfaction coefficient and the evaluation index with the same attribute. Among them, two evaluation indexes respectively represent: the larger the Better index value, the higher the satisfaction of users by providing this demand index item; The smaller the Worse index value, the higher the dissatisfaction of users if the demand index item is not provided. The formula for calculating the Better-Worse satisfaction coefficient is:

$$Better = \frac{A+O}{A+O+M+I} \quad Worse = \frac{O+M}{A+O+M+I}$$

Integrating Better-Worse satisfaction coefficient and Kano model demand index characteristic results, taking the average value of satisfaction coefficient as coordinate origin, arranging each demand index, and constructing user demand index coordinate diagram. Better-Worse satisfaction coefficient is used to evaluate the relationship between demand index and customer satisfaction, and analyze the importance between satisfaction coefficient and evaluation index with the same attribute. The calculation formula of Better-Worse satisfaction coefficient is as follows: A, O, M and I represent each evaluation index respectively. The higher the Better index value, the higher the user satisfaction when providing demand index items; The lower the Worse index value, the higher the user dissatisfaction when the demand index item is not provided. Combining Better-Worse satisfaction coefficient with KANO model demand index characteristic results, taking the average value of satisfaction coefficient as coordinate origin, the layout of each demand index is carried out, and the coordinate diagram of user demand index is formed (Fig. 8).

Fig. 8. Summary of KANO model analysis results (Photo source: Author homemade)

Aiming at the elderly group in Dongmen community, we made an in-depth analysis of the questionnaire data in order to deeply understand their suitability for community public space Demand feedback of aging renovation. Through detailed analysis, we classified the attributes of the eight demand indicators sorted out in the survey. The results show that the elderly groups in Dongmen community have a significant demand for leisure and gathering functions in the community, and they expect to enjoy personalized activity places for the elderly, which presents a unique charm attribute. In the aspect of expectation demand, according to the activity types and preferences of the elderly, more elderly residents hope to provide diversified activities in the community to improve their participation and happiness in the community. On the level of exciting demand, the old people place their expectations on the community public space, hoping that these spaces can ensure the safety and comfort of activities. This research results provide a profound and comprehensive insight into the needs of the elderly in Dongmen community, and provide a useful reference for the renovation of community public space in the future (Fig. 9).

Based on the statistical results of demand as the basic data, we use Better-Worse coefficient analysis method to calculate the survey user satisfaction coefficient and dissatisfaction coefficient of various demand indicators. By taking the average value as the origin of coordinates, a coordinate map is established, and the survey result data is substituted into it. The first quadrant represents the expected attribute (O), the second quadrant represents the basic attribute (M), the third quadrant represents the indifference attribute (I), and the fourth quadrant represents the exciting attribute (A). In terms of

Summary of the KANO model analysis results-numerical results												
Features / Services	A	O	M	I	R	Q	Results		Better	Worse		
Exercise and Fitness Function (positive) & Exercise and Fitness Function (negative)	16	3	23	36	22	0	No difference property		24.36%	-33.33%		
Chess Entertainment (positive) & Chess Entertainment(negative)	19	2	14	60	4	1	No difference property		22.11%	-16.84%		
Open-room function (positive) & Open-rest function (negative)	62	12	16	1	6	3	Charm attributes		81.32%	-30.77%		
View appreciation function (positive) & View appreciation function(negative)	22	0	36	9	31	2	Essential attributes		32.84%	-53.73%		
Reading function (positive) & Reading function (negative)	14	7	18	42	19	0	No difference property		25.93%	-30.86%		
Manual practice function (positive) & Manual practice function (negative)	38	5	25	12	19	1	Charm attributes		53.75%	-37.50%		
Dating function (positive) & Dating feature (negative)	16	2	37	23	22	0	Essential attributes		23.08%	-50.00%		
Community gathering activity function (positive) & Community gathering activity function (negative)	38	3	31	11	17	0	Charm attributes		49.40%	-40.96%		

Fig. 9. Summary of KANO model analysis results (Photo source: Author homemade)

basic needs, the elderly in Dongmen community show their safety needs for the basic public space and service facilities in the community. Among the expected needs, the elderly residents emphasize the sense of participation in community activities, pursue to meet emotional needs, and emphasize the safety and suitability of facilities in terms of physical fitness. As for the exciting demand, the elderly hope to realize the healing and viewing function through the ingenious arrangement of green landscape, so as to relieve the body and mind (Fig. 10).

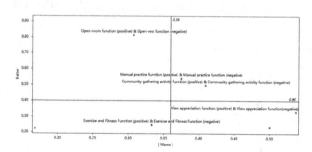

Fig. 10. Better-Worse coefficient diagram (Photo source: author homemade)

In the editing and processing of evidence-based evidence, we sort out and classify the previous data, analyze the current situation of public space in the community, and

Active aging evidence grading					Space interaction model analysis of Quanzhou aging community based on evidence-based design theory			Improve the quality of life of the elderly in the community, and promote the sustainable development of active pension in the community	
Rank	Content	Rank	Content	Topic		Design goal			
1a	Demonstration cases of active aging evaluation will be included	4	Field observation, field research	Rank	Evidence	Design criteria	Design plan	Remarks
1b	To ude controlled experimental evidence of active aging	5	Reports on professional books	1a	Fire escape in old residential areas is blocked	The fire escape is the life escape	Strictly in accordance with the fire prevention code of high-rise civil buildings	...
1c	Inclusion of active aging was not experimentally tested but was tested	6a	Government information	5	The elderly population indicators in the community are abnormal and the detection rate is high	Prevention is greater than treatment	Relevant community medical service stations have been established to provide contracted services for family doctors for the elderly	
1d	Strictly enforced single case study evidence	6b	Information on the professional forum					
1e	Original evidence incorporated into the evaluation system	6c	Engaged in the aging enterprise website information					
2	Results of the review of the relevant literature	6d	All kinds of online reviews	5b	Public property and owners' parcels are frequently lost	One-to-one assistance against fraud will be provided for the elderly	Improve the infrastructure, intelligent service system	...
3	Mainly based on practice, without experts' discussion	7	Talk and chat at will	...	...	...	...	...

Fig. 11. Evidence-based event classification and data editing (Photo source: author homemade)

sort out and summarize the current survey data. According to the design perspective of evidence-based design theory, the evidence of all parties is collected, which provides reference for the editing and strategy of evidence in the design of public space for the aged (Fig. 11).

3.3 Results of the Study

Strategies for Severely aging Population. In the elderly community, the basic needs of severely aging people mainly focus on the safety and comfort of daily travel and activities. However, in Dongmen Community, Quanzhou City, China, the elderly people show deficiencies in walking safety and comfort of public facilities. In order to realize the renewal of public space, the first task is to meet the basic security needs of the elderly.

Firstly, there is an urgent need to optimize the walking route in the community, avoid detours and turns back, ensure the safety of people-vehicles diversion, and improve the traffic comfort of the elderly in the community. Secondly, improve the barrier-free facilities in the community in an all-round way, and add barrier-free facilities that meet the specification requirements, such as barrier-free ramps and fences, to ensure the smooth walking of the elderly. At the same time, according to the usage habits of the elderly, improve the suitability of public facilities for the elderly in the areas where activities are mainly concentrated. Finally, combined with the actual situation and the needs of the elderly, provide outdoor sunshade and rain protection facilities (Fig. 12).

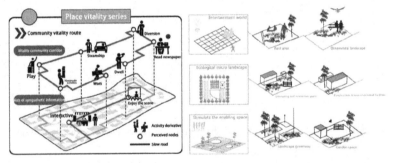

Fig. 12. Path of community activities (Photo source: homemade by the author)

Moderately Aging Population Strategy. For the moderately aging population, this group is characterized by a high degree of acceptance of the outside world, willing to actively participate in community activities and contribute their own strength to community development. The expected needs of the community mainly focus on the interaction between the elderly and others and the connection between neighbors, which highlights their urgent needs for the sense of belonging, spirit and emotion in the community. In order to cope with this situation, it is necessary to strengthen the management of public space, skillfully use community public resources and inject vitality into the community. Reasonable planning of landscape green plant layout to stimulate the use potential of public space. In the process of aging renewal, it is necessary to combine the actual activity needs of the elderly to enhance the attractiveness of community activities. Through landscape healing, it can enhance the happiness and sense of belonging to the community of the elderly, meet their needs in social dependence, and promote them to participate in community activities more deeply (Fig. 13).

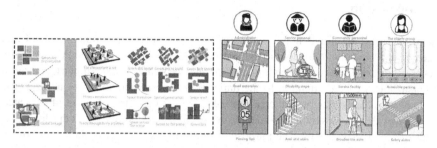

Fig. 13. Activity Strategies of the Moderately Aging Population

Strategy for Mildly Aging Population. In the community, mild elderly people have sufficient vitality and ability to act as leaders and organizers of community activities. They have their own unique talents and advantages, which are expected to stimulate the vitality of the community and tap the potential of the elderly. For this group of people, they should be provided with diversified interest activities and spaces to stimulate their empowerment potential. According to the investigation, a group of retired elderly people who are keen to participate in manual activities are especially interested in the technical performance of intangible cultural heritage. Therefore, community service providers and relevant stakeholders should pay full attention to the talents of this group of people. Through rational planning and space utilization, we can provide high-quality places for the elderly to show their talents and provide them with careful services. This kind of

Fig. 14. Effect Diagram of Community Activities of Mild Aging Population

attention and support helps to create a more dynamic community environment that gives full play to the talents of the elderly (Fig. 14).

4　Conclusion

Facing the rapid development of population aging, the old urban communities in China urgently need to solve the "double old problem" to meet the severe challenges. In the process of in-depth study on the aging-adapted renewal strategy of Dongmen Community in Quanzhou, we paid attention to the daily living habits, activity types and spiritual needs of the elderly groups in the community, and then constructed a set of evidence-based renewal strategies for aging-adapted urban old communities to meet the diversified needs of the elderly groups. The purpose of this study is to improve the quality of life and happiness of the elderly in urban communities, and provide a useful reference for the renewal design of old communities.

References

1. Lou Chengwu, Yu Hui. Active aging strategy in China: cognitive turn, realistic challenge and practical approach. Journal of Social Sciences, 1–10 [2024–01–29].
2. Yuhao, D.: Analysis of influencing factors of social network on psychological depression of the elderly–an empirical study based on CGSS2017. Oper. Manag. **11**, 126–134 (2023). https://doi.org/10.16517/j.cnki.cn12-1034/f.2023.11.010
3. Yuqi, Q.: Research on Landscape Design Based on Evidence-based Design Theory. Jilin Agricultural University (2023).https://doi.org/10.27163/d.cnki.gjlnu.2023.000147
4. Tao, Z., Liu, Y.: Business model construction and innovation path of smart pension community under "Internet of Things + Big Data." Econ. Forum **09**, 126–135 (2022)
5. Junsheng, S.: Study on Landscape Design of Community Public Space in Beihai City under the Background of Aging. Chongqing Jiaotong University (2021).https://doi.org/10.27671/d.cnki.gcjtc.2021.000737
6. Qi, Z.: Research on Community Renewal of Healing aging based on Evidence-based Design. Donghua University (2022).https://doi.org/10.27012/d.cnki.gdhuu.2022.000453
7. Hamilton, D., Xin, B.: Evidence-based design: guiding hospital design with scientific research. China Hosp. Archit. Equip. **13**(10), 37–41 (2012)
8. Shepley, M.M.: Evidence-based design for infants and staff in the neonatal intensive care unit. Clin. Perinatol. **31**(2), 299–311 (2004)

Research of Intelligent Product Design
for the Aged: The Case of Pill Box for the Elderly

Xinyang Du[1], Chen Huang[1,2], Zihao Huang[1], Chenyu Zou[1], and Mo Chen[1(✉)]

[1] College of Art and Design, Nanjing Tech University, Nanjing 211800, Jiangsu, China
mochen@njtech.edu.cn
[2] School of Design, Jiangnan University, Wuxi 214122, Jiangsu, China

Abstract. The key design features of intelligent products for seniors were achieved by literature review, and a theoretical model of the smart product was constructed. Taking a smart pill box as an example, the characteristics and demand levels of elderly people's medicine usage were explored to provide ideas for smart product design for the elderly. Specific methods are as follows: firstly, the design features of smart products for seniors were extracted based on factor analysis and multidimensional cluster analysis, and then a theoretical model of the aging-friendly design was constructed. Secondly, Anderson's Health Behavior Model (AHBM) was used to derive a hierarchy of needs of elderly users. Subsequently, the design strategy was proposed for redesigning the pill box, which it combined the theoretical model and different kinds of user needs. This strategy considered the cognitive, experience, and psychological factors of the elderly group. There are the following results. The three levels of smart product design were established, namely "acceptable, accessible and enjoyable". Then, the corresponding design strategy was established by combining the user's demand and the theoretical model of the elder. Finally, the smart pill box that included functions such as drug classification, smart reminders and step-by-step instructions was redesigned, which can eliminate users' resistance to smart products and guide them to form long-term stable medication habits and improve the phenomenon of medication non-compliance.

Keywords: Design for aged · Intelligent product · Pill box

1 Introduction

In 2022, the National Health Commission mentioned in an article in Qiushi that China is expected to enter a stage of heavy aging in 2035, which means the share of the population over 60 years old will exceed 30%. In order to cope with the rapidly accelerating aging society, the State Council issued a series of policy documents from 2018 to 2022, successively proposing the need to promote the Internet and healthcare, advance the development of elderly services, and take technological innovation as the driving force to cope with the aging population. In addition to the physiological and cognitive aspects of the aging society, such as functional decline, weakening of the senses and loss of fluid intelligence, the aging society also has to face the current social environment, which is changing dramatically. "Person-Information" interaction has become the mainstream

© The Author(s), under exclusive license to Springer Nature Switzerland AG 2024
C. Stephanidis et al. (Eds.): HCII 2024, CCIS 2115, pp. 147–159, 2024.
https://doi.org/10.1007/978-3-031-61947-2_17

trend of information acquisition. From websites to mobile devices, from structures to services, we are increasingly surrounded by a variety of "screens". Mark Weiser, the father of pervasive computing, predicted that there would be 50 billion Internet-connected devices worldwide in this century. In such an environment, it is crucial how we interact with the product.

Due to China's one-child policy, population mobility and other reasons, there is an increasing number of empty-nesters living alone. However, the functions of the smart products they face are becoming more and more massive and complicated to operate, which not only leads to problems such as anxiety and depression among the elderly, but also is one of the important factors that accelerate the widening of the gap between the elderly group and smart products, directly affecting their quality of life and social participation. There are many related reports such as "elderly people cry because hospitals can only register online", "why do the elderly prefer to queue at the counter rather than use ATMs", "the elderly encounter 'difficulty in eating' as they can only scan the code to order at restaurants" and other issues come out one after another. Under the social tide of informatization, the loss of the elderly group is apparent, which runs counter to the strategic layout of "comprehensively upgrading the level of information technology applications, making efforts to meet the general expectations of the people and to promote information technology to improve people's livelihood" emphasized in the "13th Five-Year Plan for National Informatization". Therefore, in February 2022, the State Council issued the "14th Five-Year Plan for the Development of the National Aging Career and the Aging Service System", which clearly proposes to promote intelligent services to meet the needs of the elderly. In this context, research on aging-friendly design is gradually being carried out in different fields.

2 Literature Review

In order to improve the living standards and social participation of various disadvantaged groups, relevant concepts and principles have emerged in the Design field. Currently, the more mainstream ones such as Inclusive Design, Universal Design, Design for All, etc., emphasize that all kinds of products and services should be equally and happily available to all people [1]. On the other hand, as the demographic structure changes, Transgenerational Design and Design of Aging Services have been proposed successively [2]. In response to the difficulties encountered by the elderly in using information technology products, aging-friendly design has gradually become a generalized product design criterion that takes into account the emotional needs of the elderly and the social attributes of design while expanding functional inclusiveness. Domestic research on adaptive aging mainly focuses on architectural and environmental design, but pays little attention to product design and service systems, and the concept of adaptive aging is not clearly defined. Here, we understand "adaptive aging" as "design for the aged", which aims to enable the elderly to access information, use information resources and services, and adopt information devices, so that they can actively accept and enjoy the achievements of information technology and improve their social participation. It is a design concept to improve the user-friendliness of products for the needs of the elderly.

Aldwin proposed the concept of "optimal aging", advocating that optimal aging is a multidimensional concept involving the avoidance of risk factors that cause premature disease, disability or death and the development of protective factors that promote good physiological, cognitive and mental health [3], which has guiding significance for the products designed for the aged. Although other scholars did not explicitly propose the concept of "adaptive aging", in order to enhance users' willingness to use intelligent products and service systems, a large number of studies are put forward a number of factors and key indicators that affect the acceptance and usage of intelligent products and service systems by the elderly based on the Technology Acceptance Model (TAM) and the Unified Theory of Acceptance and Usage of Technology (UTAUT). For example, all users who are exposed to information and use information devices need to possess some cognitive and technical skills. In other words, people with higher information skills are better able to access information, i.e., "Digital Literacy" [2]. Second, if a smart product is considered "unacceptable to learn," "not useful in life," or "too expensive" by the elderly, it will be difficult for users to access it, i.e., "Unacceptable". Therefore, "Acceptable" is the fundamental guarantee to ensure users use the product. "Perceived usefulness", is the users' perception that using the product/system will significantly improve their work performance. "Accessible" emphasizes that the users have a great deal of control over the product/system, and that the behavior or feedback of the product/system is consistent with the users' thought model. "Resistance to change" refers to the fact that in the face of innovation, elderly users have to change their cultivated habits. Therefore, they usually resist innovation, and the greater the change, the greater the resistance [4]. "Information redundancy" emphasizes that the same information is presented in the form of two or more channels in order to improve the validity of the information received by elderly users [5]. In addition, "Perceived behavioral self-efficacy" [6], "Trust", and "Convenience" are all key indicators to improve the access, acceptance, and utilization of information by the elderly.

Domestic research on adaptive aging can be divided into the following directions:

- Direction 1. Construction of an aging-friendly design model. Zhao Chao [7] from Tsinghua University, in view of the difficulties encountered by the elderly in using intelligent technology products and service systems, built a double-helix structure model of age-friendly design from the aspects of prior knowledge, familiarity and cultural context and used it to guide and design new old-age care products and service models; Gong Xiaodong put forward the Technology Acceptance Model for Seniors(TAMS) in his doctoral thesis, which provides a theoretical basis and experimental direction for the design of intelligent products for the elderly [8].
- Direction 2. Research on the design practice of old-age care products based on the concept of adaptive aging. For example, Huang Yueyue used Analytic Hierarchy Process (AHP) and Principal Component Analysis (PCA) to construct kitchen design factors and set up an "L-shaped aging-friendly kitchen" and "Tai Chi Concept kitchen" [9]. Liu Sijun et al. built an age-friendly mobile terminal social platform on the basis of a complete summary of the mentality and need levels of the elderly group [10]; Zhang Wenjing established a behavior model of digital poverty group acceptance for the elderly and designed an intelligent medicine box based on the lifestyle of the elderly.
- Direction 3. Aging-adaptability evaluation. Lu et al. established an aging-adaptability evaluation index system based on Improved Interval-Valued Analytic Hierarchy (IVAH) from four dimensions from the perspective of sustainable development, and studied the smart health pavilion as a case [11].

- Direction 4. Research on the adaptive aging process and cognitive matching. Scholar Chen Jiawen took optimal aging as the research basis for theoretical analysis and concluded that the positive attitude toward "aging" is the crucial factor affecting the development of optimal aging [12].

3 Building a Theoretical Model of Intelligent Product Design for the Aged

3.1 Acquisition of Age-Friendly Design Features

This study aims to improve the usability of intelligent products and enhance the experience of using intelligent products for elderly people based on the design concept of adaptive aging. In order to clarify the design direction, through the Web of Science,

Table 1. Based on the literature review, the assembled age-friendly design features

Source and meaning of characteristics	
• **digital literacy** [2, 3] experience with relevant technologies and products, and prior experience with such products • **perceived ease of use** [13] perceived by users as easy to operate • **resistance to change** [4] have developed the habit of using and thus rejecting changes in the system • **clear information** [2, 5] visible and semantic information • **cognitive directness** [2] align with the user's mental model through an intuitive, natural form of interaction • **perceived effort investment** [15] whether prior knowledge and assistance from other people are required to use the product • **actions should be reversible** [14] actions can be revocable • **avoid frustrating the user** [13, 14] align with the user's mental model to avoid wrong interactions • **respond to the user's actions** [6, 14] provide feedback based on user input • **physical control** [16] physical input method, providing hardware devices such as physical buttons and knobs to complete the input of information • **interruptible, allow users to change focus** [13] the system can switch the focus of work at any time to correspond to the transformation of user tasks • **help user recognize, diagnose, and recover from errors** [16] eliminate error-prone conditions, or check conditions and provide users with confirmation options before they perform an action	• **help and support** [14] provide clear instructions by systematically listing the specific steps to be performed to ensure the user completes the task successfully • **convention** [17] the system should follow an agreed-upon working model • **place users in control** [18] improve the user's sense of control during the use • **familiarity** [14] master the interaction techniques of the product and successfully implement your work requirements through the system • **recognition rather than recall** [19] provide options instead of input • **minimize user's memory load** [14] provide options or easily retrievable instructions to avoid recalls • **provide shortcuts** [13, 20] avoid redundant and tedious operation steps, and provide convenient ways such as one-click completion • **predictable, encourage exploration** [21] provide the necessary documentation to encourage users to explore infrequently used functional operations • **customization, individual differences** [18] users can employ customization options to help enhance the efficiency and experience of use • **consistency** [14] Internal consistency emphasizes that patterns within the system use the same design to represent the same concepts; external consistency emphasizes the need for the system to maintain the same working patterns as other systems in the industry to avoid user confusion

Table 2. Results of factor analysis

Serial number	Initial Eigenvalue			The sum of squared rotating loads		
	Eigenvalue	Variance contribution rate/%	Accumulation/%	Eigenvalue	Variance contribution rate/%	Accumulation/%
1	4.196	27.974	27.974	4.196	27.974	27.974
2	2.384	15.893	43.867	2.384	15.893	43.867
3	2.049	13.660	57.527	2.049	13.660	57.527
4	1.427	9.515	67.042	1.427	9.515	67.042
5	1.023	6.817	73.859	1.023	6.817	73.859
6	0.802	5.350	79.209			
....	......	......	......			
15	0.102	0.681	100.000			

we review the research on the keywords "characteristics of elderly users", "elderly & intelligent products", "elderly & service system", "technology acceptance model" and "usability", and list the following key design features of intelligent products for elderly users, and take them as age-friendly design features, as shown in Table 1. The criteria for feature selection were being cited in at least two other authors' articles.

3.2 Construction of Similarity Matrix and Factor Analysis

According to the age-friendly design features derived from the literature review in the previous section, although the names of some terms are different, the connotations are the same. For example, "responding to user actions" is actually a kind of "feedback", "recognizing rather than remembering" is actually "reducing the user's memory burden", "consistency" and "compliance" are all important attributes that emphasize prior knowledge for elderly people to use intelligent products. Based on expert user interviews, we classified design features from the following perspectives: 15 perspectives are identified, including "familiarity", "cognitive intuitiveness", "minimal memory burden", and "physical control". After the initial screening, the 15 design features of intelligent products for the elderly group were clustered and condensed again to guide the development and deepening of the subsequent design. This study uses the affinity relationship between every two aging-friendly feature keywords to generate a similarity matrix by comparing the identified 15 design features two-by-two through five levels, such as most similar, relatively similar, and not too similar. Subsequently, factor analysis was performed on the 15 keywords to **determine** the number of factors that should be extracted.

The degree of association between the 15 aging-friendly design feature terms can be seen in Table 2. According to the selection principle of "Factors with the eigenvalue greater than 1 should be retained, while those with less than 1 should be discarded" in factor analysis, there are five factors with eigenvalues greater than 1, and their cumulative contribution rate reaches 73.86%. On this basis, in order to optimize the clustering results, only three factors with eigenvalues greater than 2 were selected as the number of clusters.

3.3   Clustering Analysis of Aging-Friendly Design Features

Cluster analysis is to classify words with greater similarity into the same category and words with different similarities into different categories. Therefore, the categories are different from each other. In this study, a systematic clustering method was adopted to analyze the similarity matrix. The average join (inter-group) method was selected to cluster all elements into three categories according to factor analysis, and a clustering tree was obtained, as shown in Fig. 1.

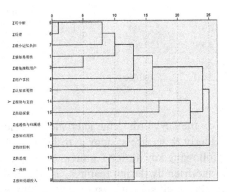

Fig. 1. Aging-friendly design features keyword clustering dendrogram

As shown in Fig. 1 and Fig. 2, the key design features of intelligent product design for the elderly can be divided into 3 categories. The keywords and aging-friendly design features of each category are shown in Table 3.

Table 3. Classification of aging-friendly design features

Category	Keywords
Category1	perceived ease of use, cognitive directness, avoid frustrating the user, place users in control, Interruptible, feedback, minimize user's memory load
Category2	perceived usefulness, perceived effort investment, familiarity, consistency, physical control
Category3	connectivity and belonging, help and support, encourage exploration

The two-dimensional coordinates of the multidimensional scale are plotted with centripetal degree and density as parameters. As shown in Fig. 2, the first quadrant is generally identified as being at the center of the study; the second quadrant has room for further development and is of greater potential importance; the third and fourth quadrants are in a marginal position and are considered to be areas with less room for development. From the behavioral process and demand degree of users using the product, it can be inferred that it reflects different levels of age-friendly design. By the progressive degree of hierarchy and based on the TAMS model and Positive Aging theory, a theoretical

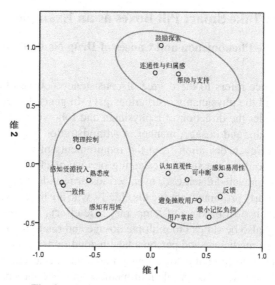

Fig. 2. Muti-dimensional scale analysis chart

model of aging-friendly intelligent product design was constructed. Categories 1, 2 and 3 are named "Acceptable, Manageable and Enjoyable" respectively. The details are as follows.

1. Acceptable. If a smart product is perceived by older people as "unlearnable" or "not useful in life", it will be difficult to enter the stage of testing and evaluation, i.e., it will not be "accepted". That is to say, "not accepted". At present, the overall system of most ageing-friendly smart products is quite perfect, but many elderly people still resist them for various reasons. For example, the APP application constructed on the basis of the intelligent platform, its own requirements for resources become the threshold of use, making it difficult for the elderly group to accept and participate in it, and whether or not the balance between payment and return, and whether or not they receive support will affect the acceptability of the elderly.

2. Accessible. It is based on acceptance of a product that the user will be willing to use it and gradually interact with it. Therefore, the ease of use of the product directly determines to a large extent whether users can master the product, or even whether they are willing to master it. Many elderly people are currently using smartphones, but only a tiny number of them can be said to have "mastered" them. A significant number of them have reluctantly accepted the use of smartphones based on the usefulness of their social needs.

3. Enjoyable. If smart products have good usability, then in the process of using and mastering them, the elderly can gradually build a connection with society, obtain behavioral pleasure, and further achieve their goals and higher needs.

4 Case Study: Take Smart Pill Boxes as an Example

4.1 Analysis of the Phenomenon and Causes of Drug Non-adherence Among the Elderly

Medication adherence refers to the degree of consistency between the way a patient uses medication and the physician's instructions [21]. In general, medications need to be administered under the direction of a physician and following certain criteria. This includes proper timing and dosage, manner of administration, and rate of administration over time. However, deviation from the requirements of medication may result in increased adverse drug reactions, weakening or loss of efficacy, which may lead to prolonged and aggravated disease, or even serious drug-induced diseases. This phenomenon is particularly prominent among the elderly, who are likely to adjust the dosage of medicines on their own because of temporary side effects or improvement in their condition, and may also be subject to multiple dosage and random dosage because of a lack of awareness of medicines and personal health conditions.

Although the phenomenon of medication non-adherence is a common phenomenon, its causes are not consistent. The problem of medication non-adherence in older adults may be due to taking more and more medications, age changes, fear of addiction, transient side effects, prolonged asymptomatic spells, and lower drive [3]. At the same time, medication perceptions can similarly affect medication outcomes in older adults. The literature suggests that low medication adherence due to forgetfulness is a key factor contributing to suboptimal medication efficacy [23] Dai et al. conducted a long term test using a large randomised controlled trial designed to address procrastination as well as a lack of motivation, and concluded that interactive reminders (devices) and goal-setting can enhance medication adherence over an extended period of time [21].

In order to circumvent the problem of non-adherence in taking medication caused by the information vulnerability of the elderly and the lack of availability of existing pill boxes, this product focuses on improving the transition to aging. It was divided into four stages according to the degree of aging: transitional aging, preliminary aging, moderate aging and aging. And the target user group of the age-friendly smart medicine box was defined as 55–75 years old group, i.e., the young elderly group, which has high requirements for quality of life and strong acceptance ability.

4.2 Survey of User Demands

In this study, semi-structured interviews were conducted with older adults who were willing to be interviewed through the Anderson Health Behaviour Model, which is the dominant model for explaining the reasons for the adoption of healthcare behaviours by individuals or families [3]. The model was investigated through three dimensions: antecedent factors, enabling factors and demand factors. It was found that the older adults studied still had a low perception of medication and did not see the need for pillboxes; in addition, a large number of older adults reported that the products were difficult to use and that they were not receptive to modern products, which was partly due to closed sources of information and a lack of understanding of the functions, and partly due to self-esteem and independence. After analysing the surface issues from the research, a user needs hierarchy diagram was drawn up, which is summarised in Fig. 3.

4.3 Elaboration of Design Strategy Based on Aging-Friendly Design Model and User Requirements and Scheme Evolution

With regard to the three levels of "acceptable, graspable and enjoyable" in the ageing design model, user research has led to the goal that "practicality is the top priority, guidance and support are needed, and scenarios need to be flexible". On this basis, in order to correctly guide users and improve the phenomenon of medication non-adherence, this study proposes the design strategies of "child-mothering + multi-scene", "naturalization + intelligent" and "guidance + supportive", and the specific design strategies of "guidance + supportive". "The specific design strategies and solutions are described below (Fig. 4).

Fig. 3. Hierarchy chart of user needs based on user survey

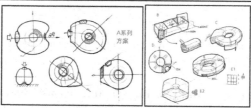

A-Series Solutions: A ring is adopted as the main shape, and a finger ring is used as a split reminder device in the middle. And the disadvantage is that there is some difficulty in loading.
B: By separating medications in the morning, midday and evening. And the disadvantage is that the opening method is not examined in depth.
C: Taking the shape of a Ferris wheel, it separates the storage part and the rotation part. The disadvantages are complex shape and poor shape affinity.
D: The reminder pill box is separated, and the pill storage part is modified into a crescent shape. The disadvantage is that it is less functional and creative.
E1/E2: It takes the design of the refillable pill compartment. With multiple replaceable storage compartments added based on the existing pill box shell case,which shows good functionality and convenience.

Fig. 4. Initial program sketch

During the initial design process, the deduction was made mainly through the divergence and combination of different ideas. From Oki Sato's point of view, that is, in the face of the problem of resistance in design, designers can adopt multiple perspectives and multiple ways of thinking to produce solutions, and make use of the strengths of different solutions to integrate a more perfect solution in the end. The final design chosen was based on the A-series solution, combining the advantages of the other solutions to improve the design as much as possible and to meet the user's needs.

The Design Strategy of "parent-Child + Multi-scene" based on the "Acceptable" Principle. On the basis of "acceptable" principle, the design insight of the early stage is transformed into two design ideas of parent-child and multi-scene.

- **Parent-child:** The pill box has a parent-child structure. The parent pill box is used for filling medicine, and the child ring is used for reminding, making it easy for the user to notice while convenient to carry. Its flexibility of use can effectively improve the perceived usefulness of the product.
- **Multi-scene:** Carrying and platform placement are two main types of scenarios. In addition, some other special situations are also included, such as first-time use, one-handed use, and prolonged fixed scenes. The goal is to improve the capacity and *separability* of the pill box when displayed in home to use, and enhance the portability and ease of operation when carried around (Fig. 5).

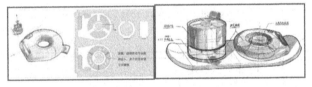

Fig. 5. Scheme refinement under the "acceptable" principle

The Design Strategy of "Naturalization + Intelligence" based on the "Accessible" Principle. On the basis of "accessible" principles, two design strategies of naturalization and intelligence are proposed.

- **Naturalization:** A simpler and intuitive way of interaction is adopted, and the overall operation does not require fine movements, etc. In addition, the presentation of information is as clear and unambiguous as possible. In addition, information is presented as clearly and unambiguously as possible. From a perception point of view, gentle colours and tactile sensations can provide a certain channel feedback, thus improving the sense of control during the medication process for the elderly.
- **Intelligence:** While simplifying the operation of physical products, the online platform provides advanced data display. User data is monitored through intelligent means and aggregated into stage-by-stage reports (Fig. 6).

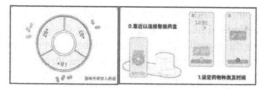

Fig. 6. Scheme refinement under the "accessible" principle

The Design Strategy of "Guidance + Support" based on the "Enjoyable" Principle. On the basis of "enjoyable" principles, two design strategies of guidance and support are proposed.

- **Guidance:** Provide detailed and clear instructions for novice users. The use of large graphics, animation effects and other methods of explanation, tolerance of the user to forget or misuse.
- **Support:** It allows family members as well as friends of the elderly group to participate in medication monitoring. Relatives can check the medication status of the concerned elderly through mobile phones. In addition, the continuous clocking and sharing mechanism for the elderly in the long-term medication process is constructed, which enhances the sense of accomplishment and control while increasing the social nature (Figs. 7 and 8).

Fig. 7. The final scheme

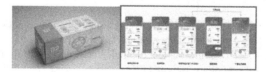

Fig. 8. Scheme refinement under the "enjoyable" principle

5   Conclusion

Ageing-friendly products are in the stage of great demand in China, but the problems of how to define ageing-friendly and how to design ageing-friendly intelligent products have not been well solved. The design of this ageing-friendly smart pill box is an attempt and exploration of ageing-friendly smart products with smart pill box as the carrier. This paper constructs a theoretical model of ageing-friendly design by combing through the literature and through the three levels of smart product design; subsequently, a hierarchical diagram of the needs of elderly users is derived through the Anderson Health Behaviour Model. And the corresponding design strategy for each level is formulated. Finally, by setting up the functions of drug classification, intelligent reminder and so on, we eliminate the users' resistance to smart products and guide them to form long-term stable medication habits, so as to improve the phenomenon of medication non-adherence.

Funding. The author(s) disclosed receipt of the following financial support for the research, authorship, and/or publication of this article: The author received the financial support from Fund program: Philosophy and Social Science Research Fund for Colleges and Universities in Jiangsu Province (2023SJYB0211) and Art Education Practice Project of Nanjing Tech University (2022MC51).

References

1. Wenying, Z., Xiliang, F.: The significance of inclusive design for the construction of public space in an aging society **28**(10), 30–35 (2012)
2. Ning, L.: Research on the design and evaluation method of the human-computer interaction interface of intelligent health detection products for elderly. Southwest Jiaotong University, Chengdu (2021)
3. Hayes, S.: Health, illness, and optimal aging: biological and psychosocial perspectives by Carolyn M. Aldwin and Diane Fox Gilmer. J. Hosp. Librarianship **15**(3), 344–345 (2015). https://doi.org/10.1080/15323269.2015.1049074
4. Al-Somali, S.A., Gholami, R., Clegg, B.: An investigation into the acceptance of online banking in Saudi Arabia. Tec Novation **29**(2), 130–141 (2009). https://doi.org/10.1016/j.tec hnovation.2008.07.004
5. Reddy, G.R., Blackler, A., Popovic, V., et al.: The effects of redundancy in user-interface design on older users. Int. J. Hum. Comput. Stud. **137**, 102385 (2020). https://doi.org/10.1016/j.ijhcs.2019.102385
6. van Deursen, A.J.A.M., van Dijk, J.A.G.M.: Modeling traditional literacy, internet skills and internet usage: an empirical study. Interact. Comput. **28**(1), 13–26 (2016). https://doi.org/10.1093/iwc/iwu027
7. Chao, Z.: Building the theoretical model for aging design: intuitive cognition, prior knowledge and familiarity in the context of technology and culture. Zhuangshi **05**, 12–19 (2022)
8. Xiaodong, G.: Research on Information Technological Life Design for the Elderly People. Beijing Institute of Technology, Beijing (2014)
9. Xinyue, H.: The Kitchen Design for Aging People based on Interactive Behavior. Jiangsu Normal University, Xuzhou (2021)
10. Sijun, L.: A Study of Age-Friendly Mobile Terminal Social Platform based on Maslow's Hierarchy of Needs Theory. Nanjing University of Science & Technology, Nanjing (2017)
11. Lu, N., Li, Y., Xu, B.: Evaluation of the suitability of smart health products for aging based on the IIVAHP-CRITIC model: a case study of smart health Kiosk. Sustainability **14**(15), 9212 (2022). https://doi.org/10.3390/su14159212
12. Jiawen, C., et al.: When you're old, what more can you do? An investigation of the optimal aging process for the elderly in Taiwan. Local Psychol. Res. **40**, 87–14 (2013)

13. Ruiz, J., Serral, E., Snoeck, M.: Unifying functional user interface design principles. Int. J. Hum.-Comput. Interact. **37**(1), 47–67 (2021). https://doi.org/10.1080/10447318.2020.180 5876

14. Nilsen, J.: Usability Engineering. 机械工业出版社 (2004)

15. Teixeira, A., Ferreira, F., Almeida, N., et al.: Design and development of Medication Assistant: older adults centred design to go beyond simple medication reminders. Univ. Access Inf. Soc. **16**(3), 545–560 (2017). https://doi.org/10.1007/s10209-016-0487-7

16. Vilar, P.: Designing the user interface: strategies for effective human-computer interaction (5th edition). J. Am. Soc. Inf. Sci. Technol. **61**(5), 1073–1074 (2010). https://doi.org/10.1002/asi. 21215

17. Kim, C., Mirusmonov, M., LEE, I.: An empirical examination of factors influencing the intention to use mobile payment. Comput. Hum. Behav. **26**(3), 310–322 (2010). https://doi. org/10.1016/j.chb.2009.10.013

18. Davis, F.D., Bagozzi, R.P., Warshaw, P.R.: User acceptance of computer technology: a comparison of two theoretical models. Manage. Sci. **35**(8), 982–1003 (1989). https://doi.org/10. 1287/mnsc.35.8.982

19. Bar-Tur, L.: Fostering well-being in the elderly: translating theories on positive aging to practical approaches. Front. Med. **8**, 517226 (2021). https://doi.org/10.3389/fmed.2021. 517226

20. Shen, Z., Xue, C., Wang, H.: Effects of users' familiarity with the objects depicted in icons on the cognitive performance of icon identification. i-Perception **9**(3), 2041669518780807 (2018). https://doi.org/10.1177/2041669518780807

21. Dai, H., Mao, D., Volpp, K.G., et al.: The effect of interactive reminders on medication adherence: a randomized trial. Prev. Med. **103**, 98–102 (2017). https://doi.org/10.1016/j.ypmed. 2017.07.019

22. Wenjing, Z.: Research on the Design of Intelligent Medicine Box based on the Life Pattern of the Elderly. Xi'an Polytechnic University, Xi'an (2017)

23. Weishan, L., et al.: The problems of modern gerontological research (literature review). Foreign Med. (Geriatrics Branch) **03**, 3–7 (1980)

24. Sato, O.: Oki Sato's Rejected Projects. Cultural Development Press (2017)

Practical Utility and Factors Driving Use of Virtual Cardiac Rehabilitation: A Patient-Centric and Disabilities View to Innovation

Helene Fournier[1]([✉]) [iD], Ehsan Etezad[2] [iD], Dana El-Mughayyar[2,3] [iD], Samantha Fowler[4] [iD], and Keith R. Brunt[2,3,5] [iD]

[1] National Research Council Canada, Digital Technologies Research Centre, Human Computer Interaction, Moncton, NB, Canada
`helene.fournier@nrc-cnrc.gc.ca`
[2] I.M.P.A.R.T. Investigator Team Canada, Saint John, Canada
[3] New Brunswick Heart Centre, Cardiovascular Unit, Saint John, NB, Canada
[4] Horizon Health Network, New Brunswick, Maritime SPOR SUPPORT Unit, Saint John, NB, Canada
[5] Dal Medicine New Brunswick, Dalhousie University, Saint John, NB, Canada

Abstract. This paper reports on research being conducted under the National Research Council of Canada's Aging in Place Program in collaboration with academic and healthcare partners. The research focuses on understanding the journey of patients through cardiac rehabilitation from the perspective of older patients with disabilities. Our approach involves engaging with patient partners having lived experiences requiring improved access to cardiac rehabilitation. Our goal is to understand the status of inclusivity, the unique needs of patients, and the strategies and techniques to bridge gaps in care, and to engineer virtual care solutions that are more inclusive and accommodative to older adult patients with disabilities. This paper emphasizes the significance of the study as an initial stride toward understanding the unique needs of older patients with disabilities. The paper also discusses likely avenues to inform the design and development of future digital health solutions informed by patient-centric perspectives.

Keywords: Virtual Care · Cardiac Rehabilitation · Patient-Centric · Disabilities · HCI · Human Factors

1 Introduction

This paper reports on collaborative research and development efforts focused on understanding the journey of patients through cardiac rehabilitation from the perspective of older patients with disabilities, under the National Research Council of Canada's Aging in Place Program in collaboration with academic and healthcare partners. The importance of involving end-users is well established in the literature [1–3] and in our context

C. Stephanidis et al. (Eds.): HCII 2024, CCIS 2115, pp. 160–167, 2024.
https://doi.org/10.1007/978-3-031-61947-2_18

considers older adults with disabilities as primary users, for design and innovative development of virtual care technologies [4–7]. Current evidence suggests that virtual care solutions have been developed and tested in isolation or in laboratory environments, and rarely *in situ*, with older patient partners in their homes [8, 9]. Such a design and development limitation frequently results in inadequate usability of virtual care technology, leading to poor user experiences, and low health economic returns from theory to practice [10]. A collaborative design process for aging-in-place technology that includes older adults in the design process from the start can improve virtual technology's usability and provide a better user experience, with diverse outcome benefits to care users, providers, and insurers [5].

Drawing from the literature and prior recommendations [1–6], this research project engages with patient partners having "lived experiences" requiring improved access to cardiac rehabilitation. At the heart of this research, our goal is to understand the status of inclusivity, the unique needs of patients, and the strategies and techniques to bridge gaps in care to make virtual care solutions more inclusive and accommodative to older adult patients with disabilities.

Recent innovations in virtual cardiac rehabilitation support provide an opportunity for further integration and utilization, particularly for eligible older adults [11, 12]. Some health disparities within virtual care arise from limits to human-computer interaction (HCI) systems, too often designed for those conceptualized as "standard persons" overlooking diversity, vulnerability and need priorities of those with varied physical, sensory or cognitive features [13–15]. A strong need for patient-centered design and web accessibility standards across platforms could remove significant barriers to access and utilization of virtual care by patients with disabilities [16].

In addressing these challenges, our study seeks to explore and contribute to the research and design process by investigating the intersection of virtual cardiac rehabilitation, older patients with disabilities, and HCI. We aim to uncover the barriers faced and needs encountered during cardiac rehabilitation to serve as a practical guide for the development of a patient-centered, inclusive, and effective virtual care solution for cardiac rehabilitation or other clinical care planned deliverables.

Population-based evidence from administrative health data across seven Canadian provinces shows that the Atlantic Provinces have the fastest-aging population in Canada. The proportion of people aged 65 years and older in the Province of New Brunswick currently surpasses Canada's national average and is expected to reach 30.5% by 2043 [17]. The incidence of cardiovascular disease (CVD) in the Province of New Brunswick is also above Canada's national average [18] and few studies have explored regional variations in cardiovascular disease, risk factors, and broader determinants of health (e.g., unemployment, diet, smoking, social isolation) [19]. Barriers and facilitators to attending different cardiac rehabilitation programs have been described in the literature [20–22], however, little is known about the patients' journey through cardiac rehabilitation from the perspective of older patients with disabilities and their experiences during the COVID-19 pandemic in particular. Our survey study aims to fill an important knowledge gap related to sociodemographic and clinical characteristics of participants expected to enroll in cardiac rehabilitation and those participants who complete the program.

2 Methodology

2.1 Survey Development and Implementation

Informed by a literature review and prior recommendations from patient-centric health-care studies, our survey study takes a patient-oriented approach in engaging with former cardiac rehabilitation patients having "lived experiences" and unique needs such as improved access to cardiac rehabilitation. The survey targets former patients with lived experience in order to gather insights on the status of inclusivity, the unique needs of patients, and the strategies and techniques to bridge gaps in care to make virtual care solutions more inclusive and accommodative to older adult patients with disabilities.

Our survey approach focuses on patient-participants with current or past experience in virtual cardiac rehabilitation across four provinces in Atlantic Canada and aims to answer the following research questions:

- What is the current state of inclusivity of the technologies that are currently being used by cardiac rehabilitation centers for older adult patients with or without disabilities?
- What are some of the barriers and challenges experienced by older adult patients with disabilities?
- What are the main characteristics of older adult patients who successfully complete a cardiac rehabilitation program vs non completion? (e.g., demographics, health, level of disability, personal preferences, options for participating, etc.)
- What other factors create barriers and challenges for older adult patients in successfully completing a cardiac rehabilitation program? (e.g., literacy, technology, COVID-19 pandemic, socioeconomic circumstances)

Phase 1 of the survey study is completed. This phase consisted of a virtual care survey pilot and validation study with subject matter experts and individuals with cardiac rehabilitation experience—as a patient or caregiver supporting a family member through the cardiac rehabilitation process. A panel of experts and collaborators reviewed and revised the survey for clarity and readability. The panel included researchers in cardiac rehabilitation, HCI, clinical and translational medicine, with survey design experience, as well as one older adult expert by experience (EBE) with both cardiac rehabilitation and survey design experience. The survey went through several iterations to simplify the language with the use of generic terminology to ensure that respondents would recognize their own experiences with cardiac rehabilitation programs. Additional pilot testers were recruited from a local patient registry to participate in a Zoom call with research staff where they completed the survey and shared their live feedback on question wording, ease of completion, etc. in exchange for a $20 honorarium. These individuals did not identify any major barriers to survey completion but provided some suggestions to ensure the survey is clear to future participants and the resulting data is accurate.

Our validated (60-item) virtual care survey contains multiple choice and open-ended questions, structured using skip and display logic to help ease the burden of duration and effort required by survey participants. Items include screening questions (3 items), demographic questions (11 items), health and disability-focused questions (8 items), cardiac rehabilitation experience (23 items), including familiarity with digital technologies, prior experience using virtual care or home health monitoring tools (11 items), privacy, security and usability of virtual care (8 items), and the intent to use virtual care tools in the future (1 item). Survey participants must meet the following eligibility criteria to proceed with the survey: be over the provincial age of majority (18–19 years of age or older), live in the Atlantic provinces of Canada, and have been advised or referred to participate in a cardiac rehabilitation program by a health professional.

Phase 2 involves patient-participant recruitment and survey implementation, including a strategy to encourage different modes of participation. The research team is currently engaging with community partners to recruit at least 300 older patients who were eligible to receive cardiac rehabilitation from 2020–2022 to participate in the current patient-centric survey study. Recruitment efforts target the following participants: older adults who are 65 years of age or older, and have gone to or used cardiac rehabilitation or have had a heart complication (e.g., heart surgery, stents placed, heart attack, etc.). Additionally, patient-participants may be recruited via a snowball sampling method whereby potential participants are first contacted by the research team via their professional networks (by email, Facebook or X), and those participants will be asked to consider publicly sharing the post with their network on Facebook or X. As our study population is not easily accessible, snowball sampling will enable the research team to reach them via the distribution of the survey to increase the number of voluntary participants in the study.

A mixed methodology (i.e., collecting both quantitative and qualitative responses in our survey) will enable us to collect sufficient quantitative data to permit inferential analysis, while simultaneously providing participants with the opportunity to have their voices heard about their disability and health conditions.

2.2 Sampling Method and Recruitment Strategy

The sample size ($N = 300$) was chosen based on (1) power analysis, the minimum required sample to conduct a robust cross-sectional study given an anticipated margin of error, confidence intervals, effect size, and the design of our study, (2) the sample size of similarly related studies in the literature [23–25] and (3) our study is aimed at comparing patient-participant "lived experience" based on their different disability and health condition, therefore, the sample size must be sufficient to include representation within each condition to ensure the internal validity of our findings. A priori power analysis was conducted to compute the required sample size for an ANOVA examining main and interaction effects across five different groups (vision, hearing, physical, cognitive, and without disability) for a study with an assumed medium effect size (derived from the literature and previous studies, f = 0.30), alpha = 0.05, and power = 0.95. The sample size required to achieve an actual power of 0.95 is 226 participants (df = 221). When we divide the final sample size by the number of groups, it leads to 18.8 (226 divided by 12), therefore, we round up the number of participants in each group to 20 which leads to a final target of 240 based on our power analysis. Based on previous research examining predictors of cardiac rehabilitation [25], we expect approximately a 25% attrition rate and missing data, leading to the desired sample size of 300 participants.

Survey participants will have the option to participate online via Qualtrics web-based survey software or they can request alternative forms of participation. Specifically, patient-participants can request a printed version (mailout) of the survey if they are eligible to participate in the survey but cannot complete the survey online. Or if the mailout option is not feasible due to any disability or limitations, patient-participants can complete the survey over the phone with the help of a research assistant. These different modes of participation in the survey study are critical to ensuring more equitable recruitment, access, and equal opportunity to participate in the survey study. Collaboration with community partners is also crucial in maximizing recruitment efforts. Regardless of their mode of participation, all participants will provide their informed consent before the survey and have the opportunity to enter a raffle to win one $50 gift card upon completion of the survey.

Preliminary survey results serve as valuable guides for refining recruitment strategies, particularly when employing snowball sampling to achieve a target sample size of 300 participants. The initial analysis of responses allows researchers to identify any demographic gaps within the current sample, enabling a more targeted approach for additional recruitment efforts. By understanding response patterns and engagement levels, researchers can determine which channels (i.e., email, word of mouth, Facebook, X) have been most successful in reaching the target audience. This insight is pivotal for tailoring recruitment messages to resonate with potential participants, and addressing specific concerns revealed in the preliminary survey.

Periodic analysis of incoming data and adjustments to the recruitment strategy based on real-time feedback contribute to maintaining momentum and achieving the desired sample size. Through this approach, we can gain insights from preliminary survey results to enhance the effectiveness of snowball sampling and successfully reach the targeted number of participants. Email campaigns can benefit from optimization based on the insights obtained from preliminary survey responses. Subject lines and email content can then be refined to align with participant interests and concerns. The engagement of initial participants will be crucial in motivating them to share the survey link within their networks amplifying the snowball effect. Implementing referral incentives can further boost participant motivation.

2.3 Data Analysis

Quantitative Analysis. Descriptive statistics will be used to answer most of our research questions (i.e., frequency table, average, SD, range, and plots). Additionally, from an exploratory perspective, participants will be divided into different subgroups and the independent sample t-test, and one way ANOVA will be conducted to compare means across different groups. In some instances, we will also use multiple regression analyses to evaluate the unique predictive ability of each independent variable in our dependent variables of interest (i.e., different components of experience with cardiac rehabilitation programs).

Independent Samples T-Test. We will compare younger adults versus older adults (over 65 years of age) across our three key dependent variables: satisfaction with cardiac rehab coordinator (likert-5); satisfaction with the cardiac rehab program (likert-5); perceived impact of cardiac rehab program (likert-7).

One-Way ANOVA. We have a few variables that include more than two groups which will be analyzed using one-way ANOVA. Independent variables: living in urban vs.

suburban vs. rural; living alone vs. living alone but support is nearby vs. living with significant other; 4 different levels of ability (example: severe vision loss, moderate vision loss, mild vision loss, no vision impairment). Our key three dependent variables: satisfaction with cardiac rehab coordinator (likert-5); satisfaction with the cardiac rehab program (likert-5); perceived impact of cardiac rehab program (likert-7).

Linear Regression. The goal of the previously mentioned analyses (T-Test & ANOVA) is to explore any significant differences between different groups of participants. We will use a linear multiple hierarchical regression to explore how much each independent variables influence our outcome of interest (i.e., their predictive ability). There will be 2 blocks of independent variables which we will run for each one of our dependent variables. Block 1 will include demographic variables including age, sex, gender, ethnicity, location, living arrangement, education, income level, occupation, level of ability. Block 2 will include factors that are related to cardiac rehab experience including *type of cardiac rehab* whether virtual or in-person and *perceived clarify of instructions*. The dependent variables will be satisfaction with cardiac rehab coordinator (likert-5); satisfaction with the cardiac rehab program (likert-5); perceived impact of cardiac rehab program (likert-7). We are interested in exploring the effects of variables in block 2 over and above the effect of demographic variables in block 1 (controlling for demographic variables).

Factorial ANOVA. Besides looking at the mean differences across different groups, we are interested in the interaction between these groups if we can successfully recruit enough patients within each group. As an example, we are interested to see how patients' satisfaction with cardiac rehab program differs based on their levels of cognitive ability and their living arrangement, but we are also interested in the interaction of these variables to see how the experience of someone who [has mild disability AND lives alone] differs from someone who [has severe disability AND lives with family]. For investigating these types of interaction effects, we are aiming to use factorial ANOVA.

Qualitative Analysis. Thematic analysis will be used to analyze the qualitative data points. It involves a systematic process of identifying, analyzing, and interpreting patterns and themes within qualitative data. Thematic analysis is a flexible method that can be applied to a wide range of research questions and data types. It involves multiple stages of data coding, categorization, and interpretation. The resulting themes provide insights into the underlying meanings, experiences, and perspectives of the participants, and can be used to inform theory development, policy and practice recommendations, and further research questions.

3 Conclusion

Informed by a literature review and prior recommendations from patient-centric healthcare studies, our survey study takes a patient-oriented approach in engaging with former cardiac rehabilitation patients having "lived experiences" and their unique needs related to improved access to cardiac rehabilitation. Our survey approach focuses on patient-participants with current or past experience in virtual cardiac rehabilitation across four provinces in Atlantic Canada and aims to inform specific research questions related to the status of inclusivity, the unique needs of patients, identifying gaps in care, and making virtual care solutions more inclusive and accommodative to older adult patients with disabilities.

Our survey study methodology emphasizes the importance of piloting and validating the survey instrument ahead of the main study, as each iteration improved item clarity and overall readability. Given our population of interest, that is older cardiac care patients with disabilities, our patient-participant recruitment and survey implementation involve special considerations, such as: working with community partners, developing a strategy to encourage different modes of participation, leveraging potential participants in further recruitment efforts, to increase the number of voluntary participants in the study. The goal is to collect sufficient quantitative data for deeper analyses of our sampling to make predictions about the cardiac rehabilitation population at large, while providing opportunities for participants to share their experiences and have their voices heard about their disability and health conditions.

Our patient-participant recruitment and engagement strategy will be closely monitored and adjusted based on initial response rates, with subject lines and email content being tailored to participant interests and concerns, along with referral incentives that could further boost participant motivation per TCPS2 guidelines [26]. Our current survey participants will also be invited to share their contact information to participate in inclusive design studies aimed at developing usable, accessible, and affordable technologies for older cardiac care adults with disabilities.

References

1. Gélinas-Bronsard, D., Mortenson, W.B., Ahmed, S., Guay, C., Auger, C.: Co-construction of an Internet-based intervention for older assistive technology users and their family caregivers: stakeholders' perceptions. Disabil. Rehabil. Assist. Technol. **14**, 602–611 (2019)
2. Matthew-Maich, N.: et al.: Designing, implementing, and evaluating mobile health technologies for managing chronic conditions in older adults: a scoping review. JMIR mHealth uHealth **4**, e29 (2016). https://doi.org/10.2196/mhealth.5127
3. Gris, F., et al.: Personalized technological support for informal caregivers of older people with dementia: a co-design approach involving potential end users and healthcare professionals in three focus groups in Italy. Healthcare (Switzerland) **11**, 2640 (2023)
4. Melles, M., Albayrak, A., Goossens, R.: Innovating health care: key characteristics of human-centered design. Int. J. Qual. Health Care **33**, 37–44 (2021)
5. Sumner, J., Chong, L.S., Bundele, A., Wei Lim, Y.: Co-designing technology for aging in place: a systematic review. Gerontologist **61**, E395–E409 (2021)
6. Walden, A., Garvin, L., Smerek, M., Johnson, C.: User-centered design principles in the development of clinical research tools. Clin. Trials **17**, 703–711 (2020)
7. Fischer, B., Peine, A., Östlund, B., Heyn, P.C.: The importance of user involvement: a systematic review of involving older users in technology design. Gerontologist **60**, E513–E523 (2020). https://doi.org/10.1093/geront/gnz163
8. Kumar, A.R., Cluff, K., McLeroy, T.: Is remote human factors testing an acceptable approach for human factors validation. Proc. Int. Symp. Hum. Factors Ergon. Health Care **10**, 152–156 (2021)
9. Mclaughlin, A.C., Drews, F.A.: Evaluating medical devices remotely: current methods and potential innovations. Hum. Factors **62**(7), 1041–1060 (2020)

10. Bitkina, O.V., Kim, H.K., Park, J.: Usability and user experience of medical devices: an overview of the current state, analysis methodologies, and future challenges. Int. J. Ind. Ergon. **76**, 102932 (2020). https://doi.org/10.1016/j.ergon.2020.102932

11. Grace, S.L., Turk-Adawi, K., Santiago de Araújo Pio, C., Alter, D.A.: Ensuring cardiac rehabilitation access for the majority of those in need: a call to action for Canada. Can. J. Cardiol. **32**, S358–S364 (2016)

12. Moulson, N., et al.: Cardiac rehabilitation during the COVID-19 era: guidance on implementing virtual care. Can. J. Cardiol. **36**, 1317–1321 (2020)

13. Abascal, J., Azevedo, L.: LNCS 4554 - Fundamentals of Inclusive HCI Design. LNCS, vol. 4554 (2007). http://www.idcnet.info/home, https://doi.org/10.1007/978-3-540-73279-2_1

14. Keates, S., Kozloski, J., Varker, P.: LNCS 5614 - Cognitive Impairments, HCI and Daily Living. LNCS, vol. 5614 (2009). https://doi.org/10.1007/978-3-642-02707-9_42

15. Prior, S.: HCI methods for including adults with disabilities in the design of CHAMPION. In: Conference: Proceedings of the 28th International Conference on Human Factors in Computing Systems, CHI 2010 2174 (2010). https://doi.org/10.1145/1753846.1753878

16. Friedman, C., Vanpuymbrouck, L.: Telehealth use by persons with disabilities during the COVID-19 pandemic. Int. J. Telerehabil. **13**, e6402 (2021)

17. Statistics Canada. Population Projections for Canada, Provinces and Territories: Interactive Dashboard (2022). https://www150.statcan.gc.ca/n1/pub/71-607-x/71-607-x2022015-eng.htm

18. Government of Canada. Prevalence of Chronic Diseases and Risk Factors among Canadians aged 65 years and older (2020). https://www.canada.ca/en/services/health/publications/diseases-conditions/prevalence-chronic-disease-risk-factors-canadians-aged-65-years-older.html

19. Filate, W., Johansen, H., Kennedy, C., Tu, J.: Regional variations in cardiovascular mortality in Canada. Can. J. Cardiol. **19**, 1241–1248 (2003)

20. Cotie, L.M., et al.: A social-ecological perspective of the perceived barriers and facilitators to virtual education in cardiac rehabilitation: a mixed-methods approach. J. Cardiopulm. Rehabil. Prev. **42**, 183–189 (2022)

21. Ganeshan, S., et al.: Clinical outcomes and qualitative perceptions of in-person, hybrid, and virtual cardiac rehabilitation. J. Cardiopulm. Rehabil. Prev. **42**, 338–346 (2022)

22. Tadas, S., Coyle, D.: Barriers to and facilitators of technology in cardiac rehabilitation and self-management: systematic qualitative grounded theory review. J. Med. Internet Res. **22**, e18025 (2020). https://doi.org/10.2196/18025

23. Eraslan, S., Yaneva, V., Yesilada, Y., Harper, S.: Web users with autism: eye tracking evidence for differences. Behav. Inf. Technol. **38**, 678–700 (2019)

24. Eraslan, S., Yesilada, Y., Yaneva, V., Ha, L.A.: "Keep it simple!": an eye-tracking study for exploring complexity and distinguishability of web pages for people with autism. Univers. Access Inf. Soc. **20**, 69–84 (2021)

25. Khadanga, S., Savage, P.D., Gaalema, D.E., Ades, P.A.: Predictors of cardiac rehabilitation participation: opportunities to increase enrollment. J. Cardiopulm. Rehabil. Prev. **41**, 322–327 (2021)

26. Canadian Institutes of Health Research. Tri-Council Policy Statement: Ethical Conduct for Research Involving Humans (2022). https://ethics.gc.ca/eng/policy-politique_tcps2-eptc2_2022.html

Cultural Dimensions Affecting Perception of Privacy and Intrusiveness of Video Monitoring Technologies for Aging at Home

Irina Kondratova[✉] [ID]

Human Computer Interaction, Digital Technologies Research Centre, National Research Council Canada, Fredericton, NB, Canada
`Irina.Kondratova@nrc-cnrc.gc.ca`

Abstract. This paper reports on research results for the project by NRC under the Aging in Place Program, working on design guidelines and prototypes for safe and usable technologies for remote mobility assessment, including video technologies. We analyzed how cultural factors affect perception of privacy and intrusiveness of video technologies for aging at home, and cultural dimensions affecting privacy perceptions by conducting a literature review, with more than 30 research papers reviewed via the scoping literature review. Results demonstrate that whilst video technology is useful for monitoring older adults' activity, assess mobility and capture and report emergency events, technology design and development needs focus on preserving privacy and minimizing intrusiveness. Adoption of video technologies strongly depends on cultural preferences by older adults and family caregivers. The paper concludes with recommendations for future work on guidelines for culture and privacy incorporated into the design of video surveillance technologies to improve technology adoption.

Keywords: Cultural Factors · Privacy · Video Surveillance · Older Adults

1 Introduction

This paper reports on research results for the project by the National Research Council of Canada under the Aging in Place Program. We work in collaboration with healthcare researchers and academic and industry partners and focus on design, evaluation and adaptation of assistive technologies for older adults living at home. We are developing guidelines and prototypes needed to create safe, usable, and affordable Aging in Place technology solutions in virtual care, research best practices to remotely evaluate the usability of virtual home care technology solutions, and develop technologies, including video technologies, that facilitate remote mobility assessment for older adults.

In Canada, taking into account the high prevalence of chronic disease among older Canadian adults [1], virtual access to care is especially important to support home-based medical services, including home care monitoring, and virtual access to a healthcare practitioner. Recently, widespread acceptance and rapid adoption of virtual care have

© His Majesty the King in Right of Canada 2024
C. Stephanidis et al. (Eds.): HCII 2024, CCIS 2115, pp. 168–174, 2024.
https://doi.org/10.1007/978-3-031-61947-2_19

been observed in many jurisdictions, including Canada [2, 3], with an additional challenge for Canada being a delivery of remote access to care in vast rural and remote areas [4].

2 Methodology

Technology-enabled mobility assessments for older adults focus on implementing community-based and remote mobility assessments. Some of the technologies we are exploring that could be used for remote mobility assessments are video-based systems. The use of video-based systems for classifying the motion capabilities of older people is not yet widespread in clinical practice, especially for clinical evaluations of motion skills [5].

There is a need to develop vision-based motion analysis systems to collect accurate kinematic data in a noninvasive and valid manner to support the mobility assessment processes of medical staff in telehealth aging in place care contexts. At the same time, it is important to develop technologies that will be accepted and adopted by older adults and caregivers. Whilst collecting data on user needs for remote mobility assessments, to improve future technology adoption potential, we also conducted a scoping literature review for culturally driven perceptions about video monitoring and privacy by older adults, with 32 recent research papers reviewed and analyzed.

We targeted published research results about cultural aspects and perceptions of older adults, related to privacy, intrusiveness and motion monitoring, including video surveillance. We reviewed research papers published in scientific conferences and journals on the topic of privacy, cultural dimensions and home technologies for aging in place, with publication dates from 2016 to 2022. The keywords we used to identify

Table 1. Keywords for Google Scholar database search

Mobility Assessment; Smart Home; Video surveillance; Older adults; Privacy; Cultural Dimensions; Cultural Factors; Healthcare; Technology adoption.
Filters: published in the academic journals and conferences, English language.

Table 2. List of topics and issues identified

Topics	Major Issues	References
Privacy	Cross-cultural perspectives Aging in place	[6–15]
Technology acceptance	Cultural dimensions Socio-technological factors	[16–23]
Video surveillance	Intrusiveness Privacy concerns Acceptance	[5, 19, 24–33]

papers for analysis are listed in Table 1. The highlights of our findings are listed below (Table 2).

3 Cultural Dimensions and Digital Technologies for Healthcare

Our analysis of video monitoring technology adoption factors that matter for different cultural audiences is based on the Hofstede theory of cultural dimensions [24], along with other complementary cultural theories related to adoption and use of digital technologies and privacy [7, 8, 11, 24]; and grounded on our past research on culturally appropriate user interfaces with a global tool developed to design culturally appropriate web interfaces [16].

Cultural appropriateness and culturally appropriate design is a cornerstone of healthcare delivery in many countries [34]. Cultural considerations encompass many aspects of healthcare delivery, including culturally sensitive communications, home care and digital healthcare services. Research demonstrates effect of culture on the user adoption of home care digital technologies, such as wearable health devices based on the perceived usefulness and perceived ease of use [17, 18], with a greater influence on adoption intention for people in individualistic, masculine, and low uncertainty avoidance cultures [15]. Cultural factors are being a corner stone for the design of the care robots for older adults in the care homes [35], and cultural factors are being researched for the introduction of video surveillance technologies to support aging in place [24, 32].

4 Privacy Considerations

Privacy matters for older adults, a recent online survey of 2,807 adults ages 18 and older conducted by AARP (American Association of Retired Persons) Research revealed that 34 percent of people aged 50 and older cited privacy concerns as a top barrier to adopting new technology [14]. Privacy is listed as one of the main concerns by older adults that contribute to fear, distrust and abandonment of assistive technologies [22]. Assistive technologies should be designed to protect users' privacy, dignity and independence. Assistive technologies for older adults are being developed into a range of "gerontologies," existing and developing technologies that cater to the needs and aspirations of aging and aged adults [36], with far-reaching implications for privacy, surveillance, and technology adoption [6]. Fearing loss of privacy, some older adults even choose to stop using technology that could compromise their privacy [6].

Research demonstrates that online privacy preferences are strongly influenced by cultural dimensions [11], with people from collectivist-oriented cultures placing greater emphasis on privacy risks in social networks in order to safeguard the collective and people from the countries with high uncertainty avoidance finding privacy risks to be more important when making privacy-related disclosure decisions. Others [10] recommend that privacy researchers must take cultural differences in contextual information norms into consideration when examining privacy decisions. At the same time, research shows that it is difficult to use only cultural dimensions such as Hofstede's [23] to discern privacy preferences, since they are rather dependent on the individual preferences within the cultural context [8].

5 Video Surveillance Technologies for Aging in Place

Video technology could be deployed as a part of the suite of home digital technologies for aging in place, including smart home technologies, for monitoring older adults' activity, assess mobility and capture and report emergency events, thus video surveillance technology design and development needs strong focus on preserving privacy [30]. Adoption of video surveillance for aging in place depends, among other factors, on privacy concerns dependent on the cultural and individual preferences by older adults and family caregivers [35]. In the literature review, we explored how cultural factors affect perception of privacy and intrusiveness of video technologies for aging at home in different countries and across cultures.

Technology Intrusiveness. Studies from Nordic countries demonstrated that whilst using surveillance cameras in the nursing home resulted in a better working environment for staff at night and improved security and integrity for older people living in nursing homes, family members and residents emphasized that privacy invasion is an important issue. Using camera-based surveillance systems could increase the risk for privacy invasion compared to non-camera-based systems. Nevertheless, the residents of the nursing home thought that video surveillance was less intrusive than physical monitoring with staff who enter their rooms, which affected their privacy and integrity [26]. Others exploring intrusiveness features of smart assistant technologies, in a study with mostly German-speaking participants, demonstrated that intrusive technology features may increase user strain through privacy invasion and have a negative impact of in-house social relationships [33].

Privacy Perceptions. Research on privacy perceptions of a video-based technology for lifelogging in home environments among German and Turkish users [32] demonstrated significant difference in acceptance of using lifelogging cameras between German and Turkish participants and suggested that cultural factors play a significant difference in technology acceptance and successful implementation of a video-based assistive technology in private environments.

Another study on using video surveillance at home with physically active older adults in Taiwan [30] demonstrated that, while safety concerns and family expectations facilitate the adoption of surveillance systems, privacy concerns serve as a barrier and highlight the need for technology redesign with older adults' participation. While some privacy preserving technologies are being developed in the area of older adults surveillance, including only storing skeletal data obtained after processing raw video, the Taiwanese users showed a clear preference for avatar-based privacy protection methods for video monitoring technology, instead of a simpler privacy protection technology such as blurring or skeletal data [30].

6 Conclusions

The scoping literature review demonstrated that perception of privacy and intrusiveness of the video monitoring technologies for aging in place, as well as technology acceptance by older adults and caregivers, strongly depend, among other factors, on the cultural appropriateness of these technologies for a target user population. At the same time, we found only few studies that address cultural dimensions of the acceptance and adoption of video surveillance technologies for aging in place, with most research studies focusing on individual user preferences.

Research demonstrated that when developing new aging at home technologies, upmost care must be taken by technology designers to make sure that technology design is culturally appropriate and that the user interface and user interactions are highly customizable to accommodate both cultural and individual user preferences related to privacy and intrusiveness.

There are gaps identified in the application of Hofstede theory of cultural dimensions, and other cultural theories, to privacy research and to incorporation of cultural factors into the design of aging in place technologies, including video surveillance technologies. New measures for cultural factors and HCI dimensions must be developed and tested in order to account for both individual and culture specific factors that affect technology acceptance and trust, leading to improved adoption of video surveillance technologies by older adults and their caregivers.

Acknowledgments. This study was funded by the National Research Council Canada under the -Aging in Place Challenge Program.

Disclosure of Interests. The author has no competing interests to declare that are relevant to the content of this article.

References

1. Public Health Agency of Canada. Prevalence of Chronic Diseases and Risk Factors among Canadians aged 65 years and older (2020)
2. Hill, J.R., Harrington, A.B., Adeoye, P., Campbell, N.L., Holden, R.J.: Going remote-demonstration and evaluation of remote technology delivery and usability assessment with older adults: survey study. JMIR mHealth uHealth 9(3), e26702 (2021). https://doi.org/10.2196/26702
3. Moulson, N., et al.: Cardiac rehabilitation during the COVID-19 era: guidance on implementing virtual care. Can. J. Cardiol. 36(8), 1317–1321 (2020). https://doi.org/10.1016/j.cjca.2020.06.006
4. Buyting, R., et al.: Virtual care with digital technologies for rural Canadians living with cardiovascular disease. CJC Open 4(2), 133–147 (2021). https://doi.org/10.1016/j.cjco.2021.09.027
5. Romeo, L., Marani, R., D'Orazio, T., Cicirelli, G.: Video based mobility monitoring of elderly people using deep learning models. IEEE Access 11, 2804–2819 (2023). https://doi.org/10.1109/ACCESS.2023.3234421
6. Carver, L.F., Mackinnon, D.: Health applications of Gerontechnology, privacy, and surveillance: a scoping review. SS 18(2), 216–230 (2020). https://doi.org/10.24908/ss.v18i2.13240
7. Engström, E., Eriksson, K., Björnstjerna, M., Strimling, P.: Global variations in online privacy concerns across 57 countries. Comput. Hum. Behav. Rep. 9, 100268 (2023). https://doi.org/10.1016/j.chbr.2023.100268

8. Ghaiumy Anaraky, R., Li, Y., Knijnenburg, B.: Difficulties of measuring culture in privacy studies. Proc. ACM Hum.-Comput. Interact. **5**(CSCW2), 1–26 (2021). https://doi.org/10.1145/3479522

9. Cockcroft, S., Rekker, S.: The relationship between culture and information privacy policy. Electron Markets **26**(1), 55–72 (2016). https://doi.org/10.1007/s12525-015-0195-9

10. Li, Y., Rho, E.H.R., Kobsa, A.: Cultural differences in the effects of contextual factors and privacy concerns on users' privacy decision on social networking sites. Behav. Inf. Technol. **41**(3), 655–677 (2022). https://doi.org/10.1080/0144929X.2020.1831608

11. Trepte, S., Reinecke, L., Ellison, N.B., Quiring, O., Yao, M.Z., Ziegele, M.: A cross-cultural perspective on the privacy calculus. Soc. Media + Soc. **3**(1), 205630511668803 (2017). https://doi.org/10.1177/2056305116688035

12. Elueze, I., Quan-Haase, A.: Privacy attitudes and concerns in the digital lives of older adults: westin's privacy attitude typology revisited. Am. Behav. Sci. **62**(10), 1372–1391 (2018). https://doi.org/10.1177/0002764218787026

13. Edward, C.B.: Older Adults Wary About Their Privacy Online. American Association of Retired Persons. https://www.aarp.org/home-family/personal-technology/info-2021/companies-address-online-privacy-concerns.html. Accessed 12 Dec 2023

14. Gochoo, M., Alnajjar, F., Tan, T.-H., Khalid, S.: Towards privacy-preserved aging in place: a systematic review. Sensors **21**(9), 3082 (2021). https://doi.org/10.3390/s21093082

15. Zhang, Z., Xia, E., Huang, J.: Impact of the moderating effect of national culture on adoption intention in wearable health care devices: meta-analysis. JMIR Mhealth Uhealth **10**(6), e30960 (2022). https://doi.org/10.2196/30960

16. Kondratova, I., Goldfarb, I.: Cultural interface design advisor tool: Research methodology and practical development efforts, vol. 5623 LNCS (2009). https://doi.org/10.1007/978-3-642-02767-3_29

17. Fritz, R.L., Corbett, C.L., Vandermause, R., Cook, D.: The influence of culture on older adults' adoption of smart home monitoring. Gerontechnology **14**(3), 146–156 (2016). https://doi.org/10.4017/gt.2016.14.3.010.00

18. Jacob, C., Sezgin, E., Sanchez-Vazquez, A., Ivory, C.: Sociotechnical factors affecting patients' adoption of mobile health tools: systematic literature review and narrative synthesis. JMIR Mhealth Uhealth **10**(5), e36284 (2022). https://doi.org/10.2196/36284

19. Kamp, S.L.: A user-centered approach to help residents make an informed decision between functionalities and privacy within a smart home using a fully implemented web interface

20. Palas, J.U., Sorwar, G., Hoque, M.R., Sivabalan, A.: Factors influencing the elderly's adoption of mHealth: an empirical study using extended UTAUT2 model. BMC Med. Inform. Decis. Mak. **22**(1), 191 (2022). https://doi.org/10.1186/s12911-022-01917-3

21. Weck, M., Afanassieva, M.: Toward the adoption of digital assistive technology: factors affecting older people's initial trust formation. Telecommun. Policy **47**(2), 102483 (2023). https://doi.org/10.1016/j.telpol.2022.102483

22. Pirzada, P., Wilde, A., Doherty, G.H., Harris-Birtill, D.: Ethics and acceptance of smart homes for older adults. Inform. Health Soc. Care **47**(1), 10–37 (2022). https://doi.org/10.1080/17538157.2021.1923500

23. Hofstede, G.: Dimensionalizing cultures: the hofstede model in context. Online Readings Psychol. Cult. **2**(1), 8 (2011). https://doi.org/10.9707/2307-0919.1014

24. Thompson, N., McGill, T., Bunn, A., Alexander, R.: Cultural factors and the role of privacy concerns in acceptance of government surveillance. Asso. Sci. Tech. **71**(9), 1129–1142 (2020). https://doi.org/10.1002/asi.24372

25. Alghamdi, S., Furnell, S.: Assessing security and privacy insights for smart home users. In: Proceedings of the 9th International Conference on Information Systems Security and Privacy, Lisbon, Portugal: SCITEPRESS - Science and Technology Publications, pp. 592–599 (2023). https://doi.org/10.5220/0011741800003405

26. Emilsson, M., Karlsson, C., Svensson, A.: Experiences of using surveillance cameras as a monitoring solution at nursing homes: The eldercare personnel's perspectives. BMC Health Serv. Res. **23**(1), 144 (2023). https://doi.org/10.1186/s12913-023-09130-2

27. Hathaliya, J.J., Tanwar, S.: An exhaustive survey on security and privacy issues in Healthcare 4.0. Comput. Commun. **153**, 311–335 (2020). https://doi.org/10.1016/j.comcom.2020.02.018

28. Li, J., Ma, A.Q., Chan, H.S., Man, S.S.: Health monitoring through wearable technologies for older adults: Smart wearables acceptance model. Appl. Ergon. **75**, 162–169 (2019). https://doi.org/10.1016/j.apergo.2018.10.006

29. Schwartz, K.M.: THE PERSONALIZATION-PRIVACY PARADOX EXPLORED THROUGH A PRIVACY CALCULUS MODEL AND HOFSTEDE'S MODEL OF CULTURAL DIMENSIONS

30. Wang, C.-Y., Lin, F.-S.: Exploring older adults' willingness to install home surveillance systems in Taiwan: factors and privacy concerns. Healthcare **11**(11), 1616 (2023). https://doi.org/10.3390/healthcare11111616

31. Kan, J.: Ethical Issues In The Use Of Surveillance Cameras To Support Ageing In Place. Simon Fraser University (2020). https://summit.sfu.ca/_flysystem/fedora/2022-08/input_data/21085/etd21193.pdf

32. Wilkowska, W., Offermann-van Heek, J., Florez-Revuelta, F., Ziefle, M.: Video cameras for lifelogging at home: preferred visualization modes, acceptance, and privacy perceptions among German and Turkish participants. Int. J. Hum.–Comput. Interact. **37**(15), 1436–1454 (2021). https://doi.org/10.1080/10447318.2021.1888487

33. Benlian, A., Klumpe, J., Hinz, O.: Mitigating the intrusive effects of smart home assistants by using anthropomorphic design features: a multimethod investigation. Inf. Syst. J. **30**(6), 1010–1042 (2020). https://doi.org/10.1111/isj.12243

34. Kim-Godwin, Y.S., Clarke, P.N., Barton, L.: A model for the delivery of culturally competent community care. J. Adv. Nurs. **35**(6), 918–925 (2001)

35. Papadopoulos, C., et al.: The CARESSES randomised controlled trial: exploring the health-related impact of culturally competent artificial intelligence embedded into socially assistive robots and tested in older adult care homes. Int. J. Soc. Robotics **14**(1), 245–256 (2022). https://doi.org/10.1007/s12369-021-00781-x

36. Chen, L.-K.: Gerontechnology and artificial intelligence: better care for older people. Arch. Gerontol. Geriatr. **91**, 104252 (2020). https://doi.org/10.1016/j.archger.2020.104252

An Exploratory Study Integrating Deep Learning in Digital Clock Drawing Test on Consumer Platforms for Enhanced Detection of Mild Cognitive Impairment

Bryan Zi Wei Kuok[1], Malcolm H. S. Koh[1], and Kenneth Y. T. Lim[2(✉)]

[1] Singapore, Singapore
[2] National Institute of Education, Nanyang Technological University, 1 Nanyang Walk, Singapore, Singapore
kenneth.lim@nie.edu.sg

Abstract. Dementia is set to become a major global health challenge. Studies show that there is a significant surge in cases of adults above 40 living with dementia. This alarming increase is due to various factors and early detection of dementia can allow for proper treatment to be administered.

There exist various screening methods, but all come with shortcomings, particularly, subjectivity in hand-scored tests. Digitalisation of the tools mitigates this concern but can bring about newer concerns such as feasibility.

The clock drawing test is a simple pen and paper test, to differentiate normal individuals from those with cognitive impairment, such as dementia. Our project aims to enhance the use of the clock drawing test, via digitalising it and equipping it with machine learning capabilities.

We aim to offer an increased potential for early detection of cognitive impairment, to overall, improve the state of dementia detection already in practice.

Keywords: Early dementia diagnosis · data acquisition and data quality · facilitation of early therapeutic intervention

1 Introduction

Dementia is a medical condition characterized by cognitive functional decline. It affects everyday life and is the seventh leading cause of death [1]. Cases of dementia are expected to almost triple, from 57 million in 2019 to 153 million in 2050, worldwide [2].

Early detection during the 'pre-clinical' period, prior to significant cognitive decline, is critical for the deployment of therapeutic intervention for patients of Alzheimer's Disease (AD) [3]. Current clinical methods of detection rely heavily on reports from patients or cognitive screening tests, such as the Mini-Mental State Examination (MMSE) or the Montreal Cognitive Assessment.

B. Z. W. Kuok and M. H. S. Koh — Independent scholar.

© The Author(s), under exclusive license to Springer Nature Switzerland AG 2024
C. Stephanidis et al. (Eds.): HCII 2024, CCIS 2115, pp. 175–181, 2024.
https://doi.org/10.1007/978-3-031-61947-2_20

These tests are also relatively insensitive to milder impairments and require hand scoring and administration. As such, this introduces subjective judgement, hindering scoring and analysis. Computerized tests have proven to tackle this issue, as seen in the CANTAB Mobile [4] and the Cogstate Brief Battery [5], through automation of the process. However, patients find it unfamiliar, hindering their confidence in the test. Combined with lengthy screening sessions, feasibility is limited, especially in older and uneducated patients.

The Clock Drawing Test (CDT) is a simple, widely used and longstanding screening method for neurological disorders. Patients are tasked to draw a clock showing a certain time [Command Clock] and then asked to replicate a specific pre-drawn clock [Copy Clock] [6]. Being a simple pen and paper test, it is non-invasive and low cost, yet providing valuable diagnostic utility. However, there persists a concern whereby its physical administration brings about inconsistency and subjectivity.

Digitalization of this tool can greatly assuage this concern as it reduces the need for human scoring. The clock drawing test has gained popularity as a candidate for digitalization. Dr. Dana Penney of Lahey Health and Dr. Randall Davis of Massachusetts Institute of Technology (MIT) developed a digital clock drawing test, later branded as DCTClock [7]. It offered significant improvement in the detection of early cognitive impairment [8]. However, development of such proprietary technology is rather expensive.

2   Aims

We aim to provide a more enhanced and streamlined method for early detection of mild cognitive impairment, via the digitalization of the test, through creating an application and also a machine learning model that is capable of detecting anomalies and flagging potential impairments.

3   Literature Review

We firstly investigated the elaborate issue of dementia in Singapore. Singapore's trajectory towards a 'super-aged' status and the alarming 1 in 10 individuals aged 60 and above having dementia emphasizes the imminent challenge that needs to be addressed [9]. Global trends also drew light to the rising trend [10] in dementia cases, and highlighted the urgent need for early dementia diagnosis [11]. Some underlying factors included low socioeconomic status and education level. [12].

A research report from the national center for biotechnology information [13] provided us with insightful review on the impediments and necessities when sharing patient-generated health data. This aspect is highly relevant in our endeavor in improving dementia diagnosis, particularly in streamlining data processing.

Advancements in cloud computing and machine learning capabilities [14] instills our confidence in the feasibility of conducting digital clock drawing tests on tablets. Data is easily collected and uploaded for processing, and such an innovation presents an opportunity for more efficient running of the application, especially on lower end devices.

A study on digital clock drawing tests conducted by Linus Health [15] corroborates the feasibility and advantages of digital tools for such a cognitive assessment. It reinforces our stance regarding the efficacy and viability of digital solutions, especially in this context.

This review underscores the urgency of proactive measures in combating dementia, as well as the transformative potential of leveraging technological advancements, particularly cloud computing and machine learning.

4 Methodology

4.1 Application Design & Development

We envisioned our application to be simple, clean and interactive to make it easy for users, in this case the medical professionals and patients, to use the app. We also envisioned for the algorithm to be written efficiently to reduce application file size and computational load.

Programming Language. We chose Swift Programming Language, a high-level general-purpose, multi-paradigm, compiled programming language developed by Apple Inc. It is fast, safe, modern, and easy to use, allowing for development of an application that can run efficiently on mobile devices [16].

Development Environment. We decided to develop a user interface for our application for iPadOS using Xcode, which is Apple's integrated development environment (IDE) for macOS. It is equipped with a comprehensive set of tools for developing our application, and supports Swift Programming Language, and has a large and active developer community that provides support and resources to developers, making our development process more rapid [17].

Interface Development. We developed 3 pages, The Start page, the Clock Drawing page, and the Result page.
Here, we show some illustrations of the interface that we have built, namely the Start page and the UI alert requesting access to the user's Photo Library.

4.2 Database

For databases, we have also explored Realm, a mobile database platform that enables us to store and manage data efficiently in our application [18].

RealmSwift. We used RealmSwift as our mobile database framework to integrate its Application Programming Interface (API) into our program.

Realm Studio. To visualise our database, we have used Realm Studio, a desktop application that provides a graphics user interface (GUI) for managing and interacting with Realm databases.

4.3 Dataset

Data Collection. We started out by sourcing an image dataset from Kaggle. However, as patient's clock drawing in clinical settings are normally associated with other forms of patient data and these images with their respective scores are not normally culled to form an image dataset, we could not find any image datasets compatible with our project. Therefore, we resorted to creating a dataset, by manually finding and extracting images of clock drawings from online journal papers on the topic of Clock Drawing Test by cognitively normal and impaired elderly. In the end, we were able to extract 52 normal clock drawing images and 63 abnormal clock drawing images. Then, we categorize the normal drawings into the 'Pass' class and the abnormal drawings into the 'Fail' class.

Data Preparation. We obeyed the 70:30 ratio commonly practiced by the data science community [19]. Validation data are automatically split from the training dataset.

4.4 Machine Learning Model

We explored the capabilities of CoreML, Apple's Machine Learning framework used across Apple products due to its ability to perform fast prediction or inference efficiently, while allowing for easy integration into our application [20]. We used this framework to train an image classification model capable of learning images of 2 classes, 'Pass' and 'Fail'.

Model Training and Deployment. Underlying the image classification model is a feature extractor, a base model that extracts image features for image classifier training sessions. In this study, we kept the iteration to 25, and enabled all augmentations - Noise, blur, crop, expose, flip and rotate every image, to expand training data by giving it more variety, as our self-collected dataset is small.

Vision Framework. The Vision Framework is a high-level API for image analysis tasks. This framework is optimised for performance on Apple's hardware, including CPUs and GPUs to ensure that computer vision tasks are executed efficiently, even on mobile devices. Each time a patient does a drawing, the image buffer of the drawing is captured. The application then passes it to a Vision image classification request. Vision resizes and crops the photo to meet the feature extractor's constraints for its image input, and then passes the photo to the model using the Core ML framework behind the scenes. Once the model generates a prediction, Vision relays it back to the app, which presents the results to the user.

5 Results and Discussion

5.1 Image Classification Model

Our image classification model achieves a high training accuracy of 100%, with a validation accuracy of 86.7% and a testing accuracy of 81%. While such results generally indicate that our model performs well in classifying drawings, a training accuracy of 100% brings about concern that our model is overfitted.

To assess the model's performance in real life, we inputted 3 abnormal clock drawing images [21] and a normal clock drawing image [22] into the model using the Preview function in CreateML. These images have been clinically assessed and are not a part of the training or testing data.

In the selection of the images, we took care to have them be representative of three common types of clock-drawing errors, each of which will now be described in turn.

Firstly, Conceptual deficits are impairments in accessing the knowledge of the attributes, features, and meaning of a clock. They encompass a range of errors due to various ways of misinterpretation, such as misinterpretation of the clock, or misinterpretation of time, our model accurately classified such images typifying this error as 'Fail' with a 75% confidence.

Secondly, a stimulus-bound response is the tendency of the drawing to be dominated or guided by a single stimulus, most often related to the verbal time-setting instructions, such as "Please draw a clock, put in all the numbers in the clock, and set the time to 10 after 11." For example, in the erroneous image, the error was that the hands were set for "10 till' 11" instead of "10 after 11". This showed that the patient had been "attracted" to the strong stimulus source (i.e. the "10"), thus failed to recode the "10" as a "2" to set the minute hand. Our model accurately classified an image typifying this error as 'Fail' with a 99% confidence.

Thirdly, spatial and/or planning deficits are due to errors in the layout of numbers on the clock-drawing. Such errors include negligence of the left hemispace, deficit in planning resulting in gaps in number spacing, numbers written outside the clock face, and more. Our model accurately classified an image typifying this error as a 'Fail' with a 100% confidence.

The normal drawing image was selected because it depicted a clock drawing with correct shape, number placement and time information, indicating full comprehension of the verbal instruction and conceptual understanding of the attributes and features of a clock. Our model was able to accurately classify the normal drawing image as a 'Pass' with a 100% confidence.

5.2 Data Input and Output Interface

Out of the 3 pages, our writing will focus on the Clock Drawing page, which serves as the data input point to our model and the Result page as the data output point. The Clock Drawing Page consists of a white blank canvas that allows patients to perform the clock drawing test. It is equipped with a refresh button to clear the drawings and a 'Save' button to save the drawings to Realm database and start the classification process. The Result page will then display the patient's information alongside the classification result.

5.3 Application Performance

Our application was intended to run at high performance whilst keeping application size and computational load low. The performance test was conducted on an iPad Pro 11-Inch, second generation with 8 core CPU and 8 core GPU, along with 6GB of RAM.

Central Processing Unit and Memory Usage. It was initially hypothesized that the Central Processing Unit (CPU) and memory usage would be highest during the image classification process due to the large number of resources required. However, it showed that the highest CPU Usage, at 76%, and memory usage, at 152.1MB, was during the drawing the clock with an Apple Pencil. Further investigation showed that it was attributed to the need of Apple's PencilKit Framework to render the strokes on the screen using the CPU and manage drawn content using the device memory [23].

Energy Impact. Similarly, energy usage is recorded at its highest during the use of the apple pencil to draw on the screen. This can be attributed to the relatively large amount of energy used to draw on more computational resources, such as CPU, GPU and memory.

5.4 Limitation

As we failed to find any datasets compatible with our project, we resorted to manually collecting images to form a mock dataset. However, the dataset suffers from lack in size and variety, which severely impacted the training result of our model.

Disclosure of Interests. The authors have no competing interests to declare that are relevant to the content of this article.

References

1. What Is Dementia? Symptoms, Types, and Diagnosis. https://www.nia.nih.gov/health/alzhei mers-and-dementia/what-dementia-symptoms-types-and-diagnosis. Accessed 12 Mar 2024
2. Air pollution may increase risk for dementia. https://www.hsph.harvard.edu/news/press-rel eases/air-pollution-may-increase-risk-for-dementia/. Accessed 12 Mar 2024
3. Applications of artificial intelligence to aid early detection of dementia: A scoping review on current capabilities and future directions. 127:104030. https://doi.org/10.1016/j.jbi.2022. 104030
4. The Paired Associates Learning (PAL) Test: 30 Years of CANTAB Translational Neuroscience from Laboratory to Bedside in Dementia Research. 449–474
5. Clinical utility of the cogstate brief battery in identifying cognitive impairment in mild cognitive impairment and Alzheimer's disease. 1:30–30. https://doi.org/10.1186/2050-7283-1-30
6. Scoring and Interpreting the Clock Drawing Test for Dementia. https://www.verywellhealth.com/the-clock-drawing-test-98619. Accessed 12 Mar 2024
7. History of the Clock Drawing Test and the Linus Health Platform. https://linushealth.com/history-of-clock-drawing-test-and-dctclock
8. DCTclock: Clinically-Interpretable and Automated Artificial Intelligence Analysis of Drawing Behavior for Capturing Cognition. 3
9. Asian dementia on the rise in Singapore. In: The Straits Times. https://www.straitstimes.com/life/home-design/asian-dementia-on-the-rise-in-singapore. Accessed 12 Mar 2024
10. Association of Socioeconomic Status With Dementia Diagnosis Among Older Adults in Denmark. 4, e2110432. https://doi.org/10.1001/jamanetworkopen.2021.10432
11. Dementia Is On The Rise Worldwide. Here's How To Stop It. https://www.forbes.com/sites/sophieokolo/2022/05/26/dementia-is-on-the-rise-worldwide-heres-how-to-stop-it/. Accessed 12 Mar 2024

12. Socioeconomic Status and Access to Healthcare: Interrelated Drivers for Healthy Aging. 8
13. Understanding the Barriers and Facilitators to Sharing Patient-Generated Health Data Using Digital Technology for People Living With Long-Term Health Conditions: A Narrative Review. 9
14. The Benefits of Cloud Native ML and AI. https://odsc.medium.com/the-benefits-of-cloud-native-ml-and-ai-b88f6d71783. Accessed 12 Mar 2024
15. Digital Alzheimer's Clock-Drawing Test Detects Biomarkers, Study Finds. https://linushealth.com/press-releases/blog/digital-clock-drawing-test-can-detect-alzheimers-biomarkers-in-individuals. Accessed 12 Mar 2024
16. Arham A (2023) "swift 2023: Exploring the pros, cons, loopholes, and improvements of Apple's powerful language." In: Medium. https://medium.com/@arham55/swift-2023-exploring-the-pros-cons-loopholes-and-improvements-of-apples-powerful-language-9c80f476977b. Accessed 12 Mar 2024
17. What is Xcode: Features, Installation, Uses, Advantages and Limitations. https://browserstack.wpengine.com/guide/what-is-xcode/. Accessed 12 Mar 2024
18. Exploring the Advantages of Realm: A Flexible and Efficient Mobile Database Platform. https://medium.com/@rishabh_verma/exploring-the-advantages-of-realm-a-flexible-and-efficient-mobile-database-platform-26655faa049e. Accessed 12 Mar 2024
19. Optimal ratio for data splitting. In: Statistical Analysis and Data Mining: The ASA Data Science Journal. https://doi.org/10.1002/sam.11583. Accessed 12 Mar 2024
20. Understand Core ML on iOS in 5 Minutes. https://medium.com/@dmennis/understand-core-ml-on-ios-in-5-minutes-bc8ba5411a2d. Accessed 12 Mar 2024
21. The clock drawing task: common errors and functional neuroanatomy. In: Journal of Neuropsychiatry and Clinical Neurosciences. https://doi.org/10.1176/appi.neuropsych.12070180. Accessed 12 Mar 2024
22. Clock drawing performance in cognitively normal elderly. In: Archives of Clinical Neuropsychology. https://www.sciencedirect.com/science/article/pii/S0887617707002454
23. High CPU usage (167%) just by scro... I Apple Developer Forums. https://developer.apple.com/forums/thread/706226. Accessed 12 Mar 2024

UX Research on Improving PPR System Usability for Older Adults

Geunhee Lee$^{(\boxtimes)}$ ⓘ, Jihee Kim ⓘ, and Sanghyun Kwon ⓘ

Hana TI Hana Institute of Technology, 127 Teheran-Ro, Gangnam-Gu, Seoul, Korea
{geunhee.lee,jihee_kim,sanghyun.kwon}@hanafn.com

Abstract. This research aims to improve the usability of the Paperless Process Reengineering (PPR) system for senior citizens. In the wake of COVID-19, the rapid digital shift in banking services has underscored the issue of digital exclusion of the elderly. For older adults compelled to go to the bank in person to handle their transactions due to their limited digital literacy, using PPR systems for processing electronic documents is notably challenging. Hence, it is imperative to comprehend the specific contexts, types of information, and input challenges that seniors encounter with PPR systems to make them more user-friendly. This study employed qualitative research methods to discover the usability shortcomings of the extant PPR system, particularly for the elderly in South Korea. Through desk research and stakeholder interviews, we pinpointed key issues such as suboptimal visibility and intricate task flows. Field observations at a bank branch further identified prevalent usability issues, including struggles with touchscreen interfaces, handwriting input inaccuracies, and difficulties in interpreting screen content. Usability tests, utilizing prototypes of two different concept designs and two rounds of in-depth interviews with fifteen users over the age of 60, revealed a distinct preference among the age groups for varied input methods depending on the data type. Overall, senior users preferred handwriting for short words over QWERTY keyboard and a two-row, large-button keypad for numeric entry over a three-row keypad. The outcomes of this study propose essential design guidelines that can significantly contribute to the banking industry's efforts to improve service experiences for the elderly at physical branches, especially in an era where the digital exclusion of this demographic is increasingly recognized.

Keywords: Paperless Process Reengineering · Older Adults · Digital Financial Service · Usability

1 Introduction

1.1 Background

As sustainability becomes increasingly emphasized in business management paradigms [1], the financial sector has adopted a Paperless Process Reengineering (PPR) system alongside the digitalization of operations. The PPR system, which replaces traditional paper forms with electronic documents, have led customers visiting bank branches to frequently use touchscreen-based devices for most banking services. Since the latter half of the 2010s, the banking sector has continued the replacement of paper forms with electronic forms, and by 2023, most commercial banks have equipped themselves with PPR systems, standardizing the writing of electronic forms through smart devices such as kiosks or tablets available at the counters during face-to-face services. Since the older adults still visit branches as they are not accustomed to mobile banking, main users using PPR systems has become the older adults with less digital experience. The older adults are required to perform even simple tasks such as deposits and withdrawals through electronic forms. This requires reassessing the user experience of the PPR system to make it easier and more comfortable for older adults to input information, emphasizing the importance of addressing the system's current weaknesses.

Previous studies have shown that older adults often visit branches for banking services due to limitations in accessing and using digital banking services. A study on commercial banks in South Korea revealed that while 54% of middle-aged and young adults use only online channels, only 8% of those over 65 do so. Conversely, 70% of the older adults engage in face-to-face transactions at branches, which is over four times more than the 16% of younger generations [2]. In this context, the bad usability of PPR systems leading to uncomfortable user experiences can not only cause digital exclusion and a decrease in confidence among the elderly but also result in a vicious cycle of declining customer experience and operational efficiency at the offline branches.

Efforts have been made to improve the usability of mobile and online banking services, automated teller machines (ATMs), and other technologies for the older adults, aiming to reduce digital financial exclusion [3, 4]. However, there is still a lack of research specifically focusing on the use of PPR systems at bank counters, especially regarding the input experiences of older adults.

1.2   Research Goals

This study aims to improve the usability of the PPR system for older adults by: (1) categorizing the main input information used in the PPR system into numbers, short words, and amounts (numbers and letters for units), and identifying the difficulties in each input experience, (2) observing performance and preferences based on input methods and verifying findings through interviews, and (3) proposing principles and directions for the input method of the PPR system, taking into account the characteristics of older adults.

2   Literature Review

2.1   Characteristics of the Older Adults and Digital Financial Exclusion

Since 1981, South Korea has classified individuals over the age of 65 as elderly according to the Welfare of Senior Citizens Act. As of 2022, the older adult population accounted for approximately 18% of the total population [5]. In addition, research focusing on physical and cognitive characteristics, such as age-related declines in information processing ability, has been conducted in developed countries for over 50 years, targeting the elderly population [6, 7]. The information processing ability of older adults decreases in vision, perception, hearing, attention, processing speed, muscular strength, and manual dexterity [8], especially notable declines are seen in vision, field of view, and cognitive functions.

Digital exclusion among the elderly highlights both the digital information gap and its impact on their limited ability to utilize digital banking services. This issue has become more significant with the transition to digital-based, non-face-to-face financial services following the COVID-19 pandemic.

The use of digital banking by older adults is influenced by more than just technical difficulties; psychological factors, such as distrust in digital services, security concerns, and resistance to change, also play a significant role [9, 10]. Moreover, digital banking services often fail to fully reflect the characteristics of the elderly, making them difficult to utilize the services. As a result, the elderly prefer face-to-face transactions despite the inconvenience, and research indicates that the elderly pay an average annual inconvenience cost of 24,600 KRW (approximately 18.5 USD) while using financial services [2].

Considering the characteristics and necessities of information required for using digital financial services, the usability of financial information input through the PPR system for the older adults holds particular significance and importance in the financial sector.

2.2 Touchscreen Experience Among the Older Adults

With the widespread adoption of smart devices featuring touchscreen interfaces, there has been ongoing usability research focused on older adults. Compared to other age groups, the elderly exhibit significantly lower performance levels [11]. Some studies have shown that while the older adults are slower in task performance on touchscreen-based interfaces compared to general adults, there was no significant difference in the level of accuracy [12]. This indicates that as people age, they accept a decrease in performance speed to maintain the same level of accuracy. Therefore, improving the usability of touchscreen products would enhance the overall performance of older users in terms of accuracy and speed.

When designing touchscreens for easy use by the elderly, it is necessary to consider the size of buttons, spacing, and slow hand movements, and from the perspective of universal design, a larger and clearer interface can aid in information perception [13–15].

3   Methods

3.1   Overview

This study adopted qualitative research methods to explore the experiences of the elderly using the PPR system. Although the scope of the research focused on one PPR system of commercial banks in South Korea, we observed most banks' PPR systems share common usability issues and tried to reflect the issues throughout the research. Desk research, including literature review and expert interviews, was initially conducted to establish the design direction. This was followed by the creation of two design concept proposals that were prototyped for further investigation with users. After that, task performance evaluations, sticker voting, observations, and interviews were carried out, and the collected data was comprehensively analyzed. The overall research process and outcomes at each stage are as illustrated in Table 1 below.

Table 1. Research process with activities and outcomes of each stages

Stage	Activities	Outcomes
Literature Review	- Analysis of seniors' digital data usage and digital transformation trend research - Analysis of current PPR systems - Benchmark research	- Understanding of seniors' characteristics - Insight into seniors' difficulties with digital devices in the context of PPR systems - Identification of potential improvements for the PPR system - Understanding of key input methods
Expert Interview	- Interviews with eight experts on PPR systems - In-depth understanding of expert experiences and expected outcomes	- Insights into seniors' difficulties using PPR systems - Understanding of the first-hand experiences of experts - Clarification of project limitations and design directions from experts' viewpoints
User Research Phase1	- Task performance and observation of current PPR system with active seniors[1] aged 65 or older - 1:1 in-depth Interviews about the system and bank visiting experience - Task performance using digital prototypes	- Understanding of the difficulties encountered in using the current PPR system - Observation of digital device usage behaviors among seniors - Collection and analysis of qualitative data
User Research Phase2	- 1:1 in-depth interviews with seniors aged 70 or older - Task performance using digital prototypes - Sticker voting conducted with 23 seniors	- Further understanding of digital device usage behaviors among older adults with less digital experiences - Identification of task performance and accessibility issues

1) Active seniors refer to individuals in their 50s and 60s who, even after retirement, engage in vibrant social activities, leisure, and consumption, aiming for an active and healthy lifestyle. This concept was introduced by Neugarten [16]

3.2 Design Direction and Prototyping

Expert interviews were conducted with four PPR system operation managers and four bankers responsible for deposit services to identify the current problems of the PPR system and to derive design concept ideas for improvement. Through two rounds of interviews with the operation managers, the issues and desired improvements of the current system were identified. Through observation and interviews with the bankers, difficulties experienced by users while using the PPR system were identified. After synthesizing interview results, the following three directions were proposed to enhance the usability of the PPR system for the elderly: (1) allowing only one piece of information to be entered at a time, (2) separating the input and confirmation areas, and (3) ensuring the entered information is clearly verified before proceeding. Following this, two design concepts were organized, and prototypes corresponding to each concept were created. The representative images of the existing design and prototypes A and B based on these directions are as shown in Fig. 1.

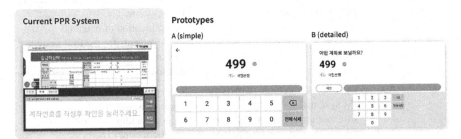

Fig. 1. A snapshot of the current PPR system and prototypes inputting numerical values for account numbers. The current PPR system uses handwriting as default input, Prototype A and B adopt a larger keypad (2x5 array) and a standard keypad(4x3 array) for comparison.

The differences between the existing design and the prototypes mainly lie in design elements (size and visibility of UI components, amount of information, UX writing, and the use of voice guidance) and the input method for each type of information. The existing design, which directly adopts paper forms, features small component sizes, a large amount of information, and the use of voice guidance that varies depending on the banker and bank environment. For bank names and account numbers, handwriting input is the default method, with an option to switch to a standard keyboard based on preference. For entering amounts, a custom-developed amount keypad that has numbers and letters for units is used.

Prototype A (simple version) and B (detailed version) are designed with larger component sizes and less information than the existing design. Specifically, Prototype A uses the largest component size and word-type guidance to minimize information. It employs the Cheonjiin keyboard for bank names and a large number keypad (2x5 array) with maximized button sizes for account numbers and amounts. Prototype B, compared to A, has smaller component sizes and provides detailed information through sentence-type guidance and voice guidance. It uses a QWERTY keyboard for bank names and a standard number keypad for account numbers and amounts.

3.3 User Research

The user research was conducted in two phases, and each phase of the research is illustrated in Table 2. Both researches targeted seniors aged 55 and above and commonly included interviews about previous bank visit experiences and current experiences with the PPR system, as well as task performance evaluations and related interviews using prototypes. Task performance included various c information input scenarios; bank name for short words, account number for numbers, amount for numbers and units. The first user research targeted 10 active seniors in their 50s and 60s (5 males and 5 females, average age 61.9 years old) with relatively high digital experience. After that, 5 seniors aged over 70 with low digital literacy (2 females and 3 males, average age 77 years old) were interviewed and a sticker voting was conducted to 17 senior customers to observe the overall difficulties and usability differences according to the level of digital experience. In both groups, most participants had previous experience using the PPR system (80% in the first group, 100% in the second group), but there was a difference in the primary method of conducting major banking tasks: mobile banking for the first group and bank branch counters for the second group.

Table 2. Stages of the 1st and 2nd user research

Stages	User Research Phase 1	User Research Phase 2
1	Interview about previous bank visit experience	Interview about bank visit experience
2	Task performance using the current PPR system[1]	-
3	Interview about the current PPR system user experience	Interview about the current PPR system user experience
4	Task performance using a prototype[2]	Task performance using a prototype[3]
5	Interview comparing task performance and user experience of the current system and the prototype	Interview comparing task performance and user experience of the current system and the prototype

1) Task scenario 1: Transfer to another bank, exchange from KRW to USD
2) Task scenario 2: Transfer to another bank (randomly conducted in the order of prototype A and B)
3) Individual information input task performance: Short text, long text, numbers

The first user research was conducted in four stages targeting 10 active seniors. In the first stage, interviews about digital banking experiences were conducted to understand participants' previous digital banking usage. In the second stage, participants performed transfer and exchange scenarios at a bank to observe their actual use of the current PPR system. In the third stage, participants performed withdrawal (transfer to another bank) tasks based on two prototype scenarios. The prototypes were created using Figma and presented to the participants through a tablet (SM-T735N) used at actual counters. This helped to understand participants' reactions and preferences for the prototypes. In the last stage, interviews were conducted to compare and evaluate experiences with the current system and the two prototype scenarios, aiming to gain a deeper understanding of participants' experiences and preferences.

The second user research was composed of sticker voting and in-depth interviews with visitors to the bank branch on the day of the research. Sticker voting presented the three input situations of numbers, short text, and long text used in the first user research, and boards were created to allow selection among the input methods of the same prototyping scenarios, which were used during sticker voting inside the branch. In-depth interviews were conducted with 5 seniors aged over 70 recruited on the spot among bank visitors. Since the interview participant group was older on average and often not proficient with digital devices, more detailed interviews about difficulties and behaviors related to bank experiences were conducted, and individual prototypes for each input situation were performed on tablets to more specifically understand the difficulties in each input situation. Additionally, understanding of bank usage experiences and difficulties was deepened, and reactions and preferences for the prototypes were confirmed.

4   Results

4.1   Usability Issues of the Current PPR System

The main problems with the current PPR system stem from simply digitizing traditional paper forms without adapting them effectively for digital use, and neglecting to create input methods suitable for the physical and cognitive needs of elderly users. Particularly, older adults find it challenging to use tablets based on touchscreen, and aging-related visual impairments and decreased manual dexterity further complicate the input of information. Interviews with experts identified the main problems as 1) the phenomenon of slipping on the touchscreen, 2) keypad errors due to insufficient recognition of screen content, and 3) situations requiring assistance from others, all of which are manifestations of these underlying usability issues and confirmed through the user research.

4.2   Preferred Input Methods upon Information Types

The preferred input methods reported by participants, based on the type of information, are as outlined in Table 2 below. For the input of short words, handwriting was preferred, while for the input of numbers, a large numeric keypad suggested by prototypes was favored (Table 3).

Short Words. Upon completion of tasks using prototypes, when participants were asked about their preferred method of input for short words, handwriting emerged as the most favored input method. Particularly, participants with lower digital proficiency expressed concerns about using keyboards instead of handwriting. Regarding the keyboard layout, participants with experience using the Cheonjiin keyboard preferred its layout, whereas those without preferred the QWERTY layout. However, due to the characteristics of the Cheonjiin keyboard, which combines consonants and vowels, individuals with limited digital experience were unable to combine these characters, resulting in situations where they could not write any letters at all. Consequently, in the second phase of user research

Table 3. Preferred input methods by type of information

Information	Input types	1st user research[1]	2nd user research - interviews[2]	2nd user research - sticker voting[3]	Total
Short words	Handwriting	6	5	16	27 (84.4%)
	QWERTY	1	0	1	2 (6.3%)
	Cheonjiin	3	N/A	N/A	3 (9.4%)
	Total	10	5	17	32 (100%)
Numbers	Large Numeric Keypad (2*5)	5	3	16	24 (77.4%)
	Standard Numeric Keypad (4*3)	3	1	1	5 (16.1%)
	Handwriting	2	0	0	2 (6.5%)
	Total	10	4[4]	17	31 (100%)

1) Active seniors, n = 10
2) Seniors with less digital experience, n = 5
3) Seniors visited the bank branch, n = 17
4) One interviewee of 2nd user research responded no particular preference, resulting in a total of 4 instead of 5

with the older adults who have generally lower digital proficiency, only handwriting and QWERTY keyboard options were provided. Although the prototype was designed to recommend auto-completion for short words within a preset list, such as bank names, with a single letter, only one participant actually used this feature. This lack of attention by older adults is a critical factor that must be considered in system design.

Numbers. For number input, the first survey showed similar preferences for prototype A with the large keypad (2x5 layout) and B with standard layouts, but in the second survey, older participants with lower digital proficiency overwhelmingly preferred the large numeric keypad. However, while the large button size of the large numeric keypad was positively perceived in terms of visual aspects and ease of touch, confusion arose due to the unfamiliar layout differing from previous experiences, and there were complaints about the difficulty in finding numbers as they were not all visible at a glance on the screen.

Amounts (Numbers + letters). To avoid errors in amount fields, Korean financial documents traditionally require handwritten letter entries, particularly for units like 'ten thousand' to prevent misinterpretations such as adding extra zeros or misreading numbers. For instance, writing "Sam (3) Man(10,000) Won(Korean Won)" clearly indicates 30,000 KRW, which helps prevent common errors like misreading it as 300,000 or altering figures to 80,000. This method is a safeguard against both input mistakes and potential forgery. Accordingly, in the PPR system, it has been noted that handwriting amounts continues as a standard practice due to this historical precedence. However, many users believed that typing amounts using a keyboard increased input accuracy when performing tasks with the prototype. Additionally, another issue with handwriting input was the difficulty in providing instructions related to its use. About half of the screen becomes filled with the handwriting recognition area for entering the amount, and even with voice or guidance, it was difficult for the older adults to immediately understand what to do.

5   Conclusion

This study aimed to enhance the usability of the PPR system for the older adults by improving the input experience. To achieve this, the study sought to understand the information and situations in which the elderly have difficulty with input in the current PPR system. Additionally, to verify whether performance and preferences vary according to the input method, the primary input methods for each type of information were set as variables to observe and conduct interviews regarding preferences. Based on the experimental results, principles and directions for input methods in designing the PPR system UX were proposed, considering the characteristics of the elderly.

The main issues with the current PPR system were identified as stemming from the direct transition of the traditional paper form structure, which is not optimized for the digital environment and the input method not being designed considering the physical and cognitive abilities of the main users, the older adults. To solve these issues, prototypes were developed, and experiments targeting the elderly were conducted, performing information input tasks that included the most common information types in banking tasks: entering short words for names of banks, numbers for account numbers, and letters and numbers for amounts.

The analysis results confirmed the effectiveness of the proposed directions for enhancing the usability of the PPR system for the elderly. The conclusions according to each direction can be summarized as follows:

Allow Only One Piece of Information to Be Entered at a Time. A preference for presenting and entering only one piece of information at a time to help the elderly concentrate on understanding and inputting information was higher than the existing method of the PPR system, where several pieces of information are presented at once.

Distinguish Between Input and Verification Areas. Higher accuracy was shown when the screen areas requiring focus for inputting and verifying information were separated, and confidence in being able to input by oneself increased.

Ensure the Content Entered is Verified Before Proceeding. When participants were allowed to recheck their input with larger UI components and texts before moving to the next step, input errors decreased, and the user experience improved.

This study has the following limitations. First, the user study was conducted with a small sample size of 10 active seniors and older adults, limiting statistical reliability and generalizability. Second, since it was not possible to adjust the bank branch and digital experience levels of the elderly users, there is a possibility that the survey results could be distorted due to varying levels of experience.

Acknowledgments. This study was conducted under a joint research agreement for the Digital Transformation of Hana Bank and Hana TI.

References

1. Kang, G.H., Jeong, W.D.: The effects of corporate efforts for the sustainable management on the corporate trust and purchase intention. EWHA Manag. Rev. **35**, 1–14 (2014). https://www.dbpia.co.kr/Journal/articleDetail?nodeId=NODE06078108

2. Park, H., Kim, H., Kim, Y.: What would be the monetary value of the financial transaction inconveniences faced by the elderly? Statistics Research Institute, 17 (2022). https://kostat.go.kr/board.es?mid=a90102010100&bid=11918&tag=&act=view&list_no=417489&ref_bid=

3. Kim, H. J.: A study on usability improvement of smart phone banking considering elderly users—focusing on usability test targeting elderly for money transfer procedure of Busan bank smart phone banking app. J. Digital Des. **15**(1), 123–132 (2015). https://www.dbpia.co.kr/Journal/articleDetail?nodeId=NODE06092303

4. Choi, Y., Choi, H.: Evaluation of ATM usability test for improving financial life of impaired elderly. J. Korea Inst. Inform. Commun. Eng. **24**(1), 77–82 (2020). https://www.dbpia.co.kr/Journal/articleDetail?nodeId=NODE09298396

5. Statistics Korea Social Statistics Planning Department (n.d.): 2022 Senior Citizen Statistics. https://27.101.222.79/ansk/?mid=a10301010000&bid=10820&tag=&act=view&list_no=420896&ref_bid. Accessed 11 Mar 2024

6. Kinoshita, Y., Ichinohe, S., Sakakura, Y., Cooper, E.W., Kamei, K.: Kansei product design for the active senior generation-A case study of mobile phone designs. Signs **6**, 9 (2007)

7. Neugarten, B.L.: Age groups in American society and the rise of the young-old. Ann. Am. Acad. Pol. Soc. Sci. **415**(1), 187–198 (1974)

8. Davidse, R.J.: Older drivers and ADAS: Which Systems Improve Road Safety? IATSS Res. **30**(1), 6–20 (2006). https://doi.org/10.1016/S0386-1112(14)60151-5

9. Lassar, W.M., Manolis, C., Lassar, S.S.: The relationship between consumer innovativeness, personal characteristics, and online banking adoption. Int. J. Bank Mark. **23**(2), 176–199 (2005). https://doi.org/10.1108/02652320510584403

10. Msweli, N.T., Mawela, T.: Enablers and Barriers for Mobile Commerce and Banking Services Among the Elderly in Developing Countries: A Systematic Review. In: Hattingh, M., Matthee, M., Smuts, H., Pappas, I., Dwivedi, Y.K., Mäntymäki, M. (eds.) I3E 2020. LNCS, vol. 12067, pp. 319–330. Springer, Cham (2020). https://doi.org/10.1007/978-3-030-45002-1_27

11. Walker, N., Philbin, D.A., Fisk, A.D.: Age-related differences in movement control: adjusting submovement structure to optimize performance. J. Gerontol. Ser. B **52B**(1), P40–P53 (1997). https://doi.org/10.1093/geronb/52B.1.P40

12. Hertzum, M., Hornbæk, K.: How Age Affects Pointing with Mouse and Touchpad: A Comparison of Young, Adult, and Elderly Users. Int. J. Hum. Comput. Interact. **26**(7), 703–734 (2010). https://doi.org/10.1080/10447318.2010.487198

13. Jin, Z.X., Plocher, T., Kiff, L.: Touch Screen User Interfaces for Older Adults: Button Size and Spacing. In: Stephanidis, C. (ed.) Universal Acess in Human Computer Interaction. Coping with Diversity: 4th International Conference on Universal Access in Human-Computer Interaction, UAHCI 2007, Held as Part of HCI International 2007, Beijing, China, July 22-27, 2007, Proceedings, Part I, pp. 933–941. Springer Berlin Heidelberg, Berlin, Heidelberg (2007). https://doi.org/10.1007/978-3-540-73279-2_104

14. Han, Y.S., Choi, J.K., Yoon, S.H., Ji, Y.G.: A study on pointing performance of elderly on smartphone. In: HCI Korea Conference, 932–934 (2012). https://www.dbpia.co.kr/Journal/articleDetail?nodeId=NODE01878366

15. Hwangbo, H., Yoon, S.H., Jin, B.S., Han, Y.S., Ji, Y.G.: A Study of Pointing Performance of Elderly Users on Smartphones. Int. J. Hum. Comput. Interact. **29**(9), 604–618 (2013). https://doi.org/10.1080/10447318.2012.729996
16. Neugarten, BL.: The Meanings of Age: Selected Papers. University of Chicago Press, Chicago, Illinois (1996)

The Application Strategy of Smart Home in Future Aging-Friendly Space Based on Chinese Retired Elderly Population - a Mixed Methods Research Protocol

Jiaxin Liu[✉] [iD] and Changming Tang

Northeastern University, Shenyang 110000, China
ljx15762258027@163.com

Abstract. To optimize the elderly care experience of the retired elderly population in China in the future and alleviate the rapidly developing aging population in China, this study proposes a hybrid method research model based on user demands. Taking sensors in intelligent living systems as an example, the study investigates the application strategies of intelligent living in future aging-friendly space based on the retired elderly population in China. Firstly, qualitative research methods such as literature review were used to collect user demands from 12 related fields; Secondly, the KANO model is used to classify and rank user demands. Thirdly, use QFD theory to transform user demands into design elements. Fourthly, resolve conflicting spatial design technology elements in QFD-HOQ through existing or innovative spatial design technology elements. The research results indicate that design elements such as "personalized customization based on lifestyle habits", "controlling the number of sensors", and "ergonomic scale" have high importance ratings, which are important design points for the future application of intelligent living in aging-friendly space. This provides forward-looking opinions for the future application of intelligent living in aging-friendly space.

Keywords: Aging-Friendly Space · Intelligent Housing · KANO Model · QFD Theory · User Demands

1 Introduction

As a residential platform, a smart home integrates facilities related to home life and constructs an efficient management system for residential facilities and family schedule affairs, which can improve home safety, convenience, comfort, artistry and achieve an environmentally friendly and energy-saving living environment [1]. Chinese elderly population is severely "not affluent before getting old" and with a structural shortage of elderly care and medical service labor force and a serious shortage of nursing staff [2]. The application of smart home in aging-friendly space can provide more accurate and efficient quality services for the elderly [3]. It enables the elderly to maintain a higher quality of life and a greater sense of well-being while remaining independent [4]. In the case study of aging-friendly renovation design for the No.1 residential complex of Beijing Lingxiu New Silicon Valley, Zhang Tianlin et al. [5] applied an aging-friendly smart home system such as intelligent lighting systems, fall monitoring systems, and emergency call systems. In this case, the use of smart home systems has greatly improved the safety, comfort, and self-care of aging-friendly homes. Therefore, the application of smart home in the future aging-friendly space will be an efficiency way to actively respond to the current aging status quo that is developing extremely rapidly in China. However, at present, the research and development of smart home mainly focuses on the technical field [6]. To help the future Chinese senior citizens carry out their daily aging activities in an intelligent way and fully enjoy the benefits that modern information technology brings to human life, this study starts with the application methods of smart homes in future aging-friendly space, and combines the problems and demands of the retired elderly population in China, with a user-oriented approach to explore the application strategies of smart homes in aging-friendly space.

Relevant studies have shown that most of the current smart home products are mainly designed for young people, ignoring the use of the elderly population in the home [7]. Therefore, the general application of smart home in the aging-friendly space still demands to go through a certain stage of development, and the improvement of the current situation is also limited by the degree of market penetration. Therefore, there is a need to be ahead of the curve regarding the application of smart home in aging-friendly space.

From a physiological perspective, as one approaches the age of 60, their physiological functions will continue to deteriorate, generally facing physiological changes such as memory decline, slower reflex speed, decreased hearing, and fragile bones [8], making it increasingly difficult to take care of oneself. In addition, from a psychological perspective, the elderly population after retirement will also experience significant changes in life centers and other aspects, directly or indirectly leading to psychological changes. The demand for respect emotions will continue to increase. Therefore, the elderly population after retirement, whether from a physiological or psychological perspective, has a significant demand for daily care and care, and their desire for these demands will continue to increase with age. Currently, the current legal retirement age for Chinese employees is 60 years for males, 55 years for female cadres, and 50 years for female workers. Based on the above analysis of the physiological changes and psychological changes of the elderly population aged 60 and above, this study proposes to discuss the application strategies of smart homes in future aging space based on the retired elderly population aged 60 and above. According to the latest data from China's seventh population census, it is expected that 225 million elderly people will be transformed into retired elderly people over 60 years old by 2030, and will be transformed into elderly people over 75 years old by 2045 [9]. This will be a challenge for China's elderly care and medical service system. Based on the current structural shortage of elderly care and medical labor in China, the Chinese government has formulated relevant policies to promote on-site elderly care for retired elderly groups. The application of smart homes in future aging suitable living space is expected to become the main elderly care assistance system for retired elderly groups in the future.

By comprehensively analyzing the current situation of smart home applications in aging-friendly space in China, the physical and mental changes of the elderly population aged 60 and above, and the future trend of China's population structure, this study proposes forward-looking and constructive suggestions for future smart home applications in aging-friendly space, based on transforming them into retired elderly populations aged 60 and above between 2023 and 2030.

2 Methods

We propose an application model for future aging-friendly smart homes that integrates qualitative and quantitative research methods (see Fig. 1). The research model used in this study effectively ensures the scientific rationality of the design strategy export process, providing ideas for the future application of smart homes in aging-friendly space.

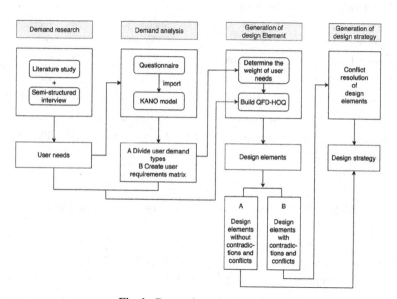

Fig. 1. Research methods model.

3 Application Strategy Research

3.1 Acquisition of User Demands

The study identified 29 personalized demands (see Table 1) of users based on the personalized demands acquisition method proposed by Tang Zhongjun et al. [10] in "Research on Personalized Demands Acquisition Method Based on Kano Model". Because the charm demand in the Kano model is usually an Attractive Quality from consumers, it is difficult for ordinary users to come up with it. Therefore, for comprehensive considerations, this study investigated 6 elderly people who will retire between 2023 and 2030 and were born between 1963 and 1970 (which will be transformed into a retirement age of 60 and above between 2023 and 2030); 2 elderly family members who meet the above restrictions; 4 interior design industry practitioners and 4 nursing home service personnel conducted semi-structured interviews. And based on the interview results, 12 demands with high relevance to the future demand for smart home applications in aging-friendly space for the Chinese quasi-retired elderly population and their families are screened and supplemented (see Table 2), providing support for further in-depth analysis of user demands.

Table 1. Summary of design requirements.

No	Demand	No	Demand	No	Demand	No	Demand
1	Health Monitoring	9	Sense of Belonging	16	Efficiency	23	Intelligent
2	Personalized Customization	10	Sensory Compensation	17	Social Participation	24	Technological Achievement
3	Ease of Use	11	Comfortable	18	Economy	25	Sustainable
4	Effectiveness	12	Stability	19	Safety	26	Thrill
5	Humanize	13	Extensibility	20	Emotional Care	27	Flexibility
6	Generality	14	Interactive	21	Standardization	28	Independence
7	Interest	15	Accessibility	22	Energy-saving	29	Silence
8	Practicality						

Table 2. Design requirements after screening and supplementation.

Type	Demand	No	Type	Demand	No
Use Demand	Ease of Use	U1	Psychological Demand	Privacy	P1
	Durability	U2		Respective	P2
	Efficiency	U3		Emotional Care	P3
	Safety	U4	Appearance Demand	Aesthetic	A1
	Autonomy	U5	Other Demand	Energy-Saving	O1
	Personalized Customization	U6		Cost-Effective	O2

3.2 User Demands Analysis Based on KANO Model

The Production of Likert's Fifth-Order Questionnaire. Based on the obtained user demands, create a Likert's Fifth-Order Questionnaire (see Table 3).

Table 3. KANO Likert Fifth Order Questionnaire.

If this requirement is met, what is your attitude? (Positive Question)					Future demands for smart home applications in aging-friendly space	If this requirement is met, what is your attitude? (Reverse Question)				
Like	Must-be	Neural	Live-with	Dislike		Like	Must-be	Neural	Live-with	Dislike
					Ease of Use					
					Durability					
					Efficiency					
					……					

Requirement Type Based on KANO Model. This survey aims to distribute and collect questionnaires for the elderly population aged 60 and above (born between 1963 and 1970) and their families who will be transformed into retirees between 2023 and 2030. A total of 38 valid questionnaires were collected. Among them, there are 14 male users, 9 female users, 7 family members of male users, and 8 family members of female users, with an age range of 54 to 59 years old.

This study uses the KANO model evaluation system to determine the attribute types of each requirement indicator (see Table 4).

Table 4. User requirement attribute type table.

Demand \ Type	A	O	M	I	R	Q	Attribute Type
Ease of Use U1	7.89%	7.89%	84.21%	0.00%	0.00%	0.00%	M
Durability U2	0.00%	7.89%	92.11%	0.00%	0.00%	0.00%	M
Efficiency U3	0.00%	89.47%	5.26%	5.26%	0.00%	0.00%	O
Safety U4	0.00%	31.58%	68.42%	0.00%	0.00%	0.00%	M
Autonomy U5	7.89%	81.58%	7.89%	2.63%	0.00%	0.00%	O
Personalized Customization U6	89.47%	5.26%	0.00%	5.26%	0.00%	0.00%	A
Privacy P1	2.63%	5.26%	89.47%	2.63%	0.00%	0.00%	M
Respective P2	18.42%	5.26%	13.16%	63.16%	0.00%	0.00%	I
Emotional Care P3	7.89%	2.63%	5.26%	84.21%	0.00%	0.00%	I
Aesthetic A1	81.58%	10.53%	2.63%	5.26%	0.00%	0.00%	A
Energy-saving O1	5.26%	78.95%	13.16%	2.63%	0.00%	0.00%	O
Cost-effective O2	7.89%	73.68%	15.79%	2.63%	0.00%	0.00%	O

The classification of demand attribute categories obtained from was analyzed as follows:

"Ease of Use", "Durability", "Safety", and "Privacy" are Must-be Quality (M) demands. Meeting M demands will not significantly improve user satisfaction, but if not met, it will lead to a significant decrease in user satisfaction. "Efficiency", "Autonomy", "Energy Saving", and "Cost-Effective" are the One Dimensional Quality (O) demands. O demands are not necessary, but the more O demands are provided, the better satisfaction customers will get. "Personalization Customization" and "Aesthetic" are Attractive Quality (A) demands, which belong to demands that exceed user expectations. The higher the degree of satisfaction of A demands, the more significant the improvement in user satisfaction will be. But when A demands are not considered, user satisfaction will not be significantly affected. Therefore, in the process of exploring future smart living application strategies for aging-friendly space, it is necessary to fully consider M demands to avoid a decrease in user satisfaction. And the O demands and A demands should also be given priority consideration to improve user satisfaction.

"Respective" and "Emotional Care" are Indifferent Quality (I) demands, and the satisfaction of such demands has no direct impact on user satisfaction. Therefore, this study will not discuss I demands.

Ranking of Importance of User Demands. The greater the sensitivity of user demands, the worthier it is to study [11], and its importance is relatively high [12]. Based on this, this study constructed a Better-Worse coefficient graph for user demands, using the absolute value of user dissatisfaction influence (Worse) as the x-axis and the value of user satisfaction influence (Better) as the y-axis, to determine the importance of different user demands by reflecting their sensitivity (see Fig. 2). By using the distance between the coordinates of each user's demand in the Better-Worse coefficient graph and the center (0,0), which is the sensitivity of user demand to rank the importance of user demand (see Table 5). It can be seen that "Efficiency", "Autonomy", and "Energy-saving" are in a high degree of importance.

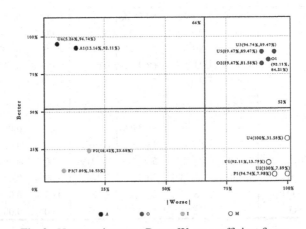

Fig. 2. User requirements Better-Worse coefficient figure.

Table 5. Ranking of Importance of user demands.

Demand	Demand Sensitivity	Importance ranking	Demand	Demand Sensitivity	Importance ranking
U1	0.93	9	U6	0.95	7
U2	1	6	P1	0.95	7
U3	1.3	1	A1	0.93	9
U4	1.05	5	O1	1.25	3
U5	1.26	2	O2	1.21	4

3.3 Design Element Acquisition Based on QFD Model

The main research directions of this study are based on the application of intelligent living in future aging-friendly space. Intelligent housing includes sensors, actuators, middleware, and networks [11]. Among them, the sensor has greater designability in terms of its spatial location, and the presentation of different sensors in different spatial locations will also have a certain degree of impact on the user's experience. Therefore, this study mainly studies the application strategies of smart home sensors in aging-friendly space.

Based on the service categories of smart homes and the sensors required for different types of services organized by Byeongkwan Kang et al. [13], this study divided sensors into "sensors that involve interacting with the retired elderly population" and "sensors that do not involve interacting with the retired elderly population", The classification is shown in Table 6.

Table 6. Sensor classification.

Sensors Involved in Interactive Behavior	Sensors Did Not Involved in Interactive Behavior	
Touch Sensors, etc.	Involved Privacy	Image sensors (cameras), video sensors (cameras), etc.
	Did Not Involve Privacy	Light Sensors, Humidity Sensors, Temperature Sensors, Infrared Sensors, Motion Sensors, Gas Sensors, PIR Sensors, CDS Sensors, Magnetic Sensors

Construction of QFD House of Quality (HOQ). Based on the particularity of different types of sensors, this study proposes spatial design elements for the application of intelligent living in future aging-friendly space according to different types of sensors, and constructs QFD House of Quality (HOQ) separately (see Fig. 3). The 1, 3, 5, and 9 scales consistent with the standard QFD method were used in the requirement function matrix diagram, where 1 represents weak correlation; 3. 5 represents moderate association; 9 represents strong association [14].

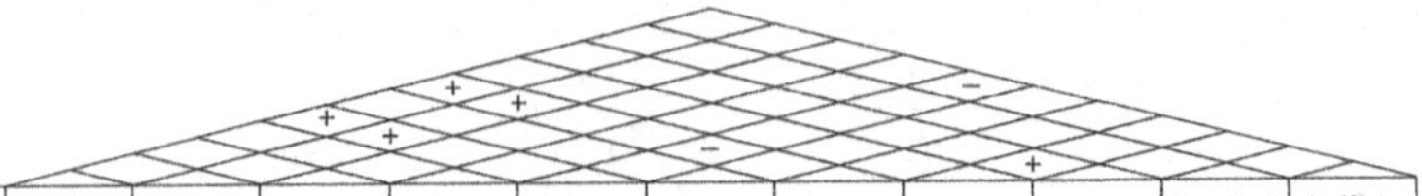

Demand	Demand Sensitivity	Ergonomic Scale	Operational Spatial Scale	Simplify Operation Flow	Scale Adjustment	High Coverage of Sensors in All Hazardous Areas	Personalized Customization Based on Lifestyle Habits	Control the Number of Sensors	Embedded Design	Minimalist Exterior Design	Sustainable and Environmentally Friendly Materials	Avoid Placing Privacy Sensors in Sensitive Spaces
Sensors that Do Not Involve Interactive Behavior but Involve Privacy												
U3	1.30					5	9	5				
U4	1.05					9						
U6	0.95						9					
P1	0.95											9
A1	0.93							3	5	5		
O1	1.25						1	9				
O2	1.21						5	9		5	1	
Importance of Design Requirements		0.00	0.00	0.00	0.00	15.95	27.55	31.43	4.65	10.70	1.21	8.55
Sensors that Do Not Involve Interactive Behavior and Privacy												
U3	1.30						9	5				
U6	0.95						9					
A1	0.93							3	5	5		
O1	1.25						1	9				
O2	1.21						5	9		5	1	
Importance of Design Requirements		0.00	0.00	0.00	0.00	0.00	27.55	31.43	4.65	10.70	1.21	0.00
Sensors Involved in Interactive Behavior												
U1	0.93	9	9	9	5		9					
U2	1.00								1		3	
U3	1.30	5	1	9	3		9	5				
U4	1.05	9	9	3	1		3		3	1	5	
U5	1.26	9	1	5	1		5					
U6	0.95				5		9					
A1	0.93							3	5	5		
O1	1.25						1	9				
O2	1.21						5	9		5	1	
Importance of Design Requirements		35.66	20.38	29.52	15.61	0.00	44.17	31.43	8.80	11.75	9.46	0.00

Fig. 3. Figure of **QFD-HOQ**.

Conflict Resolution of Design Elements. By sorting out the correlation between design elements in QFD-HOQ, this study found that there is a negative correlation between design elements, which will lead to difficulties in the application process. So this study proposes to embedding embedded technology in aging-friendly space to enhance sensor concealment and to increase the proportion of sensors placed in blind spots for the elderly population. And use sensors such as millimeter wave radar instead of image sensors to resolve the contradiction between high coverage of sensors in all hazardous areas that meet safety requirements and reducing the number of sensors that can simultaneously meet the privacy protection and respect needs of the elderly population. Solves the difficult-to-implement parts in design practice, and greatly improves the guiding role of this study in reality. And finally generate a set of strategies that can guide practice for the application of smart home in future aging-friendly space.

3.4 Application Strategies

From, it can be seen that design elements such as "personalized customization based on lifestyle habits", "controlling the number of sensors", and "ergonomic scale" have higher scores. Therefore, in subsequent design practices, design priorities can be determined by referring to the importance of design elements. This study used a series of mixed methods to study models and comprehensively developed application strategies for intelligent living in user-centered future aging-friendly space, providing constructive suggestions for subsequent design work.

4 Conclusion

With the rapid development of China's aging population in the future and the structural shortage of labor in China's elderly care service industry, achieving on-site elderly care through smart housing may become one of the main ways of elderly care in China. This study is based on the present and looks to the future. By constructing a hybrid method research model and taking sensors in intelligent living systems as an example, it explores the application strategy of intelligent living in future aging-friendly space based on the retired elderly population in China.

References

1. Yan, X., 燕雪婷 et al.: Research and Application of Elderly Adaptable Intelligent Residential System 适老性智能居住系统研究与应用. Construction Economics 建筑经济 **42**(S1), 34–38 (2021)
2. Zuo, M. 左美云.: The Meaning and Model of Smart Elderly Care 智慧养老的含义与模式. China Social Work 中国社会工作 **32**, 26–27 (2018)
3. Darianian, M., Michael, M.P.: smart home Mobile RFID Based Internet of Things Systems and Services. In: 2008 International Conference on Advanced Computer Theory and Engineering (2008)
4. Zeng, F., Chen, T.L.: A study of the acceptability of smart homes to the future elderly in China Univ Access Inf. Soc. **22**, 1007–1025 (2023)
5. Zhang, T. 张恬霖 et al.: Research on Home Aging Adaptation for the Third Age: A Case Study of Beijing Lingxiu New Silicon Valley No.1 Courtyard 面向第三年龄的居家适老化改造研究——以北京领秀新硅谷1号院住宅为例. Architectural Techniques 建筑技艺, 29 (06): 90–95 (2023)
6. Lobacaro, G., Carlucci, S., L ö fstr ö m, E.: A review of systems and technologies for smart homes and smart grids. Energies **9**(5), 348 (2016)
7. Chen, X. 陈旭, Xue, L. 薛垒. Research on Interaction Design of aging-friendly smart home Products Based on QFD/TRIZ 基于QFD/TRIZ的适老化智能居住产品交互设计研究. Packaging Engineering 包装工程, 40 (20): 74–80 (2019)
8. Li, Y. 李一洁, Tang, Z. 汤洲.: Research on Emotional Interaction Design of Household Medical Products for the Elderly 基于老年人使用的家用医疗产品的情感化交互设计研究. Art and Design (Theory) 艺术与设计(理论) **2**(03), 95–97 (2016)
9. National Bureau of Statistics. Seventh National Population Census [EB/OL] 国家统计局.第七次全国人口普查[EB/OL] (2021)
10. Tang, Z., Long, Y.: Research on personalized demand acquisition method based on Carnot model. Soft Sci. **26**(02), 127–131 (2012)
11. Li, B., Hathaipontaluk, P., Luo, S.: Intelligent oven in smart home environment. In: International Conference on Research Challenges in Computer Science (ICRCCS '09), pp. 247–250. Shanghai, 28–29 December (2009)
12. Qiang, W.: Interactive design of new energy vehicle mobile end based on Kano QFD 基于Kano-QFD的新能源汽车移动端交互设计. Packaging Eng. 包装工程. **43**(20), 212–219 (2022)

13. Kang, B., et al.: Analysis of Types and Importance of Sensors in smart home Services. In: 2016 IEEE 18th International Conference on High Performance Computing and Communications; IEEE 14th International Conference on Smart City; IEEE 2nd International Conference on Data Science and Systems (HPCC/SmartCity/DSS), Sydney, NSW, Australia, pp. 1388–1389 (2016)
14. Li, L. 李琳, Ye, Z 叶仲凯.: Research on Intelligent Public Facility Design Based on Kano and QFD Models 基于Kano和QFD模型的智能公共设施设计研究. Packaging Engineering 包装工程. **44**(16), 447–453+463 (2023)

Medication Monitoring Interactive System Based on Human Body Feature Points and Label Recognition

Siyi Qian[✉] and Yueyang Yang

Harbin Institute of Technology, No. 92 Xidazhi Street, Nangang District, Harbin, Heilongjiang, China
qsy2024_mail@163.com

Abstract. The world is facing an aging population, and the number of older people suffering from amnesia is increasing year by year. This group of patients is prone to medication errors in daily life due to cognitive decline, which poses a threat to their health. At the same time, the children of the patients find it difficult to accompany and supervise all the time due to the pressures of life. However, at present, both traditional methods and intelligent hardware are infeasible to directly and effectively monitor the medication taking of the amnesic elderly. To address the above problems, we designed an interactive system that utilizes face, arm motion, and character recognition techniques in computer vision to monitor the taking of medication by older people with amnesia. The system includes an on-site medication-taking detection, an on-site interaction, and a remote interaction unit. Besides, it is equipped with the functions of automatically detecting, reminding, and assisting the elderly in taking medication. In the specific test, we recruited 20 older people over 60 years old who suffer from amnesia to monitor their medication and found that the system can timely and accurately monitor the medication status of the elderly, effectively preventing the health problems caused by the elderly's missing of medication, and provide a certain contribution to the social care of the elderly.

Keywords: Medication monitoring · Interactive system · Human action recognition · Mediapipe Holistic · Label recognition

1 Introduction

The rapid aging of populations poses challenges for the world. Among the elderly population, the number of people suffering from amnesia, which includes cognitive disorders such as Alzheimer's disease, is increasing every year [1, 2]. These patients need to take a variety of medications at regular intervals every day to control their condition. However, due to reasons such as cognitive decline, it is easy for the elderly to miss medications and take medications incorrectly, which can cause serious health hazards to the elderly. The offspring of older people often cannot accompany and care for them all the time due to their work and life. They cannot understand and supervise the elderly's medication in time as well, which brings tremendous pressure on the family and society.

Currently, medication monitoring for the elderly population with amnesia still faces many challenges. Traditional methods, such as relying on reminder tools or communicating with children, are complex to ensure accurate monitoring of medication taking [3]. Although some intelligent hardware, such as intelligent pill boxes and wearable monitoring devices, already have pill-taking detection functions, they are either unable to detect them directly, provide real-time feedback results, or lack in comfort and ease of use, all of which are deficient [4].

Based on the above background, this project is dedicated to designing an intelligent interactive system to detect and record medication taken by the amnesic elderly in real time. The system's functions include reminding the elderly to take medicines on-site, detecting the elderly taking medication using computer vision recognition technology, and monitoring also assisting the elderly in taking medicine at the remote end. The system provides a more intelligent and comfortable medication experience for the amnesic elderly.

2 Related Work

Medication monitoring has witnessed the emergence of intelligent pill boxes, wearable devices, and other diversified means, primarily relying on indirect or contact detection. With the advancement of science and technology, computer vision and artificial intelligence have also been explored by researchers to be applied to medication monitoring to realize more accurate and non-contact monitoring.

Although smart pill boxes can remind patients to take their medication at regular intervals [5], they can't guarantee that the medication is taken to reduce the phenomenon of missed doses. Fozoonmayeh et al. developed a wearable medication motion detection system based on a smartwatch, which uses gyroscopes and accelerometers to differentiate between medication-taking and other activities [6, 7]. Still, it cannot be confirmed whether the medication has been swallowed. An intelligent necklace developed by a team from UCLA is an example of an indirect or contact monitoring system. The team developed Wearsense, an intelligent necklace that detects whether a pill has been swallowed by recognizing the swallowing motion through piezoelectric sensors [8]. However, the sensors and cables may affect patient comfort.

AiCure uses computer vision technology to capture smartphone patient medication videos to analyze medicine ingestion [9, 10]. However, this method requires the patient to actively film the pill and mouth and upload it to the server, which is not convenient enough.

The MediaPipe Holistic model introduced by Google in 2020 is more progressive [11]. The model utilizes BlazePose for low-resolution human pose estimation, then extrapolates regions of interest (ROIs) based on hand and face markers, improves the resolution of these regions through cropping, and ultimately generates a complete set of more than 540 markers.MediaPipe Holistic, through its innovative topology, enables near real-time mobile devices. Imam Nuralif et al. used the Mediapipe facial mesh model to extract the key points of the face. They used the critical point information to calculate the mouth opening size, head rotation angle, etc., for real-time driving fatigue detection [12-14]. Zacharias E et al. used the Tesseract OCR recognition algorithm to recognize text from ILU codes of trucks, achieving 80% text recognition [15].

Artificial intelligence technology brings new opportunities in the on-site of pill-taking detection. In this paper, we innovatively propose an intelligent medication detection and interaction system that can automatically detect the medication taken by the elderly, with the interactive functions of reminding, recording, and assisting in medication-taking as well.

3   System Design

3.1   Overall Architecture

In this study, we designed an intelligent medication management system for the elderly with amnesia (see Fig. 1), including an on-site medication-taking detection unit, an on-site interaction unit, and a remote interaction unit. The on-site end interaction software unit reminds the elderly to take medication on time; the medication-taking detection unit detects the accuracy of the elderly's medication taking and the medication-taking action in real-time and synchronizes the information to the remote end interaction unit; and the remote end interaction unit and the on-site end interaction software unit can be used to assist the elderly in taking their medication correctly through video and voice interaction via the Internet.

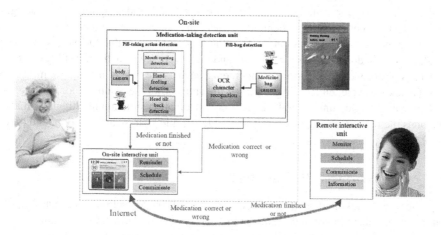

Fig. 1. System architecture diagram.

3.2   On-Site Interaction Unit

On the on-site end (see Fig. 2), we designed a series of functional modules aiming to help the amnesic elderly better manage their medication schedule, assist them in taking medication in a timely and correct manner, as well as facilitate their children to take care of them and interact with them remotely. To ensure the convenience of older people, we have designed more bright and eye-catching modules as follows:

Fig. 2. On-site interaction interface.

In the medication reminder module, when it is time to take medication, a specific video or voice message will pop up to remind the elderly to take medication. The core area contains basic information such as time, color of the medicine bag, type of medicine, etc. The font is generous and straightforward, which makes it easier for older people with degraded visual function to identify and recognize. At the same time, the system can automatically broadcast messages or prompt music. For which the elderly can adjust by clicking the volume button on the top right.

In the interaction module, older people can interact intimately with their children through video, voice, and text. The page is divided into two parts: the left side is the area for real-time video communication between offspring and the elderly, where users can quickly adjust the volume, switch call modes, set other video options, etc.; the right side is the text message area, where both sides can communicate in real-time.

In the medication information module, the page is set up so that the elderly can take medication schedules. The user can easily and intuitively see from the left side the different dates of different medication arrangements, such as the type of medicines, medicine dosage, taking cycle, etc. The right side of the area shows the results of identifying the medication detection unit to analyze the user's medication situation intelligently. It also includes the real-time state of the pill box, older people's physical condition, and other information.

3.3 Medication-Taking Detection Unit

The medication-taking detection unit comprises a pill-bag detection module and a pill-taking action detection module. They are to detect whether the senior citizen has taken the wrong medicine and whether he has finished taking the medicine.

Pill-Bag Detection Module. This module tests the accuracy of medication taken by the elderly. First, medicine bags labeled with numbers are prepared according to the medication schedule, e.g., XY, where X stands for the day of the week and Y stands for the period. Subsequently, the medication for the corresponding time is put into the corresponding bag. The medicine bag camera captures the image of the patient taking the medicine. After noise reduction and black-and-white binarization, the labeled numbers are recognized using the OCR character recognition algorithm - Tesseract. After that, the recognized numbers are compared with the numbers of the preset period. If they are consistent, the medicine is taken correctly. Otherwise, it will issue a warning. This method improves the accuracy of taking medication and protects the safety of medicines for the elderly. The principle of pill-bag detection is shown in Table 1 below:

Table 1. Principle of pill-bag detection.

Time	Medicine	Correct Med bag label number	Recognized numbers	Medicine in bag	Taken medicine bag results
Monday 7:00-9:00	Aspirin:1 pcs Amlodi-pine:0.5pcs	011	012	GV-971:3pcs	Mistaken 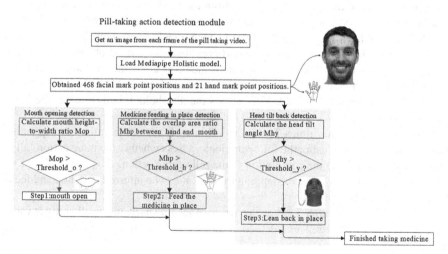
Tuesday 19:00-21:00	Donepezil:2pcs Rosuvas-tatin:0.5pcs	026	026	Donepezil:2pcs Rosuvas-tatin:0.5pcs	Correct

Pill-taking Action Detection Module. This module is used to detect the medicine-taking actions of older people. It consists of a mouth opening detection component, a medicine feeding in place detection component, and a head tilt back medicine detection component (see Fig. 3).

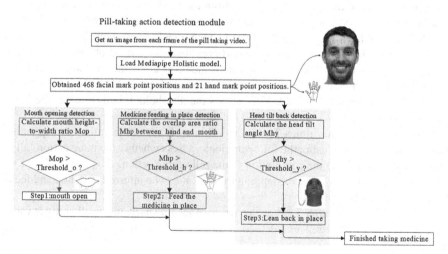

Fig. 3. Flowchart of pill-taking action detection algorithm.

The module automatically captures images of the upper half of the patient's body, loads the Mediapipe Holistic model, recognizes and obtains the location of the marking points of the human face and human hand, and then carries out the detection of the opening degree of the mouth, the detection of the overlapping degree of the palm and the mouth, and the detection of the angle of the head tilting, to carry out the real-time detection of the opening of the mouth, the feeding of the medicine and the swallowing of the medicine action, and thus determine the existence of the action of taking medicine.

The Mediapipe Holistic model recognizes 468 marker points for the face, 21 for the hand, and 33 for the body bones in real-time.

The component for detecting mouth opening measures the aspect ratio of the mouth. It obtains the coordinates of the 20 marker points on the mouth's outer contour from the model. It then calculates the average distance between the upper and lower lips, denoted as the height of the mouth. The distance from the left corner of the mouth to the right corner is calculated as the width of the mouth. The aspect ratio of the mouth, which reflects the degree of mouth opening, is obtained by dividing the height of the mouth by its width. This ratio M_{op} is compared with a preset threshold. If it exceeds the threshold, it indicates that the $Step1$ mouth opening action is completed, and the time T_1 is recorded.

The palm feeding in place detection component detects the overlap between the palm and the mouth. It obtains 14 marking points on the outer contour of the palm from the model to form the hand contour polygon $POLYH$. Similarly, it obtains 20 marking points on the outer contour of the mouth from the model to form the mouth contour polygon $POLYM$. It then calculates the overlap area of the two polygons and divides it by the area of to get the $POLYM$ degree of overlap between the palm and mouth. This overlap degree M_{hp} is compared with the set threshold value, if it is greater than the threshold value, then $Step2$ palm feeding is in place, and the time T_2 is recorded.

The head tilt back detection component measures the head tilt angle. It obtains the 14 marker points of the five sensory parts from the model, and generates a coordinate matrix of these marker points under the image coordinate system. Using the 3D Morphable Model, it fits a 3D face model. Based on the transformation relationship between the image coordinate system and the world coordinate system, it obtains the rotation matrix through OpenCV. The rotation matrix is then converted into a rotation vector and Euler angle using Rodrigues' formula to get the head tilt angle M_{hy}. This angle M_{hy} is compared with a preset threshold. If it exceeds the threshold, it indicates that the $Step3$ pill swallowing action is completed, and the time T_3 is recorded.

After the three action times T_1, T_2, and T_3 are obtained, make the corresponding timing diagrams. Then, using the following logic, assess whether the three actions align temporally to determine the completion of the pill-taking action.

$Case1$: If T_1 and T_2 have overlapping time T_4, it can be inferred that the hand feeds the medicine into the mouth;

$Case2$: If T_3 occurs after T_4, then the action of leaning back and swallowing is valid;

If both $Case1$ and $Case2$ are satisfied, it can be concluded that the pill-taking process is completed.

3.4   Remote End Interaction Unit

The remote interaction unit (see Fig. 4) is an APP application installed on the offspring's cell phone, which sends and receives information with the on-site interaction unit through WebRTC and cloud servers, and it is equipped with the functions of setting up the medication plan, displaying real-time medication information, and chatting on video calls.

The unit is divided into the home page, testing page, interactive page, and information page. It possesses various functions, like providing children with comprehensive, real-time feedback on the medication status of the elderly and, at the same time, facilitating remote interaction between the two sides.

Fig. 4. Remote end interaction interface.

On the home page, the user can enter the control and management of different kinds of medications for the elderly through the Medicine Management function module. Through this, they can set the dosage and frequency of medicines, and the data will be connected to the medication-taking detection unit. The feature is based on a calendar, which allows offspring to plan and view the number of medications for the elderly according to a specific time of the year, month, and day. Users can tap into any day to visualize and set up a quicker and more intuitive understanding of the elderly's medication process.

On the monitoring page, the user can view the progress of the elderly's medication during the day through the Medication Schedule module, where several progress bars show information based on the determination of the medication-taking detection unit. The left and right sides of the Video Record module show the time of the elderly's last medication and the detection result, respectively. The right side of the Record module shows the judgment results of whether a single dose of medicine and the quantity of medicine. In the Real-time Pill Box module, children can visually compare the photos of the status of the medicine bag before and after the time of taking the medicine, and they can also view the system's intelligent judgment on the status of older people, such as Completed or Not qualified, etc. The system will promptly communicate with them on the information exchange page.

On the interact page, the system will present the medication information of the elderly for a certain period, including automatic prompts when the elderly reach the time of the single dose of medication, such as: "Complete!" or "Not completed yet!" emergency alerts. Children can also see the timely contact of the elderly to remind them of their medication. Users can quickly click on the person button at the top of the specific conversation page to initiate a video or send a message, voice, picture, etc. When an emergency occurs, it can promptly send out real-time video of older people.

On the right side of the information page, the current status of older people is prominently displayed, including security and warnings, which can promptly draw children's attention. The function bar contains four functions: Information, Report, Suggestion, and Collection. Users can view the automatic system alerts, health reports, and tips and collect the information promptly. The Condition Analysis column at the bottom comprehensively analyzes older people's condition. In the Medication recording module, users can also view more medication records of the elderly.

4   Results

4.1   Video Dataset Test Results

ETRI-Activity3D is a large video dataset of the daily behaviors of older adults, which contains videos of 55 daily activities performed by 50 older people [16]. In the pill-taking detection module of this system, the researchers tested the videos of five daily activities in this dataset, namely pill-eating, drinking, pouring, eating, and trimming vegetables. A total of 440 videos of the frontal actions of older people were tested, which contained 120 videos of taking medicine, 40 videos of drinking water, 40 videos of pouring water, 120 videos of eating, and 120 videos of trimming vegetables.

The real-time speed of detection reached more than 20 frames per second, which satisfied the real-time requirement. The detection accuracy of pill-eating behavior is 92.5%, and the detection accuracy of non-pill-eating behavior is 98.1%. The specific detection comparisons are as follows (see Fig. 5):

Fig. 5.   Test results for ETRI-Activity3D.

4.2   Volunteer Test Results

The researchers recruited 20 people over 60 with amnesia as volunteers to test the pill-taking detection module on five occasions for each volunteer, and the detection speed reached more than 20 frames per second, which satisfied the real-time requirement. The accuracy of pill-eating action detection was 92.0%, and that of non-pill-eating action was 96.0%. The volunteer detection process is as follows (see Fig. 6):

4.3   Results of Interviews with Volunteers for the Pill-Taking Detection Module Trial

The researchers interviewed 20 volunteers on the trial results (see Fig. 7). Most volunteers gave feedback that the pill-taking detection device could intelligently recognize and

Fig. 6. Results of testing of volunteers.

analyze the situation, effectively reducing the risk of missing or wrong pill-taking and improving health protection. In addition, the sense of remote companionship and care that this technology brings to their children enhances their trust and reliance on the technology.

Fig. 7. Researchers are conducting user interviews.

4.4 Bag Testing Results

The researchers tested character recognition on 42 labeled pill bags, both when containing and when no pills were present. The character recognition accuracy was 97.6%, and the test took an average of 0.32 s.

5 Discussion

In this study, by using the computer vision MediaPipe Holistic model, we accurately captured the location of critical points of the human body. Then, we detected the actions of opening the mouth, feeding, and swallowing medicine in real-time to determine whether there were any effective pill-eating behaviors. In the test of the ETRI-Activity3D large-scale video dataset of daily behaviors of older people, the detection speed is as high as more than 20 frames per second, which meets the demand of real-time detection; at the same time, the accuracy rate of the detection of pill-eating behaviors and the detection of non- pill-eating behaviors is over 90%, and the successful differentiation of similar actions such as pill-eating and water-drinking verifies the feasibility of the scheme.

The innovations of this scheme are mainly reflected in the following: firstly, the computer vision detection method is adopted to realize the automatic detection of medicine taken by older people, which requires no additional operation, has no constraints of wearable parts, and improves the convenience also comfort of use; secondly, the human body critical point recognition model is loaded in a single pass to obtain the comprehensive and dense location of the marking points related to the medicine taking action, to realize the balance of real-time detection and high-precision detection; thirdly, a new algorithm is proposed to detect the proximity of the position of the palm and the mouth, and the overlapping area method is used to replace the traditional two-point distance method, which significantly improves the differentiation between the pill-taking action and similar actions.

However, this study still has limitations. In the case of low light or camera installation position deviation, it may lead to difficulties or misjudgment in recognizing the pill-eating action. In addition, there is a slight delay in detecting medicine bag label characters, which affects the real-time detection effect.

6   Conclusion

To address the problem of medication monitoring for elderly amnesia, this study utilizes computer vision technology to design an interactive system that contains the offspring end and the elderly end, which realizes bilateral interaction and can meet the real-time reminder and monitoring of medication taking. The face, hand, and posture recognition technologies are used to determine the medication taken, record it, and send it to the offspring. Experiments have proven that the system can effectively monitor medication, prevent potential health problems, and enhance social care.

References

1. Global action plan on the public health response to dementia 2017–2025. https://www.who.int/publications/i/item/global-action-plan-on-the-public-health-responseto-dementia-2017--2025. Accessed 14 Mar 2024
2. Slot, R.E., et al.: Subjective cognitive decline and rates of incident Alzheimer's disease and non–Alzheimer's disease dementia. Alzheimer's Dement. **15**(3), 465–476 (2019)
3. Su, Z., Liang, F., Do, H.M., Bishop, A., Carlson, B., Sheng, W.: Conversation-based medication management system for older adults using a companion robot and cloud. IEEE Rob. Autom. Lett. **6**(2), 2698–2705 (2021)
4. Casciaro, S., Massa, L., Sergi, I., Patrono, L.: A smart pill dispenser to support elderly people in medication adherence. In: 2020 5th International Conference on Smart and Sustainable Technologies (SpliTech), pp. 1–6. IEEE, Split, Croatia (2020)
5. Najeeb, P.N.J., Rimna, A., Safa, K.P., Silvana, M., Adarsh, T.K.: Pill care-the smart pill box with remind, authenticate and confirmation function. In: 2018 International Conference on Emerging Trends and Innovations in Engineering and Technological Research (ICETIETR), pp. 1–5. IEEE, Ernakulam, India (2018)
6. Fozoonmayeh, D., et al.: A scalable smartwatch-based medication intake detection system using distributed machine learning. J. Med. Syst. **44**, 76 (2020)
7. Ma, J., Ovalle, A., Woodbridge, D.M.: Medhere: a smartwatch-based medication adherence monitoring system using machine learning and distributed computing. In: 2018 40th Annual International Conference of the IEEE Engineering in Medicine and Biology Society (EMBC), pp. 4945–4948. IEEE, Honolulu, HI, USA (2018)

8. Kalantarian, H., Motamed, B., Alshurafa, N., Sarrafzadeh, M.: A wearable sensor system for medication adherence prediction. Artif. Intell. Med. **69**, 43–52 (2016)

9. AI Medication reminder service based on, AiCure. https://verticalplatform.kr/archives/6991. Accessed 14 Mar 2024

10. Bain, E.E., et al.: Use of a novel artificial intelligence platform on mobile devices to assess dosing compliance in a phase 2 clinical trial in subjects with schizophrenia. JMIR Mhealth Uhealth **5**(2), e7030 (2017)

11. MediaPipe Holistic. https://github.com/google/mediapipe/blob/master/docs/solutions/holistic.md. Accessed 14 Mar 2024

12. Sharara, L., et al.: A real-time automotive safety system based on advanced ai facial detection algorithms. IEEE Trans. Intell. Veh. (2023). https://doi.org/10.1109/tiv.2023.3272304

13. Nuralif, I., Yuniarno, E.M., Suprapto, Y.K., Wicaksono, A.A.: Driver fatigue detection based on face mesh features using deep learning. In: 2023 International Seminar on Intelligent Technology and Its Applications (ISITIA), pp. 1–5. IEEE, Surabaya, Indonesia (2023)

14. Flores-Monroy, J., Nakano-Miyatake, M., Escamilla-Hernandez, E., Sanchez-Perez, G., Perez-Meana, H.: SOMN_IA: Portable and universal device for real-time detection of driver's drowsiness and distraction levels. Electronics **11**(16), 2558 (2022)

15. Zacharias, E., Teuchler, M., Bernier, B.: Image processing based scene-text detection and recognition with tesseract (2020). https://doi.org/10.48550/arXiv.2004.08079

16. Kim, D., Lee, I., Kim, D., Lee, S.: Action recognition using close-up of maximum activation and etri-activity3d livinglab dataset. Sensors **21**(20), 6774 (2021)

Individual Characteristics Affecting Mobility of Older People and MaaS (Mobility as a Service) Design Based on These Characteristics

Toshihisa Sato[1]([⊠]) [iD], Naohisa Hashimoto[2] [iD], Takafumi Ando[1] [iD], and Yen Tran[2] [iD]

[1] Human Informatics and Interaction Research Institute, National Institute of Advanced Industrial Science and Technology (AIST), Tsukuba Central 6, 1-1-1 Higashi, Tsukuba 305-8566, Ibaraki, Japan
{toshihisa-sato,takafumi.ando}@aist.go.jp

[2] Digital Architecture Research Center, National Institute of Advanced Industrial Science and Technology (AIST), Tsukuba Central 2, 1-1-1 Umezono, Tsukuba 305-8568, Ibaraki, Japan
{naohisa-hashimoto,tran.yen}@aist.go.jp

Abstract. It is necessary to clarify how the age-related decline in physical and cognitive functions affects mobility, in order to increase the acceptance of mobility as a social system among older people. In this study, the mobility was classified into "actual mobility" and "feasibility of mobility including ability". A questionnaire survey was conducted to investigate the relationships between these mobility factors, well-being, and individual characteristics of regional residents. The results suggest that "ego-resiliency" and "openness to new people and places" had a stronger influence on the potential mobility and well-being and were found across all age groups. Based on the results of this survey, we investigated the design elements of mobility that are useful for older people.

Keywords: Mobility as a Service · Questionnaire Survey · Well-being

1 Introduction

In Japan's suburban areas, public transportation is becoming increasingly difficult to maintain as the number of residents declines due to the aging of the population. The loss of public transportation makes it difficult to provide a means of transportation for those who are forced to give up driving due to aging. Therefore, it is expected that new mobility, including on-demand transportation, will be introduced to replace existing public transportation, and MaaS will also be used to increase convenience.

In order to increase the acceptance of mobility as a social system among older people, it is necessary to clarify how the decline in physical and cognitive functions due to aging affects mobility. Mobility has two concepts: the actual frequency and extent of mobility, and the possibility of mobility as an ability. When examining the factors that influence mobility, it is necessary to identify the factors that influence actual and potential mobility. Flamm and Kaufmann used the term "motility" to describe the concept of the ability or opportunity to be mobile [1]. Motility includes "Mobility skills", "Travel self-confidence", "Openness to new people and places", "Neighborhood mobility qualities", and "Residential access qualities". It is necessary to clarify which factors, in addition to the actual frequency and extent of travel, influence the mobility components of older people by comparing them with other age groups. Based on this knowledge, it will be possible to design MaaS that are highly acceptable to older people.

Mobility is necessary for people's livelihoods and affects their well-being. Mobility and well-being are closely linked in life, and when examining the factors that influence mobility, it is necessary to consider the impact on well-being. There are various definitions of well-being, but in recent years there has been a growing focus on well-being as an individual-subjective phenomenon. There are two traditions of subjective well-being: hedonic and eudaimonic [2]. Hedonic well-being is well-being through pleasurable states and positive reports. On the other hand, eudaimonic well-being can be described as a state of being achieved through the maintenance and expansion of capabilities and self-realization.

The aims of this study are to investigate the relationships between the actual frequency and extent of mobility, motility, hedonic and eudaimonic well-being and individual characteristics, and to examine design elements of mobility that are useful for older people. The research method was a questionnaire survey among local residents.

2 Methods of Questionnaire Survey

We conducted a questionnaire survey in an area where a MaaS demonstration experiment was being conducted by the Smart Mobility Challenge [3]. The survey areas were a total of 22 regions, including the 20 MaaS demonstration areas in addition to Tukuba City and Tokyo.

2.1 Participants

A total of 20,480 residents participated in the survey. We analyzed 19268 responses from those who answered "I am not infected with COVID-19". Participants were divided into three age categories: young (N = 5551, mean age: 31.0 years; 18–39 years), middle-aged (N = 11340, mean age: 51.5 years; 40–64 years), and older (N = 2377, mean age: 70.4 years; 65– 89 years).

2.2 Contents of Questionnaire

The questions collected in this survey were as follows.

- **Demographic characteristics**: age, gender, driver's license ownership, private vehicle ownership, family income, and current employment status.
- **Life-space assessment (LSA)**: University of Alabama life-space assessment [4]. We used LSA to measure actual mobility. LSA is an index that assesses the extent of an individual's living space based on a questionnaire. LSA expressed the living space as the distance and frequency of going out in the last 4 weeks and the assistance needed to go out.

- **Motility**: mobility skills, residential access qualities, neighborhood mobility qualities, openness to new people and places, and travel self-confidence [5]. Specific questions for each component are listed below. The participants responded to these questions using a five-point Likert scale ranging from 1 (No) to 5 (Yes).

Mobility skills.

- Ease of planning a bus journey
- Ease of planning a journey to an unfamiliar location
- Ease of finding short cuts, alternative routing
- Ease of planning complex journey pattern of multiple destinations in short time framework
- Ease of using journey time for multi-tasking
- Ability to turn to strangers for directions or conversation
- Good at getting somewhere on time

Residential access qualities.

- Easily reach public transportation facilities from my house.
- Easily reach my workplace from my house.
- Easily reach the supermarket from my house on foot to buy commodities and groceries.
- Easily reach my elementary or junior high school from my house on foot.

Neighborhood mobility qualities.

- Easily reach the highway from my house.
- There are streets around my house to enjoy going for walks.
- Quickly drive around my house.
- There are streets with bicycle lanes around my house.

Openness to new people and places.

- When traveling I meet new people and learn about new places
- Traveling to new places and meeting new people is important
- Relocation, under correct circumstances can be positive
- Easy to engage in conversation when traveling
- Ease of handling the unexpected when traveling

Travel self-confidence (=Stress).

- Traveling is stressful and aware of possible dangers
- Unwilling to travel or have long absences for work
- It is stressful to travel to a new place for the first time
- Hesitation in traveling alone long distances
- Fear of harassment when traveling alone at night

Residential access qualities and Neighborhood mobility qualities were phrased as asking about physical accessibility and availability, respectively, since the original question asked whether they were important when buying a house.

- **Well-being**: eudaimonic and hedonic well-being using the Japanese version of the Hedonic and eudaimonic motives for activities scale (HEMA) [6]. The Japanese version of HEMA has three subscales: seeking happiness, seeking enjoyment, and seeking relaxation. We used "seeking happiness" for eudaimonic well-being and "seeking enjoyment" for hedonic well-being.

Seeking happiness.

- Seeking to pursue excellence or a personal ideal
- Seeking to develop a skill, learn, or gain insight into something?
- Seeking to use the best in yourself
- Seeking to do what you believe in

  Seeking enjoyment.

- Seeking fun
- Seeking enjoyment
- Seeking pleasure

- **Ego-resiliency**: ego-resiliency scale [ER89] [7].
- **Personality**: big-five personality (extraversion, agreeableness, conscientiousness emotional stability, and openness to experience) [8].
- **Subjective well-being (health)**: subjective well-being inventory Japanese edition (general happiness, inadequate mental mastery, social support, physical ill-health, family group support, deficiency in social contacts, confidence in coping) [9]. We used this assessment, especially inadequate mental mastery, social support, physical ill-health, family group support, deficiency in social contacts, confidence in coping, as one of individual characteristics.

2.3 Analysis Methods

The collected questionnaire data were analyzed in two steps. First, we used path analysis methods to examine the relationships between life space assessment, motility, well-being, and ego-resiliency. We included ego-resiliency in this analysis because our previous research has shown that the resilience has a strong influence on mobility and well-being [10].

Multiple regression analysis was then used to examine the effects of individual characteristics (extraversion, agreeableness, conscientiousness emotional stability, openness to experience, inadequate mental mastery, social support, physical ill-health, family group support, deficiency in social contacts, and confidence in coping) on each of the independent variables in the path analysis model.

These analyses were conducted for each of the three groups (young, middle, and older), and cross-sectional comparisons were made to clarify the changes among older individuals.

3 Results

3.1 Path Analysis Models

Figures 1, 2 and 3 presents the results of the path analysis for each age group. All path coefficients described in the models are significant ($p < 0.01$). Table 1 shows the results of representative model fit indices [11] obtained from maximum likelihood model estimation. The model fit indices indicate that the models of all age groups fit the observed data well.

The independent variables were "Travel Self-confidence", "Residential Access Qualities", "Neighborhood Mobility Qualities" (these are the motility factors), and "Ego-Resiliency". The independent variables were the same for all age groups. "LSA", the actual mobility, was influenced by "Travel Self-confidence" and "Neighborhood Mobility Qualities" in the models of the older and middle-aged people. On the other hand, in addition to "Travel Self-confidence" and "Neighborhood Mobility Qualities", "Residential Access Qualities" and "Openness to New People and Places" influenced the LSA of young people. Older adults' "mobility skills" were positively influenced by "Ego-resiliency", "Neighborhood Mobility Qualities", "Residential Access Qualities", and "Openness to New People and Places", and negatively influenced by "Travel Self-confidence". These effects were also found in the middle-aged model. The negative effect was not found in the model of young people.

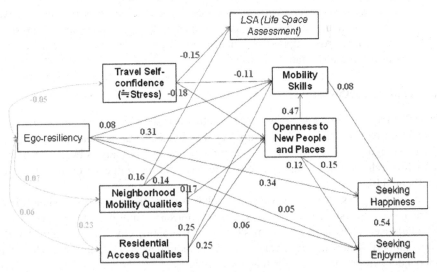

Fig. 1. Path analysis model of **older** participants. Numbers in the model indicate standardized path coefficients (blue: positive effect, red: negative effect). The measurement errors of the dependent variables (LSA, Mobility Skills, Openness to New People and Places, Seeking Happiness, and Seeking Enjoyment) are not included in this figure.

In the model of older people, 3 factors ("Mobility Skills", "Openness to New People and Places", and "Ego-resiliency") influenced "Seeking Happiness". The links between

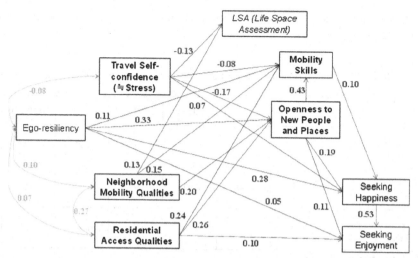

Fig. 2. Path analysis model of **middle-aged** participants. Numbers in the model indicate standardized path coefficients (blue: positive effect, red: negative effect). The measurement errors of the dependent variables (LSA, Mobility Skills, Openness to New People and Places, Seeking Happiness, and Seeking Enjoyment) are not included in this figure.

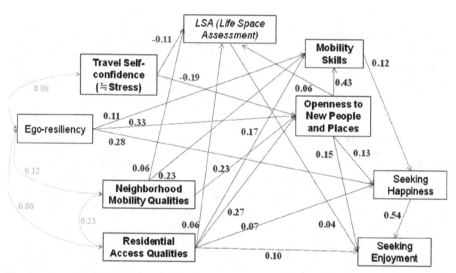

Fig. 3. Path analysis model of **young** participants. Numbers in the model indicate standardized path coefficients (blue: positive effect, red: negative effect). The measurement errors of the dependent variables (LSA, Mobility Skills, Openness to New People and Places, Seeking Happiness, and Seeking Enjoyment) are not included in this figure.

the eudaimonic well-being and the 3 factors were also found in middle-aged and young models. "Travel Self-confidence" was a factor influencing "Seeking Happiness" in the middle-aged model, and "Residential Access Qualities" was the fourth factor influencing euaimonic well-being in the young model.

Table 1. Results of model fit indices of the path analysis models in Figs. 1, 2 and 3.

	GFI	AGFI	NFI	CFI	RMSEA
Elderly respondents' model (Fig. 1)	0.987	0.957	0.975	0.977	0.064
Middle-aged respondents' model (Fig. 2)	0.992	0.971	0.985	0.985	0.054
Young respondents' model (Fig. 3)	0.995	0.982	0.991	0.992	0.04

GFI: Goodness-of-Fit Index
AGFI: Adjusted Goodness-of-Fit Index
NFI: Normed Fit Index
CFI: Comparative Fit Index
RMSEA: Root Mean Square Error of Approximation

"Residential Access Qualities" influenced two factors ("Mobility Skills" and "Openness to New People and Places") in the older model, three ("Mobility Skills", "Openness to New People and Places", and "Seeking Enjoyment") in the middle-aged model, and five ("Mobility Skills", "Openness to New People and Places", "Seeking Enjoyment", "LSA", and "Seeking Happiness") in the younger model.

3.2 Multiple Regression

Three factors were extracted as independent variables in the path analysis model. Table 2 presents the results of the multiple regression of the individual characteristics on each independent variable. Table 2 shows the results of the multiple regression of the individual characteristics on each independent variable. Table 2 shows the factors whose regression coefficients are significant and whose absolute values are greater than 0.1.

Four factors influenced "Ego-resiliency", with no differences by age. The influence of "Extraversion" was higher for middle-aged and young adults than for older adults. In terms of "Residential Access Qualities", the negative impact of "Physical Ill-health" was common to all age groups, and "Social Support" emerged as an influencing factor only for the younger age groups. For "Neighborhood Mobility Qualities", "Confidence in Coping" and "Family Group Support" were common influencing factors for all age groups, "Physical Illness" was an influencing factor for the older and middle-aged respondents, and "Openness to Experience" was an influencing factor only for the older respondents. The two factors ("Physical Ill-health" and "Inadequate Mental Mastery") influencing "Travel Self-confidence" were the same for all age groups.

Table 2. The results of influencing factors on dependent variables in the path analysis models.

(a) Dependent variable: Ego-resiliency

	Older	Middle	Young
Openness to Experience	0.363	0.323	0.313
Agreeableness	0.129	0.141	0.168
Extraversion	0.16	0.203	0.225
Confidence in Coping	0.176	0.156	0.188

(b) Dependent variable: Residential Access Qualities

	Older	Middle	Young
Agreeableness	0.111	0.13	0.084
Confidence in Coping	0.13	0.1	0.092
Physical Ill-health	-0.175	-0.181	-0.17
Social Support	0.061	0.039	0.13

(c) Dependent variable: Neighborhood Mobility Qualities

	Older	Middle	Young
Openness to Experience	0.102	0.068	-
Extraversion	0.042	0.076	0.102
Physical Ill-health	-0.106	-0.106	-
Confidence in Coping	0.147	0.13	0.144
Family Group Support	0.178	0.136	0.12

(d) Dependent variable: Travel Self-confidence(=Stress)

	Older	Middle	Young
Physical Ill-health	0.104	0.166	0.177
Inadequate Mental Mastery	0.229	0.157	0.173

4   Discussion

As in previous analyses [10], there was no direct path from LSA to well-being, and this result was the same for all age groups. For all age groups, the actual frequency and extent of travel may not be related to well-being. The factor influencing wellbeing was the motility component. This finding suggests that even if the number of users is not large, providing some level of public transportation in the community, improving information about it, and giving residents the feeling that they can get around at any time can contribute to improved quality of life.

The impact of openness to new people and places on mobility skills was high for all age groups. Ego-resiliency had a higher impact on openness to new people and places and the pursuit of happiness, and openness to experience had a higher impact on the ego-resiliency. It is suggested that enhancing adaptability to situations, including the ability to involve others, is effective in improving mobility skills, which in turn leads to eudaimonic well-being. Even if residents plan to go out in advance, there may be situations where the plans need to be changed. In such cases, it would be useful for all age groups to have information that immediately indicates when the scheduled departure time will change and alternative means of transportation. Current applications provide such functionality, but it is important to automatically provide information in response to changing circumstances. Therefore, a digital twin that recognizes the situation and predicts changes is essential.

Residential access qualities also showed a strong effect on mobility skills and openness to new people and places. Social support had a stronger effect on the residential access qualities among the younger age group, while agreeableness and confidence in coping had a stronger effect among the middle-aged and older age groups. Social support was described in the questionnaire as help from relatives and friends. With increasing age, it becomes more important to improve one's own coping skills, including cooperation with others, rather than the support of relatives and friends. Therefore, instead of an application that calls for help from family and friends, an application that allows users to solve problems on their own is needed. To motivate users to use this application, it may be essential to design an incentive that rewards users when they are able to solve problems on their own. For example, when a driver drives a car, there is a feedback mechanism that displays the fuel consumption results of his/her driving after the trip. In the case of daily transportation, it may be useful to display the task demands of the day's transportation and the results of how the resident handled it after returning home, so that the resident can see how well he/she handled the situation, thereby increasing the resident's self-efficacy.

Acknowledgments. This work was funded and supported by the Japanese Ministry of Economy Trade and Industry (METI) and the Ministry of Land, Infrastructure, Transport, and Tourism (MLIT).

Disclosure of Interests.   The authors have no competing interests to declare that are relevant to the content of this article.

References

1. Flamm, M., Kaufmann, V.: Operationalising the concept of motility: a qualitative study. Mobilities 1(2), 167–189 (2006)
2. Ryan, R.M., Deci, E.L.: On happiness and human potentials: a review of research on hedonic and eudaimonic well-being. Annu. Rev. Psychol. **52**, 141–166 (2001)
3. Sato, T., Hashimoto, M.: User's Activities when Using Mobility as a Service — Results of the Smart Mobility Challenge Project 2020 and 2021 —. IEICE Trans. Fundamentals Electron. Commun. Comput. Sci. **E106.A**, 745–751 (2023)
4. Baker, P.S., Bodner, E.V., Allman, R.M.: Measuring life-space mobility in community-dwelling older adults. J. Am. Geriatr. Soc. **51**(11), 1610–1614 (2003)
5. Shliselberg, R., Givoni, M., Kaplan, S.: A behavioral framework for measuring motility: linking past mobility experiences, motility and eudemonic well-being. Transp. Res. Part A **141**, 69–85 (2020)
6. Asano, R., Igarashi, T., Tsukamoto, S.: The Hedonic and Eudaimonic Motives for Activities (HEMA) in Japan: the pursuit of well-being. Japanese J. Psychol. **85**(1), 69–79 (2014)
7. Block, J., Kremen, A.M.: IQ and ego-resiliency: conceptual and empirical connections and separateness. J. Pers. Soc. Psychol. **70**(2), 349–361 (1996)
8. Gosling, S.D., Rentfrow, P.J., Swann, W.B., Jr.: A very brief measure of the Big-Five personality domains. J. Res. Pers. **37**(6), 504–528 (2003)
9. Sell, H., Nagpal, R.: Assessment of Subjective Well-Being. The Subjective Well-Being Inventory (SUBI). Regional Health Paper, SEARO, 24, World Health Organization (1992). https://iris.who.int/handle/10665/204813
10. Sato, T., Akamatsu, M.: What is Migration for Humans? Historical Transitions and Factors Influencing Mobility. IntechOpen (2023). https://doi.org/10.5772/intechopen.108742
11. Hooper, D., Coughlan, J., Mullen, M.: Structural equation modelling: guidelines for determining model fit. Electron. J. Bus. Res. Methods **6**(1), 53–60 (2008)

Research on Health Science Popularization Information Design for the New-Elderly Based on Subjective Evaluation Method of Cognitive Load Experiment

Yiwen Song[1], Delai Men[1(✉)], and Zhiyang Xie[2]

[1] School of Design, South China University of Technology, No. 382, Daxuecheng Outer Ring East Road, Panyu Guangzhou, Guangdong, People's Republic of China
mendelai@scut.edu.cn

[2] Shenzhen University, 3688 Nanhai Avenue, Nanshan District, Shenzhen City, Guangdong Province, People's Republic of China

Abstract. Older adults generally face difficulty accessing accurate health science information due to cognitive decline. However, few studies have explored the relationship between cognitive load and the design of health science information interfaces for older adults.

We explored the relationship between health science information design and cognitive load in New-elderly. The research objective is 1. to investigate the health science information design strategy based on cognitive aging. 2. to investigate the total cognitive load and satisfaction of older adults on the tweeted materials before and after information design. 3. to investigate three different types of cognitive loads in the health science information tweets.

We used a questionnaire for qualitative analysis. A snowball sampling method was used to recruit suitable participants for the study of a group of older adults aged 60–79 years old who were optimistic, healthy, and proficient in using smartphones, referred to as the New Older Adults (N = 40).

The results confirmed that the health science information interface after information design was effective in reducing the cognitive load and enhancing the satisfaction of the New-elderly. The study emphasizes the need to pay attention to the cognitive characteristics of older adults to develop effective health promotion design strategies.

Keywords: Health Science Popularization Information · Cognitive Load Subjective Ratings · New-elderly · Information Design

1 Introduction

In China, encouraging older adults to use the Internet and digital health technologies is an effective way to help address aging health issues in China [1]. However, information overload has been recognized as a major problem in this era [2]. Numerous studies have shown that cognitive aging is accompanied by a decline in working memory capacity and

© The Author(s), under exclusive license to Springer Nature Switzerland AG 2024
C. Stephanidis et al. (Eds.): HCII 2024, CCIS 2115, pp. 224–235, 2024.
https://doi.org/10.1007/978-3-031-61947-2_25

a decrease in the ability to suppress irrelevant information. Overloaded information and excessive cognitive load cause the elderly to perform poorly and retain negative attitudes toward the application of computer technology [3]. Fortunately, this phenomenon is widely recognized as a problem. Designing to reduce the cognitive load and enhance the experience of the elderly population in accessing health information is positive for the realization of healthy aging.

2   Literature Review

2.1   Health Science Popularization Information

Health popularization is a type of health communication behavior, which refers to the popularization of health knowledge to the public to improve public health literacy. Surveys have shown that middle-aged and elderly Chinese residents seek online health information by focusing primarily on online health accounts [4]. One of the most noteworthy promotional platforms is the WeChat official account, which is rooted in the universal social media WeChat.

At present, the effect of digital health science popularization in China has not yet reached expectations. There are relatively few studies on its specific situation. Jennifer and Caroline used the cognitive load theory to innovatively introduce the trends and uses of infographics in medicine and public health [5]. There have been no studies that consider the effects of health science from a cognitive load perspective in older populations.

2.2   Cognitive Load

Cognitive load is the total amount of mental activity imposed on an individual's cognitive system during a given operating time [6]. Cognitive load during learning can be categorized into three main types: Intrinsic Cognitive Load (IL), Extraneous Cognitive Load (EL), and Germane Cognitive Load (GL).

Il refers to the number of elements simultaneously processed in working memory [7]. El is related to the organization and presentation of learning materials. GL is the cognitive load generated when a learner, in the process of accomplishing a certain task, uses the unused residual cognitive resources for the processing directly related to learning". IL should be optimized by choosing learning tasks that match the learner, and health information design makes health information dissemination more efficient by reducing EL and increasing GL.

Currently, most researchers choose the Cognitive Load Subjective Rating to measure the level of cognitive load of the subjects. The Subjective Evaluation Scale designed by Pass and Merriënboer [8], referred to as the PAAS Scale, is the most used by researchers due to its simplicity, convenience, and operability. The PAAS scale includes both mental effort and task difficulty evaluations, both of which are rated on a 9-point scale. The reliability of this scale is high, with an internal consistency reliability coefficient of a $= 0.74$ [9]. Leppink et al. proposed a ten-item instrument to measure three types of cognitive load, and the solution was validly confirmed [10]. In the present study, we refer to the relevant research discussions, and based on them, we have prepared and modified the instrument to measure the different types of cognitive load.

2.3 Information Design for Older Adults

Information design refers to the practice of presenting information in a way that promotes efficient and effective understanding of the information. Information design for the elderly needs to consider their cognitive characteristics. Cognitive aging is mainly manifested in four aspects: perception (the ability to perceive information), learning (the ability to receive information), attention (the ability to select information), and memory (the ability to process information) [11–13]. We propose four strategies for designing health science information based on cognitive aging:

Sensory Perception - Skillful Application of Contrast and Harmony. Perceptual decline makes senior individuals less able to recognize information around them, so contrasting methods should be used effectively to highlight key information and to give variations to smooth visual memory to stimulate their visual attention and memory. On the other hand, it is also important to keep the overall visual language harmonious and unified to avoid visual noise. Typography must be beautiful and uniform to ensure that the elderly are easy to read; the overall use of color should not be messy, so as not to give the user too much stimulation but to reduce the user's ability to process information. It is worth noting that an overly strong visual style may cause older persons to become resistant. (see Fig. 1).

Fig. 1. Skillful application of contrast and harmony

Learning - Make Good use of Images and Make Analogies with Things Older People are Familiar with. Elderly people are more susceptible to the influence of proactive interference and retroactive interference in the learning process. When the learning materials are closely linked to their existing knowledge and experience, they will show better learning ability [14, 15]. Images and diagrams are not only powerful tools for conveying information, but they also complement the inadequate expression of purely verbal communication. Considering the cognitive differences of older adults, the selection of visual objects from language and choices needs to be explained in a way that is as cognitively compatible as possible with older adults, who are familiar with them. Utilizing methods such as analogies and metaphors to increase GL can make the memory more profound. At the same time should avoid the use of specialized words or network neologisms and, if necessary, should be given the necessary tips before the user operation. (see Fig. 2).

Fig. 2. Good use of images and diagrams

Attention - Rationally Organize the Information Architecture and Simplify the Information. Attention is a way of selecting a limited amount of information from a large amount of information to be actively processed [16, 17]. Individuals' ability to resist interfering information tends to decline with age [18].

Reasonably organizing the information architecture and dividing the information hierarchy are key steps in information design. We can divide the information into important information, secondary information, general information, and auxiliary information. At the same time, the Gestalt principle is effectively applied to arrange the relevant content proximally and reduce the external cognitive load through the modularized grouping layout. (see Fig. 3).

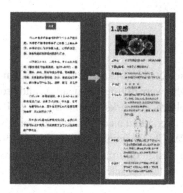

Fig. 3. Rational organization of information architecture and simplification of information

Memory - Rationally Organize Information Density to form Patterns. It has been found that the memory of senior people is mostly extracted from long-term memory, and their working memory will gradually decline with age [19].

Discovering patterns helps the brain to quickly process sensory information always received, so categorizing information into groups and using similar visual language for each group to create patterns can make it easier for users to find and remember information. The working memory of older adults has a limited capacity, so there should not be too much information presented in each group. George A. Miller suggested that the capacity of working memory is 7 ± 2 information elements or blocks [20]. In practice, however, there are fewer when processing information [21]. For older adults, we can reduce it to typically 4 ± 1 chunks, i.e., three to five (see Fig. 4).

Fig. 4. Reasonably organize information density and form patterns

3   Methods

3.1   Research Object

The study population was selected from an older group of 20 males and 20 females (N = 40) aged 60–79 years old who were optimistic, healthy, and proficient in the use of smartphones. We selected neighborhood parks around Shilou in Panyu District, Guangzhou City, Guangdong Province to conduct an offline survey using snowball sampling. A typical tweet from the health WeChat official account "Guangzhou Health Commission" is selected as a case study for design optimization, which is the most popular public number in Guangzhou. The typical tweet selected is 《Recently, acute respiratory infectious

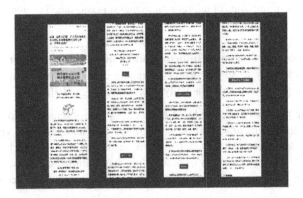

Fig. 5. The original tweet material A

diseases …control them?》, which was published by the public number on December 8, 2023, and reached a readership of 1,000,000. This experiment takes the original tweet material A and the designed tweet material B as independent variables (see Figs. 5 and 6).

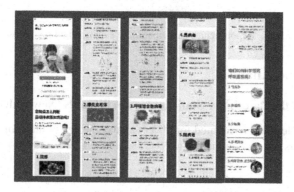

Fig. 6. The designed tweet material B

3.2 Experimental Design

To avoid potential confusion caused by item-specific order effects, the first 20 subjects browsed in the order of AB, and the next 20 subjects browsed in the order of BA. Subjects in the experiment used a uniform cell phone device to browse the tweeted material during free time, fill out the questionnaire after reading; after a ten-minute break, browse another tweet and repeat the above steps. (see Fig. 7) According to the IRB, we had to recruit participants who accepted self-disclosure in the questionnaire. Thus, participants were asked to introduce other subjects to this questionnaire by snowballing them, thus increasing self-disclosure and willingness to respond.

The questionnaire used in this study consisted of three parts: a PAAS scale, a five-point Likert scale, and a questionnaire to measure different types of cognitive load. The questionnaire measuring the different types of cognitive load consisted of 8 statements, and the subjects were asked to answer each question on a scale of 0 to 10 (0 means this is not the case at all, 10 means this is the case at all). Items 1 and 2 were used to measure IL, items 3, 4, and 5 were used to measure EL, and items 6, 7, and 8 were used to measure GL. The questions included:

1. The subject matter covered in the tweet is very complex.
2. The tweet covers concepts and definitions that I find very complex.
3. The instructions and/or design of the tweet are very unclear.
4. The instructions and/or design are very ineffective as far as learning is concerned.
5. The instructions and/or design are full of unclear language.
6. The tweet did enhance my understanding of the topic covered.
7. This tweet did enhance my knowledge and understanding of health.
8. This tweet did enhance my understanding of concepts and definitions.

Fig. 7. Experimenter participation in experimental scenarios

4 Results and Analysis

4.1 Results of the Descriptive Statistics for Participants (New-Elderly)

Males and females each accounted for 50%; the average age of the subjects was 66.55, with 60–70 years old predominating at 30 (75%) and 70–79 years old at 10 (15%) (see Fig. 8).

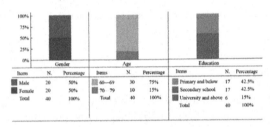

Fig. 8. Descriptive statistical results of participants' gender, age, education

4.2 Results of Measuring Different Types of Cognitive Load for Participants (New-Elderly)

The standardized Cronbach's alpha coefficients for the A and B tweeted material were 0.890 and 0.904, respectively, with good reliability. (see Table 1) The results of the different types of cognitive load in 40 subjects are available by contacting the authors. Although the sample size is rather small for a decimetric instrument, the distributional properties of the data allow for this type of factor analysis [no outliers or extreme skewness or kurtosis, and sufficient inter-item correlation; For the A tweeted material: KMO = 0.793, Bartlett χ 2 (45) = 232.801, p < .001]; for the B tweeted material: KMO = 0.839, Bartlett χ 2 (45) = 216.995, p < .001], good validity (see Tables 2 and 3).

IL was similar for A and B tweeted material, EL was significantly smaller for B tweeted material than for A tweeted material, and GL was larger for B tweeted material than for A tweeted material. This is in line with the expected hypothesis that two health tweets with the same content have almost the same IL, and the information-designed health science tweet material effectively reduces the EL, allowing more psychological resources to be devoted to the GL.

Table 1. Cronbach's Reliability Analysis-Measuring Different Types of Cognitive Load

Item count	sample size	Cronbach's alpha- Tweet A	Cronbach's alpha- Tweet B
8	40	0.890	0.904

Table 2. Measuring Different Types of Cognitive Load KMO and Bartlett's Tests for A Tweets

KMO test		0.793
Bartlett Test	Approx. Chi-Squar	232.801
	df	28
	P value	0.000

Table 3. Measuring Different Types of Cognitive Load KMO and Bartlett's Tests for B Tweets

KMO test		0.839
Bartlett Test	Approx. Chi-Squar	216.995
	df	28
	P value	0.000

4.3 Results of Total Cognitive Load and Satisfaction for Participants (New-Elderly)

The standardized Cronbach's alpha coefficients of the PAAS scale for the A and B tweet materials were 0.784 and 0.788, respectively, with good reliability. Since there are only 2 factors in the PAAS scale, the KMO value is constant at 0.5. The mental effort (mean 5.275) and learning material difficulty (mean 5) for the A tweet material are higher than that for the B tweet material (mean 2.675) and learning material difficulty (mean 2.65). This also validates the results of measuring different types of cognitive load scales in another dimension.

Subjects rated higher satisfaction with the health tweet material B after information design, with an average of 4.225 points, higher than that of the health tweet material A without information design (2.8 points). This proves that the interface of health science information through information design can effectively reduce the cognitive load of the elderly group and effectively improve the satisfaction of the elderly group.

5 Discussion

The different factors of the questionnaire were cross-analyzed using one-way ANOVA to analyze the relationship between the gender of the sample and the total cognitive load. The different gender samples would not show significant differences ($p > 0.05$)

for exerting mental effort A, learning material difficulty A, exerting mental effort B, and learning material difficulty B (see Table 4).

Table 4. Comparison of results of variance differences in PAAS scales among older adults of different genders

	Gender (Mean ± S.D.)		F	p
	Female(n = 20)	Male(n = 20)		
Mental effort A	5.45 ± 1.64	5.10 ± 1.29	0.563	0.458
Learning material difficulty A	5.30 ± 1.53	4.70 ± 1.59	1.481	0.231
Mental effort B	2.75 ± 1.07	2.60 ± 0.99	0.211	0.649
Learning material difficulty B	2.95 ± 1.28	2.35 ± 1.27	2.224	0.144

$* p < 0.05 ** p < 0.01$

Using one-way ANOVA to analyze the relationship between sample age and total cognitive load, it can be concluded that samples of different ages would not show significance ($p > 0.05$) for a total of 3 items of learning material difficulty A, mental effort paid B, and learning material difficulty B, and the other age samples showed significance ($p < 0.05$) for a total of 1 item of mental effort paid A. This may be because older adults are more sensitive to healthy tweets without information design as they age (see Table 5).

A one-way ANOVA on the relationship between the educational level of the sample and the total cognitive load shows that there is no significance ($p > 0.05$) in the three items of difficulty A, mental effort B, and difficulty B of the learning materials. There is one significant item for mental effort A ($p < 0.05$). The level of education for the psychological effort A shows a 0.01 level of significance ($F = 5.774$, $p = 0.007$). A comparison of the mean scores of the groups with more significant differences is "Elementary school and below > Junior high school > College and above, indicating that the elderly with lower education levels is more sensitive to health materials that have not been designed with information (See Table 6).

The conclusions drawn from this study are necessarily limited. We included only a specific group of older adults from a specific community, and there was some variation in their ability to access health information. Secondly, the number of participants in the experiment was small and the sample data was not large enough. There is a need to continue to analyze the specific needs of the entire elderly user community based on big data, to better guide the design of information in this area and provide better health communication services to the elderly user community.

Table 5. Comparison of results of variance differences in PAAS scales among older adults of different ages

Age (Mean ± S.D.)	60.0(n = 1)	61.0(n = 4)	62.0(n = 3)	63.0(n = 2)	64.0(n = 2)	65.0(n = 4)	66.0(n = 1)	67.0(n = 2)	68.0(n = 1)	69.0(n = 3)	70.0(n = 2)	71.0(n = 1)	72.0(n = 1)	73.0(n = 1)	78.0(n = 1)	79.0(n = 2)	F	p
Mental effort A	6.00 ± null	4.50 ± 1.29	5.67 ± 1.15	3.50 ± 0.71	7.00 ± 1.41	4.25 ± 0.96	4.00 ± null	6.50 ± 0.71	4.00 ± null	4.33 ± 1.15	5.50 ± 0.71	6.00 ± null	3.00 ± null	6.00 ± null	6.00 ± null	8.00 ± 0.00	3.030	0.020*
Learning material difficulty A	7.00 ± null	4.50 ± 1.00	5.33 ± 1.15	4.50 ± 0.71	7.50 ± 2.12	3.75 ± 0.96	4.00 ± null	6.50 ± 0.71	5.00 ± null	4.67 ± 0.58	5.00 ± 2.83	7.00 ± null	5.00 ± null	5.00 ± null	7.00 ± null	7.50 ± 0.71	2.066	0.086
Mental effort B	3.00 ± null	2.25 ± 0.50	3.33 ± 0.58	1.50 ± 0.71	3.00 ± 1.41	2.75 ± 0.96	4.00 ± null	2.50 ± 0.71	2.00 ± null	2.33 ± 1.15	3.00 ± 0.00	2.00 ± null	1.00 ± null	2.00 ± null	5.00 ± null	3.00 ± 1.41	1.459	0.237
Learning material difficulty B	1.00 ± null	2.00 ± 1.15	3.00 ± 1.73	2.50 ± 0.71	4.00 ± 1.41	2.00 ± 1.41	5.00 ± null	3.00 ± 0.00	3.00 ± null	1.67 ± 0.58	2.00 ± 0.00	2.00 ± null	3.00 ± null	3.00 ± null	6.00 ± null	3.00 ± 1.41	1.509	0.218

$* p < 0.05 ** p < 0.01$

Table 6. Comparison of results of variance differences in PAAS scales among older adults of different levels of education

	Education (Mean ± S.D.)			F	p
	Primary and below (n = 17)	junior high school (n = 17)	College and above (n = 6)		
Mental effort A	6.00 ± 1.32	5.00 ± 1.41	4.00 ± 0.89	5.774	0.007**
Learning material difficulty A	5.59 ± 1.94	4.71 ± 1.16	4.17 ± 0.75	2.523	0.094
Mental effort B	2.76 ± 1.09	2.47 ± 0.94	3.00 ± 1.10	0.697	0.504
Learning material difficulty B	2.59 ± 1.50	2.65 ± 1.06	2.83 ± 1.47	0.076	0.927

$* p < 0.05 ** p < 0.01$

6   Conclusion

We propose four information design strategies based on cognitive aging in older adults. The experimental results show that the health science information interface after information design through the above design strategies can effectively reduce the cognitive load of the New-elderly group and enhance satisfaction. Health communication researchers and practitioners can refer to them to guide their design development and further explore other design strategies.

Acknowledgments. We would like to acknowledge respondents (in a survey). This project is supported by South China University of Technology's Hundred Steps Ladder under Grant (number j2tw202402051) and Humanities and Social Sciences Research Planning Fund Program of the Ministry of Education of China (Research on Elderly-Oriented Design Countermeasures based on the Elderly's Characteristics in Sensory Perception, Grant No.19YJA760043).

Disclosure of Interests. The authors have no competing interests to declare that are relevant to the content of this article.

References

1. Sun, X., Yan, W., Zhou, H., et al.: Internet use and need for digital health technology among the elderly: a cross-sectional survey in China. BMC Public Health **20**, 1386 (2020). https://doi.org/10.1186/s12889-020-09448-0
2. Bawden, D., Robinson, L.: Information overload: An overview (2020)
3. Morris, J.M.: Computer training needs of older adults. Educational Gerontology: An International Quarterly **20**(6), 541–555 (1994)

4. Cheng, Y.U.A.N., Xiaomin, W.E.I., Xiaoyu, W.U., et al.: Habits of using online health information and eHealth literacy in middle-aged and elderly residents. Chinese General Practice **26**(16), 1989–1994 (2023)

5. Spicer, J.O., Coleman, C.G.: Creating effective infographics and visual abstracts to disseminate research and facilitate medical education on social media. Clin. Infectious Diseases **74**(Supplement_3), e14-e2 (2022)

6. Sweller, J.: Cognitive load during problem solving: effects on learning. Cogn. Sci. **12**(2), 257–285 (1988)

7. Sweller, J.: Cognitive load theory, learning difficulty, and instructional design. Learn. Instr. **4**(4), 295–312 (1994)

8. Paas, F.G.W.C., Van Merriënboer, J.J.G., Adam, J.J.: Measurement of cognitive load in instructional research. Percept. Mot. Skills **79**(1), 419–430 (1994)

9. Paas, F. Instructional control of cognitive load in the training of complex cognitive tasks. Thesis, University of Twente, Koninklijke Library: The Hague, 125–129 (1993)

10. Leppink, J., et al.: Development of an instrument for measuring different types of cognitive load. Behav. Res. Methods **45**, 1058–1072 (2013)

11. Harada, C.N., Love, M.C.N., Triebel, K.L.: Normal cognitive aging. Clin. Geriatr. Med. **29**(4), 737–775 (2013)

12. Shi-yong, X.I.A., Hua-mao, P.E.N.G.: Metrological analysis of cognitive aging in China in recent 30 years. Chin. J. Gerontol. **34**(2), 295297 (2014)

13. Lin, Y.U.: Psychological Study of Cognitive Aging. Science Press, Beijing (2014)

14. Bloemendaal, M., Zandbelt, B., Wegman, J., et al.: Contrasting neural effects of aging on proactive and reactive response inhibition. Neurobiol. Aging **46**, 96–106 (2016)

15. Clark, R., Freedberg, M., Hazeltine, E., et al.: Are there age-related differences in the ability to learn configural responses? **10**(8), PloS one e0137260 (2015)

16. Posner, M.I., Boies, S.J.: Components of attention. Psychol. Rev. **78**(5), 391 (1971)

17. Knudsen, E.I.: Fundamental components of attention. Annu. Rev. Neurosci. **30**, 57–78 (2007)

18. McDowd, J.M., Oseas-Kreger, D.M., Filion, D.L.: Inhibitory processes in cognition and aging. Interference and inhibition in cognition, 363–400 (1995)

19. Salthouse, T.A.: The aging of working memor. Neuropsychology **8**(4), 535 (1994)

20. Miller, G.A.: The magical number seven, plus or minus two: some limits on our capacity for processing information. Psychol. Rev. **63**(2), 81 (1956)

21. Cowan, N.: The magical number 4 in short-term memory: a reconsideration of mental storage capacity. Behav. Brain Sci. **24**(1), 87–114 (2001)

Understanding Seniors' Strategies for Identifying Deepfakes

Zhong Tang[1]([envelope]), Dion Hoe-Lian Goh[1], Chei Sian Lee[1], and Yihao Yang[2]

[1] Wee Kim Wee School of Communication and Information, Nanyang Technological University, Singapore, Singapore
zhong005@e.ntu.edu.sg, {ashlgoh,leecs}@ntu.edu.sg
[2] School of Business and Management, Jilin University, Jilin, China

Abstract. Deepfake videos are increasingly prevalent on social media, posing risks, especially for seniors lacking technological familiarity. The study aims to fill a gap in existing research by investigating seniors' perceptions and strategies for detecting deepfakes. The methodology involved interviewing seniors and using qualitative analysis to uncover their identification strategies when presented with real and deepfake videos. The findings reveal five strategies employed by seniors: character appearance, non-human visual elements, audio features, personal knowledge, and external sources. This study contributes insights into how seniors perceive and evaluate video credibility and addresses their unique vulnerabilities when encountering deepfakes.

Keywords: Deepfakes · misinformation · seniors · video credibility assessment

1 Introduction

Deepfake technology is a product of advanced artificial intelligence algorithms based on deep learning neural networks. They refer to synthetic media that convincingly duplicates the likeness and speech of actual people thereby blurring the line between reality and illusion [1]. Concerns have been raised regarding their abuse as tools for propaganda and manipulation [2]. This threat is particularly pronounced for seniors who may be more susceptible to deception [3]. Seniors are vulnerable due to a relative lack of knowledge about technology coupled with their difficulty in distinguishing genuine from manipulated content [4].

It is, therefore, important to raise awareness about the existence and possible consequences of deepfake technology among seniors as it continues to advance. Nevertheless, there is currently little research paid towards understanding how seniors deal with deepfakes. It is imperative to prioritize research that investigates seniors' perceptions and interactions with online videos, which can help identify approaches that are useful to them in recognizing and possibly combating deepfakes. Thus, our research objective is to identify the strategies employed by seniors in detecting deepfakes, contributing to the development of effective detection mechanisms tailored to the needs and capabilities of this demographic.

C. Stephanidis et al. (Eds.): HCII 2024, CCIS 2115, pp. 236–244, 2024.
https://doi.org/10.1007/978-3-031-61947-2_26

2 Literature Review

2.1 Societal Concerns Regarding Deepfakes

Deepfakes threaten the integrity of visual and auditory information [5], particularly in relation to mainstream media's credibility. The technology enables people to produce fake materials that cannot be distinguished from the original ones, thus leading to a loss of trust in the media and compounding misinformation [6]. This challenge extends to journalism, complicating the already complex task of discerning fact from fiction in today's information landscape [7].

Deepfakes have become tools for manipulating public opinion and influencing political narratives beyond information veracity issues [8]. This technology can create realistic videos that portray people committing false actions or saying things they never said in real life, which could potentially lead to the spread of fake news, particularly targeting prominent people. Moreover, deepfake technology is easily accessible, posing serious privacy concerns since it is possible to develop lifelike simulations of individuals in personal or compromising positions [9]. Further, deepfakes can provide avenues for malicious actors who might misemploy the technology for sinister purposes, such as blackmailing and altering the course of democratic processes [5, 10].

2.2 Senior's Challenges in Misinformation and Deepfake Detection

Seniors' susceptibility to misinformation and deepfakes is linked to their information processing capabilities. Cognitive processes, such as memory, attention, and decision-making, change with age, influencing how seniors perceive and assess information [11, 12]. Studies have delved into the intricacies of information processing in older adults, shedding light on how age-related cognitive changes may impact their susceptibility to deceptive content [13, 14]. Investigations have highlighted that declines in working memory and processing speed can impair seniors' ability to detect subtle cues indicative of manipulation, rendering them more susceptible to misinformation [15, 16].

In addition to cognitive factors, seniors may encounter difficulties detecting misinformation and deepfakes due to limited technological familiarity [17]. Given the rapid evolution of online media platforms and digital devices, seniors may struggle to navigate and discern the authenticity of content [18]. This constant evolution can make it challenging for seniors to keep pace with the latest trends and changes, leading to a potential gap in their technological knowledge. Furthermore, the prevalence of deepfakes across various online platforms further compounds this issue, as seniors may encounter misinformation without the necessary skills to identify manipulations or inconsistencies [19].

3 Methodology

Participants were seniors aged between 55 and 70. They were recruited by a combination of snowball sampling and poster advertisements. Participants were required to complete an online form, providing demographic details before the interview, including education, age, occupation, and daily online video consumption. Afterward, they received links to two real and two fake videos randomly selected from a pool of 20 across entertainment, politics, education, and sports categories. The videos, each around one minute, were reviewed 2–3 days before Zoom interviews were individually conducted. The interviews began with an introduction to the study's purpose, followed by questions about participants' identification strategies based on the assigned video.

After the interviews, a qualitative content analysis [20] was employed. The process commenced with transcribing participants' audio recordings. Subsequently, the researchers immersed themselves in the transcripts, identifying significant units that conveyed participants' narratives. These units were condensed to retain essential meaning, resulting in succinct descriptive codes. Moving forward, the analysis involved categorizing these codes, resulting in identifying categories and sub-categories of video identification strategies.

4 Findings

The research revealed five strategies for identifying deepfake videos and their corresponding subcategories, as shown in Table 1.

4.1 Character Appearance

Within the character appearance category, our research reveals two subcategories. Firstly, the facial features subcategory focuses on the analysis of facial expressions. This includes details such as eye movements, the presence of wrinkles, and the overall authenticity of facial reactions. Noteworthy aspects like blink patterns, gaze direction, and the genuine nature of eye responses to the video content were scrutinized. One participant pointed out, "As I was watching the Barack Obama video, the wrinkles caught my attention. Those wrinkles on his face just seemed off. Like, they didn't quite fit." (Participant 18, Male).

Secondly, in the posture and body movement subcategory, the examination encompasses a broader spectrum of character behavior, including posture, body language, and movements, aiming to discern any indications of unnatural, inconsistent, or strange behaviors. Examples are signs of slouching, rigidity, or abnormal positioning. A participant remarked, "Body language is what catches my eye. I want it to flow naturally with what is said in the video. If it looks rehearsed or forced, I will doubt its credibility." (Participant 3, Female).

4.2 Non-human Visual

In the non-human visual category, the first subcategory, resolution, focuses on image clarity. Seniors believed that a explicit video, comprising sharp images, indicates the content's authenticity. They argue that the absence of blurriness or lack of clarity enhances the video's credibility, as expressed by one senior, "Like that Nixon video, its image quality makes me question its credibility… it might be from a long time ago, but it

Table 1. Senior's Deepfake Detection Strategies

Categories	Sub-Categories (Definitions)
Character	**Facial Features** (Analyzing facial characteristics, such as lip, eyes, nose, ear movements, and naturalness of the face)
	Posture and Body Movement (Analyzing individuals' posture, body language, and movements in the video to detect unnatural, inconsistent, or stiff behaviors)
Non-Human Visual	**Resolution** (Evaluating the clarity of the video)
	Lighting Quality (Evaluating the video's lighting conditions)
	Scene Continuity (Evaluating any abrupt cuts, discontinuities, or irregular transitions that may indicate manipulation or editing in the video)
	Ancillary Elements (Evaluating the video items shown in the video)
Audio	**Lip-Sync Accuracy** (Assessing the synchronization between spoken words and lip movements)
	Voice Modulations (Assessing variations and naturalness in the speaker's voice)
	Sound Quality (Assessing the general sound quality of the video)
Personal Knowledge	**Knowledge of Video Content** (Utilizing personal knowledge of the video's content, topic, or speech to assess its credibility)
	Recognition of Character (Checking if the characters' backgrounds match with prior knowledge)
External Source	**Consulting People's Opinions** (Asking individuals to gather additional understandings)
	Online Search (Conducting online searches or using online tools to find corroborating or contradictory information)

is like looking through a foggy window" (Participant 11, Female). The second subcategory, lighting quality, focuses on the coherence between lighting conditions and the video's narrative. For these participants, the lighting should align with the narrative or setting. This perspective is reflected in the statement: "If the lighting feels natural and harmonizes with the story and setting, it adds to the video's credibility." (Participant 1, Female).

The third subcategory, scene continuity, aims to detect abrupt cuts, interruptions, or inconsistencies in the flow from one scene to another. One participant expressed the importance of a seamless viewing experience: "If there are too many sudden jumps or weird cuts, it throws me off." (Participant 13, Male). Lastly, for ancillary elements, seniors concentrated on background objects, analyzing their alignment with the expected context of the video. The incongruence between the video's content and background objects was considered a potential source of doubt. A participant shared an example: "I remember watching that Mark Zuckerberg video, and he was discussing something serious like data privacy. But in the background, there was a cozy living room setup with a sofa and a table. It was irrelevant to what he said, making me think it was fake" (Participant 7, Female).

4.3 Audio

Here, one pivotal subcategory is Lip-Sync Accuracy. A few seniors scrutinize how well the spoken words align with the movements of the speaker's lips believing that precise lip-sync safeguards against potential deceptive alterations in the audio. As one participant described after watching a video featuring Jeremy Corbyn, "It was like he was talking, but there was no speaking voice, and his lips were still moving. When the lip-sync is so out of whack, it is hard to trust the video" (Participant 2, Male).

Voice modulations constituted the second subcategory, with seniors identifying where the original audio might have been replaced. Any disparity between the speaker's voice and the audio track raises suspicion, leading to doubts about the video's integrity. A participant said: "You can tell if someone's voice does not match the sound in the video. It is like they used a different voice actor or something. That makes me question the whole thing." (Participant 20, Female).

The third subcategory, sound quality, captured seniors' focus on identifying background noise. This includes extraneous sounds or disruptions, such as background music or ambient noise, which could impact the overall clarity of the audio. A senior participant, reflecting on a Tom Cruise video, remarked, "When I am listening to Tom Cruise's speaking, I want complete clarity. Those little distractions made me question the video's credibility" (Participant 5, Female).

4.4 Personal Knowledge

Within personal knowledge, the first subcategory relied on seniors' knowledge of video content, subject matter, and speech to judge credibility. Seniors aligned the video's information with their expertise to detect inaccuracies. One senior used this approach by saying, "I watched that Donald Trump video where he gave a speech about his reactions and policies for attackers. I remember seeing something similar in the news a while back. When I watched the video, it matched what I remembered about the news. So, I believe it is a real video" (Participant 9, Male).

The second subcategory, character recognition, analyzes individuals' backgrounds in the videos. The seniors considered factors like characters' origin, profession, stance, and reputation. This is illustrated by one participant, "I was watching the video about Jeremy Corbyn, who I know is a UK Labor Party member. But what he said in the video supported another person from a different political party. This did not match his background, making me think it was a fake video" (Participant 15, Female).

4.5 External Sources

One subcategory focuses on gathering opinions by actively consulting with friends, family, or experts. Seniors using this approach prioritized input from trusted individuals to assess the credibility of a video. One participant highlighted this strategy by explaining, "Most of the videos you send to me are about politics. I have a friend who is studying politics, and he is like an expert to me in this domain. So, I shared the video with him and discussed it" (Participant 17, Female).

The second subcategory, online search, involves using the internet to verify video claims. Participants leveraged online platforms to find supporting evidence or contradictory information, contributing to assessing the video's authenticity. One participant shared his experience: "For the Morgan Freeman video, I am unfamiliar with him, but I somehow knew he is an actor. Being an actor, I figured it might be easy to search his info online. So, I took a screenshot of the video and uploaded it to an online Google tool called Image Search, which showed it was a fake video" (Participant 16, Male).

5 Discussion

Our findings revealed that seniors used common cues reported in the literature when identifying characteristics indicative of fake videos. In terms of character appearance, participants were adept at detecting unnatural movements or facial expressions that could signal deepfake manipulation, recognizing the importance of human faces as expressive indicators of authenticity [21]. Body language, another non-verbal communication form [22], was deemed crucial, with participants emphasizing the significance of fluid and natural movements in genuine interactions.

Examination of non-human visual attributes is also a common strategy for assessing video credibility among seniors. Participants noted deepfakes often struggle to produce consistent and realistic visuals [23], such as abrupt segment transitions or scene discontinuity. Anomalies like blurriness and unexpected lighting quality were identified as potential manipulation indicators. In the audio category, lip-sync accuracy and voice modulations were highlighted as key elements for enhancing the audiovisual experience [24] and assessing the credibility of the video content.

Moreover, seniors leveraged their knowledge and familiarity with video content to assess credibility, demonstrating sensitivity to discrepancies between it and personal knowledge or anticipated outcomes. This strategy reflected participants' self-confidence in discerning credible information, particularly when their existing knowledge aligned with the video content [25]. Additionally, seeking external sources held value in evaluating video credibility, as participants demonstrated a willingness to validate content by seeking opinions and evidence from trusted individuals or online sources. This approach fostered a more objective and critical evaluation, reducing the risk of biases and mistakes based on personal knowledge [26].

6 Conclusion

This study sheds light on the strategies employed by seniors to identify deepfakes, addressing a critical gap in research concerning this vulnerable demographic. The findings reveal the multifaceted nature of seniors' deepfake identification approaches.

Theoretically, our study contributes to the literature by providing insights on how seniors can assess the credibility of videos. The identified strategies provide a better understanding of how people perceive and evaluate multimedia content authenticity, especially when dealing with deepfakes. Moreover, our research has practical implications for digital literacy programs. Educators and policymakers can adapt the strategies to design training curricula to help seniors identify deepfakes. Similarly, digital platforms and social media companies can consider integrating strategies to enhance online content credibility assessment.

Despite the significant understanding provided by our study, certain limitations should be acknowledged. The sample size may be too small to adequately represent the various viewpoints among seniors; thus, a more diverse sample would help get a more comprehensive understanding of their strategies. Second, the rapidly evolving nature of deepfake technology may render some strategies obsolete or necessitate continuous adaptation. Therefore, ongoing research is crucial to keep pace with technological advancements and ensure the relevance of detection strategies.

Acknowledgements. We would like to acknowledge the financial support provided by the Ministry of Education (Singapore) through the Tier 2 grant (MOE-T2EP40122-0004).

References

1. Caporusso, N.: Deepfakes for the good: a beneficial application of contentious artificial intelligence technology. In: Advances in Intelligent Systems and Computing, pp. 235–241 (2020). https://doi.org/10.1007/978-3-030-51328-3_33
2. Albahar, M., Almalki, J.: Deepfakes: threats and countermeasures systematic review. J. Theor. Appl. Inf. Technol. **97**(22), 3242–3250 (2019)
3. Pirhonen, J., Lolich, L., Tuominen, K., Jolanki, O., Timonen, V.: "These devices have not been made for older people's needs"—Older adults' perceptions of digital technologies in Finland and Ireland. Technol. Soc. **62**, 101287 (2020). https://doi.org/10.1016/j.techsoc.2020.101287
4. Schirmer, W., Geerts, N., Vercruyssen, A., Glorieux, I.: Digital skills training for older people: the importance of the "Lifeworld." SSRN Electron. J. (2022). https://doi.org/10.2139/ssrn.4003089
5. Mubarak, R., Alsboui, T., Alshaikh, O., Inuwa-Dutse, I., Khan, S., Parkinson, S.: A survey on the detection and impacts of Deepfakes in visual, audio, and textual formats. IEEE Access **11**, 144497–144529 (2023). https://doi.org/10.1109/access.2023.3344653
6. Karnouskos, S.: Artificial intelligence in digital media: the era of deepfakes. IEEE Trans. Technol. Soc. **1**(3), 138–147 (2020). https://doi.org/10.1109/tts.2020.3001312
7. Giansiracusa, N., Giansiracusa, N.: Deepfake Deception: What to Trust When Seeing Is No Longer Believing. How Algorithms Create and Prevent Fake News: Exploring the Impacts of Social Media, Deepfakes, GPT-3, and More, pp. 41–66 (2021). https://doi.org/10.1007/978-1-4842-7155-1_3

8. Hameleers, M., Van der Meer, T.G., Dobber, T.: You won't believe what they just said! The effects of political Deepfakes embedded as vox populi on social media. Social Media + Society **8**(3), 205630512211163 (2022). https://doi.org/10.1177/20563051221116346

9. Li, M., Wan, Y.: Norms or fun? The influence of ethical concerns and perceived enjoyment on the regulation of deepfake information. Internet Res. **33**(5), 1750–1773 (2023). https://doi.org/10.1108/intr-07-2022-0561

10. Pawelec, M.: Deepfakes and Democracy (Theory): how synthetic audio-visual media for disinformation and hate speech threaten core democratic functions. Digit. Soc. **1**(2) (2022). https://doi.org/10.1007/s44206-022-00010-6

11. Peters, E., Hess, T.M., Västfjäll, D., Auman, C.: Adult age differences in dual information processes: implications for the role of affective and deliberative processes in older adults' decision making. Perspect. Psychol. Sci. **2**(1), 1–23 (2007). https://doi.org/10.1111/j.1745-6916.2007.00025.x

12. Fechner, H.B., Pachur, T., Schooler, L.J.: How does aging impact decision making? The contribution of cognitive decline and strategic compensation revealed in a cognitive architecture. J. Exp. Psychol. Learn. Mem. Cogn. **45**(9), 1634–1663 (2019). https://doi.org/10.1037/xlm0000661

13. Ebner, N.C., et al.: Uncovering susceptibility risk to online deception in aging. J. Gerontol. Ser. B **75**(3), 522–533 (2018). https://doi.org/10.1093/geronb/gby036

14. Calso, C., Besnard, J., Allain, P.: Study of the theory of mind in normal aging: focus on the deception detection and its links with other cognitive functions. Aging Neuropsychol. Cogn. **27**, 1–23 (2019). https://doi.org/10.1080/13825585.2019.1628176

15. Del Missier, F., Mäntylä, T., Nilsson, L.: Aging, memory, and decision making. In: Aging and Decision Making, pp. 127–148 (2015). https://doi.org/10.1016/b978-0-12-417148-0.00007-8

16. Dodson, C.S., Powers, E., Lytell, M.: Aging, confidence, and misinformation: recalling information with the cognitive interview. Psychol. Aging **30**(1), 46–61 (2015). https://doi.org/10.1037/a0038492

17. Soffer, H.: Old age and the potential for web fraud: an in-depth analysis. SSRN Electron. J. (2023). https://doi.org/10.2139/ssrn.4602538

18. Moore, R.C., Hancock, J.T.: Older adults, social technologies, and the coronavirus pandemic: challenges, strengths, and strategies for support. Social Media + Society **6**(3), 205630512094816 (2020). https://doi.org/10.1177/2056305120948162

19. Radoli, L., Langmia, K.: Of deepfakes, misinformation, and disinformation. In: Black Communication in the Age of Disinformation, pp. 1–13 (2023). https://doi.org/10.1007/978-3-031-27696-5_1

20. Erlingsson, C., Brysiewicz, P.: A hands-on guide to doing content analysis. Afr. J. Emerg. Med. **7**(3), 93–99 (2018). Sciencedirect. https://doi.org/10.1016/j.afjem.2017.08.001

21. Krumhuber, E.G., Kappas, A., Manstead, A.S.R.: Effects of dynamic aspects of facial expressions: a review. Emot. Rev. **5**(1), 41–46 (2013). https://doi.org/10.1177/1754073912451349

22. Paranduk, R., Karisi, Y.: The effectiveness of non-verbal communication in teaching and learning English: a systematic review. J. English Cult. Lang. Literature Educ. **8**(2), 145–159 (2021). https://doi.org/10.53682/eclue.v8i2.1990

23. Salvi, D., et al.: A robust approach to multimodal Deepfake detection. J. Imaging **9**(6), 122 (2023). https://doi.org/10.3390/jimaging9060122

24. Yu, P., Xia, Z., Fei, J., Lu, Y.: A survey on deepfake video detection. IET Biometrics **10**(6), 607–624 (2021). https://doi.org/10.1049/bme2.12031

25. Lucassen, T., Schraagen, J.M.: Factual accuracy and trust in information: the role of expertise. J. Am. Soc. Inform. Sci. Technol. **62**(7), 1232–1242 (2011). https://doi.org/10.1002/asi.21545
26. He, L., He, C.: Help me #DebunkThis: unpacking individual and community's collaborative work in information credibility assessment. Proc. ACM Hum. Comput. Interact. **6**(CSCW2), 1–31 (2022). https://doi.org/10.1145/3555138

Elderly of Gestures Control Design on Usability Evaluation

Ming Hong Wang[✉] and Yi Ling Hong

Department of Visual Communication Design, Southern Taiwan University of Science and Technology, Tainan, Taiwan
wming0403@stust.edu.tw

Abstract. The goal of this research is to improve the performance of man-machine interaction of elders with declining sensational, physiological and cognitive condition from observing their input, output mechanism and gesture operation on smart mobile device inter-face. Furthermore, we look forward to develop a gesture operation model to express the relation between degeneration and usability Issues. The research framework and design of simulation experiment consist of factors mentioned above. In experiment phase one, in order to prove the design principles in literatures, we invited three professional industrial designers to evaluate them with focus group methodology and thirty elders to participate in gesture operation experiment designed by us. The result turned out to be conclusive and coincided with previous literatures. Therefore, product designers could follow our research to improve interfaces for elders. In experiment phase two, we transformed the data obtained in preliminary study into graphical inter-face and merged different gesture operations systematically. In order to complete our novel gesture operation, we tested it scientifically with fuzzy theory to deduce fuzzy comprehensive evaluation data according to System Usability Scale and Jakob Nielsen's usability heuristics. It revealed the importance of design and development, we hope the novel gesture operation will meet the need of users.

Keywords: Elderly · Smart Mobile Device · Innovative Gesture Operation · Touch Gesture · Interaction Design

1 Background

Under the global trend of aging society, the European countries, the United States, Japan and other advanced countries have started to pay attention to the design in the aging society from the perspective of social welfare. Many smart high-tech products, such as mobile phones and tablet PCs, attract the public attention with the technological effects including various dazzling interface appearances, small volumes and portability. However, when the elderly is exposed to new products at the beginning, they are confused about how to use them.

The reason why some elderly people are willing to use smart products is that the time to spend with their relatives becomes less for many families gradually change to small ones under the influence of sub-replacement fertility caused by the changes in social

© The Author(s), under exclusive license to Springer Nature Switzerland AG 2024
C. Stephanidis et al. (Eds.): HCII 2024, CCIS 2115, pp. 245–254, 2024.
https://doi.org/10.1007/978-3-031-61947-2_27

lifestyle. Hence, in addition to the good performance, whether the dazzling and good-looking 3C products on the market provide the users with suitable inter-face operation gestures to convey thoughts to relatives is also relatively important. Due to the sudden change of social environment, industrial designers shall further understand the needs of this group, to design the operation gestures suitable for product interfaces by following the general design principles, which cannot only enhance the product values but also improve the life quality of this group.

In this study, the results about the effects of age on relevant abilities were found out from the previous literature, and the data were used as the suggestions needed to be considered in interface design. It is noticeable that the proportion of the elderly population in the society increases significantly and continues to grow. Hightech products and technologies are used in all aspects of our daily life to gradually improve the life quality, especially for the elderly.

However, at present, the complex and unintelligible interfaces needed to be operated in products are important cognitive and perceptual problems for the elderly in face of these products (Czaja, 2007). In order to find out the development and design elements meeting the demands, by an experiment, an exploratory factor analysis was conducted to obtain the preliminary re-sults. The users' preference for smartphones includes the following 9 factors: (1) interface element design; (2) smartphone features; (3) physical characteristics; (4) touch feedback; (5) operation design; (6) display screen; (7) connections; (8) buttons; and (9) applications (Liu and Yu, 2017). In addition, the traditional graphical user interfaces are enhanced by gesture driven interfaces combining with specific gestures, and the movements of an object are represented by tracks of hands or styluses (Studdert-Kennedy, 1992).

People are interested in the use patterns of interface design, and to some extent that a good impression will be made to the users as long as providing good equipment, software and more natural interactions. Gestures are substitute or supplement for application process control and widely used in hardware and software applications. Gestures are used as input ends, especially common in games (Nikos and Tsourakis, 2014).

2 Literature Review

2.1 Users and Technological Innovation

With the rapid development of economy and technology, the existing value cognition and belief in human society have produced a qualitative change. People are no longer satisfied with the products or services that only can be used but expect or pursue the unique pleasures and feelings or taste values during product use or service experience, and these values are an important power to encourage human behaviors. Users shall be considered in design based on the people-oriented thinking. Traditionally, design applications are mostly related to products and have no direct relationship with services. However, services have many characteristics, mainly including the experience and feel (for example, friendly, joyous and happy), products or programs, intangible technologies or modes (for example, information processing, logistical support, financial and business models) (Gallouj and Weinstein, 1997). Hence, the product focused design ideas and interpretations cannot provide complete solutions to all services.

2.2 Smart Mobile Devices

Such devices quickly became popular due to their abilities to access all kinds of information from anywhere at any time, and represent a new computing field together with the mobile computing devices such as laptops and smartphones (Wikipedia, 2018). More and more people use smartphones, and more than 1.4 billion smartphones were sold in 2015 (Liu and Yu, 2017). Mobile devices can be roughly divided into 3 types: voice, data and integration of voice and data. In face of the rapid development of technology, in such a diverse environment, visual and tactile displayers are needed as the main way to transmit information, due to the declining physiological conditions of the elderly, such as presbyopia, increased finger skin folds and tactile insensitivity. The popularity of smartphones has also brought a lot of convenience to the mass users, and mobile applications accumulated over the years also provide users with more and more diversified services. However, the operational problems are prone to be produced between technological products and middle-aged and elderly people, and cannot be ignored in today's society with aging population.

2.3 Definition of Age for the Elderly

In 1993, Taiwan had an elderly population (over 65 years old) of 1.49 million, accounting for more than 7% of the total population, and officially entered an aging society defined by the World Health Organization (WHO). Since then, its elderly population has risen year by year, and reached 3.29 million by the end of February 2018, accounting for 13.98% of the total population, which indicates that Taiwan will soon enter an aging society with the elderly population accounting for 14% (Department of Statistics, Ministry of the Interior, March, 2018). More and more attention will be paid to health as the aging conditions.

According to Chapter 1, Article 2 of the Senior Citizens Welfare Act of the Department of Social Affairs, the Ministry of the Interior published by Taiwan's Legislative Yuan, the elderly refers to the elder people over 65 years old. According to WHO, the elderly refers to the people aged more than 65 years (Organization, 2019; Senior Citizens Welfare Act, revised in 2015). In order to respect the elders, there are titles such as seniors (silver peers), wise men, old aged group, elderly people and senior citizens at home and abroad, and the aged population generally refers to the people over the age of 65. Some experts pointed out that the definitions of "the elderly" vary from study to study.

In the paper "Acquisition of computer skills by older users: A mixed methods study" by Shoemaker (2003), the elderly was represented by the people aged between 40 and 65 years old. In addition, Dyck and Gee (1998) defined the elderly as the people aged 55 years old or above in "The Changing Construct of Computer Anxiety for Younger and Older Adults".

Sociologists divided the elderly into 3 types, respectively biological aging: those who are lack of energy and unable to work due to physical disabilities. In conclusion, according to the definition of the elderly in the Senior Citizens Welfare Act, in this study, the elderly was defined as the seniors more than 65 years old as regulated by laws, for the purpose of subsequent studies.

2.4 Research Purposes

The specific aims of this study: (1) a practical observation and operation survey was conducted on the elderly using various common touch mobile devices. According to the observation, the problems arising from the elderly during gesture operation were recorded and understood, and the cognitive and identifying factors, attention and preference of the elderly in using touch control gestures were summarized. (2) The usability factors collected from the human factors survey were used as the experimental variables to make an experiment of human factors engineering on influential factors, so as to understand the gesture efficiency of the elderly in operating mobile devices. An overall subjective attitude scale was developed to examine various experimental values of gesture operation in different degrees. (3) Simulated gesture operation was used to determine the users' expectations and to develop a decision evaluation method for the elderly to use gesture operation, which can be used as a reference for future decision evaluation of design and development. It has been preliminarily found in relevant studies that the demand and cognition of smart interface device operation vary with age. Young people are better in control-ling technological products due to their best physiological conditions, and are better than the middle aged and elderly people in both the familiarity in use and the response speed to interface operation.

3 Experimental Measurement

3.1 System Usability Scale

The System Usability Scale was released by John Brooke, a British digital equipment company, in 1986. It is designed to help companies understand the overall usability of a product and compare it with previous generations of products or competitors' products. It is widely used to quickly test the usability of products. Interface usability. There are 10 questions in the system usability scale, and each question is scored on a 5-point scale for cross checking. Questions 1, 3, 5, 7, and 9 are yes, and questions 2, 4, 6, 8, and 10 are no. The full score is 100. The higher the score, the higher the user's satisfaction with the interface. Through statistics, the total score of the system usability scale is obtained, which reflects the user's comprehensive evaluation of the system usability. This scale can be used to compare the usability of different systems.

Bangor (2009) pointed out that filling in the scale requires intuitive and quick choices. If you think for a long time, you should click the "Fair" option in the middle. The scoring method is to take the raw score of all questions from 1 to 5 and then calculate the points deserved for all questions. For questions 1, 3, 5, 7, and 9, subtract 1 from the raw score of each question to get the appropriate score; for questions 2, 4, 6, 8, and 10, subtract 5 from the raw score of each question You can get the points you deserve. Finally, calculate the total score (Fig. 1) and multiply it by 2.5 to get the final score. In order to better understand the scores of the system usability scale, respectively F: 0–59, D: 60–69, C: 70–79, B: 80–89 and A: 90–100 (Fig. 2).

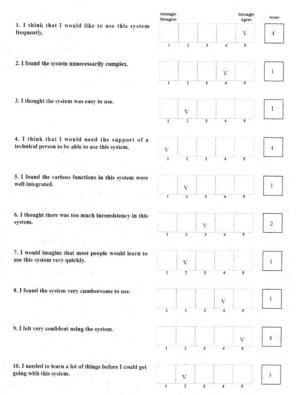

Fig. 1. Source: Brooke (1996), calculation method of system usability scale (Compiled by this study)

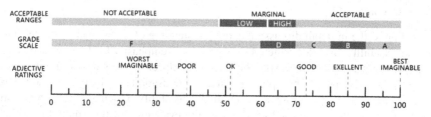

Fig. 2. Source: Bangor and Miller (2009), adjectives and mean values of grade scale (Compiled by this study)

3.2 AHP Evaluation Scale

Evaluation is the next step after the hierarchy establishment. In the AHP evaluation, the elements at the upper levels of each hierarchy are taken as the basis for the evaluation of the elements at the lower levels. In other words, with the elements at the upper levels as the evaluation criteria, any two elements of a hierarchy are used to evaluate relative contribution or importance of the two elements to the evaluation criteria.

The AHP evaluation is a pairwise comparison of every two factors of the same hierarchy, namely, the relative importance of elements is evaluated by a pairwise comparison. The ratio scale is basically divided into 5 levels: equally important, slightly important, quite important, extremely important and absolutely important, which are graded by the measurement values of 1, 3, 5, 7 and 9 with the medians of 2, 4, 6, and 8 between two scales.

3.3 Fuzzy Theory

The quality characteristics of general products can be divided into two types: measurable and unmeasurable. At present, most studies focus on the optimization of measurable quality characteristics, and there are few studies on unmeasurable quality characteristics due to the difficulty in analysis. Currently, the general practice of optimizing the parameters of unmeasurable quality characteristics is to categorize the unmeasurable quality subjectively (for example, when the product uniformity is evaluated visually, the product quality uniformity can be divided into good, fair and bad), and then to make analysis. The idea behind this theory is closely related to the information conveyed by natural language and is part of the fuzzy theory. The fuzzy theory brings scientific research and methods into this forbidden zone, to make those originally determined and accurate still remain the same, but the fuzzy nature is returned to those with fuzzy characteristics, so that the information included in the fuzzy phenomenon can be fully captured. On the other hand, the fuzzy nature softens the human-computer interface and makes the communication and relationship between human and machines closer. Control systems, text recognition (Chiu and Tseng, 1997), voice recognition (Wu and Chen, 2001), diagnostic programs, time series prediction (Mendel, 1995), intelligent robots, software engineering, decision making systems (Chaneau et al., 1987) and data offset.

3.4 Summary

According to the in-depth discussion and understanding of the human computer interface and usability, the user-centered de-sign idea is emphasized. The interface design principles help designers to design the interfaces closer to users based on the experience of others. Nielsen (1993) pointed out that the usability evaluation methods shall be used interactively, so "observation method", "usability principal scale" and "semi-structured interview" were used for the usability evaluation of this study. In addition, in order to increase the reliability and validity of the experimental design results, the System Usability Scale was used in the second stage of the experiment. The questionnaire had 10 questions in total rated on a 5-point scale and could be used to compare the usability of different systems. This study explored the usability of gesture control in the elderly and the usability evaluation method. The interface design and usability are sorted out and analyzed through the review of the previous literature. Gesture control is defined broadly, but is unable to be separated from using habits and unrestricted time and places. At present, people are using the mobile phones in a different way. They pay more attention to the freewheeling operating modes not limited by time and places but not the simply function of answering the phone. Friendly design of interface is a important bridge of communication with consumers to make gesture control closer to the elderly.

4 Case Study Analysis Results

4.1 Research Experiment

In this study, a total of 25 experts and scholars in relevant fields were invited to evaluate the preliminary elements. Specifically, 15 questionnaires recovered failed to reach the consistency score and were therefore deemed invalid. The data of these questionnaires were not included in the subsequent scoring. Therefore, 10 valid questionnaires were recovered in the first stage. The identity backgrounds of these experts and scholars are described as follows: One expert is a scholar in the field related to the elderly; two experts are developers who have more than 6 years of working experience in the field of industrial design and human-machine interface design. They have relevant working qualifications and certain knowledge of human-machine interface development procedures and user experience. Three experts are design engineers who have more than 4 years of product design experience. The last four are individuals who are 65 years old and above and have used smartphones for at least 2 years.

Snowball sampling was adopted to perform a questionnaire survey on the hierarchical elements established in the second stage, in which 16 respondents (45.7%) are male and 19 respondents (54.3%) are female. All the respondents have used smartphones for 1–5 h on a daily basis, and are familiar with the mobile phone interface. Snowball sampling obtains more information about samples through a small number of samples. The premise of this method is that there is a certain relationship between the mother samples. Without a good knowledge of the information about the mother samples, snowball sampling can collect the information about the mother samples or part of the mother samples. First, snowball sampling focuses on the survey subjects, then relies on them to provide qualified survey subjects, who then provide the third batch of survey subjects. In this logic, the size of samples grows like a snowball.

4.2 Subject Background Information

In this study, the data on the number of male and female respondents, their education level, the time to own a smartphone, and the time to use a smartphone every day was aggregated. In terms of gender, the percentage of male respondents is 45.7% and the percentage of female respondents is 54.3%. In terms of education level, 62.9% of the respondents have a university degree or above, 17.1% of the respondents have a high school diploma, and the remaining 20% have others. In terms of the time to own a smartphone, 54.3% of the respondents have used smartphones for 5 years or more, 31.4% of the respondents have used smartphones for 4 years, and 14.3% of the respondents have used smartphones for 3 years. In terms of the time to use a smartphone every day, 37.1% of the respondents use smartphones for 5 h or more every day, 14.4% of the respondents use smartphones for 4 h every day, 17.1% of the respondents use smartphones for 3 hr every day, 11.4% of the respondents use smartphones for 2 h every day, and 20% of the respondents use smartphones for 1h every day. A total of 35 respondents participated in the survey.

4.3 Experimental Process

Based on the literature review, experts and users were invited to participate in the computer simulation test to summarize the design elements in the users' single finger operation gestures, which serve as an evaluation item in the design and development of smartphone operation gestures. The fuzzy AHP adopted in this study is based on the AHP and the fuzzy theory proposed by LAZadeh (1965). It is used to analyze decision-making problems with fuzzy properties. Buckle proposed a method for dealing with fuzzy hierarchical analysis in 2001, called Lambda-Maxethod. The characteristic of this method is that it can calculate any type of fuzzy numbers, and it is quite accurate in operation and simple in calculation, which has been used by most scholars. Therefore, the Fuzzy Comprehensive Evaluation Method is adopted to perform fuzzy hierarchical analysis operations. To obtain the priority of each element, the weights of each design requirement are multiplied by the value corresponding to the technical measure in the relationship matrix, and the weighted scores of the technical measures are obtained. After the weighted scores of the technical measures are ranked, the priority of the technical measures can be obtained. According to the results of the questionnaire survey, a pairwise comparison matrix is established, and then the eigenvalue and eigenvector of the pairwise comparison matrix are obtained by a calculator. At the same time, the consistency of the matrix is tested. If the matrix consistency does not meet the requirements, the decision-makers' judgment is inconsistent, and thus the planner must clearly explain the problem to the decision-makers.

5 Conclusion and Suggestions

5.1 Conclusion

When two fingers are needed in the movement, the movement must be repeated to complete the work. For example, during the experiment, the research team asked the respondents to browse the webpage and zoom in, zoom out, or rotate the screen they browse. Although it is an intuitive action gesture considered by modern people, it is a very difficult thing for the elderly who are not sensitive to movements due to physiological degradation. The most difficult operation gestures for the elderly are: rotation, zoom in, and zoom out. The reason is that during the two-finger operation gestures, the elderly do not know whether they have touched the smartphone screen due to the aging of the skin and chose to repeat touching the screen. Alternatively, due to worsened sense of body balance, they will unconsciously shake and "mistouch". After indepth exploration, it is found that the current seemingly simple and convenient gesture operations are not so simple for the elderly. The experimental results indicate that the new operation gestures designed by the research team are favored by most elderly people. The usability evaluation scale adopted in the first stage of the research experiment includes five items, namely learnability, efficiency, memorability, error, and satisfaction, all of which reached a significant level ($P < 0.05$). In the usability evaluation, three items have helpful effects, including efficiency, memorability, and satisfaction.

5.2 Suggestions

The research results indicate that, an innovative gesture operation is proposed in this study to help the elderly use smartphones. The elderly often has inconveniences in life and actions. For example, their sensitivity to sound, touch, pressure, and fingers begins to decline, which often makes them feel psychologically frustrated and excluded from related actions. The design of services for the elderly is indeed a complicated system as when the design factors considered are increased, whether the added value of the product is relatively increased is an issue worth exploring. The design of product use patterns for the elderly also puts forward higher requirements for service designers, which include both technical requirements and thinking requirements. It is undoubtedly a new challenge for the design of service systems. Under the aging trends in the future, for the elderly and handicapped people, the product operation should focus more on the intuitive operation and work efficiency. This study suggested that the results of this study can contribute to the elderly or those with relevant needs in the future, and are relatively important issues that require special attention. According to past studies, the demand and cognition of the operation of smart devices will change with different age groups; on the contrary, younger generations will have better control of technological products. In terms of both operation familiarity and response speed, younger generations are better than the elderly. It is hoped that the human factors, thinking and cognition behaviors can be explored to develop effective data on response time and feedback time for the elderly during operation, and the final result will promote perception, memory, decision making, attention, response execution, and feedback mechanism to meet the critical lifelong mobility needs of the elderly, and help them better use smart products despite aging.

References

Bangor, A., Kortum, P., Miller, J.: Determining what individual SUS scores mean: adding an adjective rating scale. J. Usability Stud. 4(3), 114–123 (2009)

Brooke, J.: SUS-A quick and dirty usability scale. Usability Eval. Ind. 189(194), 4–7 (1996)

Chaneau, J.L., Gunaratne, M., Altschaeffl, A.G.: An application of type-2 sets to decision making in engineering. Anal. Fuzzy Inf. 2(1), 145–151 (1987)

Chiu, H.P., Tseng, D.C.: Invariant handwritten Chinese character recognition using fuzzy min-max neural networks. Pattern Recogn. Lett. 18(5), 481–491 (1997)

Czaja, S.J.:The impact of aging on access to technology. ACM SIGACCESS Access. Comput. (2007). https://doi.org/10.1145/1102187.1102189

Dyck, J.L., Gee, N.R.: The changing construct of computer anxiety for younger and older adults. Comput. Hum. Behav. 14(1), 61–77 (1998)

Gallouj, F., Weinstein, O.: Innovation in services. Res. Policy 26(4–5), 537–556 (1997)

Liu, N., Yu, R.: Identifying design feature factors critical to acceptance and usage behavior of smartphones. Comput. Hum. Behav. 70, 131–142 (2017). https://doi.org/10.1016/j.chb.2016. 12.073

Mendel, J.M.: Fuzzy logic systems for engineering: a tutorial. Proc. IEEE 83(3), 345–377 (1995)

Nielsen, J.: Usability Engineering. Elsevier (1993)

Tsourakis, N.: Using hand gestures to control mobile spoken dialogue systems. Univ. Access Inf. Soc. 13, 257–275 (2017). https://doi.org/10.1007/s10209-013-0317-0

Shoemaker, S.: Acquisition of computer skills by older users: a mixed methods study. Res. Strat. **19**, 165–180 (2003). https://doi.org/10.1016/j.resstr.2005.01.003

Studdert-Kennedy, M.: Hand and Mind: What Gestures Reveal About Thought (1992). Accessed (2017)

Wu, D., Olorenshaw, L., Menendez-Pidal, X., Chen, R.: U.S. Patent No. 6,778,959. Washington, DC: U.S. Patent and Trademark Office (2017)

Zadeh, L.A.:Fuzzy sets. Inf. Control **8**(3), 338–353 (1965)

Online Shopping Aging Design Strategy Based on Visual Attention

Yanmin Xue[(✉)], Shuting Chen[(✉)], and Yang Liu[(✉)]

College of Art and Design, Xi'an University of Technology, Xi'an 710061, China
915728096@qq.com, 1531613278@qq.com, 741048101@qq.com

Abstract. With the development of digitalization and the deepening of aging, the consumption concept of the elderly breaks the inherent cognition of the society. According to the data released by major shopping software in China, the number of users and consumption amount of the elderly population are constantly rising. However, as a special group, there is a big gap between the elderly and young people in the use of digital products, and the elderly also have different differences within themselves. In this study, the subjective and objective user research method was used to subdivide the use degree of the population and screen the target users, and then the physiological data of the young and old control group was measured through the eye movement experiment to obtain the objective preference needs. With different stimulus materials as independent variables and eye movement data as dependent variables, the experiment analyzed the differences in physiological data of users of different ages during browsing and task operation, and concluded the influence of step-by-step guidance in interactive behavior on visual attention indicators and decision time of elderly users. The experimental results show that the performance and experience of the step-by-step guided task is much higher for the elderly than that of the descriptive guided task, while the gap between the use of the young is small. Therefore, strengthening guidance and shielding non-main information in interactive behavior can significantly stimulate and regulate visual attention of visual elderly people, and can effectively improve their performance and experience.

Keywords: Online Shopping · Age-appropriate · Visual Attention · Feature Classification

1 Introduction

According to the relevant report released by Alibaba, the number of users and consumption amount of elderly people over the age of 60 in China are growing rapidly. However, as a special group, there is a big gap between the elderly and young people in the use of digital products. The current research on online shopping suitability for aging mainly focuses on behavior and intention research, shopping mode suitability for aging research, interface optimization design and interactive suitability for aging design strategy research. For example, UTAUT and IRT theories are used to explore the factors that affect the perception, acceptance and willingness of elderly Malaysians to shop online [1]. The relationship model between the color design elements of the home page interface and the usability index was built using the quantitative theory class I, and the preference of middle-aged and elderly users for the color elements of the shopping mobile terminal was found [2]. The interactive characteristics and needs of the elderly using online shopping software are analyzed, and the interface design principles and design points for improving the user experience of the elderly are summarized [3].

To sum up, many scholars have begun to pay attention to the aging of online shopping. The existing results provide a good theoretical basis and practical value, but there are still the following shortcomings: (1) The existing studies seldom carry out reasonable subdivision of the elderly population to extract the target users before user research. (2) Existing studies focus on the optimal design of visual elements of a single interface, and few studies on the visual impact of the overall functional interaction process.

In view of the above deficiencies, this study will use feature classification to subdivide the elderly population, and use physiological experiments to conduct data analysis on interface perception and interactive operation to extract visual preference needs. At the same time, relevant research hypotheses are proposed:

- H1: There are differences in eye movement indicators of free browsing in the level 1 interface of "elder version".
- H2: In the process of using functions with low familiarity, step-by-step guidance and blocking of non-relevant information have a greater impact on the visual attention of the elderly.
- H3: The completion performance of different types of tasks in the elderly group is significantly different, while there is no significant difference in the young group.

2 Theoretical Research

Visual attention, in psychology, is the ability to interpret visible light information that reaches the eye and use it to plan or act. In essence, it is a biological mechanism that can select important and required information from the complex external environment, and gradually exclude relatively unimportant information. In this way, the complex external visual scene can be simplified and decomposed, and then the important information can be further processed. As a physiological mechanism, visual attention is related to personal subjective factors, visual perception, environmental conditions and psychological feelings. Visual attention deficit is often seen as a common problem in children with autism and mental retardation. At the same time, the decline of visual attention ability has also been confirmed in the elderly population, and it has been proved that aging will cause damage to the visual attention regulatory network through a controlled experiment of dual-objective attention tasks between young and old people [4]. Experiments in elderly and young adults have shown that reduced large cell input is the main visual cause of visual attention deficit in elderly people [5].

In general, the correlation between the decline of visual attention and age has been confirmed, and most studies are based on pictorial information. However, in the process of shopping decision-making for the elderly, effectively attracting users' visual attention is also an important aspect to consider the reasonable degree of interface design. In the experiment and design, the influence of visual attention on interactive behavior of the elderly can be analyzed through visual attention time and visual fixation times.

3   Target User Establishment

3.1   User Feature Classification

The application of feature classification method can make the classification of us. The application of feature classification method can make the classification of users more scientific and specific, analyze the diversified needs of users more reasonably in the research stage, and select more typical users as subjects for the experiment stage. In this questionnaire, 7 basic questions about the degree of online shopping were scored on the 1–5 Ritke scale. The basic problem mainly focuses on the acceptance, frequency and usage of mobile shopping, which is used as the basis for the division of users with different levels of use. A total of 112 usable questionnaires were recovered in this questionnaire, and 103 questionnaires were obtained after excluding invalid questionnaires.

3.2   Characteristic Result Analysis

According to the results of the questionnaire, the different situations of the elderly's use of shopping software are preliminarily screened and the characteristics of use are classified, and the elderly online shopping group is subdivided into four categories. The first category (recorded as category A) is the elderly who have no intention of online shopping behavior due to serious physical degradation or resistance to smart products at an older age. The second category (recorded as category B) is the elderly users who use smartphones to access the Internet and occasionally have online shopping experience, but cannot complete the purchase behavior independently and are often error-prone. The third category (referred to as Class C) is the user who uses shopping software more often, thinks shopping software is necessary and is very interested in it. Such users occasionally make mistakes and misgivings in the process of making online purchases. The fourth category (recorded as category D) refers to the elderly users who can skillfully complete online shopping behavior, are familiar with the functions of shopping software and basically make no mistakes, and think that online shopping is commonly used and very important in life.

In the collected questionnaire statistics of feature classification, Class A users accounted for 5.88%, Class B users accounted for 58.82%, Class C users accounted for 23.53%, and Class D users accounted for 11.76% (Table 1).

3.3   Target Population Selection

According to the above survey, there is a great difference between the use intention and ability of the elderly, and the use ability and willingness of the elderly are not positively correlated with the growth of age. For a more objective investigation and analysis, we positioned the population in the elderly group who have a certain interest and learning tendency in online shopping, and can basically use and understand online shopping behavior. According to the screening results, we identified the BCD users as the target users for the later experiment or design. According to the survey, online shopping behavior has a certain correlation with age, and this kind of elderly group is generally between 60 and 75 years old. In addition, the elderly with the background of online

Table 1. User characteristics analysis questionnaire.

Questionnaire content	Some respondents									
	1	2	3	4	5	6	7	8	9	...
How often you use shopping apps	3	2	4	3	5	1	2	4	3	...
Is the current shopping process simple	2	3	4	3	5	1	2	3	2	...
Whether you can complete shopping independently	3	3	4	3	5	2	2	4	2	...
Whether the skip is lost when using the software	3	2	3	2	4	2	2	3	3	...
Does the operation often make mistakes	4	3	3	4	4	2	3	3	2	...
Interested in shopping online	2	4	4	4	4	1	2	4	4	...
Think shopping apps are important to your life	4	5	4	4	5	1	4	5	3	...
Total	21	22	26	23	32	10	17	26	19	...

shopping generally have the ability to live alone, have a fixed pension income, and have a certain educational background and Internet background. Such elderly people will reduce the panic caused by the unknown in the face of online trading, and have independent operation software and evaluation ability.

4 Experimental Design

4.1 Experimental Composition

The experiment adopts 2 × 2 (subjects: old subjects, young subjects × drive: interest driven, task driven) design, which is divided into two steps. The first is the interface perception experiment, which analyzes the analysis and comparison of the interface eye movement data of the "old version" of Taobao and Pinduoduo software. The second is an interactive task experiment, which analyzes the differences in completion performance and visual attention between the control group with descriptive guidance (without masking non-relevant information) and the control group with step-by-step guidance (masking non-relevant information).

4.2 Experimental Material

In experiment 1, the "home page" and "Personal Center" pages of Taobao (version 10.27.25) and Pinduoduo (version 6.75.0), two shopping software most commonly used by the elderly, were selected as the experimental materials (see Table 2). To simulate real scenarios, only the user profile picture and name are the same and the UI is not changed twice.

The stimulus materials in experiment 2 were divided into two groups. The first group was the descriptive guidance task material (see Fig. 1), which allowed the subjects to find the function independently. The second group is the step-by-step guided task material (see Fig. 2), which helps the subject to mask non-relevant information at each step of the operation and guides the user to complete the task. All stimulus materials involved in this experiment were presented on Huawei mate20 mobile device, and Pinduoduo software was simulated to avoid other variables, and the interactive interface was designed as a low-fidelity interface.

Table 2. Browse the task stimulus material freely

Home page		Personal center page	
A1-Comprehensive page	A2-Carded page	B1-Vertical list of information	B2-Information horizontal list

Fig. 1. C1 style stimulus material (Descriptive guide)

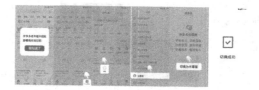

Fig. 2. C2 style stimulus material (step guide)

4.3 Experimental Subject

A total of 24 subjects were recruited from the target users, who were divided into two groups according to age: youth group and elderly group. 12 subjects in the youth group, including 8 males and 4 females, were 24 ± 1.3 years old. The aged group consisted of 12 subjects, including 6 females and 6 males, aged 63 ± 8.4 years. All subjects have normal or corrected vision, right-handed, use smart phones and have more than six months of online shopping experience, and can effectively evaluate the operation.

4.4 Experimental Procedure

First, the experimental process, equipment, precautions and experimental purpose were introduced to the subjects. Help subjects wear measuring instruments such as electroencephalography and electrodermatology. After wearing, prepare to calibrate the eye tracker, prompting subjects to sit 25–30 cm in front of the stimulation image display, put their hands on the shelves on both sides, maintain a upright posture, and look straight at the reference line of the screen with their eyes level. Under the guidance of the tester, the eyes of subjects are tracked and calibrated through the 5-point method. After the eye movement calibration was completed, EEG, eye movement, and electrodermal data were examined. After all equipment data is checked, the basic information of the subjects is recorded on the standby device, and the new experiment is created. First, sit still for three minutes and remind the subjects to close their eyes and rest. After the break, we count in the official experiment. First play the guidance, click to enter the free browsing link, play 2 home pages and 2 personal center pages in turn, each picture stimulation time is 8s. After the free browsing, there are two prompts in the link, and the experiment is carried out according to the prompts. After the completion of the experiment, the tester conducted a brief interview with them to complete the questionnaire (Figs. 3 and 4).

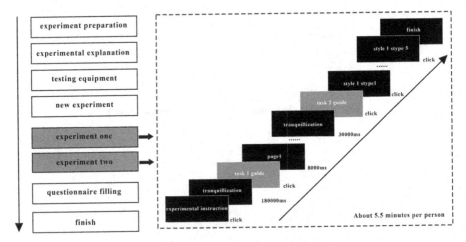

Fig. 3. Experimental procedure

Fig. 4. Experimental environment and subjects

5 Analysis of Experimental Results

5.1 Experiment 1 Results Analysis

Hot Zone Map Analysis. The hot zone map can describe the duration of the user's attention in a specific area. If the time is longer, it can be considered that the user shows more attention to the area. Different colors are used to identify areas of different attention times. The darker the color, the higher the visual attention. It can be seen from the hot zone map (see Table 3) that the visual attention of subjects to pictures and ICONS is higher than that of text information. On the A1 interface, hotspots are scattered and receive little attention in important areas such as the search box, voice search, and TAB bar. The focus on the A2 interface is the search and tagging function. In the comparison between the interface of B1 and B2, the important information related to orders in the B1 interface is not equal in steps, and the top-down information arrangement interface of B2 is more inclined. According to the analysis of the hot area map, there are differences in the visual attention hotspots of different level interfaces in the "elder version". The carded information arrangement in the comparison of home page is better than the comprehensive page, and the up-down information arrangement is better than the left and right information arrangement in the comparison of personal page. H1 hypothesis is valid.

Table 3. Freely view the task hot zone map

Home page		Personal center page	
A1	A2	B1	B2

5.2 Analysis of the Results of Experiment 2

Hot Zone Map Analysis. According to the hot area map of the elderly group and the young group (Table 4), it can be seen that the elderly group pays relatively scattered visual attention to C1 task. Since the elderly group has a low ability to remember and understand the task information on the home page, and the key information cannot attract visual attention, the elderly is easy to get lost in interactive behaviors, resulting in high cognitive load. In the young group, the visual hotspot of C1 task is more concentrated. It shows that the task information is less complex for young people, and they can quickly understand and complete the task steps. For C2 tasks, the elderly can follow the guidance and quickly focus on the task area to complete the operation, and the visual attention is not easily dispersed. On the other hand, young people tend to pay active attention to information outside the task area in highly guided tasks, and their visual attention is relatively scattered.

Table 4. Hot zone map of different style task control group

Subject population	Test	
	C 1	C 2
Older age-group		
Youth group		

Analysis of Eye Movement Related Indexes. Young people and old people were divided into AB group to complete two types of tasks. Group A completed C1 style, group B completed C2 style; Young group A completed C1 style, young group B completed C2 style.

After the completion of the experiment, three indexes of "total fixation time", "fixation number" and "saccade number" in the eye movement data were obtained for analysis. Due to the small sample size, Shapro-wilk normality test was conducted on the observed samples first, and the test results showed that the data basically obeyed normal distribution. Then, these three indicators are tested by independent sample t test, where N represents the number of subjects, M represents the mean value, SD represents the standard deviation of the mean value, and SE represents the standard error of the mean value. The formula is

$$SE = \sigma / \sqrt{n}$$

T means the degree of numerical difference, P means the level of significance, $p > 0.05$ means that there is no difference in the data of this group, $p < 0.05$ means that the data are different, and $p < 0.01$ means that the data are significantly different.

In the elderly group (see Table 5), total fixation time $t = 2.366$, significance level $p = 0.040 < 0.05$, fixation number $t = 4.622$, significance level $p = 0.001 < 0.01$, saccade number $t = 4.366$, significance level $p = 0.001 < 0.01$. Therefore, there are differences in the three indicators of total gaze time, gaze number and saccade number in the elderly group when completing tasks of different styles, among which there are significant differences in gaze number and saccade number, indicating that the elderly's performance in completing tasks of C1 descriptive guidance is much lower than that of C2 step-by-step guidance. C2 style shielding non-relevant information can effectively improve the visual attention of the elderly group. Shorten the information processing time, so the H2 hypothesis is valid.

In the youth group (see Table 6), total fixation time t = 1.337, significance level p = 0.21 > 0.05, fixation number t = 1.335, significance level p = 0.222 > 0.05, skipping number t = 0.148, significance level p = 0.855 > 0.05. Therefore, there is no difference in the total gaze time, gaze number and saccade number of young people completing different types of tasks. Compared with the elderly group, it can be seen that there are significant differences in the eye movement data of the elderly group completing different types of experiments, while the young group is small, so the H3 hypothesis is valid.

Table 5. Independent sample t test of eye movement index in elderly group

Eye movement	Testee	N	M	SD	SE	T	P
Total fixation time	Senile group A	6	53.67	18.89	7.71	2.366	0.040*
	Senile group B	6	27.67	19.18	7.82		
Number of gaze	Senile group A	6	30.83	5.23	2.13	4.622	0.001**
	Senile group B	6	20.00	2.37	0.97		
Saccade count	Senile group A	6	240.50	62.13	25.36	4.366	0.001**
	Senile group B	6	96.83	51.36	20.97		

The unit of total fixation time is second s; * indicates p < 0.05; ** indicates p < 0.01

Table 6. Independent sample t test of eye movement index in youth group

Eye movement	Testee	N	M	SD	SE	T	P
Total fixation time	Senile group A	6	14.50	3.02	1.23	1.337	0.211
	Senile group B	6	12.33	2.58	1.05		
Number of gaze	Senile group A	6	22.00	11.83	4.83	1.335	0.222
	Senile group B	6	14.83	5.74	2.34		
Saccade count	Senile group A	6	60.33	22.56	9.20	0.148	0.885
	Senile group B	6	58.83	10.44	4.26		

The unit of total fixation time is seconds

6 Discussion

According to the above eye movement experiments, we can conclude that when the elderly browse the online shopping interface, they are more inclined to the card-based layout of the information layout of the home page, and their visual habits are more inclined to the top-to-bottom order in the browsing of pages with more text function information such as personal pages. According to the results of the independent sample t test, it can be concluded that there are great differences in the control group for different guidance methods. In the process of interactive behavior, the elderly group is more inclined to step guidance, that is, to help shield non-relevant information, which can fully mobilize the visual attention of the elderly in the interaction, greatly reduce the cognitive load of the elderly users, and improve the efficiency of task completion. However, the youth group completed better in the descriptive guidance, and they could search and switch the unfamiliar functions independently according to the information on the home page. In view of this experimental conclusion, the shopping software can be designed to introduce new functions in the software, and the functional learning section can also be set up so that the elderly can fully understand and learn the use of functions under appropriate guidance, so that they can quickly pass the "novice period", so as to optimize their use experience and improve the retention of elderly users.

However, the whole survey also has certain limitations. 1. The classification of user characteristics of the elderly population in article 2.2 is only used to select target users, and no in-depth analysis is made on the characteristics and behavioral preferences of various users. 2. In the interactive experiment, the young and old control group was divided into AB group, with 6 people in each group. The sample size of each group is relatively small, which may affect the significance of the experimental data and the universality of the results. In addition, this paper analyzes the influence of visual attention on a single level in different interaction modes. In the future, we can analyze various influencing factors to build a relationship model that affects the interaction behavior of the elderly.

Acknowledgments. This paper was funded by The National Social Science Fund of China under grant 22BSH122.

Disclosure of Interests. The authors have no competing interests to declare that are relevant to the content of this article.

References

1. Soh, P.Y., Heng, H.B., Selvachandran, G., et al.: Perception, acceptance and willingness of older adults in Malaysia towards online shop**: a study using the UTAUT and IRT models. J. Ambient Intell. Humaniz. Comput. 1–13 (2020)
2. Xu, B., Lu, Z., Li, M.: Research on color design elements of online shopping APP for middle-aged and elderly users. Packag. Eng. 42(02), 210–216 (2021)
3. Yun, Z., Wang, K.: Research on the interface design of online shopping for the elderly under the guidance of technology for aging. Design 35(21), 111–113 (2022)

4. Cao, D., Liu, Z., Lai, Z., et al.: Effects of aging on regulatory networks of visual attention. Prog. Biochem. Biophys. **11**(07), 1–11 (2023)
5. Steinman, S.B., Steinman, B.A., Trick, G.L., et al.: A sensory explanation for visual attention deficits in the elderly. Optom. Vis. Sci. **71**(12), 743–749 (1994)

Integration of the Elderly into the Digital Society: A Study of Human-Machine Barriers in the Use of Kitchen Appliances

Yanmin Xue and Kai Qi[✉]

Department of Art and Design, Xi'an University of Technology, Xi'an, China
843672292@qq.com

Abstract. Population aging is a world trend. Home use of the kitchen is an important part of the life of the elderly, and in the context of digital society, the contradiction between the decline in the function of the elderly group and the function and operation of the existing kitchen appliances is acute, and it is easy to produce safety problems in use. The purpose of this paper is to enhance the user experience of the elderly group when using kitchen appliances. Firstly, the elderly subjects are categorized according to their age range, cognitive level, health degree, etc. Secondly, the human-computer interaction barriers to the use of kitchen appliances by the elderly with different characteristics are collected by constructing a user mental model and combining the observation method with semi-structured interviews, etc. Finally, the weights of barriers to the use of the factors are determined by the Analytic Hierarchy Process and the priorities are obtained, which provides a basis for the aging-adapted design of kitchen appliances. This study will improve the human-computer user experience of the elderly when using kitchen appliances and provide a reference for future ageing-friendly design.

Keywords: Kitchenware · Human-Computer Interaction · User Mental Models

1 Introduction

Population ageing is a major social problem currently facing the world. According to the latest statistics, as of 2022, there will be more than 280 million people over 60 years of age in China, accounting for 19.8% of the total population, and nearly 210 million people over 65 years of age, accounting for 14.9% of the total population. By 2035, China's elderly population aged 60 and above will exceed about 400 million, accounting for more than 30% of the total population and entering the stage of heavy aging [1]. In the context of digital society, the process of intelligence is accelerating, affecting the clothing, food, housing and transportation of the elderly.

In China, the kitchen is an important activity place for elderly people who age at home. Citespace software was used to analyze the current situation of the use of kitchen appliances by the elderly in China. China Knowledge Network (CNKI) database was selected as the data source, and the keywords of "elderly" and "kitchen appliances"

© The Author(s), under exclusive license to Springer Nature Switzerland AG 2024
C. Stephanidis et al. (Eds.): HCII 2024, CCIS 2115, pp. 266–274, 2024.
https://doi.org/10.1007/978-3-031-61947-2_29

were used to search the data. It can be concluded that the relationship between kitchen appliances and the elderly is very close, and interaction design, experience design, and universal design play a leading role in the design of kitchen appliances. However, most of the intelligent kitchen appliances on the market nowadays adopt universal design, combining with the existing intelligent technology to realize the functions of remote control and timer work, etc., which still require a lot of manual operation. The operation process also lacks consideration for the elderly, and the cognitive level and perceptual limitations of the elderly can become obstacle factors when using kitchen appliances. The interaction of kitchen appliances is too complicated, the feedback is not timely, and the operation is not convenient enough, which makes the elderly afraid to use or not use smart kitchen appliances. This reduces the user experience of the elderly in using kitchen appliances and hinders the process of integration into the digital society. Therefore, in order to make the elderly actively integrate into the digital society, it is necessary to accelerate the research on ageing-friendly design of products not only limited to kitchen appliances (Table 1).

Table 1. Keywords in the literature related to the use of kitchen appliances by the elderly

Sequences	Keywords	Frequency
1	The elderly	16
2	Interactive Design	14
3	Ageing-friendly	5
4	User Experience	5
5	Interface Design	3
6	Smart Kitchen	2
7	User Research	2
8	Mental Model	2
9	Experience Design	2
1O	Voice Interaction	2

2   Classification of Older Groups

Under the new perspective of digital society, accurate categorization of older adults is essential to better understand the barrier factors between older adults and kitchen appliances. In China, with the rapid development of the digital society, older adults mostly face the challenge of using smart devices and adapting to new technologies. Factors such as different ages, cognitive levels, health levels, technology familiarity, and living habits can lead to very different challenges and needs when using kitchen appliances, which in turn can lead to some negative emotions and resistance among the elderly when integrating into the digital society. According to the Chinese national standard

"Elderly Ability Assessment Specification" (GB/T42195–2022), the index assessment classification of the subject elderly age range, cognitive level, health and other characteristics, the classification is more in line with the study of the elderly's daily behavioral ability [2]. Through the scale measurement method, the elderly were categorized into five categories according to the scoring criteria, namely, "perfect ability, mild disability, moderate disability, severe disability, and complete disability". In this paper, 10 elderly people were assessed for their ability indexes, and were categorized as 6 elderly people with mild disability, 3 elderly people with moderate disability, and 1 elderly person with severe disability. Since the elderly people were required to operate alone during the operation process, the elderly people with "severe disability" decided to participate in the experiment or not depending on the situation. The "totally disabled" elderly group did not participate in the experiment (Table 2 and Table 3).

Table 2. Partial assessment indicators for the classification of older population groups

Assessment of indicators	Substance
Age Range	The starting point for the legal age of the elderly in China is 60 years of age, which means that citizens who have reached the age of 60 are considered to be elderly
Cognitive Levels	Attention, memory, language comprehension and expression, spatial perception, temporal orientation, etc
Health Level	Physical health (vision/hearing, etc.), self-care (eating, grooming, bathing, dressing/undressing, etc.), basic motor skills (walking on level ground, walking up and down stairs, carrying loads, etc.)

Table 3. Category of older persons

Categories	Substance
Age Range	The starting point for the legal age of the elderly in China is 60 years of age, which means that citizens who have reached the age of 60 are considered to be elderly
Cognitive Levels	Attention, memory, language comprehension and expression, spatial perception, temporal orientation, etc
Health Level	Physical health (vision/hearing, etc.), self-care (eating, grooming, bathing, dressing/undressing, etc.), basic motor skills (walking on level ground, walking up and down stairs, carrying loads, etc.)

3   User Mind Modeling

In order to better study the human-computer barriers to the use of kitchen appliances by the elderly, the nine qualified elderly subjects mentioned above were sequentially introduced into the user mind model, and observation, interviews and other research methods were used to show the behaviors and decision-making paths of the elderly users in the process of using kitchen appliance products. The user mental model is dedicated to exploring the user's behavioral logic and psychological expectations of using products, and has unique research value in the field of product design [3]. In the study, different data of elderly users are collected to analyze the actual needs, pain points, expectations, and behavioral logic of different elderly users when facing kitchen appliance products, so as to get a more comprehensive human-machine obstacle factors, and provide a basis for designing and optimizing kitchen appliance products suitable for the elderly (Fig. 1).

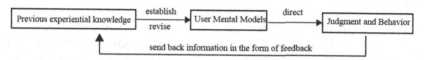

Fig. 1. Operationalization and Iteration of Mental Models

To build a mental model for the use of kitchen appliances by the elderly, combining the "ladder of inference" proposed by Chris Argyris to describe the mental modeling process, through the seven stages of "observing the information, selecting the information, assigning meaning, summarizing the assumptions, drawing conclusions, adopting the beliefs, and taking action" can truly reflect the behavior and operation of elderly users in the process of using kitchen appliances. Through the seven stages of "observing information, selecting information, assigning meaning, summarizing assumptions, drawing conclusions, adopting beliefs, and taking actions", the model can truly reflect the behaviors and operations of the elderly users in the process of use, and examine the kitchen appliance products from the perspective of the elderly users, so as to accurately explore the obstacles for the elderly to use the kitchen appliance products, instead of only relying on the designers' subjective assumptions (Fig. 2).

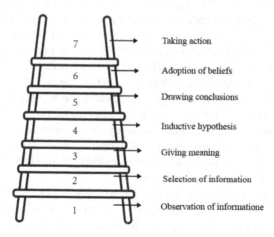

Fig. 2. The Seven Stages of Mind Modeling

The specifics of operating a user mental model of older adults' use of kitchen appliances are as follows.

- Step 1: Observation of information (Perception stage)

  Elderly users collect information about the kitchen environment through visual, auditory, tactile and other sensory channels, such as observing the layout of the kitchen and recognizing the location and appearance features of each kitchen appliance product. When observing the information, the elderly may have difficulty in reading the product icons or recognizing the features of the kitchen appliances due to their diminished eyesight.

- Step 2: Selection of information (Information screening stage)

  The brain sifts through the many perceptual information to select the focus relevant to the current task based on the cognitive ability and experience of the elderly user, e.g., deciding which kitchen appliance (e.g., rice cooker, microwave oven, etc.) to use today to complete the cooking task. When selecting information, older adults may not be able to focus quickly on the information they need due to high cognitive load, complex operating panels or too many function choices. Memory loss can also cause older adults to forget the operating procedures of kitchen appliances, etc.

- Step 3: Giving meaning (Comprehension stage)

  Based on their own experience and knowledge, elderly users understand the functions and interpret the operation of selected kitchen appliances, for example, understanding the functional meanings indicated by the various buttons and display messages on the rice cooker and determining how it should be operated in order to achieve the purpose of cooking rice. When assigning meanings, older people may have limited understanding of intelligent kitchen appliances and the instructions for using the products are too specialized or complex, leading to wrong product operation procedures.

- Step 4: Inductive hypothesis (Reasoning stage)

  Based on their understanding of how a kitchen appliance operates, older users form hypotheses about the operation of the product, for example, assuming that the rice cooker should start cooking rice at a preset time and temperature after pressing the "Start" button. When summarizing assumptions, older people's memory and logical thinking skills may decline with age, and they may not have a clear understanding of the logic and cause-and-effect relationship of the operation of a kitchen appliance.

- Step 5: Drawing conclusions (Decision-making stage)

  Combining the above assumptions, the elderly user concludes. That is, to activate a kitchen appliance product, a set of operating instructions (e.g., pressing a specific button or knob) must be executed correctly. In reaching the conclusion, older adults will overly rely on previous experience to operate the kitchen appliance product, and will not be able to make a quick decision to fight for the kitchen appliance product if it has a sudden or abnormal situation.

- Step 6: Adoption of beliefs (Confidence-building stage)

  When referring to users' adoption beliefs when using a kitchen appliance product, it can be understood that users will be assured and persist in using a product only if they accept and trust that the product will fulfill their needs and accomplish their tasks effectively. For example, when using a kitchen appliance product, older people are more likely to adopt and use the product for a long time if they form positive beliefs about the product's safety performance, ease of operation, and practicality of its functions. However, older adults still have low levels of trust in new products and are concerned about safety issues and equipment damage caused by operation.

- Step 7: Taking action (Implementation stage)

  Based on the above cognitive and decision-making processes, older users take practical actions, such as firmly pressing the "Start" button on the rice cooker and waiting for the product to start working. When taking actions, older people may have difficulties in operating the buttons due to their declining physical functions, especially when they are faced with buttons that require force and precision control.

  Nine elderly people were introduced into the user's mental model, and by observing and interviewing their behavior and decision-making paths during the seven stages of using kitchen appliances, a number of barriers to the use of kitchen appliances by the elderly were obtained. For example, the design of kitchen appliances should be based on large font displays, increased sound prompts, optimized and simplified functions, and easy operation.

4   Factor Weighting Analysis

In view of the above research affecting the elderly in the use of intelligent kitchen appliance products in the human-machine obstacle factors, through the hierarchical analysis method, systematic sorting and quantification of each obstacle factor, to determine the relative importance of their degree, so as to provide more targeted improvement recommendations for the design of kitchen appliance products for the aging, so as to make kitchen appliance products more suitable for the needs of the elderly users and their habits of use [4]. The Analytic Hierarchy Process (AHP) was proposed by Thomas L. Saaty, an American operations researcher, in the 1970s, and is suitable for decision-making problems that are difficult to quantify or contain multiple evaluation indicators. In this paper's study of the barriers to the use of kitchen appliances by older adults, the following steps can be implemented.

- Step 1: Modeling multi-level decision-making structures

  The barrier factors of the study were disassembled into several layers, such as the objective layer (the study of barriers to the use of kitchen appliance products by the elderly), the guideline layer (including but not limited to the operation interface A1, the functional design A2, the safety design A3, the design of the physical interactivity A4, etc.), and the indicator layer (the specific barrier factors to which each guideline layer belongs) (Fig. 3).

- Step 2: Constructing a judgment matrix

  For the guideline layer factors, through semi-structured interviews or questionnaires, older users and relevant experts were invited to make two-by-two comparisons to determine the degree of importance of each factor relative to the target layer, and weights were assigned to form a judgment matrix as shown in Table 5 by using the 1–9 scale method (Table 4).

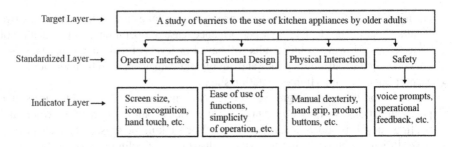

Fig. 3. Multilevel Structural Model of Barriers

Table 4. 1–9 Indicators of the Scale Method.

Value	Substance
1	The two factors are equally important when compared
3	The former is slightly more important than the latter when comparing the two factors
5	The former is significantly more important than the latter when comparing the two factors
7	The former is more strongly important than the latter when comparing the two factors
9	The former is extremely more important than the latter
2,4,6,8	The middle value of two adjacent judgments
Reciprocal (math.)	The comparative judgment of A1 to A2 is a, then the comparative judgment of A2 to A1 is 1/a

Table 5. Judgment matrix A

A	A1 (Operator Interface)	A2 (Functional Design)	A3 (Physical Interaction)	A4 (Safety)
A1	1	1/2	3	1/5
A2	2	1	3	1/3
A3	1/3	1/3	1	1/7
A4	5	3	7	1

- Step 3: Calculating weights and consistency tests

   To calculate the relative weights of the factors in the criterion layer in the target layer, the relative weights are usually derived by using the arithmetic mean method or the geometric mean method, and a consistency test is performed to ensure that the matrices are consistent. In the following example, the arithmetic mean method is

Table 6. Judgment matrix B and eigenvectors

A	A1	A2	A3	A4	ω	$A\omega$
A1	0.12	0.10	0.21	0.12	0.1375	0.5635
A2	0.24	0.21	0.21	0.20	0.2150	0.8839
A3	0.04	0.07	0.07	0.09	0.0675	0.2667
A4	0.60	0.62	0.50	0.60	0.5800	2.3850

used, and the judgment matrix is first normalized by columns, and the eigenvector values obtained are the relative weights (Table 6).

After calculating the weight values, in order to determine whether there is a logical contradiction in the relative importance between the factors, the matrix needs to be tested for consistency. The consistency index of the matrix (CI) is represented by the following formula.

$$CI = (\lambda max - n)/(n - 1)$$

where n denotes the matrix order, λ max is the maximum eigenvalue of the matrix, calculated as follows.

$$\lambda max = \sum_{i=1}^{n} \frac{[A\omega]i}{n\omega i}$$

Finally, proceed to solve for the consistency ratio of the judgment matrix (CR), which is calculated as follows.

$$CR = CI/RI$$

where RI stands for Mean Consistency Indicator, which can be found in the Mean Consistency Indicator table.

According to the consistency test formula, we get: λ max = 4.0681, CI = 0.0227, RI = 0.89, and CR = 0.0255, because the CR value is less than 0.1, which indicates that the matrix is constructed reasonably, and the weight values of the four criterion layer factors are scientific.

- Step 4: Factor weighting

  According to the hierarchical analysis method, the weights of the factors at the criterion level were calculated, and it was found that the factors at the criterion level were, in descending order, security, functional design, operation interface, and physical interaction.

- Step 5: Decision analytics

  According to the ranking results of this study, the weights of the most important guideline layer factors affecting the use of kitchen appliance products by elderly users are obtained, and safety and functional design should be taken as the primary guidelines to provide optimization suggestions and improvement directions for kitchen appliance product design. According to the above process, the specific obstacle factors in the index layer are calculated by hierarchical analysis, and the specific obstacle factor weights obtained can provide specific design solutions for the design of kitchen appliance products for aging.

5   Conclusion

This study focuses on the human-computer barriers faced by the elderly when using kitchen appliances, and provides a scientific basis for the design of kitchen appliances for aging by categorizing the elderly, constructing a mental model of the elderly, and analyzing the weights of human-computer interaction barriers with the Hierarchical Analysis Method. The method is not limited to kitchen appliances, but can be expanded to other products for the elderly.

However, there are some limitations and shortcomings in the study. First, the sample of elderly users is small, and this study does not comprehensively cover all the influencing factors, such as cultural background, education level and technology acceptance; second, some of the design suggestions, although theoretically valid, have not been verified by large-scale empirical data; finally, the article analyzes the macroscopic guideline-level factor analysis, and does not rank the weights of the specific obstacle factors. Looking forward, the study can strengthen interdisciplinary cooperation, use quantitative experiments to verify the effectiveness of design strategies, meet the needs of elderly users, and continue to optimize the experience of the elderly in the use of kitchen appliances, as well as provide a basis for the design of other products for aging and promote the integration of the elderly into the digital society.

6. References

1. Wang, W.: Development trend and response to population aging in China. Solidarity **03**, 34–37 (2023)
2. Peng, D.: Strengthening the security of elderly services and promoting the high-quality development of elderly services. China Civil Aff. **06**, 19 (2023)
3. Fei, X.: Research status and development trend of user mental modeling in product design. Art Des. (Theory) **2**(04), 84–86 (2022)
4. Jin, Y., Xu, J., Liu, Z.: Research on aging-friendly design principles of smart kitchen products based on CHC-AHP. Furniture Inter. Decoration **29**(07):42–48 (2022)

Digital Barriers in the Elderly: The Effect of Interaction Method in a Medical Registration System on Operational Stress in the Elderly

Yanmin Xue and Shuang Wang[✉]

Xi 'an University of Technology, Shaanxi 710054, China
2154575478@qq.com

Abstract. The aging of the population is increasing, and healthcare has become a hotspot for elderly services. The medical registration system uses IoT technology to optimize the medical process and interconnect information, making the medical service fast and efficient. However, the seemingly convenient, multi-approach smart registration method still has digital barrier issues for elderly users. This study collects multi-channel physiological signals from young and elderly subjects by summarizing the barriers of elderly users and designing an interactive experimental method to meet the healthcare needs of the elderly population. It was found that both elderly users and young users had slightly lower HR and SC mean indexes when auditory compensation was applied and that compensation of hearing could reduce the operating pressure of the elderly and improve the user experience; the HRV and EDA indexes of the elderly users increased more in the interactive operation, and the operating pressure of the elderly users was significantly higher than that of the young users. This study has implications for the design of intelligent products oriented to the cognitive characteristics of the elderly.

Keywords: Digital disability in the elderly · Medical registration system · Interaction method · Operating pressure

1 Introduction

Population aging is an important feature of demographic change in the world today, and China, as a large population country, is also facing a serious aging problem. At present, the proportion of elderly people in China continues to increase, and the degree of aging is still gradually deepening. In contrast, the elderly population exhibits cognitive impairment problems such as the inability to hear and see, prolonged response time, slowed information processing, and memory loss in a digitized society. Intelligent healthcare is the development trend of hospitals in China's Internet era, but the elderly population lacks interactive guidance in the necessary aspects of booking and registration and faces the problem of digital barriers that make it difficult to use equipment. Therefore, this proposal takes China's smart hospital as a typical digital scene, obtains HRV and EDA physiological indexes of elderly users in interaction behavior through multi-channel physiological experiments, and compares the effect of interaction guidance on the operation pressure of the elderly group, to explore the elderly-friendly guided interaction under the development of smart healthcare.

There have been studies that have explored the interface interaction needs of older adults, such as Park et al. Seeking feedback from older adults and their caregivers from telephone interviews and focus group sessions to understand the needs of older adults with cognitive impairments using autonomous vehicle interfaces [1].Wang et al. used the Scale of Usability (SUS) to measure users' perceived usability [2]. However, such user research methods are highly subjective and are highly susceptible to sample size and subjective user differences. Physiological measurements can reflect information about different states of the human body, provide effective feedback on the user's device operation status, and improve the effectiveness of research on emotion recognition and user experience. Skin Conductance (SC) and Heart rate variability (HRV) are commonly used physiologic measures. EDA reflects emotional and cognitive states, and SC is related to factors such as cognitive load, task difficulty, and frustration [3], and can be used to measure the usability of interactive interfaces and user experiences [4, 5]. Subjects' SC levels gradually decreased when users were navigating a preferred design interface or were in a low-stress state [6]. Yao Song used eye tracking to study the relationship between emotional expression and attention and analyzed the user's emotional arousal and stress level through electrodermal signals for robot anthropomorphic interface design [7]. HRV is a valid indicator for obtaining psychological and physiological states and can be used to study the emotional experience and psychological stress of subjects [8]. Moya-Ramon et al. measured HRV in 26 professional cyclists to assess the validity and reliability of using different smartphone apps [9]. Yang et al. obtained subjects' HRV time-domain characteristics, HR, to determine the rationality of drivers' visual attention allocation in an unfamiliar shared car [10].

This proposal is based on the cognitive impairment of the elderly group and explores the interaction methods that conform to the cognitive characteristics of the elderly group by collecting the cardiac and electrocardiographic physiological signals of the elderly and young users under each interaction guidance and comparing the stress difference between the elderly and young users in the task of booking appointments. This study is of great significance for researching the design of interaction adaptation, proposing the principles of age-friendly interaction, and alleviating the problem of barriers to medical care for elderly users.

2 Methods

2.1 Participants

The experiment recruited 12 elderly people who frequently sought medical care or suffered from chronic diseases as experimental subjects in the geriatric group (male-to-female ratio 1:1) with a mean age of 69.75 and randomly selected 12 young subjects as the experimental control group (male-to-female ratio 1:1) with a mean age of 23.75.

2.2   Experimental Equipment

The experiment used ErgoLAB EDA wireless piezoelectric sensors and ErgoLAB Chest Biosensing smart wearable chest strap sensors (Fig. 1) to collect electrocardiogram (ECG) and electrocardiogram (EDA) data from the subjects and used the human-computer environment testing cloud platform to summarize and process the data.

Fig. 1. Wearable physiological sensors.

2.3   Experimental Materials and Variable Settings

The experiment uses a computer screen as the interaction interface, draws an interaction prototype using the interaction interface of an outpatient self-service registration terminal device of a geriatric specialist hospital in China with a large flow of people as an example, and sets four different interaction guidance methods as independent variables (Table 1). The dependent variables were physiological data and operating pressure of elderly and young users with different operating reminders.

Table 1. Independent variable settings.

Task number	independent variable	Variable Settings
Task I	No interaction guide	original interoperation
Task 2	text pop-up guidance	1Pop-up guide window when user clicks on it
Task 3	Highlight after completing the interaction	After the user clicks, the icon is enlarged and deepened
Task 4	Voice Interactive Guidance	Set up appropriate voice guidance on each page

Among them, task 4 voice interaction used the more affinity AI synthesized voice as the experimental variable, in order to exclude the influence of the subjective preference of the subjects for male and female voices, eight random numbers 2, 15, 10, 3, 8, 5, 13, and 11 were generated, and the singular step was set to be the male voice, and the opposite to be the female voice. The voice guidance contents are "Please select a login method", "Please select the consultation department" etc.

2.4 Experimental Design

Experimental preparation stage: inform the subjects of the experimental process and precautions, the subjects informed and agreed to the researchers to wear the electro-cardiographic and electrocardiographic sensors for the subjects, and at the same time, calibrate the experimental equipment and observe the normal physiological data. (2) Experimental phase: First, subjects were asked to sit still for 5 min to collect resting data. Secondly, a within-subjects experiment was used so that each subject completed four interactive reminder operation tasks for appointment booking respectively. Finally, the subjects scored each task and filled out a subjective questionnaire. The experimental flow is shown in Fig. 2.

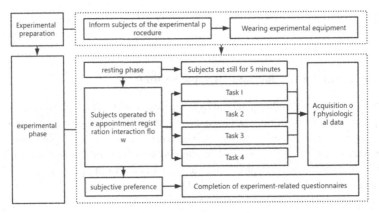

Fig. 2. Experimental flow.

The experiment was conducted using a Latin-square experimental design with rotation of the task variables, i.e., if the order of tasks for the first subject was n, n + 1, n + 2, n + 3, the order of experimental tasks for the next subject was n + 1, n + 2, n + 3, n and so on.

3 Hypothesis

The research objective of this PROPOSAL is to take the interaction obstacle problem of elderly people's appointment registration in Chinese hospital scenarios as an example and to explore the interaction methods that meet the cognitive characteristics of the elderly group by collecting the ECG and EDA indexes of the elderly users and the young users, so as to alleviate the interaction pressure of the elderly group. It is hypothesized that the auditory compensation interaction method can alleviate the operation pressure of the elderly group.

4 Results

4.1 EAD Data Analysis

The physiological sensors were used to obtain the EDA data under each interaction task for older and younger users, analyze the SC data on the EDA time domain, and plot the SC mean metrics (Fig. 3). The experimental data were based on the physiological data of the resting phase of the subjects as a baseline, and the SC mean indexes under each appointment registration operation task were compared and analyzed, it can be seen that the SC mean indexes of the elderly group were slightly higher in task one, and the operation pressure of the elderly users was relatively higher, but the SC mean indexes of each task were balanced and there was no significant difference. The youth group had slightly higher SC means when operating on Task 2 salient interaction reminders and slightly lower SC means when operating on Task 4 voice interaction reminders. Therefore, the youth group experienced the least operation pressure when experiencing voice interaction operation, and the task difficulty was slightly lower, but the SC indicators of each task did not change much, and there was no significant difference. All the SC mean value indicators in the elderly group were significantly lower than those in the youth group, which was related to factors such as thick calluses on the skin of the hands of elderly users or dry skin. An independent samples t-test found that there was no significant difference between the SC mean value indicators of the elderly and youth groups.

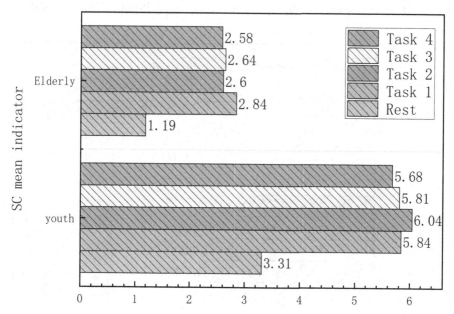

Fig. 3. Mean values of SC for young and old users with different operational reminders.

4.2 HRV Data Analysis

As shown in Fig. 4, the LF/HF mean data under each reminder task for the young and old groups after passing the Fast Fourier Transform. Comparing the LF/HF mean metrics of the older group, the LF/HF means for each interaction task, from highest to lowest, were Task 3, Task 2, Task 1, and Task 4, and the LF/HF mean for the Task 4 voice interaction was significantly lower than that for each of the other tasks. Therefore, appropriate voice reminders for elderly users in the interaction process of reservation and registration can reduce the operation pressure of elderly users and enhance the user experience. The LF/HF means under each task for young users showed the same trend as the SC means described above. Young users similarly preferred voice interaction reminders and were in a low-stress state in Task IV. The obtained physiological data on LF/HF means were analyzed by one-way ANOVA, and the results showed that there was no significant difference in LF/HF means across the different operational tasks ($p = 0.359 > 0.05$).

From the figure, it can be seen that compared to the baseline data in the resting phase, the LF/HF mean metrics of the older users operating each task increased more than the LF/HF mean metrics of the youth users. An independent samples t-test was used to further explore whether there was a significant difference between the LF/HF means generated by the different manipulation tasks in the older and younger groups. The mean values of LF/HF in the older and younger groups at rest, task 1, task 2, and task 4 phases satisfied normal distribution and variance chi-square, but there was no significant difference ($P > 0.05$). The mean values of the elderly and youth groups on Task III were 3.054 and 1.238, respectively, which did not satisfy the chi-square, Welch's T-test was used, and the significance result had a P-value of $0.034 < 0.05$, so

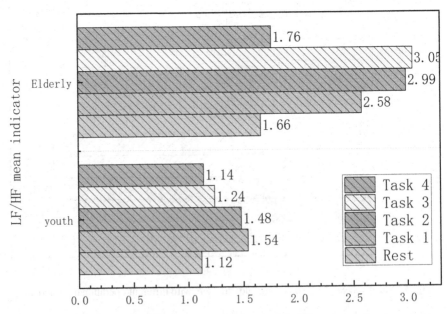

Fig. 4. Mean values of LF/HF for young and old users with different operational reminders

the statistical results were significant. Task three provides feedback and reminds users of operational behaviors by means of pop-up windows, but its textual information increases the cognitive load of the elderly. Compared to the youth group, task three caused more operation pressure on the elderly users. At the same time, task three has large inter-individual cognitive differences, and some users perceive it as a misoperation prompt, which in turn triggers nervousness; a few users believe that the pop-up window reminder can cause good operation feedback, but the overall recognition is poor.

4.3 Subjective Preference Analysis

The subjective preference data are consistent with the optimal terms of SC data and HRV data on the EDC time domain, so it can be assumed that voice interaction can alleviate the digital barriers in the booking session of elderly users and improve the user experience.

5 Conclusion

In order to alleviate the pressure of intelligent medical consultation of elderly users and meet the needs of elderly users in using intelligent devices, this proposal takes the interaction process of hospital appointment registration as an example and collects and analyzes users' ECG and piezoelectricity indexes through interaction perception experiments to explore the physiological effects of different interaction modes on the elderly users, and to compare the differences in the interaction needs of elderly users and young users. It is found that the addition of voice guidance through auditory compensation can alleviate the operation pressure and obstacle problems of the elderly group, thus proving that the hypothesis is reasonable.

Acknowledgment. This work is sponsored by the National Social Science Foundation of China (No. 22BSH122).

References

1. Park, J., Zahabi, M., Blanchard, S., et al.: A novel autonomous vehicle interface for older adults with cognitive impairment. Appl. Ergon. **113**, 104080 (2023)
2. Wang, Y., Huo, J., Wu, D., et al.: Usability of curved keyboard design on the large smartphone: an empirical study. Appl. Ergon. **113**, 104013 (2023)
3. Andreassi, J L.: Psychophysiology: human behavior and physiological response Psychology press, 2010
4. Mandryk, R.L., Inkpen, K.M., Calvert, T.W.: Using psychophysiological techniques to measure user experience with entertainment technologies. Behav. Inf. Technol. **25**(2), 141–158 (2006)
5. Pfister, H.R., Wollstädter, S., Peter, C.: Affective responses to system messages in human–computer-interaction: effects of modality and message type. Interact. Comput. **23**(4), 372–383 (2011)

6. Ward, R.D., Marsden, P.H.: Physiological responses to different WEB page designs. Int. J. Hum. Comput. Stud. **59**(1–2), 199–212 (2003)
7. Song, Y., Tao, D., Luximon, Y.: In robot we trust? The effect of emotional expressions and contextual cues on anthropomorphic trustworthiness. Appl. Ergon. **109**, 103967 (2023)
8. Rowe, D W., Sibert, J., Irwin, D.: Heart rate variability: indicator of user state as an aid to human-computer interaction. In: Proceedings of the SIGCHI Conference on Human Factors in Computing Systems, pp. 480–487 (1998)
9. Moya-Ramon, M., Mateo-March, M., Peña-González, I., et al.: Validity and reliability of different smartphones applications to measure HRV during short and ultra-short measurements in elite athletes. Comput. Methods Programs Biomed. **217**, 106696 (2022)
10. Yang, H., Hu, N., Jia, R., et al.: How does driver fatigue monitor system design affect car-sharing drivers? an approach to the quantification of driver mental stress and visual attention. Travel Behav. Soc. **35**, 100755 (2024)

Analysis of Museum Tourism Elements for the Elderly Based on Statistical Experiments

Yanmin Xue and Lu Zhang[(✉)]

School of Art and Design, Xi'an University of Technology, Xi'an 710061, China
544737327@qq.com

Abstract. This study, set against the backdrop of elderly museum tourism, employs three experimental designs: elderly cognitive strategy experiments, elderly cognitive offloading efficiency experiments, and elderly social willingness experiments. It quantitatively analyzes the internal and external interactive experiences of the elderly demographic during their travel process, aiming to enhance their mental and physical health and quality of life. The cognitive strategy experiment results reveal that within the 55–75 age group, there's a need to improve lives through external devices or digital technology, with the age demarcation for assistive technology support at 56.7 years. This need increases with age; with external technological support, offloading efficiency experiments show that the elderly's memory capacity is 69%, significantly higher than the comparison group's recall ability at 38%, with statistical expectations, variance, coefficient of variation, and skewness distributions being more favorable. Multivariate linear regression statistics indicate a high correlation between the elderly's life satisfaction and their willingness to engage socially, with social influence playing a leading role in life satisfaction. The results of this paper provide a theoretical basis for research related to the travel of the elderly.

Keywords: Older Adults · Museum Tourism · Cognitive Offloading · Statistics · Multiple Regression Programs

1 Introduction

China, as the world's largest developing country, had a population aged 60 and above reaching 296.97 million by the end of 2023, accounting for 21.1% of the total population. Among them, the population aged 65 and above was 216.76 million, accounting for 15.4% of the total population. This data marks China's formal entry into an aging society. The aging population phenomenon has begun to constrain China's economic development to some extent. Similarly, with the improvement of medical conditions and the increase in people's living standards, the same problem exists in other countries around the world, especially in developed countries in Europe and America. Therefore, providing comprehensive and three-dimensional social services for the elderly and middle-aged groups better is a hotspot of concern for the international community.

Museum tourism activities, serving as an important means for relaxation, stress relief, and quality of life enhancement, are increasingly favored by the elderly. However, studies

[2, 3] indicate that with the decline in cognitive abilities among the elderly, challenges such as memory loss, concentration difficulties, and trouble learning new things are encountered during travel. This pain point is particularly prominent in the digital and internet age, creating a dilemma for the elderly who have the desire to travel but fear the cognitive challenges it presents. Thus, effectively reducing cognitive load and easing memory burdens in the context of museum tourism for the elderly, through diverse forms of cognitive offloading [4, 5], holds significant social importance by freeing up cognitive and emotional resources, thereby aiding them in enjoying the pleasures brought by tourism.

Building on this, the study designs three experimental protocols: cognitive strategies for the elderly, cognitive offloading efficiency for the elderly, and the elderly's willingness to socialize. Through survey questionnaires, it collects the difficulties and needs of the elderly during museum tours; summarizes the commonly used cognitive offloading strategies in the visiting behaviors of the elderly; and quantitatively analyzes the internal and external interactive experiences of the elderly group during tourism. This serves as a starting point to provide a theoretical basis for subsequent research on elderly travel and tourism.

2 Experimental Program

2.1 Experiments on Offloading Strategies for the Elderly

1. Experimental Purpose

This experiment aims to discuss whether elderly people prefer external strategies or internal strategies when facing cognitive tasks, thereby verifying whether external offloading strategies can effectively reduce their cognitive load. Additionally, it investigates the elderly's attitude towards technology to determine whether digital technology should be used as the primary offloading strategy.

2. Experimental Methods

The study involves 150 elderly people aged between 55 and 75, divided into four age groups: 55–60, 60–65, 65–70, and 70–75, based on 5-year intervals. All participants are required to fill out two questionnaires: (1) the Digital Attitude Questionnaire - Capability Scale (DAQ) [6], which includes 5 items related to individuals' attitudes towards technology, using a 5-point Likert [7] scale ranging from 1 (strongly disagree) to 5 (strongly agree); and (2) the Memory Compensation Task Questionnaire [8], consisting of 20 questions. This survey asks participants to evaluate specific strategies used in daily memory tasks, categorizing data into external or internal strategies. The classification and definition of the memory compensation questionnaire are shown in Table 1.

Table 1. Memory Compensation Questionnaire

Rank		Definition	Instance
External	digital	Using digital resources to aid memory	Recording notes on a phone; setting reminders on the TV
	Physical	Using physical resources or objects to help memory	Writing in a diary; keeping notes for future reference
	Social	Seeking help from others or relying on them for assistance	Being reminded by a spouse; constantly telling others to reinforce memory
	Environmental	Using deliberately arranged environments to assist memory	Placing items near the front door; leaving labels on shelves; placing items in frequently visited spots
	Other	Undetermined type of external offloading strategy	Adding events to a calendar; making copies; writing down and highlighting; taking notes
Internal	Time	Intentionally increasing memory time, such as through repetition	Reading multiple times; asking repeatedly until a name is remembered; repeating in one's mind
	Energy	Significant increase or reference to the effort of memory intention	Making an effort to remember; focusing to avoid forgetting; listening carefully and understanding
	Mnemonic Strategies	Using complex cognitive strategies for memory	Recalling past journeys; visualizing mentally; trying to remember a mutual friend to recall a name
	Other	Undetermined type of internal offloading strategy	Reminding oneself to check the clock often; keeping things in mind; automatically remembering

2.2 Experiments on Cognitive Offloading Efficiency in the Elderly

1. Experimental Purpose

In this experiment, it is hypothesized that the more artifacts are viewed and the longer the viewing time, coupled with stronger external distractions, the more likely it is that elderly individuals will forget the content they have viewed. Therefore, they would need to rely on external strategies, such as referring to browsing records at any time, to reduce the memory burden. This experiment seeks to verify the above hypothesis.

2. Experimental Methods

This experiment is a controlled study with two groups: Group 1 is the experimental group and Group 2 is the control group. The methodology involves a "want to collect" vs "just browsing" mode. Participants in the experimental group place images of artifacts they wish to collect into a favorites folder through an operation, while the control group only views images of the artifacts. After the experiment, the experimental group is asked to recall which images were placed into the favorites folder, while the control group only recalls the images they viewed. The final comparison is based on the accuracy rate. The experiment's process is shown in Figs. 1 and 2.

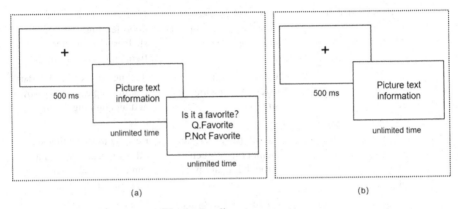

Fig. 1. Reading stage process

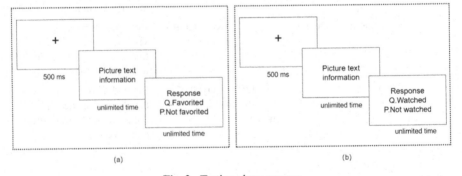

Fig. 2. Testing phase process

2.3 Experiment on Social Willingness of Older Adults

1. Experimental Purpose

This study explores whether elderly individuals are willing to engage in social sharing during museum visits and whether social participation increases life satisfaction among the elderly.

2. Experimental Methods

This study's materials consist of (1) a Social Participation Scale; (2) an Elderly Characteristics Indicator; and (3) a Life Satisfaction Scale, with sample scales and indicators as shown in Tables 2, 3, and 4.

Table 2. Social participation measurement table

Rank	Type of participation	participation criteria	Sample size	percentage
1	Get involved in an association/organization	Monthly, or with accountability	-	-
2	Do volunteer activities	Not monthly, but sometimes	-	-
3	Go to a library, museum, concert, etc.	At least once a month	-	-
4	Attend classes, meetings	At least once a month	-	-
5	Go to a cafe, tea room, restaurant	At least once a month	-	-
6	Attend a neighborhood or community gathering	At least once a year	-	-
7	Visiting family members	At least once a month	-	-
8	Visiting friends, acquaintances	At least once a month	-	-
9	Helping a family member	Helped at least once	-	-
10	Helping friends, acquaintances, neighbors	At least once	-	-

Note: The scoring range for this table is 0–1, where 0 represents 'no' and 1 represents 'yes'.

To examine the relationships between the variables and control variables, this study conducts a multivariate linear regression analysis, with the Life Satisfaction Scale as the dependent variable, and the Social Participation Scale and Elderly Characteristics Indicator as independent variables [9, 10], to explore the impact of museum social participation on the health of the elderly. This study runs two sets of linear regression models for life satisfaction scores. In the first test, the relationship between life satisfaction and social participation among the elderly is explored. In the second test, four nested models are run on top of the original regression model: Model 1 includes gender and age; Model 2 includes education level and pension; Model 3 includes physical and mental health; and Model 4 includes offspring, marital status, and living situation, to differentiate the connection between social participation and life satisfaction from broader dimensions that can affect participation and satisfaction.

Table 3. Social participation measurement table.

Variable type	Variable form	Score	Sample size	percentage
Sex	Male	1	-	-
	Female	0	-	-
Age	Elderly	1	-	-
	Low-aged Elderly	0	-	-
Education	Educated	1	-	-
	Uneducated	2	-	-
Pension	Yes	1	-	-
	No	0	-	-
Physical Health Score	Checkup at least once a year/exercise 3 times a week	1	-	-
	No medical checkups/no physical exercise	0	-	-
Mental Health Score	Rarely feel negative emotions such as loneliness/ sleep well	1	-	-
	Usually feel negative emotions such as loneliness/poor sleep	0	-	-
Offspring	No	0	-	-
	Have children	1	-	-
	At least one grandchild	2	-	-
Marital Status	Married and living with spouse	1	-	-
	Married not living with spouse	2	-	-
	Divorced	3	-	-
	Widowed	4	-	-
	Never married	5	-	-
Residence	Living with family	1	-	-
	Not living with family	0	-	-

Note: This table is scored according to variable type; sample tables have been scored accordingly.

3   Results and Discussion

3.1   Results and Discussion Experiment 1 Related Results

1. Experimental results of the DAQ

In this experiment, the relevant questions were categorized into seeking attitudes and digital learning attitudes, and the statistical results of the DAQ form for 150 older adults are shown in Table 5:

Table 4. Characteristic indicators of the elderly

Rank	score
In most respects, my life is close to my ideal	-
My living conditions are excellent	-
I am satisfied with my life	-
So far, I have gotten the important things I want in life	-
If I could live my life over, I would hardly change anything	-

Table 5. DAQ Table Statistics Results

Project/Attitude	1	2	3	4	5	Total	classification
I need computers and technology to assist in my life	2	4	27	53	64	150	Digital needs
I like to surf the web whenever and wherever I can	10	13	38	41	48	150	
I like to learn new things	67	60	20	2	1	150	Digital Learning
Technology changes quickly but I can keep up	70	72	3	2	3	150	
I can update my computer and cell phone systems	73	68	0	7	2	150	

The larger the statistical values in Table 5, the darker the color; it can be observed that the dark areas are primarily concentrated in the top right and bottom left corners of the table; This indicates that regarding the attitude towards digital needs, most elderly people show great interest, and elderly individuals of different age groups eagerly hope for new technologies and more convenient application scenarios to bring convenience to their lives; However, regarding the attitude towards digital learning, although theoretically, actively learning new digital knowledge and skills may yield more benefits, the act of learning itself is a process of dissipative system self-organization, which leads to diminishing marginal effects. Given the elderly's knowledge background and energy, it is not sufficient to support them in reconstructing a brand new cognitive system, therefore, regarding the attitude towards digital learning, most elderly individuals appear to be relatively negative.

2. Experimental Results of the Memory Compensation Task Questionnaire

The results of the memory compensation questionnaire are shown in Table 6, which groups the data in 5-year intervals, tallying the frequency of use of different strategies by the elderly aged 55–75. External strategies are abstracted into four sub-strategies based on digital, physical, social, and environmental dependencies on tools or the assistance of others, as summarized in Table 1. Similarly, internal strategies are abstracted into four sub-strategies based on time, energy, association, and others, which depend on subjective or memory-related behaviors.

Table 6. Classification results of memory compensation questionnaire

Age/statistics		55–60	60–65	65–70	70–75
external memory	Digital	1	6	8	10
	Physical	1	8	9	11
	Social	2	9	11	13
	Environmental	0	8	9	10
internal memory	Time	8	3	2	1
	Energy	6	4	2	1
	Association	3	2	1	1
	Others	0	1	0	0

To more intuitively represent the characteristics of the data in Table 6, this study plotted age on the x-axis and the statistical values of each sub-strategy on the y-axis, creating Fig. 3(a). From the figure, it is evident that, overall, older adults significantly favor external offloading strategies over internal ones, with a statistical ratio of 115:35. Furthermore, as age increases, the number of older adults using external strategies rises, while those employing internal strategies decrease. This suggests that, on an individual level, there may be a propensity to switch between strategies. This phenomenon indicates that younger individuals prefer to rely on their subjective memory to solve cognitive problems, but as they age, they increasingly require tools (such as digital technology) to facilitate their daily lives. The intersection point of the rising and falling trend lines is 56.7 years old, as shown in Fig. 3(b). Therefore, this age can be considered a statistically significant physiological demarcation point where individuals start adopting different strategies to compensate for cognitive behaviors.

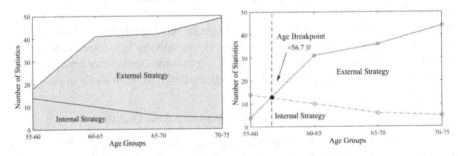

Fig. 3. Schematic diagram of classification statistics results

The age-statistical value fitting curves for different external strategies are shown in Fig. 4. It can be observed that the statistical values for all four external strategies are positively correlated with age, and the statistical results indicate that their correlation coefficients all have $R^2 > 0.75$. This demonstrates a strong linear correlation between the four external strategies' statistical values and age. Further examination reveals that the slopes of the fitting lines for each strategy range between 2.9 and 3.5, indicating a minor fluctuation in the angle of inclination between approximately 19° and 22°. This mathematical significance suggests not only a strong positive correlation between the four strategies' statistical values and age but also a consistency in trend. This indicates that as age increases, older adults' reliance on external strategies becomes more uniform; that is, regardless of the type of external strategy, as long as it has a significant offloading effect, it will be favored by older adults.

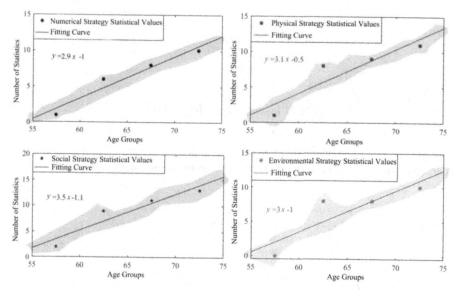

Fig. 4. Wavelet Variance Diagram and Wavelet Coefficient Diagram

This study's description reveals the trend changes in people's choices of cognitive strategies as they age. Similarly, the age-statistics fit curves for different internal strategies, as shown in Fig. 5, reveal that the statistical values for four different internal strategies are negatively correlated with age. Due to the scant statistical value of the sub-strategy "4-Other Strategies," which appears only once in the 60–65 age group, it is not meaningful for fitting. The other three sub-strategies each have a correlation coefficient $R2 > 0.82$, demonstrating good linear correlation. This further indicates that, whether considering the overall internal strategy or individual internal strategies, as people age, they gradually abandon this method of offloading, meaning no internal strategy holds an advantage with increasing age.

The comparison between internal and external strategies across different age groups is shown in Fig. 6. This figure demonstrates that with increasing age, the gap in the number of strategies widens, embodying the phenomenon of "the rich get richer and the

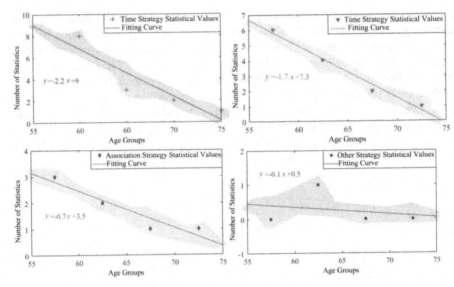

Fig. 5. Internal strategy fitting curve

poor get poorer." Mathematically, this indicates that external strategies tend to increase at an accelerating rate, while internal strategies show a trend of accelerating decline.

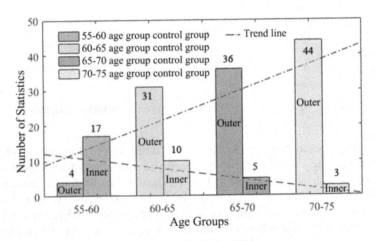

Fig. 6. Comparison of strategies in different age groups

3.2   Experiment 2 Related Results

1. Expected Value; The expected value, also known as the mean, represents the average of the statistical target. To a certain extent, it directly measures the magnitude of a set

of statistical values and serves as a fundamental indicator in this study. The formula for its calculation is:

$$u(x_i) = \bar{x} = \frac{1}{n} \sum_{n=1}^{n} x_i \tag{(1)}$$

Among them, $u(x_i)$ represents the expected value, $\bar{X}$ represents the mean, n represents the sample size, and x_i represents the sample statistic value.

Substitute the statistical data of the experimental group and the control group into Eq. 1 to calculate the expected value. The results of the two groups of experiments are shown in Fig. 7; where the expected accuracy rate of the experimental group is 38%, and the expected accuracy rate of the control group is 69%.

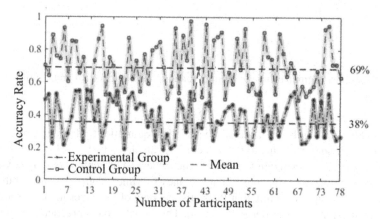

Fig. 7. Expected value of the experimental group compared to the control group

This result is consistent with expectations, preliminarily indicating that when cognitive steps reach a certain level of complexity, without effective external unloading mechanisms, solely relying on internal memory, older adults find it difficult to remember which items they have collected. This is still only a short-term experiment, lasting no more than 5–10 min, with only 3 steps in the experimental procedure. It can be imagined that in a real scenario of elderly museum tourism, with further extension of time and increase in spatial steps, their accuracy rate will inevitably decrease further.

1. Variance; variance indicates the extent to which statistical targets deviate from the expected value. Generally, smaller variances have more concentrated statistical values, making the statistical results more representative. In the context of this experiment, when the statistical means are the same, smaller variances indicate that the test population may have certain common characteristics or unloading requirements. Its calculation formula is:

$$\sigma(x) = \frac{1}{n-1} \sum_{i=1}^{n} (x_i - \bar{x})^2 \tag{(2)}$$

where $\sigma(x)$ represents the variance, and the meanings of the remaining variables are the same as before.

Substitute the statistical data of the experimental group and the control group into Eq. 2 to calculate the variance. The results of the two groups of experiments are shown in Fig. 8; where the variance of the experimental group is 0.014, and the variance of the control group is 0.025.

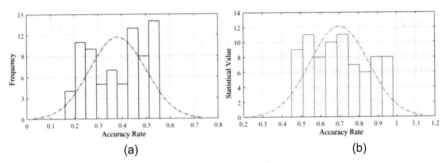

Fig. 8. Experimental group comparison group variance. (a) Experimental group, (b) comparison group.

It can be seen that the variance of the statistical quantities for both groups of experiments is less than 0.05, indicating that the mean calculated by Eq. 4.1 is representative and can reflect the overall cognitive level of the subjects. Further analysis of the variance calculation results reveals that the variance of the experimental group is smaller than that of the control group, indicating that the statistical data of the experimental group has a smaller dispersion and is closer to the mean. This conclusion is practically significant, indicating that without unloading tools, the ability of older adults to cope with complex scenarios is generally poor (tending towards the mean), and this situation cannot be improved solely by their subjective abilities. For simple scenarios, however, the variance of the experimental results is large, indicating a greater dispersion of statistical data, with varying accuracy results. This suggests that, without unloading tools, due to individual differences in quality, some older adults may have better coping abilities when facing simple scenarios. This result further underscores the necessity of external unloading for alleviating cognitive load in the elderly population. |

1. Coefficient of variation; the coefficient of variation is the ratio of the variance of a set of statistical quantities to the expected value, used to characterize the overall characteristics of the statistical quantities. The smaller the coefficient of variation, the more stable the statistical results. In this study, if the coefficient of variation is greater than a critical value, it indicates that the statistical results are unstable, meaning that there may be highly knowledgeable elderly individuals, relevant professionals, individuals with hidden cognitive defects, etc., among the subjects. Its calculation formula is:

$$C_v(x) = \frac{\sigma(x)}{u(x)} \tag{(3)}$$

where $C_v(x)$ represents the coefficient of variation, and the meanings of the remaining variables are the same as before.

Substitute the statistical data of the experimental group and the control group into Eq. 3 to calculate the coefficient of variation. In this experiment, the coefficient of variation for both the experimental group and the control group is 0.37, as shown in Fig. 10 (a). Therefore, the stability of the statistical results cannot be determined by the coefficient of variation. Hence, we further select the statistical range (the difference between the maximum and minimum values in each group of statistics) for judgment. The maximum value of the experimental group is 0.54, the minimum value is 0.18, and the range is 0.36; the maximum value of the control group is 0.97, the minimum value is 0.46, and the range is 0.51, as calculated and shown in Fig. 9 (b).

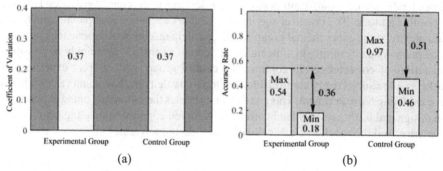

Fig. 9. Experimental group comparison group variation and range coefficient. (a) Coefficient of variation of experimental group comparison group, (b) Coefficient of extreme variation of experimental group comparison group

The range of the experimental group is smaller than that of the control group, indicating that the statistical results of the experimental group are more stable, while the stability of the control group is poorer. Attribution analysis suggests that the reason for this bias is that the unloading mode based on subjective factors is more sensitive in the control group, and it is more affected by individual differences among the subjects. This conclusion is consistent with common sense and can also be indirectly confirmed. The low accuracy rate of the experimental group is stable and universal. Therefore, intervening with external cognitive unloading methods holds both mathematical and social significance.

1. Skewness coefficient; the skewness coefficient measures the asymmetry of the distribution of statistical data. The smaller its absolute value, the more symmetrical the distribution. A skewness coefficient of 0 indicates a strictly symmetrical distribution of data. A positive skewness coefficient indicates data skewing to the right, while a negative value indicates data skewing to the left. In this study, the skewness coefficient can be used to test the rationality of the design of the experimental group (or control group), reflecting the subjects' attitudes towards the current experiment. Its

calculation formula is:

$$C_s = \frac{\sum_{i=1}^{n} [x_i - u(t)]^3}{n\sigma^3(t)} \tag{4}$$

where C_s represents the skewness coefficient, and the meanings of the remaining variables are the same as before.

The skewness coefficients of the experimental group and the control group are calculated using Eq. 4, resulting in a skewness coefficient of -0.13 for the experimental group (negatively skewed towards the left of the coordinate axis) and a skewness coefficient of $+0.16$ for the control group (positively skewed towards the right of the coordinate axis), as shown in Fig. 10. This indicates that during the testing, participants in the experimental group tend to have a negative attitude, while participants in the control group tend to have a positive attitude. The practical significance of this conclusion is apparent: due to the complexity of the experimental group's tasks, participants quickly experience cognitive load phenomena, resulting in a mentality of "complete the test as quickly as possible, regardless of correctness". In contrast, the control group, with simpler experimental tasks, is more subjectively controllable, leading to participants having more confidence in completing the experiment. This conclusion validates the rationality of the experimental design and further reveals the interrelation between cognitive unloading, application scenarios, and the psychological well-being of elderly individuals.

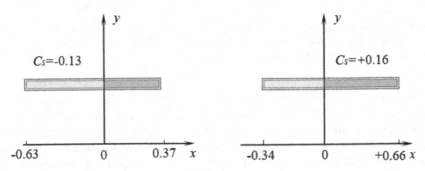

Fig. 10. Range coefficient of experimental group comparison group

3.3 Experiment 3 Related Results

1. Sexual regression model results.

The questionnaire survey results from Tables 2, 3, and 4 are scored according to the standards described earlier and summarized in Table 7. Due to the large amount of data, only 10 rows of data are listed in Table 7 for demonstration purposes, and the rest of the data follows a similar format.

Using the life satisfaction of elderly individuals as the dependent variable and social participation as the independent variable, an original regression model was constructed.

Table 7. Summary results of each scale

Rank	1	2	3	4	5	6	7	8	9	10	:	:
Life Satisfaction	14	8	12	18	14	25	13	15	13	13	:	:
Social Participation	6	4	5	8	5	10	5	7	6	5	:	:
Gender	2	1	1	1	2	2	1	2	1	1	:	:
Age	2	1	2	1	1	1	1	2	1	1	:	:
Education Level	2	1	1	1	1	1	2	2	2	1	:	:
Pension	2	2	1	2	1	1	2	2	1	1	:	:
Physical health	2	2	1	1	2	1	1	2	2	1	:	:
Mental Health	1	1	1	1	1	1	1	1	2	1	:	:
Offspring	2	1	0	1	1	1	1	2	2	2	:	:
Marriage Status	4	1	1	4	4	1	1	4	1	1	:	:
Residence	1	1	2	1	1	1	1	2	2	1	:	:

The calculation results show that there is a positive correlation between social participation level and life satisfaction. The regression equation is $y = 2.2x + 1.8$, with a coefficient of 2.2 for social participation influence and a correlation coefficient $R2 = 0.82$. This indicates that considering single-factor indicators alone, the correlation between social participation level and life satisfaction is relatively high, and social participation plays a major role in this regression model, as shown in Fig. 11.

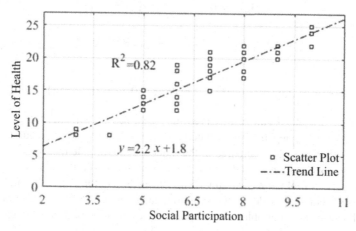

Fig. 11. The correlation between social participation and life satisfaction

The following examines the impact of other social factors on life satisfaction by adding control variables to the original regression model. The control variables and their respective models are gender and age (Model 1, purple data in Table 7); education level and pension (Model 2, red data in Table 7); physical health and mental health (Model 3, green data in Table 7); and offspring, marital status, and living arrangement (Model 4, yellow data in Table 7).

Model 1 takes the life satisfaction of elderly individuals as the dependent variable y, social participation as the independent variable x1, and gender and age as control variables x2, x3. The regression equation is established using the data from Tables 7 through Matlab, and it is as follows:

$$y = 2.21x_1 + 0.76x_2 + 0.52x_3 \tag{(5)}$$

In this experiment, the dummy variable for gender is 1 for male and 2 for female, while the dummy variable for age is 1 for older adults and 2 for younger adults. Therefore, the coefficient for gender is positive, indicating that females have higher life satisfaction. Similarly, the coefficient for age is positive, indicating that younger adults have higher life satisfaction (as the dummy variable for younger age is 2 in this example). However, further analysis reveals that even after adding these two control variables, the influence of social participation remains around 2.2, with little change compared to the original model. Additionally, the coefficients for the control variables are 0.76 and 0.52 respectively, contributing minimally to the regression equation and failing to pass the significance level test. This suggests that this type of control variable is not a major influencing factor, whereas the importance of social participation for life quality is almost absolute.

Using the same method, the regression equations for Model 2, Model 3, and Model 4 are obtained as Eq. 6 to Eq. 8, respectively:

$$y = 2.32x_1 + 0.89x_2 - 0.19x_3 \quad R^2 = 0.83 \tag{(6)}$$

$$y = 2.46x - 0.29x_2 + 0.39x_3 \quad R^2 = 0.82 \tag{(7)}$$

$$y = 2.43x_1 - 0.036x_2 + 0.48x_3 - 0.24x_4 \quad R^2 = 0.81 \tag{(8)}$$

From Eqs. 5 to 8 , it can be observed that regardless of whether the control variables are positively or negatively correlated with the dependent variable (outcome), their coefficients are very small compared to the independent variable (social participation). Additionally, none of them pass the significance test. Moreover, the addition or removal of these control variables has minimal impact on the coefficient of the independent variable itself. For further detailed discussion, each column of Table 7 can be used to individually set control variables. At this point, the correlation between the independent variable and the dependent variable, as well as between the control variables and the dependent variable, is illustrated in Fig. 12.

It is evident from Fig. 13 that the impact of each control variable on the dependent variable is almost independent of the independent variable, and the involvement of control variables does not affect the correlation between the independent variable and the dependent variable.

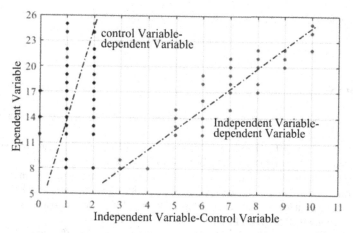

Fig. 12. Sensitivity analysis table for control variables and independent variables

4 Conclusion

1. Analysis results of the Digital Attitude Questionnaire and Memory Compensation Questionnaire indicate that elderly individuals exhibit a positive attitude towards digital services. An increasing number of elderly people are willing to enjoy the convenience brought by the digital age. However, their attitude towards digital learning is slightly negative, which is related to factors such as age, energy, and cognitive composition. Elderly individuals tend to employ more external unloading strategies than internal ones. External strategies increase with age, while internal strategies decrease with age, with a turning point occurring at 57.6 years old.

2. Unloading efficiency experiments demonstrate that as the complexity of the visiting task increases, cognitive efficiency significantly decreases. The correct recall rate for the complex experimental group is 38%, while it is 69% for the simple control group. The statistical results of the four numerical characteristics of the experiment, namely the expected value, variance, coefficient of variation, and skewness coefficient, effectively corroborate the above viewpoints.

3. A single-factor linear regression model of elderly individuals' social willingness indicates a positive correlation between social participation and life satisfaction, with a correlation coefficient R^2 value of 0.82. In a multiple linear regression model, when adding gender and age as independent variables, the correlation coefficient R^2 for social participation is 0.83; when adding education level and pension as independent variables, the correlation coefficient R^2 for social participation is 0.83; when adding mental health and physical health as independent variables, the correlation coefficient R^2 for social participation is 0.82; when adding living arrangement and marital status as independent variables, the correlation coefficient R^2 for social participation is 0.81. This indicates that social participation is a determining factor for elderly individuals' life satisfaction and should be given attention in subsequent research.

Acknowledgment. This study was supported by the National Social Science Fund of China (22BSH122).

References

1. The Seventh National Population Census Bulletin. [EB/OL], 30 Dec 2023. https://www.stats.gov.cn/. (in Chinese)
2. Korman, M., Weiss, P.L., Hochhauser, M., et al.: Effect of age on spatial memory performance in real museum vs. computer simulation. BMC Geriatr. **19**(1), 1–10 (2019)
3. Madeleine, J.R., Riley, N., Ruth, B., et al.: Memory compensation strategies in everyday life: similarities and differences between younger and older adults. Scientific **13**, 8404 (2023)
4. Gilbert, S.J.: Strategic offloading of delayed intentions into the external environment. Q. J. Exp. Psychol. QJEP **68**(5), 971–992 (2015)
5. Boldt, A., Gilbert, S.J.: Confidence guides spontaneous cognitive offloading. (1), 1–2 (2019)
6. Thomas, J., et al.: Measuring Australia's digital divide: the Australian digital inclusion index 2018. RMIT University (2018)
7. Xiaochun, Z.H.U.: The Role of Likert Scale in Civilization Index Survey. Soochow University, Suzhou (2013). (in Chinese)
8. Dixon, R.A., de Frias, C.M., Bäckman, L.: Characteristics of self-reported memory compensation in older adults. J. Clin. Exp. Neuropsychol. **23**(5), 650–661 (2001)
9. Junjie, H.E., Song, H.U., Yonggang, G.U.O., et al.: Analysis of tectonic stress in high altitude deep buried tunnel based on multiple linear regression principle. J. Disaster Prev. Mitig. Eng. **44**(1), 120–126 (2024). (in Chinese)
10. Probability and Statistics Teaching and Research Group at Donghua University. Probability Theory and Mathematical Statistics. Higher Education Press, Beijing (2017)

Interaction Behavior Based Urban Bus Stop Research on Aging Adaptive Design

Yanmin Xue[(✉)] and Chengxin He[(✉)]

School of Art and Design, Xi'an University of Technology, Xi'an, 710061, China
644635723@qq.com, 915728096@qq.com

Abstract. Along with the increasing development of digital society, smart travel has become a new direction for the development of public transportation systems. At the same time, the aging degree continues to deepen, and the elderly's own perceptual limitations are becoming more and more serious, resulting in multiple barriers to bus travel for the elderly. In this paper, from the perspective of interaction behavior, Censydiam user motivation analysis model is used to sort out the inner relationship of "demand-motivation-behavior-station" of elderly users. It proposes the key points of aging-friendly design of urban bus stops based on interaction behavior, and conducts visual experiments with eye-tracking devices to explore the influence of different interface layouts on users' task completion efficiency and preferences, and verifies the interactive relationship between the interaction behavior of the elderly and their travel decisions. The experimental results show that in the layout design, the top layout is more user-friendly and easy to operate compared with the side and mixed; in the verification of the relationship between interaction behavior and travel decision-making, there is an interaction relationship between the interaction behavior of elderly subjects and travel decision-making and the degree of the relationship is greater than that of young subjects. Based on this, this study applies the interaction behavior to the aging design of urban bus stops to enhance the willingness of elderly users to travel actively, and to promote the active integration of the elderly into the digital society and enjoy the convenience from it.

Keywords: Interactional Behavior · Bus Stops · Older People · Censydiam's User Motivation Analysis Model · Eye Movement Experiment

1 Introduction Interaction Behavior Explanation

With the rapid development of digital society and aging society, public transportation system is moving towards the direction of intelligence and aging. Scholars around the world have conducted several studies on this. Foreign scholars have analyzed the key role that public transportation can play in the transition to less car-dependent, healthier, and more sustainable modes of transportation with the loss of driving ability in old age [1, 2]. Since China has been advocating public transportation, many scholars mainly study from the optimization strategy of public transportation travel [3], senior travel behavior [4] and the design of supporting facilities [5].

In addition, interaction behavior is crucial to the daily life of older adults. With the advancement of technology and the popularity of social media, more and more older adults can achieve social support through the use of smart devices, and this change can help older adults to broaden the opportunities for interaction. This paper combines the Censydiam user motivation analysis model to sort out the relationship between "demand-motivation-behavior-station" of the elderly, and conducts experiments with eye-tracking devices to explore the influence of different interface layouts on the efficiency of users in completing tasks and their preferences, and at the same time verifies that there is an interactive relationship between the interaction behaviors of the elderly and their travel decisions. At the same time, it also verifies the interactive relationship between the interaction behavior of the elderly and their travel decision-making, with a view to providing design ideas for the study of aging-adapted design of urban bus stations.

2 Interaction Behavior Explanation

2.1 Definition of Interactional Behavior

"Interaction behavior" is the behavior of people in order to satisfy their own needs, establish relationships, obtain information or achieve common goals, which is a basic need of human beings. Necessary interaction activities are conducive to people's mental health, and in the process of communicating with each other, it also has a certain role in alleviating people's negative emotions.

2.2 Characterization of Older Adult Interaction Behavior

Interaction needs tend towards the "three-same generation". As older people age, their interaction needs change, including a tendency towards same-sex interaction, same-age interaction, same-interest interaction and intergenerational interaction. Frequency of interactions tends to decrease. Older people's frequency of interaction usually decreases, mainly due to the limitations of physical health conditions and changes in social roles. The mode of interaction shifted to multiple choices. With the advancement of technology and the popularization of social media, the way older adults interact is also changing.

3 Extracting the Demand for Aging-Adapted Design of Urban Bus Stops

In order to fully explore the various needs of elderly users at bus stops, the Censydiam User Needs Analysis Model is used to provide us with design ideas. The model consists of "2 dimensions, 4 strategies, and 8 motives". The "2 dimensions" refers to the individual and the society, and the "4 strategies" are "enjoyment/release", "control/rationality", "status/power" The "4 strategies" are "enjoyment/release", "control/rationality", "status/power", and "belonging/submission". Due to the complexity of the user's emotions and needs, in addition to these four strategies, the model is combined with two neighboring quadrants to form the final Censydiam model framework [6], as shown in Fig. 1.

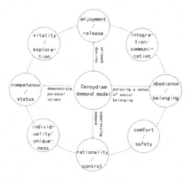

Fig. 1. Censydiam user motivation analysis model.

3.1 User Requirements Mining Application Process Based on Censydiam Modeling

User demand is the basic work, first determine the target object of this research for the elderly, and then through user interviews, questionnaires and literature analysis and other methods to obtain information on elderly users, mining emotional needs, and then fit with the model, by clarifying the required, and then guide the design of the experiments, as shown in Fig. 2.

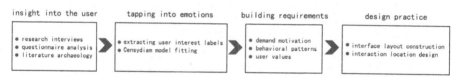

Fig. 2. Application process of user motivation mining based on Censydiam modeling.

3.2 Get User Information

Qualitative Research Interviews. The research was conducted in August-September 2023 in Qujiang New District, Xi'an City, China, with a randomly selected target group of 30 users, including 15 males and 15 females, all of whom were between 60 and 75 years old. After summarizing the results, it was found that the natural aging process of the elderly is accompanied by a decline in all aspects of the body's perceptual ability, including the physical and psychological dimensions, as shown in Fig. 3. Secondly, there is a prominent state of the elderly in the process of riding the bus, which is that they usually show a state of inactivity while waiting for the bus, looking around and waiting for the arrival of the bus. The Censydiam model was used to extract user interest labels, and it was found that the main focus was on comfort/safety, conformity/belonging, integration/communication, and enjoyment/release. Approximately the same results were obtained in qualitative literature analysis and quantitative questionnaire recovery, proving that the research results have strong objectivity.

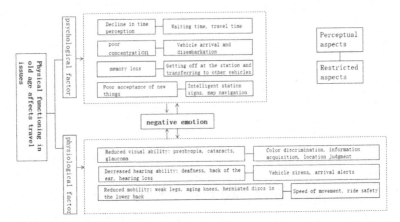

Fig. 3. Chart of perceived and ridership limitations performance in old age.

Status of Qualitative Literature Analysis. By using CiteSpace knowledge visualization software as a knowledge mapping tool, we quantify the research literature in the field of elderly public transport travel in the world, and map the related knowledge, which is distributed in the time period of 2010–2023, with a total of 302 articles, 129 in Chinese and 173 in foreign languages, which further enriches and validates the interest labels of the elderly target users, as shown in Fig. 4.

Fig. 4. Co-occurrence of keywords for elderly public transportation in China and abroad.

Recovery of Quantitative Questionnaires. In the process of obtaining user information, on-site questionnaires and network questionnaires were also used to investigate the behavioral characteristics of senior transit travel and bus stops related issues, a total of 180 questionnaires were issued and 173 valid questionnaires were recovered. The influencing factors of senior transit travel include personal factors, environmental factors and other factors, as shown in Fig. 5.

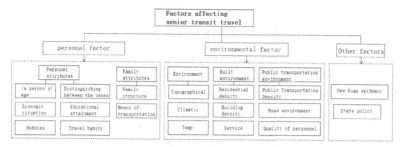

Fig. 5. Factors affecting senior transit travel.

3.3 Tapping into Users' Emotional Needs

According to the analysis of the elderly target users' public transportation information, more than 10 keywords were extracted, and the top 10 keyword tags were: safety, convenience, ease of use, comfort, communication, entertainment, shopping, intelligence, multifunctionality, and accessibility. Combining the user information keywords with Censydiam model, the keywords are selected according to the emotional tendency priority, and the cumulative scoring form is used for statistics, ★ represents the keyword label, and 1 ★ represents 1 keyword label, scoring 1 point. The more ★, the higher the total score of the keywords, representing the greater the user demand, according to which the user emotional insight table is obtained, as shown in Table 1.

Through Table 1, we get that the emotional needs of elderly bus travel users correspond to the four sub-regions of the Censydiam model: comfort/safety, enjoyment/release, obedience/belonging, and integration/communication. It can be seen that at the bus travel station, the emotional needs of elderly users do not focus on innovative exploration, nor do they care about highlighting their difference and social status by showing their advantages. Older users firstly want to get inner peace and relaxation, and be cared for (comfort/safety), and secondly, they do not restrain themselves emotionally, and actively enjoy life (enjoyment/release), in which they pay attention to following the rules of the group, do not act in a maverick way (conformity/belonging), and are always willing to integrate into the collective, and communicate with the group in an open way (integration, communication).

3.4 Building a List of User Requirements

According to the established Censydiam motivation model for elderly bus travel, the user journey diagram method is adopted to visualize the behavioral paths of elderly users waiting for buses at bus stops, and different motivation subclasses are represented by dots in different colors in the user journey diagram, from which it can be clearly seen that there is a correspondent relationship between the motivations and behaviors of elderly users, as shown in Fig. 6.

Older users are driven by motivation to produce interaction behavior, and this behavior can be based on bus stops. As a platform for older users to participate in interactions, bus stops can play a role in satisfying and triggering the motivation of older users, which in turn affects their behavior, and the correlation between user motivation, user behavior

Table 1. User sentiment insight form.

Keywords	Motivation							
	Enjoyment/Release	Rational/Control	Competence/Status	Obedience/Belonging	Vitality/Explore	Integration/Communication	Personality/Unique	Comfort/Safe
Surety		★		★		★		★
Convenient and fast	★			★		★		★
Easy use	★	★		★		★		★
Comforts	★			★		★		★
Exchanges	★	★		★		★		★
Diversion	★				★	★	★	★
Shop	★	★					★	★
Smart	★		★	★	★	★		★
Multifunctional	★						★	
Barrier-free				★				★
Mark	8	4	1	7	2	7	3	9

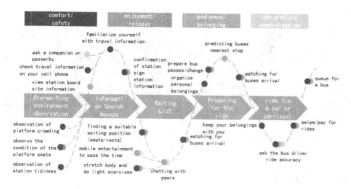

Fig. 6. Elderly bus stops waiting for the user journey map.

and bus stops forms a closed loop. Based on this, combined with the background of the obstacles encountered by elderly users in integrating into the smart society, the author proposes to set up intelligent interactive devices at bus stops to create social opportunities for elderly users, who can find and meet the needs of interaction according to their own situation.

4 Experimental Research

4.1 Experimental Purpose

Through eye movement experiments, we explored the effects of different interface layouts on users' efficiency and preferences in completing tasks, and also verified that there is an interactive relationship between older adults' interaction behaviors and travel decisions.

4.2 Experimental Hypothesis

1. The top layout method is more friendly to older users compared to side and mixed.
2. There is an interaction between interaction behavior and travel decision.

4.3 Subjects and Environment

Since bus stops are public places, the principle of universal design usually needs to be considered, and the subjects of this experiment were determined to be elderly people and young people who can accomplish the task of traveling independently. There were a total of 24 subjects, 12 elderly people aged 55–75 years old and 12 young people aged 20–25 years old, with normal visual acuity or corrected visual acuity and healthy upper limb function, who were instructed before completing the task. In addition, this experiment was conducted in an indoor laboratory, through the introduction of the pre-transit travel scenario, and then simulate the behavior of the passengers, providing bus stops and trips, etc., the user and the screen need to maintain an operating distance of about 50 cm, to try to avoid extraneous factors have an impact on the subjects, as shown in Fig. 7.

Fig. 7. Experimental scenarios and some experimental subjects.

4.4 Stimulus Material

Interface Layout. In the layout interface design, it includes top navigation, side navigation and hybrid navigation, as shown in Fig. 8.

Fig. 8. Layout and interface design.

Function Module. The function module of the intelligent interactive device is segmented to provide a variety of functions for the needs of elderly users. Including route inquiry, along the route around, real-time information and more services.

Interaction Behavior. The combination of interaction behavior and functional modules is applied in the perimeter along the route. The frequent travel destinations of elderly users, including supermarkets, parks, pharmacies, and banks, are displayed in the form of percentage of location attention, as shown in Fig. 9.

Fig. 9. Interaction behavior design.

Experimental Tasks. In the Interface Layout Test section there will be 3 interfaces, each with the same two task operations: first find Route 212 in the interface and click on it, then find the perimeter along the route and click on it. In the Verify Interaction

Behavior section, there will be 4 screens, each with the same task: select the location you are interested in from locations ABCD and click on it.

Experimental Procedure. The experiment is divided into four sessions, which are the introduction of the experiment, the introduction of the scenario, the interface layout task session, and the verification of interaction behavior task session. The subjects were required to fill in the relevant questionnaire information after the experiment, as shown in Fig. 10.

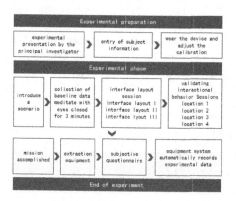

Fig. 10. Experimental flow chart.

5 Experimental Data Analysis

5.1 Eye Movement Data Indicators

This study statistically analyzes the eye movement data corresponding to the two task sessions separately. The first interface layout task session was analyzed by taking the total gaze time and the first gaze AOI time, which refers to the total duration of the user's gaze on the whole interface, while the first gaze AOI time refers to the time when the user first gazes into the area of interest (AOI). The shorter task completion time means that the interface layout is clearer, the information is presented more intuitively, and the user is able to find the required information or complete the task quickly. The second validation of the interaction behavior task is to analyze the number of gaze points and the hot zone map. The number of gaze points indicates the number of times the user has gazed at a specific area, while the hot zone map is used to visualize the hot zones that the user is gazing at, i.e., the areas that the user pays more attention to, the more gaze points, which means that the user pays more attention to and is more interested in the area.

5.2 Analysis of Specific Data

Interface Layout Task Session Data Metrics Analysis. The results were obtained by dividing the experimental segments and coding the different layouts, the top layout as

A1, the side layout as A2, and the hybrid layout as A3, as shown in Table 2. The results show that the total gaze time and the time to first AOI for the top layout, A1, were significantly less than those for layouts A2, and A3, and the results for the older and the younger groups were the same. From this, it is concluded that the top layout method is more friendly and easy to operate compared to side and hybrid, followed by side and hybrid layouts.

Table 2. Interface layout task session data metrics.

Encodings	Groups	Mean total gaze time (s)	Mean time to first AOI gaze (s)	Order of preference
A1	Geriatrics n = 12	4.65	2.93	1
	Youth n = 12	2.89	1.61	
A2	Geriatrics n = 12	5.23	3.25	2
	Youth n = 12	3.12	2.04	
A3	Geriatrics n = 12	5.51	3.43	3
	Youth n=12	3.24	2.27	

Validating the Analysis of Data Metrics for the Interaction Behavior Task Session By AOI coding of the four locations showing percentage attention in supermarkets, parks, pharmacies, and banks, supermarkets are A1, supermarkets 10% are A2, supermarkets 30% are A3, and supermarkets 50% are A4; parks are B1, parks 10% are B2, parks 30% are B3, and parks 50% are B4; pharmacies are C1, pharmacies 10% are C2, pharmacies 30% are C3, and pharmacies 50% are C4; bank as D1, bank 10% as D2, bank 30% as D3, bank 50% as D4, as shown in Table 3 and Figs. 11 and 12. The results show that the older group presented the number of gaze tendency to be high attention in all four locations: supermarket, park, pharmacy, and bank, and the darker color of the hot zone map appeared in the places with high percentage of attention. The youth group differed from the older in that the presence of the tendency to interact behavior was verified only in the location park, which may be related to the difference in the frequent travel destinations of the youth group and the older people. Thus, it was concluded that the relationship between the interaction behavior and the influence of travel decision-making was greater in older subjects than in younger subjects.

Table 3. Validation of interaction behavior task session data indicators.

Encodings		Groups	Mean number of points of attention (units)
Hypermarket	A1	Geriatrics n = 12	2
		Youth n = 12	3
	A2	Geriatrics n = 12	2
		Youth n = 12	2
	A3	Geriatrics n = 12	4
		Youth n = 12	2
	A4	Geriatrics n = 12	9
		Youth n = 12	6
Park (for public recreation)	B1	Geriatrics n = 12	2
		Youth n = 12	1
	B2	Geriatrics n = 12	3
		Youth n = 12	3
	B3	Geriatrics n = 12	6
		Youth n = 12	4
	B4	Geriatrics n = 12	11
		Youth n = 12	7
Pharmacies	C1	Geriatrics n = 12	2
		Youth n = 12	2
	C2	Geriatrics n = 12	3
		Youth n = 12	2
	C3	Geriatrics n = 12	5
		Youth n = 12	3
	C4	Geriatrics n = 12	8
		Youth n = 12	6
Banks	D1	Geriatrics n = 12	3
		Youth n = 12	3
	D2	Geriatrics n = 12	3
		Youth n = 12	6
	D3	Geriatrics n = 12	4
		Youth n = 12	3

(*continued*)

Table 3. (*continued*)

Encodings		Groups	Mean number of points of attention (units)
	D4	Geriatrics n = 12	9
		Youth n = 12	5

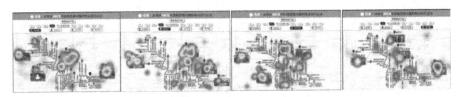

Fig. 11. Geriatric groupt hot zone map.

Fig. 12. Youth groupt hot zone map.

6   Conclusion

This paper analyzes the bus travel needs of elderly users through the Censydiam User Motivation Analysis Model, and obtains the motives of comfort/safety, obedience/belonging, integration/communication, and enjoyment/release, from which we find that the social interaction behavior of elderly users is found, and that bus stops, as a platform for elderly bus travel stops, have high quality that will lead to a chain of interaction behaviors among the elderly. Based on the interaction behavior, we propose a design experiment to study the aging of urban bus stops, and verify the feasibility of the design through eye movement experiments. However, in the design of the main points are mainly aimed at the platform waiting activities stage, the elderly users stay at the platform of other phases have not been systematically designed, these issues will be an important object of subsequent research.

Acknowledgments. This study was funded by The National Social Fund of China under grant 22BSH122.

Disclosure of Interests..   The authors have no competing interests to declare that are relevant to the content of this article.

References

1. Karekla, X., Tyler, N.: Maintaining balance on a moving bus: the importance of three-peak steps whilst walking on the lower-deck. Transp. Res. Part A, **116**, 484–496 (2018)
2. Suman, M., Mingqi, Y., Ritchie, S.G.: Gender differences in elderly mobility in the United States. Transp. Res. Part A **154**, 203–226 (2021)
3. Zhao, T.: Strategy of digital design of bus shelter under aging. Design **14**, 126–127 (2018)
4. Xu, G.C.: A preliminary study on the improvement of urban transportation under the background of aging: a case study of the travel characteristics of the elderly in Wuxi. Transpoworld **22**, 13–15 (2022)
5. Li, R., N., Zhu, L.L.: Optimization design of auxiliary facilities of public transportation system in aging society. China Transp. Rev. **39**(08), 74–79 (2017)
6. Wang, Z.Y., Yan, L.L.: Research on user demand mining and application of product design based on Censydiam model. Changzhou Inst. Technol. **35**(01) (2022)

A Study on Narrative Visualization of Health Information for Elderly Osteoporosis Guided by Health Needs

Yanmin Xue[✉] and Yuting Shi[✉]

School of Art and Design, Xi'an University of Technology, Xi'an 710061, China
2488400679@qq.com, 915728096@qq.com

Abstract. Analyze the user needs of smart health equipment for elderly osteoporosis communities, and study the impact of the form of elderly osteoporosis health information materials on information processing performance based on physiological experiments such as EEG and eye movement. By using literature analysis and semi-structured interviews, the original demand for smart health care equipment in elderly osteoporosis communities was identified. Combining survey questionnaires and Kano models, three demand dimensions for smart health care equipment in elderly communities were analyzed. Visualize health information in the dimensions of health education using theories such as visual selective attention and information visualization, and validate experimental hypotheses through physiological experiments such as eye movement. Based on the analysis of experimental results, it can be concluded that elderly people have different performance in processing osteoporosis health information in different material forms. Therefore, an innovative design direction is proposed for the smart health care equipment for elderly osteoporosis communities.

Keywords: Health information visualization · Kano model · Visual selective attention · Elderly osteoporosis

1 Introduction

Osteoporosis is a preventable and treatable chronic disease, and identifying the risk factors associated with osteoporosis can help prevent and treat osteoporosis more effectively. Due to the presence of one or more chronic diseases among the elderly, they are more likely to overlook osteoporosis and have a lower awareness and perception of the disease [1]. Therefore, it is necessary to strengthen health education on osteoporosis among the elderly. This article uses the Kano model to analyze the health needs of elderly people for osteoporosis, and combines information visualization, visual selective attention, and information processing theory to visualize the health information of osteoporosis. Through experiments such as eye movement, the study analyzes the effect of visual intervention on improving the performance of elderly people in processing health information.

2 Theoretical Basis

2.1 Information Visualization

Information visualization can be seen as the mapping process from information to form and then to human perception systems. Unlike scientific visualization, which focuses on the representation of physical data, information visualization focuses on abstract information. In most cases, since the type of information itself does not have a clear corresponding physical representation, this type of information cannot be directly mapped to geometric physical space. This requires designers to explore new visual structures to represent information.

2.2 Visual Selective Attention

Visual Selective Attention is a cognitive processing method that focuses limited psychological resources on the most significant information at a specific time [2]. The selectivity of visual attention is the foundation, mainly reflected in the efficient processing of key visual information, capturing and discarding some information. From a human perspective, it is the process of selecting objects from the scene to observe, which is called visual selective attention (see Fig. 1).

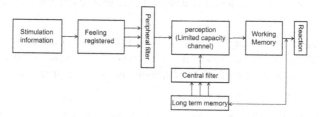

Fig. 1. Triesman's attenuator model.

3 Analysis of Health Needs for Elderly Osteoporpsis

3.1 Original Health Needs for Elderly Osteoporosis

Firstly, by consulting relevant literature and visiting the Osteoporosis Department of Xi'an Honghui Hospital, Zaoyuan Street Comprehensive Elderly Care Service Center, and Xiguan Street Comprehensive Elderly Care Service Center, the actual living conditions of the elderly were understood from relevant personnel in hospitals and nursing homes. Based on the research results, the elderly were divided into two types: diseased and non-diseased, To understand the basic health needs of elderly people for osteoporosis through semi-structured interviews, considering that different individuals have limited knowledge of the disease, describe and communicate the problem in detail as much as possible, in order to obtain the most authentic user health needs. Sort out and analyze the original health needs for elderly osteoporosis (see Table 1).

Table 1. Health demand items for smart health equipment in elderly osteoporosis communities

Health education	Health assessment	Health management
Disease nursing education	Osteoporosis prevention	Nutritional dietary planning
Mental health education	Self screening of osteoporosis risk	Home care
Health knowledge education	Pathological stage evaluation	Sports prevention planning
Health information is easy to read		Personalized maintenance

3.2 Analysis of Demand for Smart Health Care Equipment in Elderly Osteoporosis Communities Based on Kano Model

Kano Model Questionnaire Design for Smart Health Care Equipment in Elderly Osteoporosis Communities. To further clarify the health needs of elderly osteoporosis, a Kano model survey questionnaire was designed around the relevant issues of 5 design requirements to obtain data on the functional requirements of target users for the product. To ensure the reliability of the questionnaire data, the Kano survey questionnaire is distributed to elderly people aged 60 and above. Considering the special characteristics of the survey users, the questionnaire design should ensure that the questions are clear and easy to understand.

Data Calculation and Analysis. A total of 60 Kano model questionnaires were distributed, and the collected questionnaires were processed. Invalid questionnaires were removed, resulting in a total of 54 valid questionnaires. The proportion of functional

Table 2. Health demand attribute analysis of smart rehabilitation equipment in elderly osteoporosis communities based on the Kano model

Requirements	A	O	M	I	R
Disease nursing education	18.18%	1.82%	50.91%	18.18%	10.91%
Mental health education	10.91%	3.64%	14.55%	50.91%	20%
Health knowledge education	29.09%	30.91%	16.36%	14.55%	50.91%
Health information is easy to read	48.48%	21.21%	6.06%	21.21%	3.03%
Osteoporosis prevention	16.36%	49.09%	14.55%	12.93%	7.27%
Self screening of osteoporosis risk	6.09%	10.27%	50.91%	22.73%	10%
Pathological stage evaluation	20%	9.09%	27.27%	41.82%	1.82%
Nutritional dietary planning	25.45%	14.55%	40%	18.18%	1.82%
Home care	12.73%	1.82%	49.09%	30.36%	6%
Sports prevention planning	10.91%	20%	21.82%	40%	7.27%
Personalized maintenance	21.82%	0%	10.91%	43.64%	23.64%

Explanatory note: A represents charismatic type, O represents expected type, M represents basic type, I represents undifferentiated type, R represents reverse type.

requirement item attributes was calculated according to the Kano model evaluation classification comparison table (see Table 2). In the attribute analysis table of elderly osteoporosis health needs in the positive Kano model, it was found that functional needs under the dimension of health education mostly belong to basic, charismatic, and expected needs. Among them, health knowledge education is expected, and health information is easy to read as charismatic needs. Therefore, it can be seen that elderly people are more eager to learn about osteoporosis through simple and easy to understand methods, Therefore, in order to improve the readability and sensitivity of health information, the following experiments are designed to verify the effectiveness of health information visualization in enhancing the awareness of osteoporosis in the elderly.

4 Health Information Readability

This article needs to quantify the readability of health information, and evaluators need to independently evaluate it. Therefore, it is advisable to select widely used readability formulas as the calculation basis for experimental stimulus materials. Drawing on the formula constructed by Ke Qing [3] in the study of health information readability, determine the formula for health information readability in this study, as shown in formula (1). Among them, R represents the readability value of health information. The smaller the R value, the easier the material is to read, and the lower the readability; The larger the R value, the more difficult the material is to read and the higher its readability. $X1$ represents the total number of words in the reading material; $X2$ represents the average sentence length (total word count/sentence count); $X3$ represents the proportion of professional terms (total word count of professional terms/total word count of materials). After quantifying the readability of osteoporosis health information, this article visually maps the content of health information.

$$R = 17.5255 + 0.0024 \times X1 + 0.04415 \times X2 - 18.3344 \times (1 - X3) \qquad (1)$$

5 Experimental Study

5.1 Experimental Purpose

To objectively verify and evaluate the processing performance of elderly people on different forms of osteoporosis health information through eye movement experiments and data comparison analysis.

5.2 Experimental Hypothesis

1. The Forms of Health Information on Osteoporosis and Visual Selective Attention

H1a: Without replacing the professional terms in the original stimulus materials, participants in eye movement experiments read osteoporosis health information in pure text format for a longer period of time;

H1b: Without replacing the professional terms in the original stimulus materials, participants in eye tracking experiments showed different durations of attention to the layout forms of the upper, lower, left, and right interfaces.

2. The Forms and Processing Performance of Health Information on Osteoporosis

H2a: Without replacing the professional terms in the original stimulus materials, the accuracy of user search results for osteoporosis health information in graphic and textual form in the high R value group is higher than that in pure textual form in the low R value group;

H2b: Without replacing the professional terms in the original stimulus materials, the accuracy of user answers for osteoporosis health information in pure text form will be lower.

5.3 Experimental Subjects and Environment

The selected elderly participants in the experiment meet the following conditions: there is a certain aging phenomenon in their physical functions, and compared with their youth, various physiological indicators have decreased. However, their lifestyle behavior is no different from that of ordinary people, they can independently carry out various activities to meet their needs, are willing to accept new things, and have a certain learning ability as self-help elderly people; Having a certain level of education, able to read independently. The selected young experimental subjects meet the following conditions: they are able to independently read materials and complete relevant experimental operations, and have no color blindness or color weakness. The final participants in this experiment were 12 elderly participants aged 55–75 and 12 young participants aged 19–25 (see Fig. 2).

Fig. 2. Experimental Object and Environment

5.4 Stimulative Materials

1. Selection of Health Information for Osteoporosis

   The experimental stimulation materials are from "Osteoporosis" edited by Li En. Six health information sections were selected from the book, including the introduction, classification, prevention, and treatment of osteoporosis, ensuring that there is no duplicate content between the six health information sections and they are relatively independent. Calculate the readability R value of 6 health information texts according to formula (1). The experiment selected materials A ($R = 8.2445$) and B ($R = 8.2858$) with the highest R value in the calculation results as the high R value group, as well as materials C ($R = 3.6926$) and D ($R = 3.6812$) with the lowest R value as the low R value group.

2. Visualization and transformation of osteoporosis health information

For the selected four groups of materials, material A is selected for health information visualization in the high R-value group, and material C is selected for health information visualization in the low R-value group. The principle of visualization in this experiment is not to delete medical terminology in the health information text, only to visualize and process its content, and finally obtain visualization materials A and C (see Figs. 3 and 4).

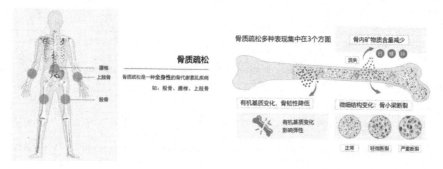

Fig. 3. Visualization of Osteoporosis Health Information Material A.

Fig. 4. Visualization of Osteoporosis Health Information Material C.

6 Experimental Data Analysis

6.1 AOI Related Fixation Analysis

The first fixation time, number of AOI fixation points, and task duration of the two groups of subjects were all lower in the form of graphic and textual stimuli than in the form of textual stimuli. The subjects were able to cognitive process the most significant information within a specific period of time (see Table 3). The experimental results showed that the subjects needed more time to read textual stimuli and find the key information to read, confirming the experimental hypothesis H1a. The experimental results of the high R-value group showed significantly higher differences than those of the low R-value group, and the first fixation time and number of fixation points of the high R-value (text) AOI were lower than those of the low R-value (text). It is speculated that visualizing health information with higher complexity can significantly improve the participants' understanding ability of complex health information.

Table 3. Eye movement experiment results.

Eye movement indicators	AOI first fixation time/s Experimental Task 2		Number of AOI fixation points		Task duration	
Grouping	Elderly	Youth	Elderly	Youth	Elderly	Youth
High R value (text)	80.714(±0.380)	44.194(±5.510)	224.783(±4.609)	150.778(±1.347)	143.667(±69.365)	63.333(±15.911)
High R value (graphic and textual)	41.187(±5.488)	24.660(±4.248)	167.036(±20.387)	110.5(±1.364)	107.083(±50.669)	48(±12.764)
Low R value (text)	54.474(±2.250)	42.547(±0.443)	195.964(±2.516)	133.706(±5.881)	108.333(±48.882)	51.250(±12.578)
Low R value (graphic and textual)	38.240(±2.463)	21.057(±1.767)	147.144(±1.319)	92.963(±4.595)	78.334(±28.279)	42.750(±12.871)

6.2 Analysis of the Percentage Difference in AOI Total Visit Duration

The percentage of AOI total visit duration related indicators reflect the degree of attention allocation [4] and processing difficulty of participants towards stimulus materials. The experimental results were analyzed using mean data from the elderly and young groups of participants (see Fig. 5). Sixteen AOIs were divided into four groups of stimulus materials, all of which were professional terms. The comparison results showed that the percentage of total AOI visit duration in the high and low R-value (text) groups was higher than that in the high and low R-value (text) groups, indicating that the subjects were able to more easily distinguish professional terms and focus their attention on understanding professional terms while reading visual osteoporosis health information. The accuracy results of the experimental tasks completed by two groups of participants showed that the task accuracy of graphic and textual stimulus materials was significantly higher than that of textual stimulus materials, and the answering results were significantly improved. The experimental results verified hypotheses H2a and H2b. Combining the percentage of total AOI visit time and the accuracy of experimental tasks, participants are more likely to observe and understand professional terminology while reading visual health information materials, improving their performance in processing osteoporosis health information (Table 4).

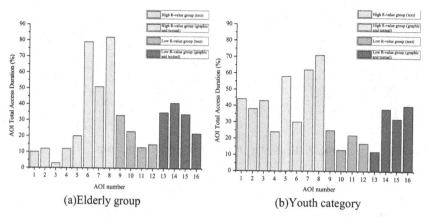

(a)Elderly group (b)Youth category

Fig. 5. AOI Total Access Duration Percentage.

Table 4. Experimental task accuracy

Experimental tasks		Task 1	Task 2	Task 3	Task 4
Accuracy	Elderly	19.445%	63.889%	29.67%	79.167%
	Youth	69.445%	83.334%	75%	95.834%

6.3 Hotspot Map Analysis

The hotspot map reflects the position and time of the subject's visual attention, and the darker the color (red), the more focused the subject's attention is and the higher the visual hotspot. The hot spot maps of four stimulating materials are (see Figs. 6 and 7). In pure text materials, the focus trajectory of the subjects is more scattered and more concentrated on the left side of the text information, with a more scattered focus at the beginning of each line. In visualized health information materials, hotspot images

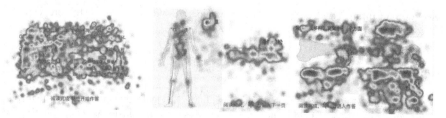

Fig. 6. Readability R-value high group hotspot map.

are more concentrated in the textual description section, and the reading attention time for the image section is shorter, which can prove that the image information is better understood by the subjects and does not require more time to memorize.

Fig. 7. Readability R value low group hotspot map.

7   Conclusion

This article aims at health education, guided by the health needs of smart health equipment in elderly osteoporosis communities, and applies the Kano model to conduct qualitative research on health needs. The research results show that the health needs of the elderly mainly focus on the dimensions of health education and health care. Specifically, the goal of improving the readability of health information in the dimensions of health education is analyzed, and combined with information visualization theory and visual selective attention theory, osteoporosis health information is visualized and mapped. Eye tracking experiments are conducted to verify that visualized health information can improve information processing efficiency and solve the problem of strong professionalism in health information that is difficult for the elderly to understand. In subsequent research, specific design specifications for visualizing osteoporosis health information will be refined, and narrative theory will be combined to improve the universality of osteoporosis health information and the disease awareness of the elderly towards osteoporosis.

Acknowledgments. This paper was funded by The National Social Fund of China under grant 22BSH122.

Disclosure of Interests..   The authors have no competing interests to declare that are relevant to the content of this article.

References

1. Sun, L., Wang, Y., Chen, S., Liang, J., Ying, W., Jun'e, L.: Qualitative study on stress perception and coping experience of empty nest elderly spouses with chronic disease comorbidities. Mil. Nurs. **39**(07), 33–36 (2022)

2. Sternberg, R.J.: Cognitive Psychology, 3rd edn. China Light Industry Press (2006). Beijing Translated by Yang Bingjun et al.
3. Ke, Q., K., Ding, S., Qin, Q.: Eye tracking experimental study on the impact of health information readability on user cognitive load and information processing performance. Data Anal. Knowl. Disc. **5**(2), 70−82 (2021)
4. Li, S.: Eye Movement Experiment Design and Research on the Impact of Risk Perception Ability. Harbin Institute of Technology (2023)

Towards an Understanding of How Computer Skills Relate to Online Safety Across Older Adults

Jikun Yin[✉], Emilene Zitkus[✉], and Martin Maguire[✉]

School of Design and Creative Arts, Loughborough University, Loughborough, Leicestershire, UK

{j.yin,e.zitkus,m.c.maguire}@lboro.ac.uk

Abstract. In the United Kingdom, older adults aged sixty-five and above who lack essential digital skills are on the edge of being digitally excluded. To investigate the crucial digital skills that might motivate older adults to engage more online, an exploratory study was conducted through a questionnaire survey with 31 participants and a semi-structured interview with 13 participants. The results indicated that potential risks on the web make older people overly guarded and therefore undermine their confidence in enjoying online services and applications. They mistrust the internet, are concerned about information safety, and lack basic digital literacy. This paper aimed to understand how older adults' digital skills and literacy influenced their attitudes towards cybersecurity and privacy problems.

Keywords: Digital skills · older adults · online safety · ICT · digital literacy

1 Introduction

Technology has permeated every aspect of people's lives. Technological advancements are putting new demands on consumer's comprehension of the fundamental application methods of technology. However, people who are slower to learn the new Information and Communication Technology (ICT) will suffer digital exclusion, including older adults [1]. Senior adults withdrawing from the digital working environment have gradually lost their ICT skills [2], resulting in some older people lacking in self-confidence when facing daily life-based digital tasks.

In the last 3 years, the pandemic forced daily services to be transferred online, from that time on, online services became the norm [5]. Older people have to suddenly adapt to the use of various applications and e-services related to their daily lives. As the UK Office for National Statistics reported in 2019 [6], people over 65 years old are the main group that does not participate on the internet, which means that they use fewer facilities such as online banking, online government services and medical appointments. If older people are unable and unwilling to improve their digital skills, this can exacerbate inequalities in the digital sphere and widen the digital divide [7].

In this research, in order to improve older adults' digital skills, inclusive design can be used to obtain an understanding of the older individual's digital skills and literacy level, studying style and attitude towards ICT.

C. Stephanidis et al. (Eds.): HCII 2024, CCIS 2115, pp. 324–334, 2024.
https://doi.org/10.1007/978-3-031-61947-2_34

1.1 Cybersecurity Threats to Older Individuals

During the COVID-19 pandemic, many older adults concentrated on learning the usage of applications they ignored, including privacy, data protection, and data hygiene. More identity theft incidents occurred [8]. In Grilli's study [9], the findings showed that in suspicious phishing emails, even seniors in a good cognitive state were also at greater risk of internet fraud. The Special Eurobarometer 480 regarding Europeans' attitudes towards Internet security [10] reported that almost 80% of European respondents were worried about being victims of cybercrime. The precautionary steps taken by older adults in this context entail a deliberate reduction in their online involvement. Furthermore, adults over the age of 65 are less likely to take additional safety precautions following identity theft [11], and they may be less inclined to report or seek aid if they become a victim of cybercrime [12]. As a result, the number of victimized seniors being reported may be greater than the available data.

The United Kingdom National Cyber Security Centre (NCSC) [13] listed six kinds of cyber problems: being hacked, being infected with ransomware, being infected with a virus or malware, having a username and password stolen, receiving suspicious email or text, and having banking details stolen. In response, the NCSC proposed guidance for individuals and families. It suggested six actions for being safe online, including the method to create a strong and long enough password, manage and store passwords, use a separate password for email, back up data, install and update the latest version of software and apps, and turn on 2-step verification (2SV). These precautions are the basic measures that need to be taken proactively for online safety. However, online dangers can be hidden in various scenarios. When a user is passively affected by a dangerous situation, it is up to the user to be aware of the danger and save the situation.

1.2 Research Gap

Previous studies have concentrated mostly on investigating the causes and consequences of older adults' low levels of digital literacy and skill. The current inclusive design research calls for increased experimental validation of the effectiveness of practical examples of better understanding the dilemmas faced by older people using the internet based on real-world scenarios and an evolving alignment with contemporary needs.

There is an agreement that older people should be considered a heterogeneous group [14]. Many existing inclusive design studies conceptualize the heterogeneity of older adults as reasons for different digital skills rather than a starting point for the enhancement of their digital skills.

The primary research objective of this paper is to explore whether inclusive design principles can empower older adults to be independently resilient to cyber risks. The question of where inclusive design can intervene in the scenarios and process cyber dangers for older adults is also worth exploring in this study.

2 Research Objectives

1. To understand the skills that older adults have and are lacking in using IT in general.
2. To understand their capabilities and needs in relation to online safety.

3   Literature Review

The review covered the literature from the past six years. The literature review presents a summary of papers from Scopus and Web of Science to explore the digital skills and literacy levels of older people in the UK and the cybersecurity threats to older individuals. The literature searching strategy is to limit the literature range by some keywords such as 'older adults', 'online safety', 'skills', 'inclusive design', and 'learning methods and their synonyms. During the search, the literature was sorted by citations and relevance and filtered by browsing the abstracts individually. The table (see Table 1) showed the record of literature review sources and the volume.

Table 1. Literature review search terms and results

Database	Keywords	Results	Useful article
Scopus	Older adults AND Online Safety	16	5
	Older adults AND ICT skills	12	5
	Older adults AND Digital skills	13	5
	Research Methodology	17	6
	Age related factors AND Online engagement	6	3
	Older adults AND Digital divide	8	4
	Older adults AND digital services	9	5
Web of science	Older adults AND cybersecurity AND digital	10	7
	Older pe- AND digital AND skills	5	2
	Older adults AND Safety AND digital skills	17	4
	Older adults AND Safety AND digital literacy	26	4
	Cyber security AND Threats AND Older adults	2	2
	Cyber security AND Older adults	25	6
Online resources	Cyber security threat		15
	Online privacy protection		5
In total		166	78

3.1   UK Older People's Digital Skills Level

In terms of prior career experiences, motivation for utilizing technology, and computer literacy, older persons make up a highly heterogeneous population of technology users [14]. The UK Government Essential Digital Skills Framework 2018 [15] categorises essential digital skills needed for an individual's life and work. The five categories are problem-solving skills, communicating skills, handling information and contents skills, transacting skills, and being safe, legal, and confident online skills. The framework provides a basis for assessing digital skills [13].

The Lloyds Bank's 2021 report [16] aligned with the Framework, conducted a survey on the digital skills level of 2,000 UK residents. The data reveals that a mere 14% of individuals aged 65 and above possess proficiency in all foundational digital skills. Breaking down the demographic, there are 49% of people over 65 years old who have foundation level digital skills, and 47% have life EDS. Furthermore, only 28% of people over 75 years old have acquired foundation level skills, and 26% have life EDS.

However, it is worth noting that the way the Lloyds Bank measures participants' digital skills is that a person can be rated as having a certain level of skill (foundation level, life EDS and work EDS) if they have fully performed the tasks in each category. Older adults have different experiences with using ICT. Those who possess a high level of partial digital competence may nevertheless lack the essential cybersecurity knowledge and skills.

3.2 The Importance of Online Safety Skills for Older Adults

Senior ICT-hesitant individuals would be potentially advantaged by more online participation [17]. The use of ICT will also enhance seniors' autonomy and independence. However, older adults with less digital literacy and skills generally have a slower realization of online scams, fraud, and identity theft [12, 18, 19].

The main concern is that the data has been stolen or misused. Forty three percent of participants are anxious that their privacy will be used by a third party [20]. In the United States and Canada, older adults, to protect cybersecurity and privacy, refused to use apps and online services, and those who were on the internet would share a minimum of their information online [21, 22].

According to Kantar TNS Research Express [27], which sampled 1,367 people aged 65 and above in the UK, nearly five million (43%) adults over the age of 65 have reported being the target of scams. Although they are extremely careful, they are frequently vulnerable as well. Some of them do not have basic digital knowledge of being safe online, so they have a harder time identifying the early indicators of a scam or cyberattack and they are the target group of the scammers [28].

The Adults, Data, and Emerging IDentities (AUDID) project was organized by the United Kingdom, Portugal, Croatia, Greece, Italy and Slovenia. This project offered a real-world application practice highly related to the day-to-day situation for people aged above 55 who are vulnerable to shaping and protecting an appropriate online identity [20]. It aimed at enhancing senior citizens' digital skills for protecting their online identities. This included preventing personal information from being stolen and sold, being scammed, and having an online identity attacked. The program has 28 daily scenarios. The user needs to watch characters perform online actions in cybersecurity scenarios. After that, users need to respond with 'correct' and 'incorrect'. The application will provide feedback at the end of 28 scenarios on the security information for the operation [20]. The results showed that 70 percent of respondents felt that this program had increased their knowledge of Internet safety, and the same percentage of them indicated that they would continue to improve their online knowledge in the future. More than half of the respondents expressed that they would change their online behavior in the future. The program had been approved and provided a creative and interactive learning source for ICT beginners.

Research in behavioural cybersecurity consistently demonstrates that users constitute the most vulnerable links within any cyber framework. This vulnerability comes from the fact that cyber attackers can exploit users as susceptible targets [23–25]. Therefore, enhancing users' digital proficiency within all cyber frameworks is paramount, as it not only fortifies their resilience against potential cyber threats, but also maximizes the efficacy of digital applications in safeguarding against exploitation by cyberattacks.

3.3 Older Adults Learning Preference

Professionals generally use ICT terminologies such as phishing, viruses and malware, by contrast, non-professionals usually use daily words like hacker to describe security issues. Nicholson and his team recruited 15 females and 7 males from community internet users, mainly around 72 years old, to attend a semi-structured interview in Newcastle, UK. They found that older users in the UK prioritize sources of cyber security and privacy assistance based more on availability than expertise. Older adults prefer media like TV and radio over the internet when seeking cybersecurity and privacy advice [26]. However, news reports typically use everyday language and terms that the public can easily understand when discussing events related to internet security [26]. This can cause confusion among older people in terms of blurring the concepts of the cyber problems they encounter.

There is a large body of research suggesting that older people prefer face-to-face tuition. However, offline training is relatively limited by time, place, or staffing constraints. By contrast, online resources can be provided through networks and devices that are instantaneous and stable.

4   Exploratory Study

This study is an exploratory study that aims to learn about older people's digital skill levels to help develop the focus of the research. In this study, a questionnaire survey and a semi-structured interview were used as research methods.

Thirteen participants were from the U3A (University of the Third Age) who filled out an online questionnaire. The other 18 were from a local community centre, John Storer House who filled out a paper questionnaire and were also interviewed.

All of the participants come from Loughborough and towns nearby. This study was mostly conducted at John Storer House (offline) and U3A (online). John Storer House built in the 1990s, is the largest charity and activity centre for older people in Loughborough. It has a daily number of visits of around 100 older people. Therefore, taking open sampling first at John Storer House was a good way to reach potential participants within the target user group.

The study gained ethical approval from Loughborough University through the LEON ethical system. Before the study took place, the researcher let participants know the nature of the study, the information they needed to provide, and the possible effects of the study on them. No sensitive personal information was collected. Participants needed to sign the Informed Consent Form and read the Participation Information Sheet before the research started.

4.1 Data Collection

The aim of the questionnaire was to investigate older adults' basic ICT experiences based on UK Digital Skills Framework tasks. It consisted of 16 questions.

The questionnaire was divided into three parts. Firstly, the questions will start with asking participants basic information, which includes age, gender, residence town, current employment status, previous working experience, and education experience. Secondly, participants were required to share their previous experience of using computers, phones, and tablets, their confidence when facing computers, and how they will deal with the difficulties and learning difficulties. The third part was the self-assessment based on UK digital skills framework tasks in five categories. The format of the quiz in this part was modelled on the UK Digital Skills Framework's digital skills tasks, giving participants the choice of whether it was 'Yes', 'No', 'Partly' or 'No, but would like to learn it'. Finally, there was an open question about commenting on how easy it is for participants found it to learn digital skills and the fundamental digital skills that they thought could drive them to learn more.

The interview was to explore the main reasons that affect the motivation for older adults to attempt and develop their essential digital skills. And older adults have different situations and experiences when interacting with ICT. Thus, semi-structured interviews were found to be more adaptable than structured interviews and unstructured interviews.

4.2 Data Analysis

The analysis was carried out by Microsoft Excel on the results of 31 questionnaires of people aged 65 and above. The thirteen interview transcripts were coded in N-vivo. The average interview length was 20 min. Twelve times, a one-to-one interview was carried out and a group interview was conducted with six people over a one-and-a-half-month period. Thirteen participants attended both the questionnaire and the interview.

Participant Demographic. All the participant demographic data comes from a questionnaire survey. The wide-ranging representation included age, gender, educational background, working experience, ICT experience, digital skills learning experiences, and the learning barrier to improving their digital skills. The demographics of the participants were defined to ensure the sample represented a broader population. The figure below (see Fig. 1) illustrates the age range and number of participants who attended the questionnaire survey and interview. Twelve participants were aged below 65 and forty-two of them were 65 or older. The younger group was included for comparison.

The following section is a summary of the results from both the survey and interviews.

4.3 Results

From the survey, it was found that 26 (81%) of the participants had used computers in their work. This reported that most of older adults aged 65 or older in this study has gained computer skills from their work. The average confidence self-rating score (5 points in total) with computer working experience was 3.2, compared with people without 2.8.

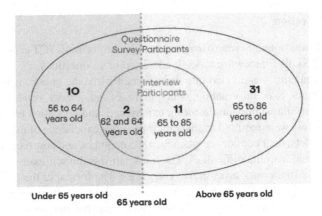

Fig. 1. Age structure of Study 1 participants

This indicated that people who use computers in their work are more confident than those who do not.

The number of tasks that participants self-assessed that they knew the least in order were transacting, handling information and content, and being safe and legal online. However, online shopping and banking were the second most frequently used internet functions. Although older adults are less adapting online transactions, they could be assisted by getting help from others. They were found to be very cautious, and they tended to only trust 'more professional people'.

Besides, being safe online is a common concern for older people. Only 56% of participants thought they could manage passwords to enhance account security; 72% of participants did not set privacy settings on their social media; and 34% of them believed they could improve the computer system's safety. In terms of being safe online, most of the older interviewees expressed that they use the same password on all platforms, they felt that they needed to do this because their memory was less reliable than it was. Thirteen participants in Study 1 brought up their concern about making mistakes when using ICT. This was because they lacked knowledge of which errors could cause unsafe results.

In addition, it was found that some participants may have the misconception that with antivirus software, they don't need to have the knowledge and skills to prevent it themselves. Older adults with negative attitudes showed greater insecurity about advances in technology, they considered themselves to be vulnerable to online fraud and aggression and were both dependent on and sceptical of antivirus software.

4.4 Discussion

It was discovered through the interview that when a strange online environment requires participants' privacy information, the majority of the participants are hesitant to provide personal information. On online social platforms, they also do not want to show their personal lives to the public. Three participants expressed in the interview that the reason they engage less online is because the less they expose themselves online, the hacker will know less about them, so the cyber dangers pose less of a threat to them.

Most of the participants were found to be very cautious about their online presence, they would rather avoid using some 'high-risk' functions like online banking and shopping on their own. When they need e-services like transactions or government services, some seniors who are less confident in operating themselves would rather rely on librarians or bank staff to help them apply for banking services, which is idealistic but may be a naive mentality. However, some scammers will hide behind a secure identity. An elderly woman had been scammed by fake members of the National Anti-Fraud Squad. Crossler et al. (2013) found that seniors proactively protect their financial information, but they did not understand the danger of sharing identification information with strangers [23].

The cultivation of basic digital literacy alongside the enhancement of digital skills among older adults is important. Basic digital literacy can help older users comprehend their circumstances and communicate their needs using appropriate ICT language. On the one hand, digital literacy may enable older ICT users to gain assistance when they need it urgently; on the other hand, digital skills empower older users to avoid risks or escape danger. The difference between a Wi-Fi connection and data, the meaning of applications and software, the size of files, the concept of cloud storage, and two-factor authentication (2FA) became the most common problems for the elderly.

Older adults need a better way to manage their online identity. From the interview open questions, a number of seniors expressed that they have a single password on all platforms, which they know poses a security risk for their online accounts, but they thought that they could only remember one password.

Older people are cautious and don't want to take any risks. They need appropriate cybersecurity knowledge to recognize safe and fake links and web features. Further research is needed to test if they can determine the safety of a website based on some features. Besides, setting privacy on social media helps older individuals establish online boundaries, preventing them from being easily influenced by spam and nuisance messages, provided they know how to do this.

According to the online safety skill data collected by respondents' self-assessments, being safe online is clearly important to older users. Although the results for 'being safe online' were generally positive, further research and testing are needed to understand this area of knowledge and skills better.

While in Study 1 the people who responded to the recruitment posters were willing to talk about their digital skills and their confusion with ICT, it did not include those less willing to come forward and share their experiences. As for the semi-structured interviews, many participants tend to mention online safety communication and online transactions of life EDS. As a result, in future interviews, participants should be guided to talk about more aspects to ensure data is collected completely and diversely.

5   Conclusion

The findings of the exploratory study show that the participants' digital skills level is related to previous digital skills training from learning or working experience. Most of them have computer using skills, which builds participants good confidence when they are facing ICT. However, when they retire from the work environment, their evaluation of their digital skills may be influenced by the results of comparisons with those around them, such as family and friends, while the convenience and availability of some participants to instantly access assistance from family, friends, and neighbours to meet the demands of their normal online activities may result in a biased evaluation of their own digital skills. In terms of cybersecurity, some conservative older adults choose to minimise their involvement online in order to avoid encountering cyberthreats. They express fear and concern when newer technologies emerge.

Most of the older adults taking part in the study lack fundamental digital skills and need basic digital literacy to determine their online situation and understand concepts relating to online safety, e.g., identity theft. Meanwhile, having basic digital skills and literacy can help older adults gain assistance and respond to urgent circumstances when they are applying for e-services. It is also important for them to be able to identify cybersecurity threats, which include phishing emails and fake websites, and privacy threats, which refers to oversharing on social media. If they follow the online fraudster's instructions without awareness, they can end up losing their private information or money to web criminals. The study indicated that future research is needed to show how inclusive design principles can help older users understand security threats better and take actions to be able to avoid and deal with them.

References

1. Statista Daily Data: Infographic: Where 5G Technology Has Been Deployed (2022). https://www.statista.com/chart/23194/5g-networks-deployment-world-map. Accessed 5 Mar 2024
2. Statista: 5G subscriptions 2019–2028. https://www.statista.com/statistics/1199693/north-america-5g-subscriptions/. Accessed 5 Mar 2024
3. Friemel, T.N.: The digital divide has grown old: determinants of a digital divide among seniors. New Media Soc. **18**(2), 313–331 (2016)
4. Barnard, Y., Bradley, M.D., Hodgson, F., Lloyd, A.D.: Learning to use new technologies by older adults: perceived difficulties, experimentation behaviour and usability. Comput. Hum. Behav. **29**(4), 1715–24 (2013). https://linkinghub.elsevier.com/retrieve/pii/S0747563213000721. Accessed 31 Dec 2023
5. Heponiemi, T., Kaihlanen, A.M., Kouvonen. A., Leemann. L., Taipale, S., Gluschkoff, K.: The role of age and digital competence on the use of online health and social care services: a cross-sectional population-based survey. Digit. Health **8**, 20552076221074485 (2022)
6. UK Office for National Statistics: National population projections: 2018-based. Data and analysis from Census 2021, October 2019. https://www.ons.gov.uk/peoplepopulationandcommunity/populationandmigration/populationprojections/bulletins/nationalpopulationprojections/2018based
7. McCosker, A., Critchley, C., Walshe, J., Tucker, J., Suchowerska, R.: Accounting for diversity in older adults' digital inclusion and literacy: the impact of a national intervention. Ageing Soc. **43**(11), 2629–2649 (2021)
8. Ray, H.: Towards understanding usable privacy concerns among older adults, 1 January 2022. http://hdl.handle.net/11603/28477. Accessed 8 Jan 2024
9. Grilli, M.D., et al.: Is this phishing? Older age is associated with greater difficulty discriminating between safe and malicious emails. J. Gerontol. Ser. B Psychol. Sci. Soc. Sci. **76**(9), 1711–1715 (2021)
10. European Commission: Migration DG for, Affairs H. Europeans' attitudes towards cyber security. European Commission (2020)

11. Identity Fraud in Three Acts: A Consumer Guide | Javelin. https://javelinstrategy.com/res earch/identity-fraud-three-acts-consumer-guide. Accessed 5 Mar 2024

12. Parti, K.: "Elder Scam" risk profiles: individual and situational factors of younger and older age groups' fraud victimization. Int. J. Cybersecur. Intell. Cybercrime 5(3), 20–40 (2022). https://vc.bridgew.edu/ijcic/vol5/iss3/3. Accessed 31 Dec 2023

13. National Cyber Security Centre: Information for individuals and families to keep safe online. Individuals & families. https://www.ncsc.gov.uk/section/information-for/individuals-families. Accessed 31 Dec 2023

14. van Boekel, L.C., Peek, S.T., Luijkx, K.G.: Diversity in older adults' use of the internet: identifying subgroups through latent class analysis. J. Med. Internet Res. 19(5), e180 (2017)

15. UK Government: Essential digital skills framework. Department for Education, April 2019. https://www.gov.uk/government/publications/essential-digital-skills-framework

16. LLOYDS Bank: Essential Digital Skills Report 2021, Third Edition – Benchmarking the Essential Digital Skills of the UK (2021)

17. Alagood, J., Prybutok, G., Prybutok, V.R.: Navigating privacy and data safety: the implications of increased online activity among older adults post-covid-19 induced isolation. Information 14(6), 346 (2023)

18. Phibbs, C.L., Rahman, S.S.M.: A synopsis of "the impact of motivation, price, and habit on intention to use IoT-enabled technology: a correlational study". J. Cybersecur. Priv. 2(3), 662–699 (2022). https://www.mdpi.com/2624-800X/2/3/34. Accessed 8 Jan 2024

19. Sugunaraj, N., Ramchandra, A.R, Ranganathan, P.: Cyber fraud economics, scam types, and potential measures to protect U.S. seniors: a short review. In: 2022 IEEE International Conference on Electro Information Technology (eIT), Mankato, MN, USA, pp. 623–627. IEEE (2022). https://ieeexplore.ieee.org/document/9813960/. Accessed 31 Dec 2023

20. Zanchetta, C., Schiff, H., Novo, C., Cruz, S., Vaz de Carvalho, C.: Generational inclusion: getting older adults ready to own safe online identities. Educ. Sci. 12(10), 715 (2022)

21. Quan-Haase, A., Elueze, I.: Revisiting the privacy paradox: concerns and protection strategies in the social media experiences of older adults. In: Proceedings of the 9th International Conference on Social Media and Society, Copenhagen, Denmark, pp. 150–159. ACM (2018). https://dl.acm.org/doi/10.1145/3217804.3217907. Accessed 31 Dec 2023

22. Ray, H., Wolf, F., Kuber, R., Aviv, A.J.: 'Woe is me': examining older adults' perceptions of privacy. In: Extended Abstracts of the 2019 CHI Conference on Human Factors in Computing Systems, Glasgow, Scotland, UK, pp. 1–6. ACM (2019). https://dl.acm.org/doi/10.1145/329 0607.3312770. Accessed 31 Dec 2023

23. Crossler, R.E., Johnston, A.C., Lowry, P.B., Hu, Q., Warkentin, M., Baskerville, R.: Future directions for behavioral information security research. Comput. Secur. 32, 90–101 (2013). https://www.sciencedirect.com/science/article/pii/S0167404812001460. Accessed 7 Jan 2024

24. Hu, Q., Dinev, T., Hart, P., Cooke, D.: Managing employee compliance with information security policies: the critical role of top management and organizational culture*. Decis. Sci. 43(4), 615–60 (2012). https://onlinelibrary.wiley.com/doi/abs/10.1111/j.1540-5915.2012.00361.x. Accessed 7 Jan 2024

25. Warkentin, M., Willison, R.: Behavioral and policy issues in information systems security: the insider threat. Eur. J. Inf. Syst. 18(2), 101–5 (2009). https://doi.org/10.1057/ejis.2009.12. Accessed 7 Jan 2024

26. Nicholson, J., Coventry, L., Briggs, P.: 'If it's important it will be a headline': cybersecurity information seeking in older adults. In: Northumbria University. Association for Computing Machinery, Inc. (2019)

27. Kantar, T.N.S.: Research express polling for age UK. Nearly five million older people targeted by scammers (2017). www.ageuk.org.uk
28. Yu, K., Wu, S., Chi, I.: Internet use and loneliness of older adults over time: the mediating effect of social contact. J. Gerontol. Ser. B **76**(3), 541–550 (2021)

Application of Virtual Reality in Empathy Training for Elderly Care Personnel

Jiawen Zhang(✉)

Department of Service Design, School of Design, Royal College of Art, London, UK
jiawenzhang17769046992@gmail.com

Abstract. As the aging population continues to grow, the demand for elderly care personnel has significantly increased. Establishing effective training models for these caregivers is a critical step in realizing an active aging strategy. Traditional training methods are costly, limited, and vary in educational quality. Virtual reality (VR) technology, due to its spatial and temporal flexibility and cost-effective simulation capabilities, has rapidly evolved in the healthcare and education field. This study introduces empathy design theory into the development of virtual simulation systems for elderly care, defining a potential framework for empathy training among elderly care personnel. Based on Daniel Goleman and Paul Ekman's "Three Types of Empathy" theory, this framework categorizes empathy training strategies in virtual simulation systems into three levels: Cognitive Empathy intervention, Emotional Empathy intervention, and Compassionate Empathy intervention. By combining traditional empathy training practices, the specific methods for each type of empathy intervention are elucidated. This research offers new insights into the application of VR technology in the elderly health industry, delivering substantial value to both the geriatric and digital technology sectors.

Keywords: Virtual Reality · Elderly Care · Empathic Care · Empathy Training

1 Introduction

The global population structure is rapidly undergoing an aging transformation. The World Health Organization (WHO) defines the elderly as those aged 60 and above. According to their statistics and projections, the global population of people aged 60 and over was 1 billion in 2020, and it is expected to increase to 1.4 billion by 2030. By 2050, the number of people aged 60 and above is projected to reach 2.1 billion, constituting 22% of the global population.[1] Concurrently, there is a rising trend in non-communicable chronic diseases and disabilities among the elderly [7]. The rapid growth of the elderly population, coupled with the loss of functional abilities due to various health issues [10], is driving the

---

[1] https://www.who.int/news-room/fact-sheets/detail/mental-health-of-older-adults.

C. Stephanidis et al. (Eds.): HCII 2024, CCIS 2115, pp. 335–342, 2024.
https://doi.org/10.1007/978-3-031-61947-2_35

demand for elderly care and talents. In this context, exploring innovative and timely methods of caregiver training holds significant value for achieving the strategic goal of active aging.

This study delves into the interdisciplinary integration of virtual reality (VR), psychology, caring education, and health informatics, aiming to delineate the potential uses of VR technology in the training of elderly care personnel. The training content focuses on a critical component of elderly care work-empathetic care. Based on existing theories of empathy and experiments in empathy capability training, a design framework and methods for empathy training in a virtual simulation training system are proposed. These are intended to enhance the empathetic caregiving capabilities of care personnel, improve the effectiveness of caring practices, and ensure the quality of life and physical and mental health of the elderly being cared for.

2   Empathetic Care in Elderly Care

Empathy is considered one of the fundamental qualities of nursing personnel, a key factor in primary care [15], and has even been described as the essence of therapeutic nurse-patient interaction [17]. The elderly population presents its own set of unique challenges, such as widespread physical decline, diminished sensory sensitivity, and chronic illness in terms of physical health. In terms of mental health, they are prone to loneliness, depression, neglect, and low self-esteem. In cognitive health, there is a decline in comprehension, memory, learning ability, and reaction speed, with a high incidence of cognitive impairments. In elderly care practice, possessing a higher level of empathy for these characteristics has been proven to facilitate the improvement of communication processes, understanding of the care recipients' perspectives and needs [16], thereby enabling personalized care, enhancing the quality of caring practices [27], establishing better nurse-patient relationships [26], improving patient cooperation [19], and ultimately achieving better caring outcomes [2]. For the caregivers themselves, empathy can also help address professional burnout or depression [28]. Therefore, in addition to routine living and medication care, empathetic care is a crucial aspect of elderly care.

2.1   The Meaning of Empathetic Care

Empathy is a complex and multidimensional concept [1], with numerous definitions within the field of empathy research. Emotional theorists Daniel Goleman and Paul Ekman broadly categorize empathy into three dimensions: "Cognitive Empathy", "Emotional Empathy", and "Compassionate Empathy". The specific meaning of empathy also varies according to the context in which it is applied. In caring practice, empathy can be seen as a professional form of interaction (a skill or ability) [16], involving a combination of emotional, cognitive, and practical skills [18]. Integrating the descriptions of clinical empathy by Morse [17], Powell [20], and others, in the context of elderly care within this study, the specific meanings of the three types of empathy are as follows:

- **Cognitive Empathy**: Involves caregiver adopting an open attitude, intellectually recognizing, understanding, or assessing another person's situation and inner world.
- **Emotional Empathy**: Concerns the internal subjective response of the caregiver, integrating the experiences of others with their own to gain an emotional experience.
- **Compassionate Empathy**: Involves the professional ability of caregiver to make timely actions and provide help based on rational judgment and professional ethics.

2.2   Empathetic Care Training

Practice shows that empathy is a teachable ability [22], which can be enhanced through targeted instructional methods [16]. Common empathy training approaches include: (1) Experiential empathy training, such as role-playing and simulation games; (2) Mindfulness training, including mindfulness-based relaxation, cognitive therapy, and compassion cultivation [12]; (3) Using videos and other multimedia to stimulate empathy; (4) Instructional training focusing on theory and concepts; and (5) Skill application training that provides practical opportunities [14]. These methods of empathy training have been applied in nursing training and have been validated for their effectiveness through empathy ability evaluation methods such as JSPE-HP and IRI-C [9].

However, traditional training methods face numerous limitations. For example, there is often a lack of available clinical sites [2], and as a result, practice is usually achieved through role-playing with other students and standardized patients (SP: trained actors hired to simulate patients and assess practitioners' performance in interviews). This leads to the arrangement of simulated experiences requiring extensive resources, and it is challenging to enable practitioners to independently repeat practices [5,13].

3   Empathetic Care Training in VR

VR employs computer technology to create and sustain an environment that facilitates user interaction via a virtual embodiment [6]. It is increasingly applied in the realms of caring practice and education, where users have reported acquiring valuable, essential knowledge and caring skills [29]. In contrast to applications focused on knowledge and skill training, this study proposes a framework for empathy training aimed at enhancing the empathetic care capabilities of elderly care practitioners from cognitive, emotional, to behavioral dimensions.

3.1   Why VR Is Suitable for Empathetic Care Training

Immersive VR possesses the capability to substitute the first-person perspective, engendering a perceptual illusion of "embodiment" or "body ownership" [4], immersing oneself in roles detached from their real-world self. This capacity for perspective-taking aligns directly with the essence of empathy, which involves "putting oneself in another's shoes." Studies have shown that, compared to traditional role-playing methods reliant primarily on imagination, VR allows for an in-situ experience of roles, more effectively fostering empathy [21,30]. Moreover, VR facilitates sensory immersion in scenarios, enhancing user engagement. This results in a higher degree of stimulation and empathic effect for the learners with content delivered through VR compared to the same material presented in non-VR formats [24]. United Nations immersive VR 360° video projects like Clouds Over Sidra and The New York Times VR documentary "The Displaced," though placing viewers in a third-person perspective, have profound impacts [25]. VR technology also supports the creation of interactive virtual patients (VPs) and real-life simulated environments allowing learners to practice repetitively without constraints of location and time. This could be a solution to the high costs associated with using standardized patients (SPs) and the scarcity of clinical practice opportunities [8]. Even in testing scenarios, learners' responses to VPs exhibit more empathy compared to their responses to SPs, as they feel lower interaction pressure in virtual scenarios, enabling a greater focus on reflecting upon their responses [13]. Overall, the features of VR present it with the potential to develop a standardized, effective, easily repeatable, and low-risk, low-cost empathetic care training system.

3.2   Empathetic Care Training Strategies in VR

Based on the "Three types of empathy" theory by Daniel Goleman and Paul Ekman, traditional empathy training methods, and the characteristics of VR, the following strategies, as shown in Fig. 1, can be utilized within a virtual simulation training system to intervene in the empathetic abilities of elderly care personnel:

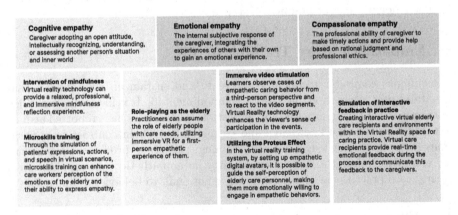

Fig. 1. Empathy training strategies in VR for elderly care personnel.

- **Enhancing Cognitive Empathy**
  Intervention of mindfulness: Mindfulness training involves teaching learners to become relaxed and mindful, that is, to be in a state of non-judgmental awareness, following meditation practices and engaging in positive thinking. VR technology can provide a relaxed, professional, and immersive mindfulness reflection experience. This enables individuals to focus their attention on subconscious cognitions, such as various implicit biases towards the elderly. Some argue that the impact of mindfulness on empathy might be indirect, facilitating friendly behavior by helping to reduce criticism and negative emotions [14].

  Microskills training: Microskills are a common approach used in counseling, encompassing active listening skills, questioning skills, and the recognition of a consultee's feelings and emotions through their non-verbal expressions. These skills are often crucial for empathetic communication [11]. Through the simulation of patients' expressions, actions, and speech in virtual scenarios, microskills training can enhance care workers' perception of the emotions of the elderly and their ability to express empathy.
- **Enhancing Cognitive Empathy and Emotional Empathy**
  Role-playing as the elderly: Practitioners can assume the role of elderly people with care needs, utilizing immersive VR for a first-person empathetic experience of them. This method stimulates emotional empathy and significantly enhances the ability to "understand patient feelings." Additionally, considering the use of visual, tactile, and auditory synchrony to guide perceptual illusions can intensify the sense of role immersion [4].
- **Enhancing Emotional Empathy and Compassionate Empathy**
  Immersive video stimulation: Video stimulation allows learners to observe cases of empathetic caring behavior from a third-person perspective and to react to the video segments during or after viewing [14]. VR technology enhances the viewer's sense of participation in the events, enriching their subjective experience and guiding them to reflect on empathy in caring practice.

  Utilizing the Proteus effect in simulation games: In a virtual environment, digital avatars can influence users and lead their behaviors to align with those of the avatar. This behavioral adjustment is known as the Proteus effect [31]. For example, computer games that induce users to engage in pro-social behaviors can make it more likely for the users to perform helpful actions in the real world after the game ends [23]. This means that in the VR training system, by setting up empathetic digital avatars, it is possible to guide the self-perception of elderly care personnel, making them more emotionally willing to engage in empathetic behaviors.
- **Enhancing Compassionate Empathy**
  Simulation of interactive feedback in practice: Creating interactive virtual elderly care recipients and environments within the VR space for caring practice. Virtual care recipients provide real-time emotional feedback during

the process and communicate this feedback to the caregivers. This allows them to practice empathetic care skills without the risk of negatively impacting the real elderly. Training in this manner also enhances related empathetic abilities such as communication and interpersonal skills [3].

4   Conclusion

Enhancing the empathetic caring capabilities of caregivers directly and positively impacts the quality of life for the elderly, holding significant social value. With the widening gap in caring personnel and the implementation of active aging strategies, leveraging digital technology for caring talent training presents a new perspective in research on aging issues. Virtual simulation empathy training systems should have tremendous commercial potential in the future, yet this study also has its limitations: the effectiveness of VR in enhancing empathy compared to traditional methods requires further empirical validation. Additionally, this research focuses on proposing a theoretical framework, but the details regarding specific training types for different trainees, scientifically structured training cycles, and duration remain vague and necessitate development and experimentation. Moreover, how to prevent caregivers from losing "emotional distance" due to immersive experiences, a potential risk where excessive emotional empathy could harm their personal psychological health, is also an important consideration.

References

1. Batson, C.D.: These things called empathy: eight related but distinct phenomena (2009)
2. Bauchat, J.R., Seropian, M., Jeffries, P.R.: Communication and empathy in the patient-centered care model-why simulation-based training is not optional. Clin. Simul. Nurs. **12**(8), 356–359 (2016)
3. Bearman, M., Palermo, C., Allen, L.M., Williams, B.: Learning empathy through simulation: a systematic literature review. Simul. Healthcare **10**(5), 308–319 (2015)
4. Bertrand, P., Guegan, J., Robieux, L., McCall, C.A., Zenasni, F.: Learning empathy through virtual reality: multiple strategies for training empathy-related abilities using body ownership illusions in embodied virtual reality. Front. Robot. AI **5**, 326671 (2018)
5. Brydon, M., et al.: Virtual reality as a tool for eliciting empathetic behaviour in carers: an integrative review. J. Medi. Imag. Radiation Sci. **52**(3), 466–477 (2021)
6. Burdea, G.C., Coiffet, P.: Virtual reality technology. John Wiley & Sons (2003)
7. Chatterji, S., Byles, J., Cutler, D., Seeman, T., Verdes, E.: Health, functioning, and disability in older adults-present status and future implications. Lancet **385**(9967), 563–575 (2015)
8. Dean, S., Halpern, J., McAllister, M., Lazenby, M.: Nursing education, virtual reality and empathy? Nurs. Open **7**(6), 2056–2059 (2020)
9. Gholamzadeh, S., Khastavaneh, M., Khademian, Z., Ghadakpour, S.: The effects of empathy skills training on nursing students' empathy and attitudes toward elderly people. BMC Med. Educ. **18**(1), 1–7 (2018)

10. Han, W.J., Shibusawa, T.: Trajectory of physical health, cognitive status, and psychological well-being among Chinese elderly. Arch. Gerontol. Geriatr. **60**(1), 168–177 (2015)
11. Ivey, A.E., Daniels, T.: Systematic interviewing microskills and neuroscience: Developing bridges between the fields of communication and counseling psychology. Int. J. Listen. **30**(3), 99–119 (2016)
12. Jazaieri, H., et al.: Enhancing compassion: a randomized controlled trial of a compassion cultivation training program. J. Happiness Stud. **14**, 1113–1126 (2013)
13. Kleinsmith, A., Rivera-Gutierrez, D., Finney, G., Cendan, J., Lok, B.: Understanding empathy training with virtual patients. Comput. Hum. Behav. **52**, 151–158 (2015)
14. Lam, T.C.M., Kolomitro, K., Alamparambil, F.C.: Empathy training: Methods, evaluation practices, and validity. J. Multidiscip. Eval. **7**(16), 162–200 (2011)
15. Lewis, J.R.: Patient views on quality care in general practice: literature review. Social Sci. Med. **39**(5), 655–670 (1994)
16. Mercer, S.W., Reynolds, W.J.: Empathy and quality of care. Br. J. Gen. Pract. **52**(Suppl), S9-12 (2002)
17. Morse, J.M., et al.: Exploring empathy: a conceptual fit for nursing practice? Image: The journal of nursing scholarship **24**(4), 273–280 (1992)
18. Moudatsou, M., Stavropoulou, A., Philalithis, A., Koukouli, S.: The role of empathy in health and social care professionals. In: Healthcare. vol. 8, p. 26. MDPI (2020)
19. Ogle, J., Bushnell, J.A., Caputi, P.: Empathy is related to clinical competence in medical care. Med. Educ. **47**(8), 824–831 (2013)
20. Powell, P.A., Roberts, J.: Situational determinants of cognitive, affective, and compassionate empathy in naturalistic digital interactions. Comput. Hum. Behav. **68**, 137–148 (2017)
21. Quay, C., Ramakrishnan, A.: Innovative use of virtual reality to facilitate empathy toward older adults in nursing education. Nurs. Educ. Perspect. **44**(5), 300–302 (2023)
22. Richardson, C., Percy, M., Hughes, J.: Nursing therapeutics: teaching student nurses care, compassion and empathy. Nurse Educ. Today **35**(5), e1–e5 (2015)
23. Rosenberg, R.S., Baughman, S.L., Bailenson, J.N.: Virtual superheroes: using superpowers in virtual reality to encourage prosocial behavior. PLoS ONE **8**(1), e55003 (2013)
24. Schutte, N.S., Stilinović, E.J.: Facilitating empathy through virtual reality. Motiv. Emot. **41**, 708–712 (2017)
25. Sirkkunen, E., Väätäjä, H., Uskali, T., Rezaei, P.P.: Journalism in virtual reality: Opportunities and future research challenges. In: Proceedings of the 20th International Academic Mindtrek Conference, pp. 297–303 (2016)
26. Spiro, H.: Commentary: the practice of empathy. Acad. Med. **84**(9), 1177–1179 (2009)
27. Teófilo, T.J.S., Veras, R.F.S., Silva, V.A., Cunha, N.M., Oliveira, J.d.S., Vasconcelos, S.C.: Empathy in the nurse–patient relationship in geriatric care: an integrative review. Nurs. Ethics **26**(6), 1585–1600 (2019)
28. Thirioux, B., Birault, F., Jaafari, N.: Empathy is a protective factor of burnout in physicians: new neuro-phenomenological hypotheses regarding empathy and sympathy in care relationship. Front. Psychol. **7**, 205258 (2016)
29. Wang, J., et al.: Effectiveness of virtual reality on the caregiving competence and empathy of caregivers for elderly with chronic diseases: a systematic review and meta-analysis. J. Nurs. Manage. **2023** (2023)

30. Wiederhold, B.K.: Embodiment empowers empathy in virtual reality (2020)
31. Yee, N., Bailenson, J.: The proteus effect: the effect of transformed self-representation on behavior. Hum. Commun. Res. **33**(3), 271–290 (2007)

Author Index

Printed in the United States
by Baker & Taylor Publisher Services